MW01505280

"This well-conceived book fills a m literature that exists on rural living and governance. The authors explore numerous topics from economic development strategy to public budgeting challenges to public safety and others. A theme that is present in many of the chapters is the lack of financial support for healthcare, non-profits, broadband, and public services. For all those interested in local government management, you will find this volume enlightening even if your focus is on urban governance."

Douglas J. Watson, *Retired City Manager and Professor,*
The University of Texas at Dallas, United States

LOCAL GOVERNMENT ADMINISTRATION IN SMALL TOWN AMERICA

In government administration and leadership, rural community leaders face unique challenges in delivering public services including (but not limited to) education, health care, and public safety. Meanwhile, residents who live in smaller and more isolated rural settings often face greater difficulties accessing provisions and services or commuting to work, among other economic development challenges. These factors may affect a community's resiliency to and recovery from shocks such as the COVID-19 pandemic. *Local Government Administration in Small Town America* devotes some overdue scholarly attention to the governance and administration of public programs in small towns and rural communities in the United States.

The chapter contributors to this volume analyze some of the unique challenges rural communities face, as well as the policy tools that their governments employ to address them. The book explores ways that small town governments collaborate with one another, the state, and the federal government, and examines how local government officials use knowledge of people and place to improve policy performance. The chapters are designed to provide cases and strategies for students and practitioners in public administration to use in a small town environment, while also considering a community's distinctive social and political culture, which determines how local political leaders and government practitioners might respond to demands and challenges they face. *Local Government Administration in Small Town America* is an essential resource for undergraduate and graduate students studying local government, as well as for rural practitioners navigating evolving challenges unique to their communities.

James C. Clinger is a professor in the Department of Political Science and Sociology and serves as director of the Master of Public Administration program at Murray State University. He teaches courses in state and local government, Kentucky politics, intergovernmental relations, public policy analysis, and public budgeting and finance.

Donna M. Handley serves as Master of Public Administration Director and associate professor at Southern Utah University. Prior to her academic career, she served as an assistant director of community development for the City of Auburn, Alabama. Her research interests include online learning, rural community governance and leadership, and women and leadership.

Wendy L. Eaton currently serves as the Program Chair of the Master of Public Administration program at Franklin University (Ohio). Prior to her academic career, she served as an assistant city manager and has over twelve years of experience in local government management.

LOCAL GOVERNMENT ADMINISTRATION IN SMALL TOWN AMERICA

*Edited by James C. Clinger,
Donna M. Handley, and
Wendy L. Eaton*

Routledge
Taylor & Francis Group

NEW YORK AND LONDON

Designed cover image: © halbergman / Getty Images

First published 2024
by Routledge
605 Third Avenue, New York, NY 10158

and by Routledge
4 Park Square, Milton Park, Abingdon, Oxon, OX14 4RN

Routledge is an imprint of the Taylor & Francis Group, an informa business

© 2024 selection and editorial matter, James C. Clinger, Donna M. Handley, and Wendy L. Eaton; individual chapters, the contributors

The right of James C. Clinger, Donna M. Handley, and Wendy L. Eaton to be identified as the authors of the editorial material, and of the authors for their individual chapters, has been asserted in accordance with sections 77 and 78 of the Copyright, Designs and Patents Act 1988.

Library of Congress Cataloging-in-Publication Data
Names: Clinger, James C., 1958– editor. | Handley, Donna M., editor. | Eaton, Wendy L., editor.
Title: Local government administration in small town America / edited by James C. Clinger, Donna M. Handley and Wendy L. Eaton.
Description: New York, NY : Routledge, 2024. |
Includes bibliographical references and index. |
Identifiers: LCCN 2023018785 (print) | LCCN 2023018786 (ebook) |
ISBN 9781032263311 (hardback) | ISBN 9781032263281 (paperback) |
ISBN 9781003287766 (ebook)
Subjects: LCSH: Local government–United States. | County government–United States. | Local government–United States–Case studies. | County government–United States–Case studies. | Public administration–United States. | Public administration–United States–Case studies.
Classification: LCC JS331 .L59 2024 (print) | LCC JS331 (ebook) |
DDC 320.0973–dc23/eng/20230602
LC record available at https://lccn.loc.gov/2023018785
LC ebook record available at https://lccn.loc.gov/2023018786

ISBN: 978-1-032-26331-1 (hbk)
ISBN: 978-1-032-26328-1 (pbk)
ISBN: 978-1-003-28776-6 (ebk)

DOI: 10.4324/9781003287766

Typeset in Sabon
by Newgen Publishing UK

CONTENTS

FIGURES

TABLES

CONTRIBUTORS

Narine Badasyan is an associate professor of economics and the chair of the Department of Economics and Finance at Murray State University. Her teaching and research primarily focus on the economics and public policy of the telecommunications industry. She has served as a consultant to USAID, NTIA, and ConnectKentucky.

Stephanie L. Bellar is an experienced community leader who is currently serving as the dean of the School of Graduate Studies at Salem State University. Her research interests are focused on community building in rural areas, leadership, and policy implementation.

Deborah A. Carroll is Director of the Government Finance Research Center (GFRC) and professor of public administration at the University of Illinois Chicago. Her research focuses on local and state financial management and fiscal policy, particularly related to taxation, revenue diversification, revenue stability, and urban economic development.

Roger R Carter is an assistant professor in the public administration program at Southern Utah University. Prior to joining the faculty in 2020, he served for more than 20 years as a city manager. Appointed by the federal courts, Carter oversees the restructuring of the local governments of Hildale, Utah, and Colorado City, Arizona.

Xiaoou Cheng is a doctoral student in the Department of Political Science at Texas Tech University. Her research interests include local government, collaborative management, and economic and environmental policy.

James C. Clinger is a professor in the Department of Political Science and Sociology and serves as director of the Master of Public Administration program at Murray State University. He teaches courses in state and local government, Kentucky politics, intergovernmental relations, public policy analysis, and public budgeting and finance.

Wendy L. Eaton serves as Professor and Director of the Master of Public Administration program at Indiana Wesleyan University, National & Global. Prior to her academic career, she served as an assistant city manager and has over 12 years of experience in local government management.

Jayce L. Farmer is an assistant professor in the School of Public Policy and Leadership at the University of Nevada, Las Vegas. His research focuses on local public finance, urban sustainability, county government administration, state and local relations, and interlocal collaboration.

William A. Fischel is a professor of economics, emeritus, at Dartmouth College. He taught economics at Dartmouth College from 1973 to 2019. Among his five books are *The Homevoter Hypothesis: How Home Values Influence Local Government Taxation, School Finance, and Land-Use Policies* (2001) and *Zoning Rules! The Economics of Land Use Regulation* (2015). He serves on the Hanover, NH, zoning board.

Clara Gerhardt is Distinguished Beeson Professor at Samford University in Alabama. She is a licensed clinical psychologist, a licensed marriage and family therapist, and has authored several textbooks, book chapters, over 140 articles in the popular press, and a regular column for the National Council on Family Relations.

Kathleen Hale is a professor of political science at Auburn University where she directs its Election Administration Initiative and Graduate Program in Election Administration. She also directs Auburn's partnership with The Election Center (National Association of Election Officials) to professionalize the public administration of elections through its national certification program.

Jeremy L. Hall is Professor of Public Administration and Director of the PhD Program in Public Affairs at the University of Central Florida. An international expert on public management, performance and accountability systems, and evidence-based practice and policy, Hall is Editor-In-Chief of *Public Administration Review* and a National Academy of Public Administration fellow.

Donna M. Handley serves as Master of Public Administration Director and associate professor at Southern Utah University. Prior to her academic career, she served as an assistant director of community development for the City of Auburn, Alabama. Her research interests include online learning, rural community governance and leadership, and women and leadership.

Matthew L. Howell earned his PhD in public policy and administration from University of Kentucky and is an associate professor of government at Eastern Kentucky University. His teaching and research interests focus on local government, urban politics, and public policy.

Janet M. Kelly is a professor of urban and public affairs at the University of Louisville where she teaches in the Master of Public Administration program. Her research interests focus on state and local government finance and economic development.

Elise Lael Kieffer serves as program director and assistant professor of nonprofit leadership studies at Murray State University. She also serves as the executive director of the Nonprofit Resource Center which provides technical support for nonprofit organizations across Western Kentucky.

Jiseul Kim is an assistant professor in the Department of Public Affairs and Planning at the University of Texas at Arlington. Her research focuses on public budgeting, finance, and financial management, with an emphasis on fiscal policy, performance management, capital budgeting and management, and governmental accounting and financial reporting.

Sung-Wook Kwon is an associate professor in the Department of Political Science at Texas Tech University. He has conducted research in the areas of urban management, regional governance, and interlocal collaboration, including the topics of local political institutions, economic development, service delivery, environmental sustainability, and land use.

Clement Lau is a departmental facilities planner with the Los Angeles County Department of Parks and Recreation where he works on a variety of data-driven, equity-focused park planning projects, including master plans and needs assessments. He holds a Doctorate in Policy, Planning, and Development from the University of Southern California.

Jamie Lawrence currently serves as the city administrator of Sac City, Iowa. He received his master of public administration degree from Murray State University.

Martin K. Mayer is an assistant professor at the University of North Carolina at Pembroke in the Department of Political Science and Public Administration. In this position, he teaches a variety of courses, primarily in the graduate school, in public management and health policy.

Clinton McNair is a doctoral student at the University of Oklahoma. His professional work has focused on nonprofits, community leadership, workforce development, housing, and economic development.

John C. Morris is a professor of political science at Auburn University. He is the author/editor of 12 books, and has published more than 120 journal articles, book chapters, and other publications. His research interests include collaborative governance, multisectoral partnerships, water policy, and state comparative public policy.

Sue M. Neal is an assistant professor in the Department of Political Science at Arkansas State University. Her research interests include public administration ethics and animal welfare.

William C. Rivenbark is a professor of public administration in the School of Government at the University of North Carolina at Chapel Hill, specializing in performance and financial management. He has published in numerous academic and professional journals and has coauthored two books. He also has prior working experience in local government.

Scott E. Robinson is the Bellmon Chair of Public Service at the University of Oklahoma. His research and teaching focus on the management of public service organizations as they cope with various forms of disasters or extreme events.

Simone Silva is a professor of economics, the director of MS in Economic Development Program, and a senior fellow at the Initiative for Community Economic Development (ICED) at Murray State University. Her research interests include regional economic development, applied econometrics, and statistics and data analysis.

Mary Ellen Travers received both her graduate degrees (Master of Public Health and Master of Science in Geography) from West Chester University of Pennsylvania. She is passionate about improving health in communities and public health education. When not writing or brainstorming sustainable solutions to public health problems, Mary Ellen can be found hiking with her dog or reading.

Jaymes Vettraino holds an MBA from Lehigh University and a BA in Political Science from Michigan State University. After 17 years as a city manager, he joined Rochester University as a faculty member and director of civic engagement. He also provides consulting services to local governments in human resources and strategic planning.

Kim Wallace holds a master's degree in public administration from Murray State University. Her wide-ranging career in public safety and city management spans three decades. She currently works at Hopkinsville Community College as an instructor and the Criminal Justice Program Coordinator.

FOREWORD

Ann O'M. Bowman

America's landscape is filled with small towns. Drive along an interstate highway in any part of the country and you will pass signs announcing the exit to a town that, unless you are from those parts, you have never heard of. Perhaps, if you are not running late to your destination, you decide to exit the highway, drive along a two-lane road and explore the town of "Smallville." You might be surprised by what you find. Some of these communities are bucolic havens, surrounded by vast acres of farmland. The town itself may be relatively isolated, with no other towns nearby, but the residents are connected. Local folks gather at the coffee shop on Main Street to shoot the breeze and they turn out at high school football games on Friday nights to cheer on the hometown team. These places are often low-change, that is, many routines and activities are a lot like they were 30 years ago. And Smallville residents might be quite content with that. It is a durable community, one that has maintained itself over time.

However, your excursion off the interstate highway may take you to a very different kind of small town, one that is located on the fringes of a metropolitan area that is expanding outward. This small town is likely to have a growing population and a strong commercial corridor of shops and restaurants. Basically, this Smallville is experiencing significant change as it transitions from a rural area to a more suburban-like milieu. Large tracts of land that once produced bountiful crops are being sold for residential development; rumors that Starbucks plans to open a store in town send a buzz through the community. Some of these booming small towns, especially those that are located just beyond the existing suburbs of large cities, risk losing the small town ambience that once epitomized them.

Still other small towns are experiencing change but of a less positive variety. This will be evident from the moment you pass the faded "Now Entering Smallville" sign and reduce your speed from 60 mph to 25 mph. These are the small towns that are losing population, perhaps a major employer has scaled down its operations or closed completely. The formerly robust downtown area is characterized now by vacant storefronts, potholes in streets go unrepaired, and homes that could benefit from a fresh coat of paint do not get one. You may want to stop for lunch but there are no restaurants open anymore; "for lease" signs are posted on their front doors. A sense of the town's former glory may be recalled on the historical markers that are located near the town hall building, but in general, you drive away somewhat disconsolate about the future of this Smallville.

The preceding discussion clarifies an important reality: small towns are not all alike. Even among the three general types described above, variations exist; diversity is apparent. But one feature that small towns possess regardless of their condition is a local government. And this is a key point: A well-functioning local government can make the difference between a small town that flourishes and one that struggles. Of course, local government is not the only factor influencing a town's destiny, but it is a central one.

In reading this book, remember that, despite the media attention accorded big cities, three-quarters of incorporated places in the United States have fewer than 5,000 residents. That is about 15,000 really small towns. Place matters, and while each small town has its own norms and culture, they all need a government, ideally one with committed leaders at town hall. Those who build their careers in small town government know the place and the people; they can witness the impact of their work first-hand. The policies that local officials debate, adopt, and implement affect their communities in meaningful ways.

Additionally, these towns can benefit from an engaged local citizenry that will help sustain the community and determine the town's future path. For residents, one of the advantages of living in a small town is the opportunity to participate in the democratic process beyond simply voting for elected officials. Small-scale democracy makes it easier for people to be heard on pressing community issues, especially if they create groups and organizations to supplement individual effort. People who live "out here" can become active in shaping their communities.

The primary audience for *Local Government Administration in Small Town America* is students who are considering working in small local governments once they graduate. For these students, small town government offers an ideal setting in which they can apply the knowledge and skills they have learned in the classroom—and see the results more immediately. These students can become sources of community renewal as they introduce fresh ideas and approaches appropriate for and tailored to the town.

The editors of this book have assembled a stellar set of scholars and practitioners to write chapters and case studies reflective of contemporary small town America. The themes and topics that are covered are relevant and forward looking. Not only do they acquaint readers with the challenges facing small towns, they also provide the knowledge that will help address those challenges. For example, many small communities are facing resource constraints or other capacity-related limitations. Leaders and managers have the opportunity to develop and pursue innovative strategies and approaches to deal with these constraints. In some cases, this may involve rallying local residents to participate in a brainstorming session; in others it could necessitate collaboration with nearby local governments or engagement with nonprofit organizations. Problem solving is a start, but looking ahead is also required.

As I write this, I am reminded of Smithville, a town of nearly 4,000 people in central Texas. The 2011 film, *The Tree of Life*, starring Brad Pitt, Sean Penn, and Jessica Chastain, was filmed in Smithville. And the four-square-mile town has a quirky side: At one point, Smithville held a Guinness World Record for baking the largest gingerbread man. More seriously, its collective vision for the future is stated on the town's website: "Our vision is to maintain a small-town sense of community while encouraging positive growth and continually improved standards of living for the citizens of Smithville, Texas." That sounds like a worthwhile course for a small town to chart.

PART I

Government Structures

1

THE NETWORK OF INTERESTS, INSTITUTIONS, AND INDIVIDUAL INTERACTIONS IN SMALL TOWN GOVERNANCE

James C. Clinger, Donna M. Handley, and Wendy L. Eaton

Introduction

In the US, metropolitan cities are often typified as prosperous while rural areas are thought of as economically distressed. The ideological chasm between the two goes beyond economic differences to include political, cultural, demographic distinctions as well. Over the past decade, medium and large cities experienced significant population growth (Bishop, 2021), are convenient units of study, and are often the focus of study and attention.

However, approximately three-quarters of the US is considered rural. In 2020, 46 million US residents lived in rural areas, comprising 14 percent of the nation's population. And, while urban dwellers may have lost an appreciation for rural America, it serves all Americans as a key source of affordable energy, safe food and water, and accessible outdoor recreation. Because of this, strong rural communities benefit all Americans.

In terms of government administration and leadership, rural community leaders face unique challenges that are not shared by their urban counterparts. Education, health care, unemployment, public safety, immigration, and poverty are just some of the issues that have rural distinctives. Furthermore, "residents who live in smaller and more isolated rural settings often face greater difficulties accessing provisions and services or commuting to work, among other economic development challenges. These factors may affect their resiliency to and recovery from shocks such as the COVID-19 pandemic" (Dobis et al., 2021, p. 2).

The purpose of this volume is four-fold. The first important goal is to devote some scholarly attention to the administration of smaller, often

DOI: 10.4324/9781003287766-2

neglected units of government. Second, we seek to provide a helpful resource for students as they study this segment of local government. Third, we hope to provide insights to rural practitioners who must navigate evolving challenges unique to rural governments. Finally, we will underscore the importance of social networks, collaboration, and intergovernmental interactions in rural communities.

Local Governmental Forms and Structures

No matter their size or geographical location, each government is organized with particular institutional arrangements that provide a structure for their operations and governance. Certain standard sets of arrangements are often referred to as particular "forms of government," although in practice many of those governments do not quite fit perfectly within the categories that those forms represent. Particular forms of government tend to be more common in certain types of government (e.g., cities, counties, special districts, etc.).

Municipal governments generally have the ability to choose how they are organized, either by writing their own charters or by adopting a form of government approved by the state government in municipal incorporation statutes. Other forms of local government usually have less discretion. Most municipalities adopt one of two basic forms: the council-manager form or the mayor-council form. There are variations within each form, and there are also other lesser-used forms of government including commission, town meeting, and representative town meeting. Each municipal form of government addresses differently the importance of political leadership and administrative leadership. Furthermore, each establishes structure, functions, values, lines of authority, electoral representation, and accountability.

The International City/County Management Association (ICMA), as part of its ongoing research and advocacy of professionalism in local government administration, conducts annual surveys to understand the evolution of municipal government management. As a part of that ongoing effort, ICMA has conducted its municipal Form of Government survey since 1974. Its latest survey on municipal form, conducted in 2018, found the council-manager form (48 percent) to be slightly more popular than the mayor-council form (38 percent).

Different Forms of Government Defined

Mayor-Council Form of Government

In cities with this form of government, an elected council or board serves as the legislative body. The mayor serves as the chief elected official and is often a full-time paid employee. The mayor is often elected separately from the council and has significant administrative and budgetary authority. This form is intended to promote political responsiveness (Box, 1995, p. 11) "between the mayor and council" (Svara, 1990, p. 11). Since the mayor is the designated leader in both the political and administrative realm, this also increases the chances that decisions involving public services and operations are inevitably made using a political lens. As a result, election details seem to matter. Partisan elections, all other things being equal, tend to increase voter turnout and ward or district elections tend to increase the representation of racial minorities (Abott & Magazinnik, 2020).

Council member behavior has also been found to be influenced by district elections (Clingermayer, 1990, 1993; Clingermayer & Feiock, 1990, 1994). Council members are often, but not always, elected in partisan races from districts or wards. More than half of all mayor-council cities employ a chief executive, sometimes called a chief administrative officer (CAO) whose responsibilities vary greatly (ICMA, 2018). Some cities have institutionalized the role of the CAO by including it in the city charter, while other cities have a more informal approach (Nelson, 2002) which can make it difficult to identify the distribution of administrative responsibilities between the mayor and the CAO. As a result, the administrative structure of the mayor-council form of government can differ greatly across local governments regardless of their size.

According to ICMA (2018), the mayor-council form is most popular among small cities with populations of 5,000 or fewer residents. While limited national data are available on smaller communities, the common belief is that they primarily use the mayor-council form, in large part because they cannot afford a professional city manager.

Council-Manager Form of Government

In council-manager governments, an elected council or board serves as the legislative body along with the chief elected official/mayor. Therefore, political power is concentrated in the elected officials (including the mayor). Structurally, political power is separate from the administrative duties associated with the day-to-day management and operations of the city government (Choi, Feiock & Bae, 2013; Montjoy & Watson, 1995; Svara, 1985, 1990). The legislative body appoints a professional administrator/ manager to serve as the chief administrative officer who serves at the pleasure of the legislative body. The manager advises the legislative body on policy matters and is responsible for the daily operations of the city. The council-manager form is not based on separation of powers because the legislative body can select, direct, and remove the manager if it is not pleased with his or her performance (Svara, 1990). The council-manager form is traditionally characterized by professional management, apolitical decisions, and efficiency (Alford & Scoble, 1965; Box, 1995; Svara, 1990). Employing this structure is viewed as an effort to encourage the professional separation of politics from administration in a more formal way that helps to reduce the influence of politics in administrative decisions that serve local citizens.

Commission Form of Government

In this form, members of an elected board of commissioners serve a dual role as both department heads (such as police, finance, and public works) and members of the legislative body. One commissioner is generally designated to preside over meetings. Historically, county governments have used this structure to manage larger county jurisdictions, and the small five to seven member commission is elected by county residents and granted both legislative and executive authority in running the county. They serve with other elected positions including the county sheriff, coroner, and clerk (NACO, 2012, p. 5). The commission form was once used by a number of US cities, but has slowly been abandoned since World War I (Adrian & Fine, 1991).

Today, examples of the commission form of government can be found in cities like Decatur, Georgia (population 24,000) and Daytona Beach, Florida (population 68,000). Commissioners serve in capacities that are similar to city council members, as noted on the City of Decatur's website:

> The City Commissioners determine the policies of the city and enact the local laws necessary for the protection of the public health, safety, and welfare. They provide leadership in identifying community needs and developing programs to meet community objectives. They oversee the delivery of services to citizens and are responsible for adoption of an annual budget and the levying of taxes necessary to finance local government operations.
>
> *(City of Decatur)*

In Daytona Beach, six commissioners serve alongside a mayor, and each is elected based on their respective zones to represent their constituents (City of Daytona Beach).

Town Meeting Form of Government

In this form of direct democracy, all qualified voters residing in the community participate in policy making and budgetary decisions. Acting as a legislative body, the voters select a board to carry out the policies.

Alternatively, they may delegate the day-to-day management of the municipality to an appointed manager/administrator. Currently, towns and townships operate in approximately 20 US states, in three regions of the country: New England, the Mid-Atlantic, and the Midwest (Michigan Townships Association, n.d.). "Because they often serve rural areas, Midwestern townships tend to focus on providing roads and bridges, fire and rescue, and other basic services to scattered populations" (Michigan Townships Association, n.d.).

Representative Town Meeting Form of Government

This form is similar to the town meeting form except that voters select residents to represent them at the town meeting. All residents may attend and participate in meetings and policy debate, but only elected representatives may vote.

Other Units of Local Government

Municipalities are not the only units of local government, nor are they the most numerous. Interestingly, these other units often have organizational structures that resemble municipal governments, share jurisdiction with municipalities, and often share tax bases and service responsibility with municipalities.

County Government

Counties are general-purpose governments that are typically larger in geographic area than municipalities. Legally speaking, they are generally considered "arms" of the state government, rather than "creatures of the state." Typically, state governments have plenary authority over county functions and organization, although some states have provided for county home rule just as they have permitted that status for municipalities. In the absence of home rule, county governments normally follow state templates for structure and policy responsibilities. Most counties are governed by a legislative body called a commission, board of supervisors, a fiscal court, or a county council. The chief executive may be called a county mayor, judge, or judge-executive. Some counties have a professional manager, much like a city manager in council-manager cities, but many others, particularly in rural areas, do not. Usually, the county executive is fragmented among several officers, such as the sheriff, county clerk, property tax assessor, and county attorney, many of whom are directly elected.

Special Districts and Public Authorities

Special districts and public authorities are limited-purpose governments with geographic jurisdictions that overlay those of city and county governments. Special districts generally provide water and sewer services, hospitals, libraries, electric power, and mass transit. Independent school districts are a particularly notable form of special district, although they are in many ways field offices for state public education systems. In rural areas, water districts and fire protection districts are particularly common and important. Public authorities are similar to special districts and in some cases the terms authority and district are used interchangeably. However, usually special districts have taxing authority, often levying property taxes, while authorities generally may not tax but instead receive most of their revenue from intergovernmental aid. Both special districts and authorities may impose user charges in exchange for services. Common policy responsibilities for local public authorities are public housing, airports, and community colleges. Usually both special districts and public authorities are governed by boards of trustees who appoint an executive director. In most public authorities, the board members are appointed to fixed terms by the chief executives leading the municipalities and counties in the authorities' service area. A larger percentage of board members of special districts are elected, although some districts have only appointed boards. These elections generally have very low voter turnout. In general, districts and authorities operate with little public notice and very little media attention. Board meetings are sparsely attended and press coverage is minimal (Burns, 1994). Nevertheless, the variation in organizational form (e.g., having elected rather than appointed members) may affect policy choices, particularly when issues become salient (Mullin, 2008).

Cooperatives

Many parts of the country, particularly rural areas, are served by cooperatives that are not truly governmental, but have a special status under state statutes and federal tax law. These cooperatives have members that are also service recipients. Farm cooperatives, for example, provide many different services, such as use of farm equipment for harvesting crops and fertilizing fields. The coop may employ the truck drivers and farm implement operators as well as the equipment (Grashuis & Su, 2019).

Rural electric cooperatives provide electric service and often auxiliary services such as satellite or cable television and internet provision within a particular service area. Unlike an electric power district, the electric cooperative considers its customers to be members who have voting rights in board elections. Rural electric cooperatives are normally granted powers of eminent domain to take title to property for purposes of power distribution. Electric cooperatives, electric power districts, and municipally owned electric power systems are granted first available options to purchase power from federal hydropower plants. Additionally, cooperatives enjoy unique tax privileges compared to for-profit, investor-owned utilities. The absence of corporate taxation and the access to relatively cheap hydropower reduces the cost of delivering services to rural cooperative customers (see Berry, 1994; Peterson, 1991).

Research on Form of Government

Every city has a unique history built on the qualities that give it a distinctive identity and character. Its economy, geography, population, diversity, demographics, political leaders, community activists, churches, clubs, and various civic and business organizations all contribute to each city's distinctive essence. At the heart of each city are its values and its vision for future generations. Furthermore, each community has its own set of social networks linking individuals to individuals and organizations to organizations. These values are profoundly felt in the way the city is organized and structured through its form of government. Form of government serves as the basis by which policy decisions are made and is a central concern to citizens, public administrators, and elected officials as well as a valuable topic for academic inquiry (e.g. Svara, 1990).

The significance of governmental form is not lost on scholars. Since the inception of council-manager government, scholars have studied and debated the normative aspects of municipal government (see, e.g., Adrian, 1988; Box, 1995; Fannin, 1983; Frederickson et al., 2004; Hassett & Watson, 2007; Kim, 1997; Lyons, 1978; Montjoy & Watson, 1995; Nalbandian, 1987; Svara, 1990, 2001; Watson & Hassett, 2003). Local government form is an outgrowth of citizen attitudes toward government and values held by community residents. Therefore, governmental structure and activities "gain authority" through representing the values that "underpin political culture" of the community (Nalbandian, 1990, p. 660). Furthermore, the form sets the stage for the provision of local public services (Crain & Rosenthal, 1966, Farnham & Bryant, 1985; Lyons, 1978; Morgan & Pelissero, 1980). A closely related line of inquiry pursued by scholars has been to identify reasons why communities select one form over another (Alford & Scoble, 1965; Dye & MacManus 1976;

Farnham & Bryant 1985; Knoke 1982; Lineberry & Fowler 1967; Watson et al., 2006; Wolfinger & Field 1966).

Recent trends suggest that the traditional forms of government are not as differentiated now as they once were (Carr & Karuppusamy, 2008; DeSantis & Renner, 2002; Frederickson et al., 2004). Because cities have long struggled to balance the governmental roles of elected and appointed officials, along with the authority, responsibility, accountability, responsiveness, and checks and balances associated with those roles, many cities have modified their structure to one that better suits their values. So, while all municipalities officially embrace a particular form of government, few operate exactly as prescribed by a textbook model.

These modifications and structural adaptations in governmental form occur for a variety of reasons. Calls for accountability and responsiveness are heard from an increasingly diverse and vocal citizenry. As a result, fewer and fewer cities operate in their pure form. This is particularly the case in council-manager and mayor-council forms. Council-manager cities have evolved to take on features of the mayor-council form to become more politically responsive, and mayor-council cities have adopted features of the council-manager form to become more professionally managed and efficient. While citizens in council-manager cities agree that a professional manager is important for the efficient functioning of a city, they also desire a strong political leader. Nalbandian (1987, p. 4) comments, "A strong mayor symbolizes politics, whether good or bad, and people like this." Similarly, mayor-council cities recognize the value of an experienced and professional local government manager. For that reason, a growing number of mayor-council cities now employ a chief administrative officer (CAO) who works for the mayor and is responsible for managing the daily city government operations.

These modifications are becoming commonplace in cities across the country. In fact, a growing number of scholars argue that the terms "mayor-council" and "council-manager" no longer accurately describe the hybrid forms that have evolved and are in place today. As a result, a body of literature describing "adapted cities" (Carr & Karuppusamy, 2008; Frederickson et al., 2004) has developed that attempts to more accurately describe municipal reforms as a convergence of the mayor-council and council-manager forms of government. These authors promote a new framework and put forth a typology of five different hybrid structures that combine the two traditional forms in various ways.

This convergence challenges scholars and researchers who attempt to classify cities that have adopted structural modifications. Such classification is made even more complex by differences in the number of council members, the method by which the mayor is chosen, the authority of the mayor, the use of at-large or district/wards, partisan and nonpartisan elections, full-time/part-time status of elected and appointed officials, and the length of terms served by elected officials.

While it may be more difficult to tell the two forms of government apart, there remain underlying value-based differences that distinguish the two. In council-manager governments, professional city managers are trained to take a nonpartisan, objective approach to city management and service delivery. They aim to be responsive to the will of the council and respond to citizens and interest groups in an efficient, fair, and uniform manner. On the other hand, as elected officials, mayors have a more difficult challenge to balance both their political and administrative duties. They must build political support and develop relationships with individuals and groups to be re-elected (Svara, 2009). As a result, mayors typically feel the need to be politically responsive to their supporters, a challenge that is not experienced in quite the same way by city managers.

Significance of Form of Government

Structural adaptations aside, the underlying structure of a city's government is the foundation of all other aspects of municipal government, and its significance cannot be overstated. While the variability in and among municipal government structures makes it difficult to analyze the differences between them (Nelson & Svara, 2010), examining some of the research attempting to do so provides an analysis of the nuances of the underlying forms and the inherent challenges associated with each. The way the political and administrative functions are designed deeply influences governmental outcomes and the intrinsic political and administrative incentives of the council-manager and mayor-council forms of government (Feiock, Jeong, & Kim 2003; Frant 1996; Nelson & Svara, 2012).

In their research on municipal government decision making, Nelson and Nollenberger (2011) found that form of government, including district elections, was an important factor in the levels of conflict and cooperation in local governance. Nelson and Afonso's (2019) inquiry into a link between form of government and corruption found that municipalities with a council-manager form of government are "57 percent less likely to have corruption convictions than municipalities with the mayor council form" and "having a mayor elected at-large is found to reduce the risk of corruption" (p. 591). Form of government was also found to influence local budgetary decision making (Carr & Karuppusamy, 2008).

In his research on municipal government form and budget outcomes, Jimenez (2020) concluded that form of government influences the motivations of chief executives in each form in very different ways. For example, the mayor in the mayor-council form is motivated to be re-elected which increases responsiveness to voters' demands. This can lead to budgetary insolvency as the mayor attempts to follow through on projects popular with voters, but not always fiscally prudent. On the other hand, the chief executive in council-manager cities is motivated by career advancement in which leading a fiscally responsible city is a large part. As a result, council-manager cities were found to have stronger budget solvency than mayor-council cities.

In their work in local government management and performance, Nelson and Svara (2012) found that innovation rates are higher in cities with council-manager governments. Even controlling for variations in form, these researchers found that form of government best explained the adoption of innovative practices in municipalities. Of particular importance for this volume, Folz and Abdelrazek's (2009, p. 553) research on small cities with populations between 5,000 and 25,000 found that cities having a professional city manager and an adaptive or administrative type of local government structure are somewhat more likely to provide qualitatively higher levels of municipal services, suggesting that professional managers play an important role in advancing the level of service provided in the communities they serve.

Changing Form of Government

There is clearly not a one-size-fits-all form of government model for municipalities. The ways cities can be structured are more varied than in the past. Today, more than ever, local government leaders have the ability to create a future using a structural framework and adaptations to that structure that is as unique as the city they govern.

As cities grapple with policy disputes, political tensions, increasingly diverse citizenry, fiscal challenges, leadership missteps, and divisive controversies, the question about how best to conduct municipal government operations often arises. As a part of that conversation, governmental form can be debated. One interesting aspect of local governmental form is that it is never permanent. Cities are able to change the form of government they use. Other units of government typically do not have that autonomy.

While form of government changes are not common occurrences, they can and do happen. According to ICMA, municipal attempts to change the form of government are rare. However, when these attempts occur, they are generally successful (ICMA, 2018). Hassett and Watson (2007) suggest that the council-manager and mayor-council forms emerge from two dissimilar ways of looking at governing and describe them as completely separate paradigms. When structural change happens, the community's value-based paradigm shifts. On one end of the value continuum is the strong-mayor form headed by a political chief executive. At the other end is the council-manager form.

In most communities, both value paradigms are simultaneously present. The community's dominant paradigm serves as the basis by which local policy decisions are made. When demographics and other defining factors change in communities, it seems to be more likely that the question of governmental structure will arise.

Changing Form of Government: Two Small City Examples

One small city that changed its form of government was Daphne, Alabama, a rapidly growing community on Mobile Bay. Daphne, with a population of under 12,000 in 1990, adopted council-manager government, but then abandoned it in the mid-1990s after a string of three city managers encountered ethical or performance issues leading to their removal. As a result of the city's constant turmoil since its adoption of council-manager government, the city decided to return to the mayor-council form (Watson & Hassett, 1997). Daphne has continued to grow since that time and is a city of approximately 26,500 residents, according to the 2018 Census.

With a 2018 population of only 15,000, Talladega, Alabama, is best known as being home to the famous Talladega Superspeedway. Efforts to change that city's form of government were led by a coalition of business owners and government reform groups. Interestingly, the catalyst for changing to the council-manager form was based on the prospect that a former mayor who had been imprisoned for illegal activities while in office was considering another run for mayor. He had staunch support in the community among those who felt he was wrongfully convicted, and his voting rights were eventually restored. In spite of that, council-manager government was adopted in 2004, and Talladega remains one of the few cities in Alabama operating with a council-manager form of government (Hassett & Watson, 2007).

Institutions, Interests, and Ideas

Governmental research is rooted in a body of scholarship focused on political institutions. In fact, many social scientists who discuss politics and policy change rely not only on institutional variables, but also other explanatory concepts, such as interests and ideas (see, e.g., Hall, 1997;

Mukand and Rodrik, 2016; Mukand and Rodrik, 2018; Shearer et al., 2016). Institutions provide the structure of decisions and the constraints upon behavior that individuals must consider as they pursue their interests. Interests provide the motivation and incentive for action. While ideas are invariably thought to be important, this importance manifests in different ways. Some see ideas as having the same motivating force as interests. Others see ideas as merely a lens through which individuals perceive the world around them. Others view ideas in instrumental terms, as a tool that some political entrepreneurs use to persuade others to join them in pursuing their own personal objectives. Institutions, interests, and ideas emerge throughout this volume and point to key distinctives of rural places.

The Network of Small Town Governance

In the chapters that follow, we examine strategies that small American towns and rural communities use to serve their constituents within the institutions, ideas, and interests that impact how they govern. This includes how local administrators and leaders operate within the context of their respective units of government, various political influences, and fiscal constraints. But we also add other concepts to the mix, particularly the individual and organizational interactions in which interests, institutions, and ideas are embedded. These personal interactions and interrelationships are often described by social scientists as social networks. The implications of these networks have been discussed by many scholars, some of whom are contributing to this volume.

Individuals with whom anyone interacts are part of that person's social network. But the network does not end with those who directly interact with one specific individual. Linkages that the first order contacts have with each other and with others are all part of that network. These linkages become the conduits through which information can flow. They reflect the exchanges of money, time, and effort through which collective action can occur. Social networks may work within and sometimes around formal government institutions.

Scholarship has classified different types of networks as dense or loose, based on how interconnected the linkages are between different members of the network. Scholars also have characterized different unique connections between members of a network as strong or weak, depending upon the frequency and salience of the interactions between the linked members. Most notably, Mark Granovetter (1973, 1983) has argued that, while strong ties often found in tight-knit families, work teams, neighborhoods, and communities may have some appeal, the weak ties in a social network may provide the greatest access to information and influence because the weak ties normally act as bridges to individuals, groups, and organizations that are different from one another. Networks of strong ties normally connect individuals to other individuals who have the same information and the same kinds of resources, so strong-tie linkages may not encourage innovation or access to outsiders.

Of course, strong ties and tightly knit relationships can be of use, too. Repeated, multi-faceted, mutually beneficial interactions between individuals and groups can encourage trust and a reputation for cooperative behavior (Axelrod, 1984). This trust can make interpersonal commitments more credible. This can become the basis for norms of conduct that can facilitate collective action directly or which can support formalized institutional arrangements which can encourage collective action and identify and sanction uncooperative behavior (Ostrom, 1990). Formal institutions may supplement or supplant the role of informal social ties, and vice versa (Granovetter, 1985).

This perspective may inform our thinking about governance in small towns and rural communities. It may be a stereotype or, more generously, an overly broad empirical generalization, to believe that small towns are full of close, tight-knit social networks of people who know each other and one another's business (Catlaw & Stout, 2016). Unlike the weak ties of their counterparts in more urban locales, small town and country folk have dense networks. This may foster many attractive outcomes, but it may also encourage parochialism and ignorance of opportunities for progress. Governance in these communities may emphasize knowledge of local people and places, but not expertise in technical fields or the politics of distant governmental bodies. Small communities also generally have small local bureaucracies, which may be more characterized by trust, pride, and perceptions of high ethics than are larger bureaucracies (Morrison & Clinger, 2021). This may prove a disadvantage in handling complex policy problems (Berardo & Scholz, 2010).

The "Rural" Lens

Historically, defining "rural" has been a challenge. The US Census Bureau does not actually define "rural." Instead, it refers to rural places as geographic areas that are "not urban—that is, after defining individual urban areas, rural is what is left" (Ratcliffe et al., 2016). Essentially, this means that all areas and populations that exist outside urban areas and urban clusters are considered rural.

In the 1950 census, the Census Bureau began officially classifying urban areas as those with a population of 50,000 or more residents (Ratcliffe et al., 2016). Beginning with 2000, the Census Bureau expanded the classification of urban areas to include urbanized areas and urbanized clusters, which meant that urban clusters included areas with more than 2,500 residents but fewer than 50,000 residents (Ratcliffe et al., 2016). Further, "to define an area as urban, the Census Bureau uses criteria including total population thresholds, density, land use, and distance. Census blocks are the 'building blocks' for urban areas" (Ratcliffe et al., 2016). When focusing on urban vs. rural census blocks, the classifications range between (1) completely rural, (2) mostly rural, and (3) mostly urban (Ratcliffe et al., 2016). Understanding how the US Census Bureau classifies rural illustrates the difficulty that local governments and service providers can have based upon urban-rural classifications.

While the chapters that follow are designed to provide cases and strategies for students and practitioners in public administration to use in a small town environment, we strongly encourage readers to explore and consider the unique nature of small towns and their social and political cultures. We recognize the important influence of a community's distinctive social and political culture and how that alters how local political leaders and government practitioners respond to demands and challenges they face. To follow or accept the prescriptions in this volume without considering the unique cultures of the small town in which you live and/or work would be a tremendous handicap in your efforts to make informed and effective decisions regarding administrative and governance decisions otherwise.

References

Abott, C., & Magazinnik, A. (2020). At-large elections and minority representation in local government. *American Journal of Political Science*, 64(3), 717–733.
Adrian, C. R. (1988). Forms of city government in American history. In International City Management Association (Ed.). *The Municipal Yearbook 1988*. International City Management Association, 3–11.
Adrian, C. R., & Fine, M. R. (1991). *State and Local Politics*. Wadsworth.
Alford, R. R., & Scoble, H. M. (1965). Political and socioeconomic characteristics of American cities. In O. F. Nolting & D. S. Arnold (Eds.), *The Municipal Yearbook 1965*. International City Managers Association, 82–97.
Axelrod, R. (1984). *The Evolution of Cooperation*. Basic Books.
Bauroth, N. G. (2015). Hide in plain sight: The uneven proliferation of special districts across the United States by size and function. *Public Administration Quarterly*, 39(2), 295–324.
Berardo, R., & Lubell, M. (2016). Understanding what shapes a polycentric governance system. *Public Administration Review*, 76(5), 738–751.
Berardo, R., & Lubell, M. (2019). The ecology of games as a theory of polycentricity: Recent advances and future challenges. *Policy Studies Journal*, 47(1), 6–26.

Berardo, R., & Scholz, J. T. (2010). Self-organizing policy networks: Risk, partner selection, and cooperation in estuaries. *American Journal of Political Science, 54*(3), 632–649.

Berry, C. (2008). Piling on: Multilevel government and the fiscal common-pool. *American Journal of Political Science, 52*(4), 802–820.

Berry, D. M. (1994). Private ownership form and productive efficiency: Electric cooperatives versus investor-owned utilities. *Journal of Regulatory Economics, 6*(4), 399–420. https://doi-org.ezproxy.waterfield.murraystate.edu/10.1007/BF01418234

Bishop, B. (2021, July 14). In the last decade, rural counties saw slight decline in population while rest of the nation grew. *The Daily Yonder.* https://dailyyonder.com/in-the-last-decade-rural-counties-saw-slight-decline-in-population-while-rest-of-the-nation-grew/2021/07/14/

Bourdeaux, C. (2007). Conflict, accommodation, and bargaining: The implications of using politically buffered institutions for contentious decision making. *Governance, 20*(2), 279–303.

Bourdeaux, C. (2008). Politics versus professionalism: The effect of institutional structure on democratic decision making in a contested policy arena. *Journal of Public Administration Research & Theory, 18*(3), 349–373.

Box, R. C. (1995). Searching for the best structure for American local government. *International Journal of Public Administration, 18,* 711–741.

Burns, N. (1994). *The Formation of American Local Governments: Private Values in Public Institutions.* Oxford University Press.

Carr, J. B., & Brower, R. S. (2000). Principled opportunism: Evidence from the organizational middle. *Public Administration Quarterly, 24*(1), 109–138.

Carr, J. B., & Karuppusamy, S. (2008). The adapted cities framework: On enhancing its use in Empirical research. *Urban Affairs Review, 43*(6), 875–886.

Carr, J. B., & Karuppusamy, S. (2010). Reassessing the link between city structure and fiscal policy: Is the problem poor measures of governmental structure? *American Review of Public Administration, 40*(2), 209–228.

Catlaw, T. J., & Stout, M. (2016). Governing small-town America today: The promise and dilemma of dense networks. *Public Administration Review, 76*(2), 225–229.

Choi, C. G., Feiock, R., & Bae, J. (2013). The adoption and abandonment of council-manager government. *Public Administration Review, 73*(5), 727–736.

City of Daytona Beach. (n.d.). City commission. www.codb.us/384/City-Commission

City of Decatur. (n.d.). City commission. www.decaturga.com/citycommission

Clingermayer, J. C., & Feiock, R. C. (1990). The adoption of economic development policies by large cities: A test of economic, interest group, and institutional explanations. *Policy Studies Journal, 18*(3), 539–552.

Clingermayer, J. C. & Feiock, R. C. (1994). Campaigns, careerism, and constituencies: Contacting council members about economic development policy. *American Politics Quarterly, 22*(4), 453–468. https://doi.org/10.1177/1532673X9402200403

Crain, R. L., & Rosenthal, D. B. (1966). Structure and values in local political systems: The case of fluoridation decisions. *Journal of Politics, 28*(1), 169–195.

Crew, M., & Kahlon, R. (2014). Guaranteed return regulation: A case study of regulation of water in California. *Journal of Regulatory Economics, 46*(1), 112–121.

DeSantis, V. S., & Renner, T. (2002). City government structures: An attempt at clarification. *State and Local Government Review, 34*(2), 95–104.

DiMaggio, P. J., & Powell, W. W. (1983). The iron cage revisited: Institutional isomorphism and collective rationality in organizational fields. *American Sociological Review, 48*(2), 147–160.

Dobis, E. A., Krumel, T. P. Jr., Cromartie, J., Conley, K. L., Sanders, A., & Ortiz, R. (2021). *Rural America at a Glance.* USDA.

Dye, T. R., & MacManus, S. A. (1976). Predicting city government structure. *American Journal of Political Science, 20*(2), 257–271.

Fannin, W. R. (1983). City manager policy roles as a source of city council/ city manager conflict. *International Journal of Public Administration, 5*(4), 381–399.

Farnham, P. G. & Bryant, S. N. (1985, July). Form of local government: Structural policies of citizen choice. *Social Science Quarterly, 66*, 386–400.

Feiock, R. C., Jeong, M. & Kim, J. (2003). Credible commitment and council-manager government: Implications for policy instrument choices. *Public Administration Review, 63*(5), 616–625.

Feiock, R. C., Lee, I. W. & Park, H. J. (2012). Administrators' and elected officials' collaboration networks: Selecting partners to reduce risk in economic development. *Public Administration Review, 72*, S58–S68.

Folz, D. H., & Abdelrazek, R. (2009). Professional management and service levels in small U.S. communities. *American Review of Public Administration, 39*(5), 553–569.

Frant, H. (1996). High-powered and low-powered incentives in the public sector. *Journal of Public Administration Research and Theory, 6*(3), 365–381.

Frederickson, H. G., Johnson, G. A., & Wood, C. (2004). The changing structure of American cities: A study of the diffusion of innovation. *Public Administration Review, 64*(3), 320–330.

Granovetter, M. S. (1973). The strength of weak ties. *American Journal of Sociology, 78*(6), 1360–1380.

Granovetter, M. (1983). The strength of weak ties: A network theory revisited. *Sociological Theory, 1*, 201–233.

Granovetter, M. (1984). Small is bountiful: Labor markets and establishment size. *American Sociological Review, 49*(3), 323–334.

Granovetter, M. (1985). Economic action and social structure: The problem of embeddedness. *American Journal of Sociology, 91*(3), 481–510.

Granovetter, M. (2005). The impact of social structure on economic outcomes. *Journal of Economic Perspectives, 19*(1), 33–50.

Grashuis, J., & Su, Y. (2019). A review of the empirical literature on farmer cooperatives: Performance, ownership and governance, finance, and member attitude. *Annals of Public & Cooperative Economics, 90*(1), 77–102. https:// doi-org.ezproxy.waterfield.murraystate.edu/10.1111/apce.12205

Hager, M. A., Galaskiewicz, J., & Larson, J. A. (2004). Structural embeddedness and the liability of newness among nonprofit organizations. *Public Management Review, 6*(2), 159–188.

Hall, P. A. (1997). The role of interests, institutions, and ideas in the comparative political economy of the industrialized nations. In M. I. Lichbach and A. S. Zuckerman (Eds.), *Comparative Politics: Rationality, Culture, and Structure*. Cambridge University Press, 174–207.

Hassett, W. L., & Watson, D. J. (2007). *Civic Battles: When Cities Change their Form of Government*. PrAcademics.

International City-County Management Association (ICMA). (2018). *2018 Municipal Form of Government Survey*. International City-County Management Association.

Jimenez, B. S. (2020). Municipal government form and budget outcomes: Political responsiveness, bureaucratic insulation, and the budgetary solvency of cities. *Journal of Public Administration Research & Theory, 30*(1), 161–177.

Kim, J. (1997). Changes in Municipal Governmental Forms and their Impact on Local Government Policy Outputs: Theory, Evidence, and Implications (unpublished dissertation). Cleveland State University.

Knoke, D. (1982). The spread of municipal reform: Temporal, spatial, and social dynamics. *American Journal of Sociology, 87*(6), 1314–1339.

Konisky, D. M. (2009). Inequities in enforcement? Environmental justice and government performance. *Journal of Policy Analysis & Management, 28*(1), 102–121.

Konisky, D. M., & Teodoro, M. P. (2016). When governments regulate governments. *American Journal of Political Science, 60*(3), 559–574.

Lindsay, C. M. (1976). A theory of government enterprise. *Journal of Political Economy, 84*(5), 1061–1077.

Lineberry, R. L., & Fowler, E. P. (1967, September). Reformism and public policies in American cities. *American Political Science Review, 61*, 701–717.

Lubell, M., Mewhirter, J., & Berardo, R. (2020). The origins of conflict in polycentric governance systems. *Public Administration Review, 80*(2), 222–233.

Lubell, M., Mewhirter, J. M., Berardo, R., & Scholz, J. T. (2017). Transaction costs and the perceived effectiveness of complex institutional systems. *Public Administration Review, 77*(5), 668–680.

Lyons, W. (1978). Reform and response in American cities: Structure and policy reconsidered. *Social Science Quarterly, 59*(1), 118–132.

Menzel, D. C., Ed. (1996). *The American County: Frontiers of Knowledge*. University of Alabama Press.

Montjoy, R. S., & Watson, D. J. (1995). A case for reinterpreted dichotomy of politics and administration as a professional standard in council-manager government. *Public Administration Review, 55*(3), 231–239.

Morgan, D. R., & Pelissero, J. P. (1980). Urban policy: Does political structure matter? *American Political Science Review, 74*, 999–1006.

Morrison, J. S., & Clinger, J. C. (2021). Agency design and state administrators: Political insulation and managers' views of their workplace. *International Journal of Public Administration, 44*(7), 557–563.

Mukand, S., & Rodrik, D. (2016). *Ideas versus Interests: A Unified Political Economy Framework*. Available at https://drodrik.scholar.harvard.edu/files/dani-rodrik/files/ideasinterestsapr10sm_dr.pdf

Mukand, S., & Rodrik, D. (2018). *The Political Economy of Ideas: On Ideas versus Interests in Policymaking*. NBER Working Paper No. w24467, Available at SSRN: https://ssrn.com/abstract=3154249

Mullin, M. (2008). The conditional effect of specialized governance on public policy. *American Journal of Political Science*, 52(1), 125–141.

Nalbandian, J. (1987). The evolution of local governance: A new democracy. *Public Management*, 69(6), 2–5.

Nalbandian, J. (1990). Tenets of contemporary professionalism in local government. *Public Administration Review*, 50(6), 654– 662.

National Association of Counties (NACO). (2012). *History of County Government Part I*. www.nvnaco.org/wp-content/uploads/History-and-Overview-of-Cou nty-Government-n-the-U.S.-NACo.pdf. Accessed June 25, 2023.

Nelson, K. L. (2002). Assessing the CAO position in a strong-mayor government. *National Civic Review*, 91(1), 41+. *Gale Academic OneFile*, link.gale.com/ apps/doc/A86389601/AONE?u=anon~24405cac&sid=googleScholar&xid= 946e57a4. Accessed Aug. 28, 2022.

Nelson, K. L., & Afonso, W. B. (2019). Ethics by design: The impact of form of government on municipal corruption. *Public Administration Review*, 79(4), 591–600.

Nelson, K. L., & Nollenberger, K. (2011). Conflict and cooperation in municipalities: Do variations in form of government have an effect? *Urban Affairs Review*, 47(5), 696–720.

Nelson, K., & Svara, J. H. (2010). Adaptation of models versus variations in form: Classifying structures of city government. *Urban Affairs Review*, 45(4), 544–562.

Nelson, K., & Svara, J. H. (2012). Form of government still matters: Fostering innovation in U.S. municipal governments. *American Review of Public Administration*, 42(3), 257–281.

Nelson, B., & Wood, C. (2010). Repercussions of reform: The effect of municipal form of government on citizen participation strategies. *Journal of Public Administration*, 3(3), 25–43.

Ostrom, E. (1990). *Governing the Commons: The Evolution of Institutions for Collective Action*. Cambridge University Press.

Petersen, H. C. (1991). Rates and tariff structures: Investor-owned utilities vs. rural electric cooperatives. *Agribusiness*, 7(6), 597–601. https://doi.org/10.1002/ 1520-6297(199111)7:6<597::aid-agr2720070609>3.0.co;2-h

Ratcliffe, M., Burd, C., Holder, K., & Fields, A. (2016). Defining rural at the U.S. Census Bureau. *American Community Survey and Geography Brief*. Accessed 1 Nov. 2022.

Scholz, J. T., Berardo, R., & Kile, B. (2008). Do networks solve collective action problems, credibility, search, and collaboration. *Journal of Politics*, 70(2), 393–406.

Shearer J. C., Abelson, J., Kouyaté, B., Lavis, J. N., & Walt, G. (2016). Why do policies change? Institutions, interests, ideas and networks in three cases of policy reform. *Health Policy Plan*, 31(9), 1200–1211.

Shi, Y. (2018). An empirical assessment of local autonomy and special district finance in the US. *Local Government Studies*, 44(4), 531–551.

Svara, J. H. (1990). *Official Leadership in the City: Patterns of Conflict and Cooperation.* Oxford University Press.

Svara, J. H. (1985). Dichotomy and duality: Reconceptualizing the relationship between policy and administration in council-manager cities. *Public Administration Review, 45*(1), 221–232.

Svara, J. H. (2001). Do we still need model charters? The meaning and relevance of reform in the twenty-first century. *National Civic Review, 90*(1), 19–33.

Svara, J. H. (2009). *The Facilitative Leader in City Hall: Reexamining the Scope and Contributions.* CRC Press.

Watson, D. J., & Hassett, W. L. (1997). Conflict comes to Daphne. In D. J. Watson (Ed.), *Innovative Governments: Creative Approaches to Local Problems.* Praeger Publishers, 97–125.

Watson, D. J., & Hassett, W. L., Eds. (2003). *Local Government Management: Current Issues and Best Practices.* M. E. Sharpe.

Watson, D. J., Hassett, W. L., & Caver, F. R. (2006). Form of government and community values: The case of Tuskegee, Alabama. *Politics & Policy, 34*(4), 794–813.

Wholey, D. R., Christianson, J. B., & Sanchez, S. M. (1992). Organization size and failure among health maintenance organizations. *American Sociological Review, 57*(6), 829–842.

Wolfinger, R. E., & Field, J. O. (1966). Political ethos and the structure of local government. *American Political Science Review, 60*(2), 306–326.

CASE STUDY: STARTING OUT AS A PROFESSIONAL ADMINISTRATOR IN A SMALL TOWN

Jamie Lawrence

People often ask, "how can you do this job?" My answer is that the immeasurable rewards of seeing a community flourish offsets all the stress associated with this career. As a public administrator working in a rural community, I inherited several challenges. First, I am directly responsible for the overall city finances, including the general fund, special funds, and all utilities funds. Secondly, I often serve as an official representative of the city. These duties often involve serving as an advisor on various boards and commissions, representing the city at various Chamber of Commerce events, and being a member of a local club. Indirectly, as a leader in the community, I also feel that it is important to develop a strong network and support group with other community leaders. Thirdly, when I took the position in Sac City, IA, I was very lucky to inherit an experienced city council; often this is not the case in rural communities. With an experienced city council, I tend to take the position that the council is the policy maker, and I enforce that policy. Fourth, building those personal and organization networks in smaller cities is vitally important. Lastly, and perhaps most importantly, I view continuing education through my professional organization (ICMA) as vital to becoming an effective public administrator.

As the city's chief financial officer, I propose the city's fiscal year budget, and throughout that year manage that budget to the best of my abilities. Larger cities often have a separate finance officer to carry out those duties. Smaller rural communities typically can't afford multiple administrative staff, which is the case in Sac City.

DOI: 10.4324/9781003287766-3

Budgeting activities often begin in September. Ideally, at this point I start asking department heads to submit their proposed departmental budgets. In Sac City, our supervisors include the chief of police, natural gas superintendent, water department superintendent, wastewater department superintendent, director of public works, and the city clerk. At this time, I also begin informal talks with city council members and the mayor on what items they would like to see prioritized in the upcoming budget. From December through March, more formalized discussions include committee meetings, council work sessions, public hearings, and ultimately budget adoption. In Iowa, cities are required to certify and submit their annual budget by March 31.

Budgeting can be very difficult and time consuming. In my case it was especially difficult as I saw the need to make several changes that would impact not only the city, but other community organizations as well. In Sac City, community organizations can apply for city funds as long as the city deems them for a "public purpose." Sac City historically awards funds to the local community center, day care facility, senior center, Sac City Chamber/Main Street, and other organizations. Many of these "community requests" were funded by our utilities. Examination of the finances indicated these utilities were losing money, but still awarding these grants. The fund balances of the Gas Department, Water Department, and Wastewater Department were shrinking. This unstainable situation had to be corrected.

In my first year I proposed cutting the funds to our community programs substantially. I suggested that these funds should not be used for year-to-year operation and maintenance, but for special projects that needed some matching funds. I also suggested these organizations work to develop plans to wean themselves from dependency on local funds. As most would guess, my proposal was very unpopular with the public. I received many phone calls telling me that there were other areas in the city budget that could be cut, and that we had too many employees. During this time the mayor and council were supportive and in the end the cuts were made. As a side note, all these organizations are still functioning effectively and have actually improved their financial health.

It would also be important to mention that in my first year, our wastewater department was hemorrhaging money. An unfunded mandate that ordered improvements to our plant forced the city to incur nearly $5 million in debt funded through a utility bond. A contract executed prior to my arrival precluded refinancing and placed other restrictions on the debt. Additionally, sanitary sewer fees were already very high. There was not support to further increase these fees. Our only option at that time, then, was to pay off the entire debt, which the state would allow, and refinance it into general obligation debt. This allowed us to levy a tax for a portion of the debt with the balance being paid by the wastewater plant. This allowed the plant to become solvent.

These are just a couple of examples of the decision-making process that the city council and I have gone through. Stressful situations that must be handled with an impact on many people's lives. Many times, there are no easy answers. Taxing for general obligation debt potentially raises the overall tax rate and can affect future development; raising utility rates can inordinately impact low-income individuals. Maintaining the tax rate prior to incurring GO bond debt would have required cutting some existing programs. These ethical dilemmas are not unique to Sac City; most new administrators that take a position as a city administrator in a rural community are going to face these types of decisions. It is vitally important to have a solid understanding of budgeting and finance prior to becoming employed as a public administrator in a rural community.

I think most of us who enter into this profession understand that we are going to be a leader in the community. What many may not realize is what that means. In my case, and most likely many others, the city council wanted to hire a candidate who was not necessarily local. It was their belief, in my opinion, that someone who was not from this region would bring fresh ideas and new management methods to the community. It appears hiring me brought a substantial amount of excitement to the community. I was the new guy, and this meant getting bombarded (in a good way) by various special interests in the community. It also meant getting inundated by those individuals who had been attempting to get the city to mitigate their personal issues (i.e., dead trees, neighbor issue, leaks, etc.). This process, although sometimes overwhelming, did allow me to quickly understand many issues that needed to be addressed in the city.

During my first few months I attended nearly every committee and commission meeting, attended most of the various special events I was invited to, and joined the country club. After about six months of employment, I was approached by a council member who told me that he was impressed with all my community activity, but reminded me to remember that family comes first. He advised me to make sure that my work did not take away from my home life. My wife was new to the community and did not know many people. We moved here with intentions of her finding work later on. After speaking with this council member I did change a few things. First, I prioritized which meetings I would attend and informed that chair of each committee and commission that I may not be at all their meetings, but if they needed me please let me know. Secondly, I didn't want my wife to be sitting at home alone all the time so I started asking her to attend certain functions with me. I also asked her if she would be interested in doing some volunteer work. This change increased the happiness in our family and in turn made my job less stressful.

After approximately eight months after moving to Sac City my wife was able to find employment, and approximately four years after our move my wife has found employment related to her degree. She now works at a local bank. It would seem to me that a spouse will often have a difficult time finding appropriate employment initially in a small town or rural area. It is my guess that often professional employers are mostly looking for long-term employees and those employers want to ensure that the city administrator intends on staying for an extended period of time before hiring their spouse.

One meeting that I was always required to attend was the city council meeting. As I stated earlier, I inherited a very experienced council. This council also seemed to be proactive, progressive, and educated. I was very lucky indeed. Although the city council was experienced, the mayor was new to the process. The city's Rules of Conduct names the city administrator as the parliamentarian in the absence of the city attorney. In my case, that was most meetings as our city attorney did not attend unless requested.

I feel that it is important to meet with the mayor prior to every council meeting to make him aware of items on the agenda and the processes that must be followed during the council meeting. We often review the process of passing ordinances, resolutions, and motions. Should we have a public hearing, we will discuss how that hearing needs to be run. As additional support, I am seated next to the mayor to offer assistance or advice during the council meeting. At meetings I offer my advice and opinion, but I always balance that with the fact that I am not there to create policy, only manage it. Occasionally I offer ideas on new policy ideas, but it is always my intention to ask the council how they would like those policies written.

Regarding the mayor and city council, our Rules of Conduct state that the mayor and council will not take problems, issues, or disciplinary concerns directly to the employee. It is understood that, should they have any problem with an employee of the city, that problem must be directed to the city administrator. I strongly support this policy and actually put the same requirements in my employment contract with the city. It is always important that employees know who to go to with employment-related issues.

In a rural community, personal networks are critical to maintaining a positive relationship with the general public. Although I don't personally know everyone in Sac City, I strive to get to know as many as I can. When I envision working in a larger more metropolitan area, I see separation from the public. When managing a rural city of approximately 2,000, close networks are much more important. A city manager who chooses to work in a rural city must be aware that when my spouse and I go grocery shopping, watch their children play football on Friday night, go to church, play golf, and practically any other public function, most community members know us, and more often than not, they will want to strike up a conversation about city business. I will often try and answer their questions, but if it takes over two or three minutes to discuss I will politely ask them to give me a call when I am in my office. When given suggestions from citizens I meet around town, I often pass them on to the mayor and city council members. Small town life is built on personal networks. Networks build trust in small communities and if the people don't know their leaders, mistrust and suspicion will grow quickly. We live in an era of growing mistrust in government, so it's important to be open, honest, and friendly.

In addition, my professional development training has helped me accomplish two things: first, review and training on new or upcoming state and federal laws as well as case studies and best practices. Secondly, the networking I have participated in is immeasurable. Networking with other city managers and administrators throughout the state is an excellent way to learn how to properly handle certain situations; it also serves as therapy in a way. Being able to talk with colleagues about the stress of work or just telling stories of various experiences often helps reduce stress. It is helpful talking with my wife about stressful events, but sometime the true help is when I am able to talk with people who have gone through the same problems I have. I always encourage anyone getting into the public administration profession to be involved in your state and national professional organization.

Recently, I concluded my one-year term as Sac City Kiwanis Club president. This was a fun year and afforded me the opportunity to build new relationships. I enjoyed my time working with children on bicycle safety, baking potatoes for the local "potato bake" fund raiser, working in the Kiwanis booth at the county fair serving food, making pancakes for the kids at our local schools and the community at large, listening to various speakers at local club meetings, and just having great fellowship with our members.

My time in Sac City has been satisfying. I think many administrators start in a smaller community with the intentions of moving to larger communities. Others find satisfaction in staying in a small community and managing that community until retirement. For me, I haven't quite decided what my future will bring. I really enjoy working in a small town, but at times I would like to try my hand at managing a larger city. Whatever my future brings, I do know this, demand for city administrators in Iowa is only growing and the future is bright for anyone desiring to get into this profession.

Being a public administration professional cannot be accomplished without the assistance of family, friends, community, and colleagues. I rely on them each day. When asked how can I do this job, my answer is the reward comes with knowing that I've made a difference in a community. I don't take all the credit though, it's a group effort, I just try and help guide the process to reach our ultimate goal of creating a strong vibrant community.

2

THE ORIGIN AND PERSISTENCE OF AMERICAN COUNTY BOUNDARIES

Courthouse Competition and the Road to Reapportionment

William A. Fischel

The Puzzle of Stable County Boundaries

The 50 United States are blanketed by 3,139 counties, including the county-equivalent parishes of Louisiana, boroughs of Alaska, 35 "independent cities" of Virginia (and three in Maryland, Missouri, and Nevada), and the non-governing but still demarcated counties of Connecticut, Rhode Island, and most of Massachusetts. Of this number, only 74 have been created since 1920, and those are concentrated in a handful of states: 13 in Florida in the 1920s; 19 boroughs in Alaska since statehood in 1959; and 17 independent cities in Virginia. Even as the US population has tripled in the last one hundred years, there have been no counties created in 37 states.

The stasis of American counties contrasts with sizeable changes in the number and boundaries of other units of local government. In most metropolitan areas, the number of general-purpose municipal governments greatly increased as suburban populations grew and spread out (Teaford, 2020). In contrast to cities, local school districts radically declined from about 200,000 mostly one-room school districts in 1930 to fewer than 1,500 multi-grade districts in 1970 (Fischel, 2009). The number of single-purpose districts for fire protection, water provision, and the like has skyrocketed since the 1960s (McCabe, 2000), as have private governments such as homeowner associations and business improvement districts (Nelson, 2002).

Counties' numerical stagnation is not the product of declining importance. Every native citizen's birth is accounted for by a county. Legal

DOI: 10.4324/9781003287766-4

documents are housed in a county courthouse, where the state's judiciary holds trials of first impression. Counties organize elections and report votes, and their borders are the templates to apportion state legislatures and the US House of Representatives. The US Census organizes its geographic data along county lines, which also define metropolitan areas. Weather maps, business statistics, unemployment rates, and pandemic data are organized and visualized by county.

For these purposes, steady county boundaries are a virtue. Researchers have some confidence that the county-based data in 1950 are from the same geographical unit in 2020. But for local governance and for state and national legislative apportionment, a configuration of counties that was created when most Americans lived in rural areas is puzzling. England redrew its counties in the twentieth century to facilitate urban government (Chandler, 2007), but no American counties have been similarly reconfigured since Greater New York City was created at the end of the nineteenth century.

American Beginnings: The Scramble to Establish State Control

Counties are the steadiest units of government of the twentieth century, but one would not have predicted it from their eighteenth- and nineteenth-century origins. The original thirteen colonies were divided into counties by their colonial governors. After independence, the American territories such as the Old Northwest were likewise divided into counties before statehood. Eventually, governors and state legislatures decided on the boundaries of American counties.

But county establishment was hardly regular. As the Newberry Library's maps demonstrate, new states (hereinafter to include English colonies and America's pre-state territorial governments) cast a coarse net of large-area counties over most of their territory and then filled in the spaces by subdividing the original counties into smaller units. In some cases, remote land was designated a "non-county area" but temporarily attached to an organized county for judicial purposes. Governors and legislatures were eager to establish a network of counties, however thin, across all of their territory.

The process of subdivision of original counties was seldom regular. Typical of the process was Lincoln County, Kentucky (named for the Revolutionary War general John, not Abraham). When Kentucky was separated from Virginia as a new state in 1792, Lincoln County occupied almost a third of the entire state as one of Kentucky's nine original counties. Over the next half century, scores of counties were carved from Lincoln's original territory, and by 1842 Lincoln was reduced to its present size of

344 square miles, just above the average size of Kentucky's present 120 counties.

In the process of subdividing original counties, boundaries were frequently redrawn as new counties shouldered their way in. Only in a few states, notably Iowa, did there appear to be a prearranged plan that was mostly adhered to, and even their county lines were often revised to coincide with the Public Lands survey, which laid a standard property-line grid across the nation in states west of the Appalachians.

The reason for the hasty creation of counties, sometimes without much population or knowledge of terrain, was that new state governments needed to establish authority over their entire territory, not just selective bits and pieces. Territorial governors could not afford to wait for localities to be settled and municipalities established; a legal apparatus had to be established. The failure of the US government to create counties or establish Native American tribal control over the Oklahoma panhandle was cautionary. Without courts and a sheriff, the area in the late 1800s became a "no-man's land" refuge for outlaws and fugitives from justice until it was annexed to Oklahoma (Turner, 1994).

The creation of smaller counties from large ones was distinctly different from establishing municipal governments, which were almost always promoted by local groups or entrepreneurs. Municipalities were created to serve local demands, not statewide necessity. New cities established borders that then grew outward if they were successful, and the spaces in between them were "unincorporated" land governed by counties.

The county governance system initially mimicked English practice and nomenclature: judges, court clerks, coroners ("agents of the crown"), and sheriffs ("shire reeves"). Counties also have officials to record property lines and deed transactions, marriages, births, and deaths; agents to monitor and build roads; and property assessors and tax collectors. Without these offices, state governments would not know how many citizens they had and what and whom they could tax and how to control crime and disorder. Municipal governments do many of these things, too, but unless municipalities cover the entire state (as they do in most New England states), they cannot be relied on to perform these vital state functions.

County Proliferation: Creatures of the State?

It is a mantra in legal circles that all local governments are "creatures of the state." Counties are the paradigm of this claim, but they also mirror it back to the state legislature. From the earliest days of the Republic, counties constituted the electoral districts for the state legislature in almost all states outside New England, where the town was the fundamental building block (Durfee, 1945). Forming a county around a rural hamlet gave that locale direct influence in state politics. Counties usually collected state taxes as well as those to finance local expenditures, and American democratic mores that connected taxation with representation were not merely a slogan: Local self-government required that those taxed should also elect state representatives.

The government center of a county is the "seat" where the courthouse, jail, and other offices are located. A town that became a county seat greatly improved its chances for prosperity and long-term survival. This was most evident in the sparsely populated areas of the Midwest and Great Plains. Tiny towns competed with nearby towns to win the countywide vote to be the seat or have it removed from its incumbent location. Those that lost the competition usually lost population relative to the winners and not infrequently became ghost towns and disappeared beneath the plow (De Arment, 2006; Shockley, 1904).

Most of the seat competition took place among towns within pre-existing county boundaries, as described in a later section. But entrepreneurial landowners also looked to the legislature to modify county boundaries to their advantage—typically making their land closer to the center of a resurveyed county or creating an entirely new county (Ward, 1973). Numerous towns in settled places and near the frontier of settlement did everything they could to convince the legislature to create a new county for which they could become the county seat. The authors of a geographical history of Indiana governments, George Pence and Nellie Armstrong (1933, p. 21), found that "Speculators in land values gambled on the probable location of new county boundaries to lay out towns which might logically become county seats, and county boundaries were juggled to favor towns already established."

One might ask why the Indiana legislature was so compliant in creating new counties. After all, new counties created additional legislative seats and reduced the influence of existing counties and their representatives. The main clue was discovered by Naomi Lamoreaux and John Wallis (2020). They found that before 1851, the legislature of Indiana—and those of just about every other state—was almost entirely occupied with the passage of private bills. Legislators largely logrolled their pet projects through. County creation was one of those pet projects that served a local constituency. There was little thought given to the overall effects of these bills. The exuberant creation of counties was a problem created by this undisciplined process. Counties looked less like passive creatures of the state than a prize for local influence in the legislature.

Apportionment Problems

The creation of excessive numbers of counties had a profound effect on state politics. The nearly universal rule was that each new county got to elect at least one legislator. But the original territorial "organic acts" (laws provided by Congress) as well as most early state constitutions required proportional representation in both upper and lower houses of state legislatures (Keith & Petry, 2014). A county with twice as many people was to get twice as many representatives. But existing small counties did not want to lose their political influence by combining their legislative delegations with newcomers; to insist on it would have caused stiff resistance by the earlier established counties from which the new ones were carved.

As new counties were created, legislatures could have expanded their membership, giving more representatives to the more populous counties as smaller ones were admitted. But this would have created legislatures with unwieldy numbers. The path chosen in most states was to short-change the more populous counties in at least one house of their bicameral legislatures. This malapportionment—malign both in democratic theory and contrary to their own constitutional ideals—became ever more problematic as urban counties gained population more rapidly than rural counties as the twentieth century rolled on. Even though few counties were created after 1900, the shift in population to cities without a corresponding shift in legislative representation continued to undermine democratic ideals.

The US Supreme Court put an end to state malapportionment in *Reynolds v. Sims*, 377 U.S. 533 (1964). Much of the complaint about the system was laid at the feet of rural legislators, who were unwilling to give up their positions. But in a more fundamental sense, it appears that the skewed representation was the product of excessive county creation and an unwillingness to leave a new county at a disadvantage with respect to others. Counties were extensions of state authority, and every state relied on the cooperation and participation of local voters, who taxed themselves and elected county officers to serve the state. To disenfranchise any county or treat them as second-class units would undermine the state's system of governance.

Capping County Numbers

Lamoreaux and Wallis (2020) found that a series of fiscal crises in Indiana that stemmed from failed canals and other public projects in several states brought about state constitutional reform in the 1850s. The leading reform was in the legislative process, which banned "local and special" legislation of the sort that had gotten the states into fiscal trouble. A provision in Indiana's 1851 constitution that was consistent with this reform was a ban on the creation of new counties that would result in land area smaller than 400 square miles for either the new or the old counties from which it was carved. This and related constraints on voting majorities and minimum populations and tax base effectively put an end to county proliferation. Only one of Indiana's 92 counties, Newton, was created after 1851.

Indiana's constitutional reforms inspired similar constraints on county creation throughout the eastern part of the nation (here meaning east of the 100th meridian). A minimum size of 400 square miles seemed to be the baseline, though Iowa and Kansas upped it to 432, the size of twelve townships. Minimum size grew in more western states where rural population was thinner: Missouri, 500 square miles; Arkansas and Alabama, 600; Texas and Wisconsin, 900 (Fairlie, 1906; Hough, 1872).

Most states in mountainous and arid territory west of the 100th meridian did not bother with any minimum county land area. This reflected their eagerness to promote rural development almost anywhere. In sparse rural areas, counties were both vessels for self-government and agents of economic development. Montana and Idaho both went on a country-creation tear in the early twentieth century in response to increased settlement by farmers and miners who took advantage of the world-war-driven demand for grain and minerals. World War II was probably responsible for the creation of Los Alamos County, New Mexico in 1947, whose land area is much smaller than other counties in the state. The county's original radio station, KBOM, was an unsubtle reference to Los Alamos's main industry, nuclear weapons development.

The ideal of 400 square miles for counties is often explained as the product of county seat access. A one-day ride by horseback would get one from the farthest reaches of a square county of that size to a centrally located courthouse and back. But the lightly populated territory of the West did not have enough people or tax base in 400 square miles to support a county government.

West of the 100th meridian, where the precipitation is typically too low to support row crops, ranching and timber were the dominant rural occupations, and there were fewer people than range animals. County land area in the inland West is on the order of four times larger than those in the East. Horses were not faster out West; people just didn't get to the county seat very often if they lived at the edges.

The automobile and road network of the twentieth century changed such calculations, making the courthouse accessible in a day's drive from even the largest counties. It is tempting to see the coincidence between the end of county formation in the 1920s and the dawn of the automobile age. But an examination of individual states undermines the case for transportation determinism with respect to counties. Their formation in most states came to a halt long before automobiles arrived. The average year in which the last county was formed in the 50 states was 1885, well before automobiles became widespread. It was constitutional constraints, particularly the minimum land area requirement, not technological change, that ended county proliferation.

County Dominance in the South

The old South adopted a different role for counties that persists to the present. It has long been claimed that the South was different from the North because it imported the English parish system of government (Fairlie, 1906). But both North and South were settled by English emigrants who took their local government cues from the mother country and established counties from the very beginning.

The difference was what happened after original American counties were laid out. In the North, towns and townships soon blanketed the settled areas. Northerners wanted local self-government. Their wealth was tied up in land, and they used their town governments to protect and enhance land values (Monkkonen, 1990). The Northern county was undermined from within by reliance on towns, so much so that Tocqueville (1835) could declare (with some exaggeration) that in America "the township was organized before the county, the county before the State, the State before the Union."

In the South, local government more often took the form of carving out a new county. Promotion of land wealth, which small towns and school districts were good at, was subsumed to promotion of slave-based wealth by the plantation aristocracy (Wright, 2006; Fischel, 2009). State appointment of county judges and a limited voter franchise allowed counties to be the most effective unit to protect plantation taxpayers from populist enthusiasms such as free schools. Establishment of a network of Northern-style townships would make state control more difficult and require a wider local voter franchise to function (Farbman, 2017).

County proliferation continued in the South long after county formation in the North had petered out. In nine northern states—six in New England plus New York, Pennsylvania, and New Jersey, only ten new counties were formed after 1850. (Three were in Maine and three were the product of the formation of Greater New York.) In the Confederate states south of the Ohio and east of the Mississippi (but including Louisiana) there were 253 counties formed after 1850. The disparity of 253 new counties in the South to ten in the North is striking, even allowing for the later admission dates of four of the Southern states.

Southern counties continued to be the crucial unit of local government throughout the twentieth century. Municipalities could be formed but generally had fewer functions than the county. A marker of their minor roles are the hundreds of "circle cities" of Georgia and the Carolinas (Schretter, 1963). Rather than formally measure city boundaries, circle-town founders would simply declare that all the territory within the radius of, say, one mile of the railroad station or courthouse was within the city. Without the federal Public Land Survey's premade township rectangles (not delineated in the original states), a circle was a reasonable if substandard boundary for minor civil divisions. That the circumference left many properties on the edge of the city both within and outside the city boundaries was not much of a bother, since it was the overlying county that mattered for most government services.

Counties in the twentieth century also served as school districts in the South. Relentless school segregation created substantial diseconomies of scale: separate schools, teaching staffs, and transportation systems were redundancies best internalized by a large unit (Bond, 1934; Fischel, 2009). And close state supervision of segregation's rules was best accomplished by a county district, whose school boards were usually appointed by state or county officials rather than directly elected.

County Seats and County Persistence in the Rural West

If the Southern county remains the fundamental unit of local government, as enforced by the state government's fear of localism, the Western county persists because the county seat is a vital economic and political conduit for rural life. The characteristic of "West" here is a county both lightly populated and distant from a heavily populated area. It is best characterized as not being within a Census-designated metropolitan statistical area; MSAs may include lightly populated counties that are nonetheless far from suburbs of a big city. Most truly rural counties are in states west of 100th meridian, but some are in the remote regions in eastern states such as the upper Great Lakes and the Appalachia.

In the 1990s, Dayton Duncan (2000) traveled through counties that met the 1890 frontier density of less than two persons per square mile. Frederick Jackson Turner (1893) had famously lamented the closing of the frontier, but Duncan found that, by population density, plenty of modern counties met the frontier criteria (Turner & Faragher, 1999). He wrote a nuanced appreciation of the ongoing trials and glories of life in America's outback. In contrast to the South's attention to the county as a whole, the rural West's counties are reliant on their county seats. These seats are fully formed municipalities, not pawns of the state government, and in the modern frontier counties, rural life would be nearly impossible without them.

As previously mentioned, early American landowners sought to enhance their town property value by having the legislature create a new county to win the county seat. More frequently, however, town-founders competed with other locations in the same county to obtain the courthouse. When a new county was created, the state or territory might designate a seat near the geographic center of the county, but in most states the seat could be relocated by a countywide vote.

In a frictionless equilibrium, repeated majority voting would cause the county seat to be located near the population center of the county. This would not necessarily be in the largest city. Applying the majority-rule principle to the relocation of *state* capitals, Engstrom et al. (2013) found a clear tendency for capitals to move to a city near the population center of the state. Sometimes this was the largest city near the geographic center, as in Denver, Indianapolis, and Des Moines, but often it split the difference between large cities located in different parts of the state. The small capital city of Harrisburg is in fact near the population center of Pennsylvania; the big metropolitan areas of Philadelphia and Pittsburgh are on the edges.

Because counties were laid out early in the process of rural settlement, the population center of the county was either not clear or could change over time. This resulted in keen political competition between rivals. An off-center town might claim better natural advantages—in the West, this meant water—or location along a transportation corridor such as a river or railroad.

Where centrality was contested, an enterprising town might adopt a name that would indicate its aspiration (Ashton, 1954). More than 15 percent of American county seats have a name that repeats in some fashion the name of its parent county, such as Bowman, the seat of Bowman County, North Dakota, and Bentonville in Benton County, Arkansas. (Only two American state capitals, Indianapolis and Oklahoma City, share their names with their states.) Although some counties took their names from their previously established principal city (especially in California's coastal counties), the usual sequence was that the county was named by the legislature and towns were later strategically renamed. When a likely county-seat name was already taken by another city, town-founders invoked clever associations. Examples were the Kansas towns of "Horace" and "Tribune," competitors for the seat of Greeley County, named for Horace Greeley, the famous editor of the *New York Tribune*. A town named "Greeley" had previously been established in another county in Kansas.

Another competitive device was the establishment of oversize courthouses, which both upped the ante in competition and made relocation of facilities more difficult. Local landowners often donated property and erected the buildings in the hope that winning the seat would enhance their town's property values (Visher, 1955). Newly built railroads could upset previous competitive results and cause new locations to become more central in terms of travel time (Ward, 1973). More than one prospective county seat, however, would pick up its buildings and move them to a location next to the railroad. The western Kansas City of Tribune moved itself a mile to the south to be next to the new railroad and defeat its rival, Horace, in the 1888 vote to become the seat of Greeley County.

County seat competition could sometimes involve the threat of violence. A pre-existing seat that lost a later vote might resist orders to remove the contents of its courthouse to the winning location, and armed partisans might face each other down and sometimes fire shots (Schellenberg, 1981; DeArment, 2006). More frequently, the referendum on the location involved ballot-box stuffing and related frauds, but usually the state would step in and demand recounts or revotes to determine the majority's preference.

It would seem that this messy competitive process produced county seats that were optimally located *for the existing county's boundaries*. Repeated majority votes produced seat locations more efficiently than their rivals. This could often be near the center of the county if population was more or less evenly spread, but seats could be moved to locations nearer the edges if that's where population growth occurred or if new transportation modes—railroads or major highways—made travel times to a different location lower for a majority of county residents. The Minnesota town of "Lac qui Parle" was the original seat of the county of that name ("lake that speaks"), but the main railroad passed it by, and the county seat moved along with it to the centrally located but prosaically named city of Madison in 1889.

Preserving Rural Counties

The county seat in isolated rural areas is vital to the economy and political standing of its area. It is typically where shopping, entertainment, medical services, and public education are centered. It provides the social infrastructure for the county. Proposals to merge the inefficiently small (in population) rural counties would undermine if not destroy these nongovernment functions even if consolidation made the provision of original county services—courts, road building, elections—less costly.

Merger of two adjacent rural counties would be destructive for both county seats if both county's seats had been optimally located. After merger, a new site would become optimal for the now-larger-area county. But recreating a new seat for the larger county would be nearly impossible in the rural West. Nearly all of them have declining populations. This is largely because agricultural productivity has continually risen, requiring fewer workers. Most rural county seats depend on the county government for a stable core of jobs and spillover businesses, such as hotels and newspapers of record. Without this core, the seat's population would decline below the level of viability. The town would meet the fate of its bygone rivals, becoming a mere hamlet or even a ghost town.

One might object to this solicitude on economic welfare grounds. It is people, not acres that count, a point hammered home by the US Supreme Court in the *Reynolds* decision that demolished the inequitable county-based system of apportionment. The wellbeing of people in the rest of the state—be it Kansas or Montana or any others that have underpopulated, isolated counties—is tied to the existence of county seats and other small rural towns in large-area places.

This is not because the people who live there constitute a large fraction of the US population. The 300 counties (10 percent of the total) with fewer than 5,000 people have about 900,000 people, or about one-quarter of 1 percent of the US population. Looked at from the other end, 80 percent of the US population lives in urban areas, which account for only 2 percent of the US land area.

Yet America's national psyche is predicated on those lands of spacious skies and amber waves of grain. Gertrude Stein (1936) famously remarked, "In the United States there is more space where nobody is than where anybody is. That is what makes America what it is." The people living in that big sky country amidst seemingly endless plains and forests keep alive values that are widely shared. Rural counties and their towns preserve an important part of America's heritage (Duncan 2000; Jacobson, 2002).

It may not be necessary to mount a normative defense of rural counties' geographic integrity. They actually seem to be doing pretty well on their own. For over a century, none has been combined with another despite losing much of their population and most of their representation in state legislatures over 50 years ago. Yet some are still aware of the risk.

Located on the High Plains of far western Kansas, Greeley County is the smallest in the state by population (1,284 in 2020) and surely a candidate for merger with neighboring counties by the state legislature. Greeley's leaders are aware of this vulnerability. In 2007, they persuaded the state legislature to allow the city of Tribune to join with the balance of the county—excepting the city of Horace (population 80), perhaps still smarting from its loss to Tribune in the county seat vote in 1888—to create "Unified Greeley County" (*Garden City Telegram*, November 7, 2007).

The only other county to have done so in Kansas was Wyandotte on the opposite side of the state, which joined Kansas City with most of the county's other towns. On February 11, 2021, Dan and Jan Epp, publishers and editors of the Greeley County *Republican*, an estimable weekly published in Tribune were contacted. These individuals were among the leaders of the unification effort. When asked whether unification created fiscal efficiencies, which were the rationale for the legislation allowing the merger, Dan responded, "Not many." However, it did have a singular political advantage: A unified county is considered a "home-rule" unit in Kansas, and, unlike other counties, it cannot be disbanded or merged with other counties without a vote of its residents.

References

Ashton, W. E. (1954). Names of counties and county seats. *Names*, 2(1), 14–20.

Bond, H. M. (1934). *The Education of the Negro in the American Social Order*. Prentice Hall.

Chandler, J. A. (2007). *Explaining Local Government: Local Government in Britain since 1800*. Manchester University Press.

DeArment, R. K. (2006). *Ballots and Bullets: The Bloody County Seat Wars of Kansas*. University of Oklahoma Press.

Duncan, D. (2000). *Miles from Nowhere: Tales from America's Contemporary Frontier*. University of Nebraska Press.

Durfee, E. (1945). Apportionment of representation in the legislature: A study of state constitutions. *Michigan Law Review*, 43(6), 1091–1112.

Engstrom, E. J., Hammond, J. R., & Scott, J. T. (2013). Capitol mobility: Madisonian representation and the location and relocation of capitals in the United States. *American Political Science Review*, 107(2), 225–240.

Fairlie, J. A. (1906). *Local Government in Counties, Towns and Villages*. Century Company.

Farbman, D. (2017). Reconstructing local government. *Vanderbilt Law Review*, 70, 413–498.

Fischel, W. A. (2009). *Making the Grade*. University of Chicago Press.

Hough, F. B. (1872). *American Constitutions* (Vol. 2). Weed, Parsons.

Jacobson, D. (2002). *Place and Belonging in America*. JHU Press.

Keith, D., & Petry, E. (2014). *Apportionment of State Legislatures, 1776–1920*. Brennan Center for Justice at New York University School of Law.

Lamoreaux, N. R., & Wallis, J. J. (2020). *Economic Crisis, General Laws, and the Mid-Nineteenth-Century Transformation of American Political Economy* (no. w27400). National Bureau of Economic Research.

McCabe, B. C. (2000). Special-district formation among the states. State and Local Government Review, 32(2), 121–131.

Monkkonen, E. H. (1990). *America Becomes Urban: The Development of US Cities and Towns, 1780–1980*. University of California Press.

Nelson, R. H. (2002). *The Rise of Private Neighborhood Associations: A Constitutional Revolution in Local Government.* Edward Elgar Publishing.

Pence, G., & Armstrong, N. C. (1933). *Indiana Boundaries: Territory, State, and County.* Indiana Historical Bureau.

Schellenberg, J. A. (1981). County seat wars: Historical observations. *American Studies*, 22(2), 81–95.

Schretter, H. A. (1963). Round towns. *Southeastern Geographer. 3*, 46–52.

Shockley, E. V. (1914). County seats and county seat wars in Indiana. *Indiana Magazine of History*, 1–46.

Stein, G. [1936]. *The Geographical History of America.* Random House (2013).

Teaford, J. C. (2020). *Post-Suburbia: Government and Politics in the Edge Cities.* JHU Press.

Tocqueville, A. (1835) *Democracy in America.* Saunders & Otley.

Turner, F. J., & Faragher, J. M. [1936] (1999). *Rereading Frederick Jackson Turner: "The Significance of the Frontier in American History."* Yale University Press.

Turner, K. R. (1994). *The Creation of No Man's Land.* Brochure Series, 1. No Man's Land Historical Society.

Visher, S. S. (1955). The location of Indiana towns and cities. *Indiana Magazine of History*, 341–346.

Ward, D. M. (1973). *A Spatial Analysis of County Seat Location in Nebraska: 1854–1930.* University of Nebraska-Lincoln.

Wright, G. (2006). *Slavery and American Economic Development.* LSU Press.

PART II

Public Functions in Rural Government Systems

Subsection: Economic and Community Development

3
PLACEMAKING AS AN ECONOMIC DEVELOPMENT STRATEGY FOR RURAL GOVERNMENTS

Janet M. Kelly

Introduction

Rural economic development strategies traditionally centered around recruiting potential employers, often in the manufacturing, retail, or warehousing sectors. Attraction of new business remains a component of the rural economic development portfolio, but evidence of a lasting economic benefit to the local government is underwhelming (Reese, 2014). An alternative approach called placemaking is focused on enhancing the quality of life for residents as a means to attract new residents. Placemaking has gained momentum in rural economic development in the recent past. Building on the community's existing natural and cultural assets, it invites stakeholders to collaboratively define what makes the community unique and attractive for residents and visitors, then build on those features that offer the best opportunity for growth.

Rural communities are less likely to have a diverse economic base and often struggle to adjust following the loss of a major employer. They face economic challenges with limited infrastructure, sometimes outdated facilities, and a workforce whose skills may be less adaptable to other endeavors (Pender et al., 2012). Incentive-based recruitment efforts put rural communities in competition with each other for existing jobs and can exacerbate demands on the local tax base as service needs increase and ability to pay for them diminishes. This alternative recommends adjusting the local economy to fit a dynamic economic environment, using limited resources to their best advantage, and relying on distinctive assets to

DOI: 10.4324/9781003287766-7

attract residents, visitors, and small business (Environmental Protection Agency, 2015).

Is it reasonable to compete for new residents as a growth plan? Along with devastating job losses and employment insecurity, the COVID pandemic was also a sweeping social experiment in the nature of work. Futurists once opined that technology would result in "distributed work" (Hinds & Kieslar, 2002) where workers contribute from any location. Suddenly the future was present, and roughly 60 percent of workers worked remotely, most of whom had little or no remote work experience (Brenan, 2020). Many unanswered questions remain about remote work, but early studies suggest that the space/place construct associated with traditional work may be outdated, allowing at least some percentage of workers to choose their work location based on quality of life and work/ life balance. Rural communities should be ideally placed to compete for these worker-residents so long as the technology infrastructure is present. Attracting mobile worker-residents results in economic growth and is the essence of placemaking.

Rural Placemaking

The origin of placemaking traces back to a strand of economic development literature called the "creative class" (Florida, 2003) which asserts that attracting well-educated persons engaged in creative professions fosters economic prosperity. The idea is appealing because it promises benefits for exiting citizens as well as new residents with relatively modest investment of public funds. Creative placemaking as a rural economic development strategy has been gaining attention in both the practitioner and academic literature for a decade (Gallagher & Ehlman, 2020). The grounding principle is "use what you have" to create an authenticity of place that appeals to mobile in-migrants and reflects the values and priorities of current residents.

Evidence for the success of placemaking is mixed, but most of the tests have been in the largest urban places with a few notable exceptions (McGranahan & Wojan, 2007; Rickman & Rickman, 2011). Rural places were assumed to lack the diversity (and therefore, tolerance), cultural climate, and entertainment amenities associated with the creative class, though those characteristics might not be as relevant for targeted population growth in smaller cities (Kelly et al., 2017).

The more limiting factor was technology-based innovation slowed by the reach of broadband and high-speed internet services. In general, scholars have been less optimistic about placemaking as an economic development strategy than practitioners (Hatcher et al., 2011). As economic development policies gradually become more endogenous, recognizing the distinctive features of place and the workforce in the place, the evidence for successful outcomes grows (Donegan et al., 2008; Mathur, 1999). Support for attracting business and residents by marketing quality of life grows as nonmetropolitan cities and counties report better than expected economic growth because of their placemaking efforts.

Anecdotal success stories abound. In Eagle Butte, South Dakota, the creative arts and history of indigenous peoples attracted business and visitors (Housing Assistance Council, 2018). Huntington, West Virginia's farmer's market, Wild Ramp, anchors the old central city's commercial corridor and was instrumental to downtown revitalization (Environmental Protection Agency, 2017). Harland County, Kentucky, focused on public art to engage residents and attract visitors (Mountain Association, 2019). Roanoke, Virginia, used its abundant natural resources to create a network of hiking and biking trails and launched an annual *Go Outside* Festival that attracts visitors and businesses that specialize in outdoor recreational products (Murray, 2012).

Geospatial relations are an important element of placemaking. Indeed, understanding how and where citizens and visitors engage with the physical environment is an important element in a placemaking strategy, but a physical space is shaped by the social relations of the people who use it (Balassiano & Maldonado, 2015). A space becomes a place when people who use it share socially and culturally specific goals (Tuan, 1991). They become attached to the space, impart meaning and value to it, and are more likely to be engaged in their rural community affairs as a result (Alkon & Traugot, 2008).

The Placemaking Process

Managers and professional staff can't "placemake" on behalf of their citizens. Managers can help create a collaborative environment where development professionals, planners, and citizens deliberate the values that guide the evolution of shared physical space into placemaking. A management team interested in placemaking should first secure basic information that will later be shared with the larger, more representative team. For clarity, the small team (maybe three to five people) may be called the inquiring team and the larger team the exploratory team.

The first stop for the inquiring team to start gathering information about rural placemaking is the US Department of Agriculture's Rural Development website (www.rd.usda.org). Rural Development has several grant and loan programs for placemaking, along with searchable cooperative publications with USDA staff and university partners. The next stop should be the state land grant university's cooperative extension service. There are dozens of state guides to rural placemaking and most of them are quite well done. A state guide will have information to guide the exploratory process. Many cooperative extension staff are willing to travel to confer with rural governments considering a placemaking initiative, and some might even be willing to facilitate the public meetings needed to assemble a placemaking plan.

Because state-based guides are good and plentiful, what follows is a brief overview of the process common to most of them.

Assemble an Exploratory Team

This is a larger team, primarily comprised of staff, representatives of regional planning agencies, and other well-informed stakeholders. Department heads from public works, codes enforcement, planning and zoning, safety services, and finance can all contribute from their special perspective. Elected officials should certainly be made aware of exploratory meetings, but members of the exploratory group need to be committed to the kind of advance preparation, time commitment, and frank discussion that will set the stage for a successful process. The team leader should distribute placemaking resources secured by the inquiry team for review and, if feasible, engage someone with placemaking expertise or experience to talk with the exploratory team about best practices and reasonable expectations.

Review Existing Long-Range Plans

The exploratory team's focus at this point is growth patterns, growth potential, and growth goals. Some cities and counties may have a strategic plan, a long-range growth plan or master plan already in place. Strategic plans will help the team identify the priorities that drove the plan and consider how a placemaking effort could help realize the vision. A long-range growth plan is likely to have two parts, a forecast of residential growth and a forecast of economic growth. Both will be based on previous location decisions by firms and citizens. Mapping the existing development and forecasted growth can suggest development corridors or proximities to amenities that business and residents find attractive.

Produce an Economic Assets Inventory

The word "economic" might appear to limit the types of assets included but it should not. Placemaking is an economic growth plan, so any asset that helps create a unique sense of place (some call it "authenticity") should be included. Granted, the easiest to name are the tangible assets like natural resources or an attractive town square, but cultural resources like social networks and arts organizations are an economic asset as well. The inventory should also include a systematic evaluation of how places are used, which may or may not be consistent with their intended use (see Schneekloth & Shibley, 1995; Cooper & Francis, 1998).

Think broadly, as when citizens become involved the scope will likely expand further. One exploratory team identified a well-traveled scenic highway that connected their town to two larger towns as an asset and used it as a way to draw travelers into their historic downtown.

Engage the Community in a Second Assets Inventory

This is both the most critical and most challenging part of the placemaking process. Critical, because collectively citizens know vastly more about how public spaces are used than the team. Challenging, because it is difficult to draw a diverse group into meetings and keep them engaged. A special challenge can arise when advocacy groups compete, especially if funding is a possibility. Every process will be different depending on the characteristics of the community involved, but there are some common guidelines:

- Reach out broadly, using the team's network of contacts. Everyone may be welcome, but a general appeal might not produce a workable number of participants with diverse interests and perspectives.
- Use a professional facilitator from another place. A good facilitator will prevent one individual or group from dominating the discussion and can guide the group away from unproductive sidetracks.
- Participants should talk to each other, not to the facilitator or members of the exploratory team. Breakout groups are essential. Be aware that participants will tend to form groups with persons with common backgrounds and interests. This is sometimes called a "caucus," and can be useful when the spokesperson from the group shares results with the whole group. A good facilitator will ensure that the work of each breakout group is afforded the same consideration.
- Listen meaningfully and record ideas. The exploratory team should be quietly present and making notes, mentally comparing the results of their asset inventory to the community process results. Along with the facilitator, the team should look for common themes in the assets inventory.
- Report back and follow through. The meeting should end with a summary of progress to date and next steps. The team should reassemble

and draft a communication for all participants about common themes, timelines, and next steps. One person should be designated as a contact point for the public.

With these suggestions in mind, team members should draft a participation plan that identifies community groups associated with different items in the asset inventory and targets groups that might not otherwise be represented or inclined to participate. The team can use its service network to contact potential members and personally invite them, explaining the purpose of the project and how the community can benefit from their participation. As the team moves forward, a second meeting to discuss approaches around a consensus set of community assets may help keep participants engaged. The most important consideration for the team is making sure the participants know that their input drove decisions throughout the process.

Factors that Support Placemaking for Rural Communities

Having established what placemaking is and how to approach it, it is time to step back and ask a very reasonable question. Since rural communities always had a package of desirable amenities why didn't new residents and businesses respond to them by locating there? One answer is that they did, to a limited extent. Population growth in nonmetropolitan counties (especially those adjacent to metropolitan counties) rose over the last decade. A better answer is that a national pandemic and advances in technology infrastructure produced changes in the labor market that could redound to the benefit of rural communities more than ever. Telework and broadband access can make rural communities competitive for the creative class, those educated workers presumed to be high amenity seekers. Though intuitively it would seem that places with a younger college educated workforce might be more likely to attract their footloose counterparts, smaller cities with a higher percentage of college educated residents aged 25–34 were no more likely to attract new young knowledge workers than small cities with a lower percentage of young knowledge workers (Kelly et al., 2017). In other words, rural places that have experienced brain drain need not remove themselves from competition.

Economic geography, or the spatial location of economic activities, explains the formation of large cities around concentrated economic activity, especially transportation points. Glaser and Gottlieb (2008) contended that local economic development policies aimed at attracting skilled workers have the best chance for improving the fortunes of stressed urban areas. The same reasoning should apply to rural areas when the playing field is leveled by transportation factors and information flows. In other words, if the commute time is no longer a dominant factor in the location decision and technology removes the necessity for physical proximity to be a factor in innovation and idea-sharing, we might expect productivity gains to become more comparable across rural and urban spaces.

Recall that about 75 percent of the landmass in the US is considered rural but only about 15 percent of the nation's population lives there. Rural places produce food, provide energy and clean water, and offer natural amenities and physical space for recreational activities. They have a lower cost of living and fewer undesirable externalities associated with density (i.e., traffic, crime). The question is whether post-pandemic changes in economic geography might redistribute economic activity across regions. Leamer and Storper (2001) caution that every major improvement in transportation and telecommunications has been associated with increased, not decreased urbanization. But what makes this different is a lingering effect of the pandemic, called "social scarring" or fear of crowds (Florida et al., 2021). Popular media chronicled a pandemic-driven exodus from cities to rural places, but it is too early to draw finite conclusions. We must wait for migration data over the relevant period to become available before any urban to rural trend can be established.

Telework

Telework was already growing for some workers in the years leading up to the pandemic. The Bureau of Labor Statistics (BLS) 2015 American Time Use Survey found that roughly a third of workers in professional, financial, and managerial occupations did some or all the work for their main job at home (BLS, 2016). Percentages for other occupational categories (sales, services, support) remained relatively constant or decreased over the ten-year period 2006–2015. The COVID-related shift to home-based work was stunning. Brynjolfsson et al. (2020) estimated that about one third of all workers who were employed in early March 2020 had shifted to remote work by the first week of April 2020.

BLS 2020 American Time Use Survey brought the disparate impacts associated with telework into sharper focus. BLS estimated that 67.5 percent of workers with a college degree had the ability to telework, as opposed to 24.5 percent of those with a high school diploma only (Dey et al., 2020). In general, larger metropolitan areas tended to have the highest ability-to-telework rates. However, the difference between smaller metropolitan areas (39.6 percent) and nonmetropolitan or rural areas (31.8 percent) was modest, and only about 10 percentage points behind the largest metropolitan areas (Dey et al., 2020). The age, race, and gender differences in telework noted in the 2015 study mitigated throughout 2020 and vanished by 2021, holding industry and occupation constant (Lee et al., 2021).

Remote work is stratified primarily by education (Fan & Moen, 2021). Dingel & Neiman (2020) estimated that 37 percent of all jobs can be performed entirely at home but most of these jobs require a college degree. There is some evidence that, when employers have the expectation of a quick response during traditionally nonwork times, those workers are more likely to telecommute regardless of education. Expectations about availability and responsiveness may also increase work demands and work hours (Kelly & Moen, 2020).

Finally, the 2020 BLS American Time Use Survey introduced the term "takeup rate." The takeup rate is the difference between the percentage of workers for whom telework is feasible, less the percentage of workers in those jobs who work from home. For example, in rural areas the overall ability to telework rate is 31.8 percent but the takeup rate is 10.8 percent, indicating that 20 percent of rural workers who could telework are not doing so (Dey et al., 2020). There may be multiple reasons for the low rural takeup rate, but the most glaring is the rural digital divide.

Broadband

The great equalizer across urban and rural places is access to high-speed internet service. Rural areas have historically lagged behind in broadband diffusion, but the digital gap is closing (Perrin, 2019). About 75 percent of rural Americans report having a broadband internet connection at home (Pew Research Center, 2021) and about 25 percent of rural residents identify access to high-speed internet as a major problem (Vogels, 2021). Some rural economists opine that a federal broadband support policy for rural places could be the most important economic development investment in rural places in decades (Low, 2020). In a study of Tennessee counties, Lobo et al. (2020) found that broadband speed was correlated to lower unemployment rates in Tennessee, disproportionately so in rural areas. Specifically, they concluded that broadband speed, especially 100 Mbps or higher, can reduce unemployment by 0.2–0.3 percentage points, which can amount to hundreds of jobs in rural counties.

State broadband policies tend toward extremes. About half of states have some policies or programs that encourage rural broadband expansion while the other half have policies to restrict potential broadband service providers, especially electrical cooperatives and municipalities (Chamberlain, 2019). When rural municipalities build their own networks, they can challenge incumbent private internal service providers to reach areas that may not be profitable for the private provider to serve. Enabling and restrictive state broadband policies have a "measurable impact" (p. 11) on broadband diffusion in rural areas in the United States (Whitacre & Gallardo, 2020).

Recent changes in federal broadband policy may close state policy gaps, and the urban–rural digital divide. The American Recovery and Reinvestment Act of 2009 charged the Federal Communications Commission (FCC) to make broadband capability available in all US households (FCC, 2010). The FCC's authority to draft a plan for universal broadband was not in dispute, but their authority to implement it was. With the enactment of the Infrastructure Investment and Jobs Act of 2021 (Pub. L. 117–58, 135 Stat. 429), $65 billion was targeted to broadband access. The largest portion ($42.5 billion) offered subsidies to internet service providers to expand to unserved areas. An additional $2 billion in grants and loans was targeted to rural areas to build or expand broadband networks. The remainder was split between subsidies for low-income households or households who lost income due to the pandemic.

Tax Considerations

Remote work options open the door for new place-based economic development in rural communities, but an emerging redefinition of workplace has already created some serious problems. First, what are the tax obligations of the employee when the worker and workplace are in different jurisdictions? State and local income and employment taxes are clearly an issue. Some larger cities rely on employment income taxes to support their service functions. Will they be able to tax the worker because the employer is physically located in the city though the worker is not?

State corporation business taxes may also be in play. Some states take the position that remote employees (even a single remote employee) create a sufficient nexus to subject the business to the state's business taxes (see *Telebright Corp. v. Director, New Jersey Division of Taxation*, 424 N.J. Super. 384, 2012). As of this writing, sixteen states have provided COVID nexus relief, which means an employer located outside the state who has an employee working from home as a result of COVID safety protocols is not required to pay the taxes (income, franchise, sales, and use, payroll, etc.) as would a business located within the state (Megally et al., 2022). When the pandemic ends, how will continuing remote workers affect a business's state tax status?

Conclusions

As the pandemic stretches forward, businesses, government and individuals continue to invest in the infrastructure of remote work. For the most part, these are sunk costs and it would be only prudent to update the processes that make remote work possible. In fact, businesses are likely to conclude that some of these changes are more efficient and effective than traditional working arrangements (Brynjolfsson et al., 2020). Similarly, individuals may conclude that remote work has a positive impact on their work-life balance (if, for no other reason, down time spent commuting can be spent on work or life). It is almost self-evident that the changes with this new model of work will have a lasting impact.

This chapter argued that rural governments can benefit from telework and technology changes as they reconsider their economic development focus. Conversely, one also must be aware that the same economic forces that drove manufacturing jobs from rural areas to offshore locations may also threaten telework that is 100 percent remote. However, most telework is not 100 percent telework, and online meeting technologies may surpass in-person service arrangements to the benefit of all parties. Rather than think in terms of remote workers and in-person workers as two distinct economic bases, it would be wise to consider that the task bundles of almost all workers are being adjusted based on what we learned from the pandemic.

We don't know as much about rural governments as we do about metropolitan governments even though about one in five people in the US live in a rural area (Catlaw & Stout, 2016). Rural governments have their own special challenges and opportunities, though more emphasis has been given to the challenges than opportunities (Helpap, 2019). Despite limited evaluative studies in rural economic development policy outcomes, it is prudent to conclude that one approach is not sufficient. Placemaking that works well in one place fails to deliver the expected results in another comparable location. The theory of the creative class seems to hold in rural governments, particularly when they are endowed with attractive outdoor amenities (McGranahan et al., 2011). But Reese and Yi (2011) ask the hard question: Are these positive outcomes simply attributable to "place luck?" (p. 223).

The answer to this question matters because a rural government needs to be honest in its evaluation of the features—natural, social, and cultural— that might make a placemaking approach to economic development a reasonable choice. Indeed, historical patterns and geographic location do not bend to policy choices, but they can support certain policy choices like placemaking when the technology infrastructure permits. Place-based policies require a different kind of investment, but it needs to be no less intentional. The starting point should always be policies that start with collaboratively identifying a set of public services that is appropriate to the place and affordable to the residents.

References

Alkon, A. H., & Traugot, M. (2008). Place matters, but how? Rural identity, environmental decision making, and the social construction of place. *City & Community*, 7(2), 97–112.

Balassiano, K., & Maldonado, M. M. (2015). Placemaking in rural new gateway communities. *Community Development Journal*, 50(4), 644–660.

Brenan, M. (2020). U.S. workers discovering affinity for remote work. https://news.gallup.com/poll/306695/workers-discovering-affinityremote-work.aspx

Brynjolfsson, E., Horton, J. J., Ozimek, A., Rock, D., Sharma, G., & Hong-Yi T. (2020). Covid19 and *Remote Work: An Early Look* at US Data. National Bureau of Economic Research. www.nber.org/system/files/working_papers/w27344/w27344.pdf

Bureau of Labor Statistics (BLS). (2016). 24 percent of employed people did some or all of their work at home in 2015. *TED: The Economics Daily*. www.bls.gov/opub/ted/2016/24-percent-of-employed-people-did-some-or-all-of-their-work-at-home-in-2015.htm

Catlaw, T. J., & Stout, M. (2016). Governing small-town America today: The promise and dilemma of dense networks. *Public Administration Review*, 76(2), 225–229.

Chamberlain, K. (2019). *Municipal broadband is roadblocked or outlawed in 25 states*. Broadband Now. https://broadbandnow.com/report/municipal-broadband-and-roadblocks/

Cooper M. C., & Francis, C. (1998). *People Places: Design Guidelines for Urban Open Space*. John Wiley & Sons.

Dey, M., Frazis, H., Loewenstein, M. A., & Sun, H. (2020). Ability to work from home: evidence from two surveys and implications for the labor market in the COVID-19 pandemic. *Monthly Labor Review*. US Bureau of Labor Statistics. https://doi.org/10.21916/mlr.2020.14

Dingle, J. I., & Neiman, B. (2020). How *Many Jobs can be Done* at *Home?* Becker Friedman Institute for Economics at University of Chicago. https://bfi.uchicago.edu/wp-content/uploads/BFI_White-Paper_Dingel_Neiman_3.2020.pdf

Donegan, M., Drucker, J., Goldstein, H., Lowe N., & Malizia, E. (2008). Which indicators explain metropolitan economic performance best? Traditional or creative class. *Journal of the American Planning Association*, 74(2), 180–185.

Environmental Protection Agency. (2015). How *Small Towns* and Cities can *Use Local Assets* to Rebuild their Economies. EPA 231-R-15-002. www.epa.gov/sites/default/files/2015-05/documents/competitive_advantage_051215_508_final.pdf

Environmental Protection Agency. (2017). *Local Foods, Local Places Toolkit.* www.epa.gov/sites/default/files/2017-10/documents/lflp_toolkit_508-compli ant.pdf

Fan, W., & Moen, P. (2021). Working more, less or the same during COVID-19? A mixed method intersectional analysis of remote workers. *Work and Occupations.* https://doi.org/10.1177/07308884211047208

Federal Communications Commission. (2010). *The National Broadband Plan.* https://transition.fcc.gov/national-broadband-plan/nationalbroadband-plan.pdf

Florida, R. (2003). *The Rise of the Creative Class.* Basic Books.

Florida, R., Rodriguez-Pose, A., & Storper, M. (2021). Cities in a post-COVID world. *Urban Studies.* https://doi.org/10.1177/00420980211018072

Gallagher, B. K., & Ehlman, M. P. (2020). When in doubt, go to the library? Libraries and rural creative placemaking. *Journal of Rural and Community Development, 15*(2), 95–113.

Glaeser, E. L., & Gottlieb, J. D. (2008). *The Economics of Place-Making Policies.* National Bureau of Economic Research.

Hatcher, W., Oyer, M., & Gallardo, R. (2011). The creative class and economic development as practiced in the rural US south: An exploratory survey of economic development professionals. *Review of Regional Studies, 41*(2), 139–159.

Helpap, D. J. (2019). Public management in rural local governments: an assessment of institutional differences and implications. *State and Local Government Review, 51*(1), 6–18.

Hinds, P. J., & Kiesler, S., Eds. (2002). *Distributed Work.* MIT Press.

Housing Assistance Council (2018). *Native American Creative Placemaking.* https://ruralhome.org/wp-content/uploads/storage/documents/publications/rrreports/rrr-native-placemaking.pdf

Kelly, E. L., & Moen, P. (2020). *Overload: How Good Jobs Went Bad and What we can Do about it.* Princeton University Press.

Kelly, J. M., Ruther, M., Ehresman, S., & Nickerson, B. (2017). Placemaking as an economic development strategy for small and midsized cities. *Urban Affairs Review, 53*(3), 435–462.

Leamer, E. E., & Storper, M. (2001). The economic geography of the internet age. *Journal of International Business Studies 32*(4): 641–665.

Lee, S. Y., Minsung, P., & Shin, Y. (2021). Hit harder, recover slower? Unequal employment effects of the COVID-19 shock. *Federal Reserve Bank of St. Louis Review*, 367–383. https://doi.org/10.20955/r.103.367-83

Lobo, B. J., Alam, M. R., & Whitacre, B. E. (2021). Broadband speed and unemployment rates: Data and measurement issues. *Telecommunications Policy, 44*(1), 1–44. https://doi.org/10.1016/j.telpol.2019.101829

Low, S. A. (2020). Rural development research and policy: Perspectives from federal and state experiences with an application to broadband. *Review of Regional Studies, 50*(3), 311–322.

Mather, V. K. (1999). Human capital-based strategy for regional economic development. *Economic Development Quarterly, 13*(3), 203–216.

McGranahan D. A., & Wojan, T. R. (2007). Recasting the creative class to examine growth processes in rural and urban counties. *Regional Studies, 41*(2), 197–216.

McGranahan D. A., Wojan, T. R., & Lambert, D. M. (2011). The rural growth trifecta: Outdoor amenities, creative class and entrepreneurial context. *Journal of Economic Geography, 11*(3), 529–557.

Megally, S., Ohlenforst, C., Baker, M., LeDoux, W. J., & Wagner, M. S. (2020). COVID-19: State tax implications of remote working arrangements. *National Law Review, 12*(8) www.natlawreview.com/article/covid-19-state-tax-implicati ons-remote-working-arrangements

Mountain Association. (2019). Appalachia's New Day: The arts in Eastern Kentucky. https://mtassociation.org/training-ideas/appalachias-new-day-arts/

Murray, J. (2012, November). The best midsized mountain town. *Blue Ridge Outdoors Magazine.* www.blueridgeoutdoors.com/outdoors-travel/the-best-mid-sized-mountain-town

Pender, J., Marré, A., & Reeder, R. (2012). Rural Wealth Creation Concepts, Strategies, and Measures. US Department of Agriculture. www.ers.usda.gov/ publications/err-economic-research-report/err131.aspx

Perrin, A. (2019). Digital Gap between Rural and Nonrural America Persists. Pew Research Center. www.pewresearch.org/fact-tank/2019/05/31/digital-gap-betw een-rural-and-nonrural-america-persists/

Pew Research Center (2021). *State Broadband Policy Explorer.* Pew Research Center. www.pewtrusts.org/en/research-and-analysis/data-visualizations/2019/ state-broadband-policy-explorer

Reese, L. A., & Minting, Y. (2011). Policy versus place luck: Achieving local economic prosperity. *Economic Development Quarterly, 25*(3), 221–236.

Reese, L. A. (2014). If all you have is a hammer: Finding economic development policies that matter. *American Review of Public Administration, 44*(6), 627–655.

Rickman, F., & Rickman, S. D. (2011). Population growth in high amenity nonmetropolitan areas: What's the prognosis? *Journal of Regional Science, 51*(5), 863–879.

Schneekloth, L. H., & Shibley, R. G. (1995). *Placemaking: The Art and Practice of Building Communities,* John Wiley & Sons.

Tuan, Y. F. (1991) Language and the making of place: A narrative-descriptive approach. *Annals of the Association of American Geographers, 81*(4), 684–696.

Vogels, E. A. (2021). Some *Digital Divides Persist* between *Rural, Urban* and *Suburban* America. Pew Research Center. www.pewresearch.org/fact-tank/ 2021/08/19/some-digital-divides-persist-between-rural-urban-and-suburban-america/

Whitacre, B., & Gallardo, R. (2020). State broadband policy: Impacts on availability. *Telecommunications Policy, 44*(9), 1–11. https://doi.org/10.1016/ j.telpol.2020.102025

Subsection: Election Administration

4

THE MECHANICS OF DEMOCRACY

The Critical Role of Local Governments in Supporting Election Operations

Kathleen Hale

Local election offices face particular challenges. These offices typically have few full-time staff, and are vulnerable to disruptions in ways that larger offices are not, simply because backup is so limited. Rural areas are also vulnerable to changes in the USPS practices which have closed rural post offices. As jurisdictions move to voting by mail to reduce other costs such as poll workers, the local office may find that the mail service timetables for their area are not aligned well with state deadlines for mailing and returning ballot applications and completed ballots. In other words, it may not be possible for the USPS to process ballots in a timely fashion. In tribal areas, local election offices may have no mail service. For rural counties that cover large areas, or mountainous terrain, it can be challenging to travel to poll sites (or to deliver services to poll sites when issues arise), making the option of voting by mail very attractive, but subject to these limitations which are outside the control of a local election office. Rural residents may also have less confidence in election administration when they believe that electoral processes of their county favor urban political interests (Rinfret et al., 2018).

The role of local government in supporting election operations is undeniably critical. Localities have been the hub of American elections since the earliest colonial times (Ewald, 2009; Keyssar, 2000). Every elected office—regardless of the state or territory in the United States—depends upon the work of a local election office, whether that election is held for mayor, governor, city council, senator, president, school board, or any of the countless offices which are filled by election. An estimated 8,000 local election offices operate in counties, municipalities, towns, and townships

DOI: 10.4324/9781003287766-9

around the country,[1] holding thousands of elections each year. Although the federal government enforces non-discrimination in registration and voting, and state election offices have stepped in on certain administrative issues, elections have always been essentially a local enterprise. Yet, in spite of this elemental foundation, these local operations are not well understood.

This is not surprising. From childhood, we have voting experiences that are very simple and that show immediate results—show of hands, slips of paper in a bowl, press a response on a touch screen. To almost everyone, the process of voting for elected office appears quite straightforward. Voters register to vote. On Election Day, they go to designated locations such as schools and churches and community centers in their neighborhoods where they check in with poll workers who verify their eligibility and hand them their ballots. Voters mark their ballots and submit them. Sometime later that evening, results are announced.

The reality is far more complex and varied, both in the general approaches to voting and the local administrative processes that are used (Hale et al., 2015). This has always been the case, given the constitutional authority vested in states to determine how, when, and where elections are held. In addition, significant changes have occurred over the past 20 years, both in the ways we vote and the equipment that we use. The way we vote has changed from a one-day in-person experience to include some form of early voting and voting by mail.[2] In years past, voters might close a curtain behind them to cast a ballot using a lever or a punch card and stylus. Today, many voters cast ballots on electronic voting machines, which appears to be associated with fewer reported voting problems (see Burden et al., 2017; Kropf et al., 2020). In the past ten years, it has become common to be able to register to vote online. It has also become more commonplace to vote in the days prior to the traditional election day, and to receive a ballot by mail and return it either by mail or drop box. Most recently, the security of electronic equipment and the personal safety of election office staff have become priorities.

In response to these changes in technology, culture, and public policy, the complexity of the work of local election officials has intensified. It is now more important than ever to understand the local election office and the knowledge, skills, and abilities that are required, given the considerable controversy about election administration practices that arose during the 2020 election cycle and which continue today. It is critical to understand the role that local government plays in supporting these offices.

This chapter aims to demystify the local election office as a crucial institution of local government, and demonstrate the essential role of local government in American elections. The chapter first provides an overview of the local election environment, including typical local functions, institutional structures, staff and development, and budgets. As with most aspects of local law and regulation, local election requirements are established by state law through legislation and, in some cases, through constitutional provisions. Points of national commonality arise over time (e.g., expansion of suffrage, the secret ballot, adoption of various types of voting equipment), however, administrative practices are distinct across states and often across jurisdictions within states. The details demonstrate the complexity of election administration, the deep reliance on local government to the exclusion of other levels of government, and the strains on local government capacity. The chapter considers the unique challenges faced by local election offices in rural areas and small towns and offers observations about the potential to influence local capacity in ways that can reinforce democratic institutions.

The Local Election Office: Functions

Broadly speaking, the activities of the local election office are organized around the election cycles and election formats that it administers. Today, elections are conducted in person on election day and early voting days, and by mail.[3] These activities can be classified over time into pre-election day (pre-balloting), election day (during balloting), and post-election day (post-balloting) activities (Hale et al., 2015; Montjoy, 2008).[4]

Before Election Day/Pre-Balloting

Prior to election day and throughout the year, local office staff are involved in registering voters and maintaining voter registration lists for accuracy. Voter registration involves direct interaction with voters and also coordinated interaction with other public offices, including drivers' license bureaus, social services offices, and offices that provide disability services.[5] In some states, local election offices also coordinate voter registration data with the National Change of Address system of the US Postal Service and other cross-state matching services.

Staff also identify election precincts and other boundary lines. In some offices, staff collect candidate campaign filings including petitions for ballot access and campaign finance reports. Staff work with vendors to create and verify ballots. If required, ballots are mailed in advance if required, either to all voters or to those who are permitted to request them. Poll sites are identified, and permission is secured to use them. Poll workers are recruited, trained, and assigned. Drop box locations for mail ballots are identified and drop box equipment is installed along with supporting equipment such as surveillance cameras. Voting equipment is pre-tested, including electronic poll books that hold voter registration lists, voting systems that receive cast ballots, and tabulators that count ballots. Prior to election day, equipment is gathered from storage locations and transported to poll sites along with the support technology; poll sites are also supplied with ballots and all the other materials needed to conduct the election. Throughout, local offices attend to risk management including cybersecurity issues.

Election Day/During Balloting

On election day, poll sites are set up early in the morning and then open to receive voters. Poll workers—local residents who are paid a nominal rate or who volunteer—verify voter eligibility, and direct voters to the correct voting location, which may be another poll site. Voters cast ballots. Poll workers field voter questions and also field complaints, run interference with site monitors and observers and the media. Voting systems providers deploy technicians to assist with equipment functionality should issues arise. Ballots received by mail are collected, opened, reviewed for appropriate signatures and other process requirements, and counted. Whether ballots are cast in person or returned by mail, provisions exist in every jurisdiction to resolve ballot discrepancies (e.g., provisional ballots) such as mismatched signatures, lack of specific forms of identification, and minor administrative errors. Poll site staff work with voters to gather information to resolve these issues. During the day, office staff are engaged in working with poll site staff, the media, and fielding questions from voters, candidates, advocacy groups, and the general public. The poll workers may also carry out the unpleasant task of telling prospective voters that they are not eligible to vote, or must cast a provisional ballot that will not be counted until their legal status as a voter is confirmed. In a study in Missouri after the state enacted a voter ID law, researchers found that poll workers in smaller jurisdictions had fewer voters check in without photo IT than in larger, more urban jurisdictions (Anthony & Kimball, 2020).

After Election Day/Post-Balloting

Poll sites close at designated times, and materials are inventoried and returned to storage. Votes are tabulated, counts are reviewed and certified, and an accounting is conducted of all ballots issued (whether or not these can be counted); some jurisdictions also require audits of various types. Results are communicated to the state election office and become available to the press, candidates, and the public. On occasion, results trigger state laws that require ballot recounts or run-off elections. Staff are debriefed, and data are analyzed to troubleshoot the next election.

It is worth noting that local election offices must also comply with cross-cutting requirements such as the Voting Rights Act of 1965 (VRA) prohibition on discrimination in registration and voting, and the Americans with Disabilities Act (ADA) provisions on access to public services.[6] Moreover, in many localities, elections are conducted in English and in other languages as required by federal, state, or local law. The VRA[7] requires that local jurisdictions provide language assistance for registration and voting where the population exceeds a threshold in designated language groups (Spanish, Asian, American Native, and Alaskan Native), and where significant numbers of residents are not proficient in English. Language assistance may also be offered beyond federal requirements if states or localities choose. As examples, the Los Angeles County Voter Multilingual Services Program in California now offers language assistance in 18 languages in addition to English through a combination of state and local requirements; in New York City, by mayoral order, translation assistance is provided in Russian and Haitian Creole in addition to language assistance that is federally required (Hale & Brown, 2020). Rural communities experiencing an influx of language minorities may have a particularly hard time finding translators to assist non-English-speaking voters (Minnis, 2021).

Some of the administration necessary to address VRA, ADA, and other cross-cutting requirements may be housed in local government generally (i.e., a county general office) or at the state level. Nevertheless, local administrative effort is necessary in order to address the provisions that apply specifically to elections.

The Local Election Office: Institutional Structure

Most voters are served by county-level election offices.[8] The configurations vary. A local election office may be responsible for voter registration and election administration (the most common arrangement, e.g., Florida, Ohio). The structure of a local office may be limited to voter registration, or to election day operations (e.g., Texas). Election operations may also be housed in an administrative unit charged with additional responsibilities such as the office of county clerk (e.g., Colorado). Here, the work of these more general offices extends beyond election operations to include administration of business records, licenses, and court filings.[9]

At the state level, each state has a chief election officer. This position is typically held by the Secretary of State or an appointee of that office. The state election office is not involved in the day-to-day operation of local election offices, and does not conduct elections. State offices provide support for local offices by maintaining statewide electronic voter registration databases through data collected by local offices. State offices also serve as pass-through administrators for federal grant funds, and may also administer financial reimbursements for some election expenses (discussed more fully in the next section). Training is also an important state office function. Some state election offices also collect data about local operations.

The workload of a local election office reflects office structure. There is no systematic research to catalog the array of work responsibilities at the office level, and only limited information has been collected from local election officials. By any measure, the workload is diverse across many functions. About one-third of respondents to a national survey of local election officials indicated that all or almost all of their workload was devoted to election responsibilities. One-quarter indicated that they had other responsibilities; and nearly half reported that election-related work was less than half of their workload (Adona et al., 2019). This distribution of office structures (comprehensive election duties, election duties plus other duties, and voter registration or election administration only) varies by size. Offices tend to become more specialized as they increase in size. Similarly, as offices decrease in staff size, the range of duties increases.

The Local Election Office: Staff and Staff Development

The "typical" office of full-time staff ranges from one or two people to more than 1,000.[10] In 2011, the Congressional Research Service profiled the typical local election official as white, female, approximately 50–60 years old, with an annual salary of $60,000, and a high school degree, and had served in the position for at least ten years. Findings from a national sample conducted in 2018 (Adona et al., 2019) reinforce that profile, with an upward adjustment in educational attainment and length of service (about half had completed a college degree, and about half had worked for 15 years or more).

There is no clear educational path to become a local election official. Interest in democracy and political processes is logical, but not required. Most arrive in an election office through public service that began elsewhere in local government; their careers eventually lead them to election administration. It is not uncommon for the chief local election official to be elected (e.g., Supervisor of Elections in Florida, County Clerk in Colorado). Some local election officials have political experience with campaigns and advocacy activities. In rural communities and small towns, many of these election officials are related by blood, marriage, or friendship with many party officials, candidates, and voters.

Basic administrative skills such as project management, communications, and logistics are always part of the work. Technology related to election security and risk management are increasingly important. As a result of rising complexity and increasing technical responsibilities, specific education programs are beginning to emerge. Public administration programs can provide education in many of these areas. Auburn University offers a graduate certificate in election administration adjacent to its MPA Program; the University of Minnesota offers a non-degree certificate in the field.

It is quite common for local election officials to be involved in job-specific training. State election offices and state professional associations of election officials offer regular training (annual or more frequently) on state election law, policy, and procedure. The National Association of Election Officials (the Election Center) offers a national certification program for election officials and election system stakeholders, which has served thousands of local officials. This professional program earns continuing education credit from Auburn University and includes standards of conduct and an ethical code, along with education in law, policy, operations, and administration. Across the board, training and professional development providers have responded to national conditions including the need to educate, train, and prepare on issues of election cybersecurity and the potential for violence at poll sites and election offices.

The Local Election Office: Budget

Local election offices are funded through several sources. These include the general fund of the local unit of government in which they are housed, election expense reimbursements from other units of government, direct support from the state election office, and federal grants (Hale & Brown,2020). County general funds are the most significant source of local funding by far. To receive general fund appropriations, local election offices compete with every other local office for funding (Mohr et al., 2019; McGowan et al., 2021). The results are striking. In a study of county funding for election administration, Hale and Brown (2020) found that the average proportion of local election office budgets represented 0.5 percent (0.005) of the administrative expenses of a county budget.[11]

Local election offices are typically able to recoup some expenses from state election offices. These reimbursements range widely in amount and expense category, as well as the election years for which reimbursements can be claimed. As one example, reimbursement to local election jurisdictions might be permitted for the cost of printing ballots for a presidential election; as another, reimbursement might be allowed for election expenses required to set up poll sites in any election during any year. Reimbursements might be limited only to expenses incurred in special (unplanned or unscheduled) elections.

These funds are not a reliable or significant source of operating revenue. Local offices also receive reimbursements from "coordinating" jurisdictions such as school boards or other local political subdivisions within the jurisdiction of the election office that do not conduct their own elections.

Local election offices may receive direct continuing support from the state election office (typically, the Secretary of State), although this is rare and considered an innovation in the field.[12] Finally, local offices may receive federal grant funds. To date, these have been directed at specific purposes. The first tranche of federal funds was distributed under HAVA to the states for an overhaul of the nation's election equipment as well as training. Since that $3.5 billion, federal funds were not appropriated until recently, in response to specific needs such as cybersecurity monitoring and defense, and pandemic-related needs such as personal protective equipment. The EAC has chosen to send federal grant funds to state election offices that then make the determinations (whether, how much, when) about local funding, rather than directly to local election offices.

In the 2020 election cycle, private philanthropy entered the local funding picture. Grant programs established by various private sources offered funds to local election offices. Groups such as the Center for Tech and Civic Life (a pass-through for funds from Facebook CEO Mark Zuckerberg and Priscilla Chan), the Schwarzenegger Foundation at the University of Southern California, and others responded to meet shortfalls related to the pandemic. Some grantors targeted their grants at jurisdictions with particular voter registration profiles and others made their funds available to any jurisdiction who asked. Local election office response has been mixed. Some offices accepted private grant funds with open arms, and some refused. Interestingly, following 2020, some states have passed laws to prohibit such third--party funding.

Unique Challenges for Local Election Offices

Local election administrators are constantly buffeted by several challenges. These include 1) legislative pressures, 2) constant public oversight, 3) relatively unique intergovernmental relationships; and 4) concerns about capacity. All public servants face these challenges to some degree; in the decades since Election 2000, it is difficult to find another area of local administration that has experienced a greater concentration of pressures across all of these fronts.

Legislative Policy Pressures

Local election offices operate at the mercy of state legislatures, and the legislative pace in this area has been furious. Across the states, legislatures responded to the 2020 election with a flurry of bills. In 2021, nearly 450 bills (440) were drafted in nearly every state. The number that passed in 2021 exceeded more than one-third of all such bills passed in the previous ten years (Brennan Center for Justice & Benenson Strategy Group, 2022). Collectively, states imposed harsher voter identification requirements, reduced time periods for requesting mail ballots, limited the use of mail ballot drop boxes, and made it easier for citizens to be removed from voter rolls. In 19 states, legislators made changes that addressed the authority to make decisions about election operations, the ability to vote by mail, and generally created additional administrative requirements (Weiser, 2021). These additional requirements are generally perceived to make it more difficult to vote, although there is nuance in actual implementation.

The volume of state election legislation is daunting for local election officials to digest and implement. Each of these changes represents hundreds of decisions that have to be made in local offices. Deadlines are inflexible. And these state legislative changes are not accompanied by state (or federal) funding.

Equally but differently daunting is the understanding where the authority lies to make changes in local election processes. This question rose to the forefront during the pandemic in early 2020. Local election officials fielded directions from multiple sources, from the first widespread announcement of the spread of disease during the March primary season. Changes in practice continued into voter registration periods and early voting periods in some states. Governors issued emergency and executive orders to cancel or reschedule elections, expand opportunities to vote by mail, and implement various personal protective equipment measures. Chief election officers (CEOs) did the same, sometimes in accordance with their governor, and sometimes not, setting up new conflicts. Given that state CEOs are most typically elected as secretaries of state, or appointed by governors, charges of partisan politics inevitably ensued. State legislatures worked to establish new election policy—again, sometimes in concert with other state officers. State courts became involved in resolving disputes, as did the US Supreme Court. To date, decisions have not established a clear or universal rule of authority for changes in local election operations; as with the other aspects of election operations, states vary in their constitutional treatment of election law and authority.

Public Oversight

Local election offices conduct their work in the public eye. Some oversight is mandatory under state election law. Election observers and poll watchers from political parties, candidates, advocacy groups, and the general public watch voters cast their ballots. They also watch ballot counting and the adjudication of discrepancies and disputes such as signature mismatches and ballots rejected from or damaged by voting equipment.

For the typical election office, these observations are routine. And transparency is a bedrock value of public administration across the board—public offices should be transparent in the work that they do. The presence of the media is expected. However, the circumstances of the 2020 election captured on national news and social media demonstrate what happens when the number of observers rises beyond the capacity of local election offices to accommodate them.

As a result of the experiences of the 2020 election, local election officials report serious concerns about their personal safety directly related to media and to personal interactions with the public at the polls and at their offices including threats of violence (Brennan Center for Justice & Benenson Strategy Group, 2022). Reports indicate that skilled election workers are leaving the field and significant institutional memory is disappearing with them.

Unique Intergovernmental Relationships

Unlike many other areas of local public service, local election office operations are not subject to a federal administrative compliance regime. State authority over elections is long established under the US Constitution; until the civil rights legislation of the 1950s that led to the VRA, federal authority in this area was essentially non-existent.[13] Today, federal enforcement of the VRA focuses on primarily on litigation over claims of discrimination.

The federal agencies with responsibilities that relate to election operations are empowered to collect information and to offer advice and guidance, but have no regulatory authority. The Election Assistance Commission (EAC) operates an information clearinghouse and works with other federal offices to develop voluntary voting system guidelines. Established in 2002 through Help America Vote Act (HAVA), the EAC distributed approximately $4 billion to convert the nation's punch card and lever voting machines to electronic voting systems, as well as other funds targeted at cybersecurity and pandemic relief. The Department of Homeland Security has played a role in cybersecurity in the election arena since 2017 when election operations were declared to be critical infrastructure.

Within and adjacent to DHS, the Cybersecurity and Infrastructure Security Agency (CISA), the Center for Internet Security (CIS), and the Election Infrastructure-Information Sharing and Analysis Center (EI-ISAC) all provide information and guidance on cyber and infrastructure security and risk management. However, these roles are purely advisory. Although lack of federal regulation means greater local flexibility, it may also mean fewer opportunities for federal dollars to flow to local budgets to support elections, and fewer opportunities for interactions between federal, state, and local officials that showcase innovations as well as needs.[14]

Increasing Concerns about Capacity

Local election offices do a great deal with very little. Resources are constrained, and little funding is available beyond direct appropriations from local government general funds, regardless of mounting pressures posed by new laws and changing technology. These pressures are deeply rooted and not easily addressed. The significance of these pressures on the capacity of local election offices—and local government generally—cannot be underestimated. Capacity in government and in public offices means the ability to do what is intended (Burgess, 1975; Gargan, 1981; Honadle, 1981); failure to address the factors outlined in this chapter places the local election function in jeopardy. By extension, citizen trust in local government is at risk.

The "double whammy" of 2020 illustrates the essential fragility of the funding that supports local offices. First, the COVID-19 pandemic exploded in March 2020 as the primary election season moved into full swing. Every local election office scrambled to create safe environments for in-person voting and to create alternative methods of voting (e.g., expanded use of mail, drop boxes, early voting days). Governors issued executive orders about PPE (personal protective equipment), canceled or rescheduled primaries, and adopted broad plans to increase voting through the US mail. The federal government eventually issued funding for PPE and related expenses as part of some pandemic bills.

Although welcome, these resources only scratched the surface. The supply chain issues generated by the pandemic that affected the general public—shortages of everything from paper towels to furniture—were readily observable and highly publicized. Less visible, the various supply chains for election operations were also under stress. As one example, the massive transition to voting by mail required paper for ballots and envelopes and high-speed scanners among other tools.

Local election officials found solutions to protect public safety and maintain election integrity. Yet funds were not budgeted nor readily available. Some requests were swallowed up in controversy over which state or local office could make or enforce decisions about operations. Private philanthropy entered the arena with $100s of millions in grant funds for pandemic relief for local election offices. As Persily and Stewart noted (2021), it is "embarrassing and tragic" that the amount of private grant funds exceeded the funds that the federal government was willing to provide for local election administration in 2020. Their commentary implies that the federal government *should* be a more significant source of local funding; however, local governments bear responsibility in their allocation decisions.

The capacity of local election offices also relates to the technology used to administer elections. A sea change in local election technology occurred following the 2000 election and the passage of HAVA, which authorized approximately $3.5 billion in federal funds to replace the nation's paper punch card and lever systems with electronic voting systems. The systems were developed by private industry in keeping with a voluntary testing regime (the Voluntary Voting System Guidelines) established by the EAC. For the most part, these funds have purchased a single round of equipment, and voting system providers have updated hardware and software to reflect technological advances. The useful life of a voting system is estimated at 10–20 years, and most are on the edge of that (or past it) today (Hitt et al., 2017). Local jurisdictions have also purchased commercial off the shelf (COTS) technology such as iPads and printers to use in poll sites to support new approaches to voter check-in and voter registration.

The current voting system environment presents several related challenges (Brennan Center for Justice & Benenson Strategy Group, 2022). First, the voting system industry is constrained by few opportunities for sales, the lack of a stable funding stream, and the high cost of technological innovation. Local election office budgets (and even county or state budgets) are not equipped to bear the cost of voting system replacement, which is estimated in billions of dollars (Hitt et al., 2017). Standardization has been elusive. Local needs for multilingual information vary considerably, as do local ballot styles.[15] Innovation has been incremental at best, with the most significant overhaul of a voting system occurring in Los Angeles County, CA, the nation's largest election jurisdiction (Hale & Brown, 2020).[16] There, a public private partnership evolved over at least ten years to design and create a new voting system at a total cost approaching $1 billion. The system was rolled out in full during the 2020 election season.

The comparatively low level of public-sector investment in local technology is also an impediment. Local election offices are rarely in the position to have full-time technology support on staff; and even county administrative offices are unlikely to have technology staff devoted specifically to election equipment (Bennett, 2019). In about half of the states, decisions about voting technology are made at the state level; local election office input (where the equipment will be used) can be thin or non-existent (Hale & Brown, 2020). Thus, local offices rely significantly on voting system vendors for hardware and software support, at the expense of system development by these same vendors, and at the expense of creating even greater reliance on the private sector.

Enhancing Critical Local Capacity

The local election office is the heartbeat of American elections. Preserving and enhancing local capacity is critical. The following are several broad suggestions about how to begin to shore up and enhance local election offices within the context of local government.

A reliable pool of additional, sustained public funding seems an obvious solution. Private funds are not a viable long-term solution even if motives are pure, but the sources of public funding are less clear. County commissioners and county supervisors should answer the call in this arena to provide greater local support for election operations. One approach may be to encourage civic leaders to develop local initiatives to support election funding in county budgets as a point of civic pride. Local election offices already conduct significant community outreach in the ordinary course of holding elections and throughout the year—local leaders (private sector as well as public) can reciprocate by showcasing their election operations, and featuring their levels of confidence and trust in local government. After all, local elections are run by and for the community—local election office workers are neighbors and fellow community members. State legislatures and Congressional representatives can also be encouraged to support and coordinate sustainable funding legislation, although partisanship may be a more significant impediment beyond the local level.

The area of professional development is a specific area that can be targeted for developing and sustaining capacity. As the discussion of election office functions, structure, and staffing indicate, local election administration involves deep knowledge of domain specifics. Local election administration also depends on broad awareness of major themes in public administration. Successful governance of the local election office requires political acuity inside and outside the office (Hale & Brown, 2020). Risk management requires broad awareness of security risks posed by natural and intelligent (man-made) disasters including mis- and disinformation (Brown et al., 2020; Williamson et al., 2020), and threats of violence toward election officials (Brennan Center for Justice & Benenson Strategy Group, 2022) and other election system stakeholders such as private industry voting system providers.[17] The rise of mis- and disinformation has made communications with the media and multiple stakeholders (voters, volunteers, legislatures) an ascendant obligation (Praetz, 2022). Professional development should be targeted at these broad themes of public service, as well as to specific technical issues.

Last, and related to both, local offices should focus on building access to election technology including voting systems and ancillary equipment. This is particularly crucial for small towns and rural communities that are often the last to accept new technologies. This can be accomplished with relative independence in larger offices, and may require significant support from state election offices in some cases. Collaborations across local election offices may be fruitful. Voting system vendors demonstrated excellent performance in the 2020 election season, but more can be done to increase public confidence—and more means more resources.

Elections cannot happen without local election offices. And local election offices cannot function well without the support of local government. Local election officials want to run smooth operations and worry that they may be inhibited by ageing technology and mis- and disinformation, let alone the ever-changing thicket of election laws and administrative responsibilities in a resource-poor environment. Voters are concerned about whether their votes are properly counted, and whether they are confident in the operations they participate in and observe. Research indicates that voters who report problems in the voting process will have lower confidence in the elections as a whole (Alvarez et al., 2021). Understanding the intricacies of election operations is a necessary first step but alone is not sufficient. Capacity in this arena requires investment to meet multiple challenges; enhanced funding for operations, professional development, and technical expertise are worthy of careful consideration by local election offices and the local governments that support them.

Notes

1   This estimate reflects the number of counties and the number of cities, towns, and townships that also conduct elections (Hale et al., 2015).
2   Stewart and Fortier (2021) find that in 2020 the methods that voters chose for cast ballots divided fairly evenly between election day voting, early voting, and voting by mail.
3   Here, voting by mail encompasses a range of practices including absentee voting (whether ballots are requested or not, and whether excuses are required or not) and methods by which all voters are mailed ballots.
4   The term "election day" here refers to the single day historically identified for in-person polling place voting in a particular election.
5   The National Voter Registration Act of 1993 mandates that these offices offer and accept voter registration forms when providing services; that information is then provided to the local election office.

6 The ADA has established specific requirements for poll site accessibility.
7 Language assistance requirements were included in reauthorizations of the VRA beginning in 1970.
8 City, town, and township election offices are found primarily in Michigan, Minnesota, Wisconsin, and much of New England.
9 See Hale et al. (2015) for a catalog of these.
10 Little systematic research has been conducted about the demographic profile of local election office staff around the country. As a result, much more is known about the range of various metrics than other descriptive statistics.
11 Based on six states using data from the National Association of Counties and state budgets. See Hale and Brown (2020) for additional detail.
12 Hale and Brown (2020) found such an arrangement in Colorado, which resulted from a legislative overhaul spearheaded through more than a decade of political collaboration between the Secretary of State and county clerks; broad systematic study of this area of election office administration has not been conducted.
13 The Civil Rights Act of 1955 began a thread of federal involvement in local election operations by establishing the US Civil Rights Commission. Commission hearings around the country cataloged inequities in registration and voting across Southern states. Evidence from these hearings supported the eventual adoption of the Civil Rights Act of 1964 and the VRA.
14 The Federal Election Commission (FEC) is authorized by Congress to regulate, but that authority is directed at candidate and campaign fundraising, expenditures, and reporting. Prior to HAVA, the FEC housed information related to election administration in its clearinghouse. HAVA was adopted without transferring any regulatory authority to the EAC.
15 A ballot style is the unique combination of races and issues specific to a voter based on their address.
16 For perspective, in 2020 LA County had 6.1 million people eligible to vote, and 5.8 million were registered.
17 For a comprehensive account of the threats to personal security of voting system providers, see the defamation litigation filed by Dominion Voting Systems, Inc., and Smartmatic, Inc. against the allegations of election fraud levelled at these companies by members of the media and other individuals.

References

Adona, N., Gronke, P., Manson, P., & Cole, S. (2019). *Stewards of Democracy*. The Democracy Fund and Reed College.
Alvarez, R. M., Cao, J., & Li, Y. (2021). Voting experiences, perceptions of fraud, and voter confidence. *Social Science Quarterly*, *102*(4), 1225–1238.
Anthony, J., & Kimball, D. C. (2020). Implementing voter ID: Lessons from Missouri, USA. *Policy Studies*, *41*(2/3), 210–229.
Bennett, D. A. (2019). Technology procurement in election administration. In Mitchell Brown, Kathleen Hale, and Bridgett King (Eds.), The Future of Election Administration: *Cases and conversations*. Palgrave Macmillan, 203–210.
Brennan Center for Justice and Benenson Strategy Group. (2022). *Local Election Officials Survey*. Brennan Center for Justice at New York University School of Law.
Brown, M, Hale, K., Forson, L. Smith, B., & Williamson, R. (2020). Shifting focuses in US election administration: Election system security and contingency planning. *Election Law Journal: Rules, Politics, and Policy*, *19*(2), 180–199.

Burden, B. C., Canon, D. T., Mayer, K. R., Moynihan, D. P., & Neiheisel, J. R. (2017). What happens at the polling place: Using administrative data to look inside elections. *Public Administration Review*, 77(3), 354–364.

Burgess, P. M. (1975). Capacity building and the elements of public management. *Public Administration Review*, 35, 705–716. https://doi.org/10.2307/974607

Congressional Research Service. 2011. *How Local Election Officials View Election Reform: Results from Three National Surveys (R41667)*. Congressional Research Service.

Ewald, A. (2009). *The Way we Vote: The Local Dimension of American Suffrage.* Vanderbilt University Press.

Gargan, J. J. (1981). Consideration of local government capacity. *Public Administration Review*, 41(6), 649–658.

Hale, K., & Brown, M. (2020). *How we Vote: Innovation in American Elections.* Georgetown University Press.

Hale, K., Montjoy, R. S., & Brown, M. (2015). *Administering Elections: How American Elections Work.* Palgrave.

Hitt, L., Ahluwalia, S., Caulfield, M., Davidson, L., Diehl, M. M., Ispas, A., & Windle, M. (2017). The Business of Voting: Market Structure and Innovation in the Election Technology Industry. Penn Wharton Public Policy Initiative. https://trustthevote.org/wp-content/uploads/2017/03/2017-whartonoset_ind ustryreport.pdf

Honadle, B. W. (1981). A capacity-building framework: A search for concept and purpose. *Public Administration Review*, 41(5), 575–580.

Keyssar, A. (2000). *The Right to Vote: The Contested History of Democracy in the United States.* Basic Books.

King, B., & Hale, K. (2016). *Why Americans Don't Vote: Causes and Consequences.* ABC-CLIO.

Kropf, M., Pope, J. V., Shepherd, M. J., & Mohr, Z. (2020). Making every vote count: The important role of managerial capacity in achieving better election administration outcomes. *Public Administration Review*, 80(5), 733–742.

Manson, P., Adona, N., & Gronke, P. (2020). Staffing the stewards of democracy: The demographic and professional profile of America's local election officials. Paper presented at the Annual Conference of the Southern Political Science Association, San Juan, Puerto Rico.

McGowan, M. J., Pope, J. V., Kropf, M. E., & Mohr, Z. (2021). Guns or butter … or elections? Understanding intertemporal and distributive dimensions of policy choice through the examination of budgetary tradeoffs at the local level. *Public Budgeting & Finance*, 41(4), 3–19.

Menger, A., & Stein, R. M. (2018). Enlisting the public in facilitating election administration: A field experiment. *Public Administration Review*, 78(6), 892–903.

Minnis, A. T. (2021). Voting is a universal language: Ensuring the franchise for the growing language minority community in Minnesota. *Minnesota Law Review*, 105(6), 2597–2622.

Mohr, Z., Pope, J. V., Kropf, M. E., & Shepherd, M. J. (2019). Strategic spending: Does politics influence election administration expenditure? *American Journal of Political Science*, 63(2), 427–438.

Montjoy, R. S. (2008). The public administration of elections. *Public Administration Review, 68*(5), 788–799.

Persily, N., & Stewart, C., III. (2021). The miracle and tragedy of the 2020 election. *Journal of Democracy, 32*(2), 159–178.

Praetz, N. (2022). Empowering the election workforce and protecting critical infrastructure. *Journal of Election Administration Research & Practice, 1*(1), 2–6.

Rinfret, S., Barsky, C., & Scott, S. (2018). Public perceptions, elections administration, and the role of street level bureaucrats. *Public Administration Quarterly, 42*(4), 493–515.

Sellers, J. S., & Michalski, R. (2021). Democracy on a shoestring. *Vanderbilt Law Review, 74*(4), 1079–1135.

Stewart, C., III. (2022). *The Cost of Conducting Elections.* MIT Election + Data Science Lab.

Stewart, C., III, & Fortier, J. (2021). *Lessons Learned from the 2020 Election: Report to the U.S. Election Assistance Commission.* MIT Election + Data Science Lab.

Weiser, W. (2021). New York: Brennan Center for Law and Justice at New York University School of Law.

Williamson, R., Hale, K., & Brown, M. (2020). Security and integrity: Administrative structure, capacity, and American elections. *Journal of Political Institutions and Political Economy, 1*(2), 189–207.

Subsection: Public Budgeting and Finance

5

PUBLIC BUDGETING IN SMALL LOCAL GOVERNMENTS

Jiseul Kim

Public Budgeting Overview

Public budgets reflect a government's choices regarding what it will and will not do. According to Peterson (1981), there are three main policy functions of local governments: developmental policy, redistributive policy, and allocative policy. Developmental policies dictate spending that enhances a community's economic position. Redistributive policy redistributes resources through governmental revenue and expenditures. An example is when governments provide public housing to the lower-income population by imposing taxes on those who are better off financially. Allocative policy addresses the fact that the market cannot efficiently allocate public goods, necessitating local governments to intervene and provide services such as police and fire protection. To achieve these policy goals, a budget is used to align spending with policy priorities.

Perspectives on How the Budget Shapes the Decision-Making Process

Because the needs and demands of citizens always exceed revenue availability, governments ask V. O. Key's (1940) fundamental budgeting question: "On what basis shall it be decided to allocate x dollars to activity A instead of activity B?" There are four different perspectives in budgetary decision-making. The first perspective is the rational (economical) perspective. Resources are scarce, and "budget analysis is comparison of the relative merits of all alternative uses of funds" (Lewis, 1952, p. 69).

DOI: 10.4324/9781003287766-11

Marginal benefit, or utility, of spending is analyzed. Then, the comparison of relative merits is based on "the relative effectiveness in achieving a common objective" (Lewis, 1952, p. 69).

The second perspective is the political perspective in the budgetary process. The budgetary process is a fundamentally political process of deciding who gets what and how much from governments (Wildavsky, 1961). Budget decisions cannot avoid the comparison of different goals (e.g., building a playground for young families with children vs improving a road for all drivers). Recognizing the different values and goals of budgetary participants, Wildavsky implies that "the most significant way of influencing the budget is to introduce basic political changes" (p. 185). Political change does not occur every year, hence the budget is incrementally changed from one year to the next by considering the small number of politically feasible alternatives and reducing the burden of calculation.

The third perspective is the reform perspective. There are three main budgetary functions: planning, management, and control functions, and "every reform alters the planning-management-control balance" (Schick, 1966, p. 245). The first stage of reform dates back to 1920–1935. In this stage, the main emphasis was on developing an adequate system of expenditure control, which is "predominant during the execution and audit stages" (p. 244). Governments use line-item budgets which only report information on inputs, but do not contain any information on outputs or outcomes associated with spending. The second stage of budget reform emphasized a management orientation which "involves the programming of approved goals into specific projects and activities" (p. 244). The performance budget allows decision-makers to better evaluate their options by allocating funds to measurable outputs. In the 1960s, the planning-programming-budgeting system (PPB) was developed, which incorporated planning into budgeting and multi-year project expenditures. "One of the major aims of PPB is to convert the annual routine of preparing a budget into a conscious appraisal and formulation of future goals and policies" (p. 244). In this budget format, governments organize activities into programs, identify alternative means of achieving programmatic goals, and evaluate the costs and benefits of each alternative.

The last perspective of budgeting is the organizational lifecycle perspective: organizations are created, they grow, and sometimes they shrink and die. For example, Levine (1978) focuses on the organizational decline or zero growth stage. He developed the four typologies of public organization decline. The first type is a political vulnerability, caused by the organization's young age, the lack of a base of expertise, and the absence of a positive self-image and history of excellence. The second type is an organizational atrophy; declining performance may be due to inconsistent incentives, role confusion, inappropriate rules. The third type is a problem of depletion, mainly caused by demographic shifts, problem redefinition, and policy termination. The last type is an environmental atrophy which "occurs when the capacity of the environment to support the public organization at prevailing levels of activity erode" (p. 318). For instance, cities may experience fiscal stress due to weakened economic bases. Levine (1978) suggested cutback management tactics in each of the four different circumstances.

Overall, these four classical perspectives are fundamental to understanding local government budgeting regardless of their size. In the case of smaller local governments, there is limited information in the literature to explain how they budget and make decisions. However, Sokolow and Honadle (1984) noted that state law often determines local budget preparation roles, such as defining the "auditor" as the "budget officer" (p. 380). In the absence of a strong mayor or a professional manager, the city clerk or other administrative staff may find themselves compiling departmental budget requests and presenting them to the Commission or the Council for review and approval. In other cities, towns, or counties, selected commissioners may contribute to the budget preparation process as well as present the budget and vote on ultimate approval of budget numbers. In this sense, Sokolow and Honadle (1984) noted that "administration and policy in the rural community thus are not assigned to distinct and separate roles but overlap substantially" (p. 381).

Other factors to consider in smaller rural government budgeting can include the history and traditions that are in place for who prepares the budget, such as the city clerk; the skillset and ambitions of rural government employees to have a role in the budget process, such as if someone has an interest or a related job background they are recruited to help; and the overlap of administrative roles and functions for staff members that may limit the city administrator's authority over the budget (Sokolow & Honadle, 1984). A 2006 survey of elected officials in Southeastern South Carolina (Dluhy & Kwon, 2006, p. 10) found that over half of the respondents said their budget processes were zero-sum, and therefore more likely to be influenced by politics, in that each year the budget process started from scratch and departments were not guaranteed the same amounts or incremental changes from the previous year.

Operating Budget vs Capital Budget

In local budgets, there are two main types of spending: operating spending and capital spending. Operational spending is typically used for basic governmental operations. On the other hand, capital spending is used for budget items that will have significant economic impacts on an organization and typically last for more than one year (e.g., new construction and/or improvements for infrastructure, buildings, and facilities).

While local governments generally have different definitions of capital spending and operating spending (Kim & Ebdon, forthcoming), capital spending is typically much larger than operating spending. In local governments, capital budgeting encompasses the process of reviewing projects and ranking them based on the government's missions and goals.

Public Budgeting in Small Communities of Oregon

As seen in Table 5.1, Oregon has 241 incorporated cities, and 161 cities (66.8 percent) have less than 5,000 people. In other words, more than half of the incorporated cities in Oregon fall within the small cities. Of those small cities, 77, or 47.8 percent, have fewer than 1,000 people; 56 cities, or 34.8 percent, have more than 1,000 and fewer than 2,500 people; 28 cities, or 17. 4 percent, have more than 2,500 and fewer than 5,000 people.

Overview of the Selected Cities

In this study, six Oregon cities are selected to understand their budgeting practices and tools by comparing their similarities and differences. A content analysis method is used, based mostly on the six city governments' official documents available on their websites. Specifically, three of the cities, Wood Village, Lafayette, and Boardman, have populations of just under 5,000. The three other cities, Myrtle Point, Rogue River, and Lakeview, have populations just under 2,500. Data come from the 2021 *Annual Oregon Population Report* published by the Population Research Center.

These six cities were selected because of their potentially different forms of government. According to the Oregon Blue Book (2021), cities with

TABLE 5.1 The Number of Small Cities in Oregon

Population	Less than 1,000	More than 1,000–Less than 2,500	More than 2,500–Less than 5,000	Total Small Cities	Total Incorporated Cities
The Number of Cities	77 cities	56 cities	28 cities	161 cities	241 cities
% of the Total Small Cities	47.8%	34.8%	17.4 %		
% of the Total Cities	32%	23.2%	11.6%	66.8%	

over 2,500 people typically have the council-manager form of government; most small cities with less than 2,500 people have the mayor-council form of government (McCauley, 2021). Based on the analysis of 490 sample cities, research implied that the presence of a city manager in the council-manager form could promote innovative practices in a government (Nelson & Svara, 2012). More recently, by analyzing 655 mid-sized and large city governments in the United States, Jimenez (2020, p. 161) suggested that "council–manager cities have stronger budgetary solvency compared with mayor–council cities," mainly because "the appointed executive in the council–manager form is interested in career advancement" while elected executives in the mayor-council form have incentives to maximize votes by creating fiscal imbalance.

Table 5.2 includes each city's location, population size, and form of government. The selected cities are located in various regions in Oregon, including the northwest (Wood Village), northwest (Lafayette), northcentral (Boardman), southwest (Myrtle point, Rogue River), and southcentral (Lakeview). Wood Village has 4,478 residents; Lafayette has 4,446; Boardman has 4,338; Myrtle Point city has 2,479; Rogue River has 2,435; Lakeview has 2,428. Their major industries vary and include agriculture, wine, tourism, accommodation and food services, lumber, and/or manufacturing.

In 1906, the Oregon voters adopted one constitutional amendment, and according to Article XI, section 2, the people of every city or town have the right to enact and amend their municipal charters (Oregon Municipal Handbook, 2020). Based on the six cities' charters, all but Lakeview city

TABLE 5.2 Overview of the Selected Six Cities

City	Location	Population	Form of Government	Mayoral Selection	Manager Appointment
Wood Village	Northwest	4,478	Council-manager	Appointed by council	Council
Lafayette	Northwest	4,446	Council-manager	Directly elected	Council
Boardman	Northcentral	4,338	Council-manager	Directly elected	Council
Myrtle Point	Southwest	2,479	Council-manager	Directly elected	Council
Rogue River	Southwest	2,435	Council-manager	Directly elected	Council
Lakeview	Southcentral	2,428	Mayor-council		Council

have a council-manager form of government, and their city managers are appointed and removed by the council. Only Wood Village's mayor is elected and appointed by the council, while other cities' mayors are elected by the general public with two-year terms except for Boardman that grants four-year terms. The Town of Lakeview has a mayor-council form of government with a town manager who is appointed and removed by its council.

Budgeting Process and Tools

Municipal governments in Oregon are typically limited by Oregon Local Budget Law with a few exceptions. The *Oregon Local Budgeting Manual* 150-504-420 (Rev. 05-12) provides a budgeting process guideline for its local governments. First, appointed budget officers prepare their city budgets. Second, they have budget committees, including citizen members whose main roles are reviewing, revising, and/or approving budgets. The basic idea of having a budget committee is to increase citizen involvement in its budgeting process. Appointed citizen budget committee members participate in reviewing, modifying, and approving the proposed budget. Public meetings/hearings are required. Third, a city council adopts a budget, makes appropriations, and imposes taxes. Another public hearing is held by the city council.

All six cities use annual budgets for the fiscal year from July 1 to June 30. For instance, Wood Village's budget is developed annually, and the budget is prepared by the city's management team. The budget committee approves the budget officer's proposed budget and the tax rate or levy. The budget committee consists of five city council members (mayor, council president, three council members), five citizen members, five staff members (city manager, finance director, an accountant, public works director, and assistant to the city manager) (Adopted Budget 2021/22). The committee must approve the proposed budget before it is submitted to the city council for its consideration. According to the content analysis, however, these six cities don't have any participatory budgeting mechanism in the budget prioritization process or the budget preparation stage.

The document review suggests that all six cities use a line-item budget format, which only focuses on expenditure controls. In relation to the balanced budget, the *Oregon Local Budgeting Manual* implies that:

> the budget officer must present a balanced budget to the budget committee. To be in balance, the resources in each fund must be equal to the expenditures and other requirements in that fund. The estimates of resources and expenditures must be made in "good faith." That is,

they should be reasonable and reasonably likely to prove correct, based on the known facts at the time.

(p. 13)

In Rogue River, for instance, the city estimates revenues by using four-year historical trend data and reflecting expected population growth, inflation, and economic changes (Proposed Budget Fiscal Year 2019–20). The city uses a conservative approach to create some reserves. It may be that the city uses an incremental approach of resource allocation by suggesting that "city services are funded at adequate levels ... the level of service provided by the proposed is similar to that currently enjoyed by the community" (p. 1).

At least two cities, including Wood Village and Rogue River, disclose their goals and missions in their budgets, and imply the use of planning. According to the Wood Village's adopted FY 2021–22 budget, the major long-term goals are identified and adopted by the city council. Once adopted, the goals lead to the creation and adoption of an Annual Performance Plan (APP). APP is developed for implementing projects and tasks, and attaining the city's goals, based on which budgetary needs are included in the Budget Official's budget recommendation or they can be included for consideration by the Budget Committee. Also, Rogue River's proposed budget for FY 2019–20 suggests that the city prepares a budget by reassessing its plans and overall goals. Given the limits to the disclosed information, the researcher is not able to evaluate to what extent these cities link their several plans to budgets.

At least, two governments including Rogue River and Lafayette suggest that they develop a Capital Improvements Plan (CIP). Rogue River implies in its proposed budget for FY 2019–20 that the city has a five-year CIP, and the proposed capital expenditures (11.1 percent of the budget) are designed to stay on course with its CIP (p. 3). The city's proposed capital spending would be funded by grants, loans, revenue reserves for capital improvements, and new projects for the 2019–20 Budget include:

Construction of Rooster Park, improvements to Palmerton Park, Water Treatment Plant Building improvements, safety improvements and Cathodic Protection to the reservoirs, replacement of the Ultraviolet Light Disinfection system at the wastewater treatment plant, sidewalk and storm drain upgrades on Oak Street from First St. to Fourth St. and an LED lighting project for streets and public buildings.

(p. 3)

Lafayette suggests that it has CIP in the proposed budget for FY 2022–23, yet it is not clear whether the city has a multi-year CIP. Given limited information, the researcher is not able to evaluate whether they have systematic prioritization processes, and they consider lifecycle costs of assets and allocate resources for the fair-cost sharing between the current and future taxpayers.

Major Revenues and Expenditures in the General Fund

While cities typically have several funds, this analysis focuses on only revenues and expenditures for the general fund. The general fund in these six cities includes both operating expenditures (e.g., personal services, and materials and services) and capital expenditures (e.g., improvements and equipment purchases). Myrtle Point's adopted budget document is not available on its government website, so the analysis focuses on the other five cities. Throughout the five cities, the major public services provided by the general fund for operating expenditures are police, fire, and administration. These cities rely heavily on property tax, franchise tax, state revenue sharing, and grants. The following is the specific illustration of each of the five cities' revenues and expenditures.

- The city of Wood Village's total general fund in FY 2021–22 is $5,484,173. Approximately 47 percent comes from the beginning balance, and 17.6 percent comes from property tax. The city's total adopted general fund for the operating budget is $2,047,821, and the major revenue sources for the operating budget are property tax (39.71 percent), franchise tax (14.01 percent), and the City's share of the Multnomah County Business Income Tax (12.58 percent). In relation to the general fund for operating expenditures, about half of the budget is allocated for public safety (police, fire, 911 service), 12.11 percent for administration and finance, and 10.5 percent for building, followed by parks, public works, and recreation.
- Lafayette's adopted general fund is $2,393,012 in FY 2021–22, and the major revenue sources for the general fund are franchise fees, state revenue sharing, and grants. The city's general fund for operating budget is $2,003,181, and about 38.22 percent is used for administration, 21.21 percent for law enforcement (e.g., deputy sheriff, emergency communication, property abatement), and 17.92 percent for fire department, followed by planning, parks, building inspection, and court.
- Boardman's adopted general fund is $9,887,520, and the major revenues include property taxes, franchise fees, grants and loans, and revenue sharing from the state budget. In FY 2021–22, the adopted budget for taxes is about 23.88 percent and that of franchise fees

and permits is about 7.6 percent. The city lists various line-items in its general fund but does not have a clear separation of total capital spending. The major general fund expenditures include public safety-police (21.57 percent), facility (3.95 percent), and general government (3.38 percent), followed by code compliance and other spending items like community development.

- Myrtle Point's adopted total general fund revenue in FY 2021–22 is $2,188,863, which is mainly driven from property tax, revenue sharing from the state budget (e.g., cigarette, liquor, recreational marijuana taxes), grants, and various franchise fees. The biggest spending item for general fund operating spending is police (38.59 percent), and other services include public works (6.32 percent), administration and finance (5.38 percent), and parks and recreation (1.35 percent).
- Lakeview's adopted total general fund revenue in the FY 2021–22 is $2,159,612.01, and the property tax is the largest revenue source (37.42 percent), with other revenue sources like franchise fees and various grants. The major general fund expenditures include town hall expenses (59.39 percent), fire (26.83 percent), and legal services (4.9 percent).

Overall, there are variations in the types and levels of expenditures and revenues among the cities. Their definition of public services and spending vary. Thus, comparing their budget practices is extremely difficult, and the content analysis does not find any specific relation between the number of

TABLE 5.3 Major General Fund Expenditures

City	Top 1	Top 2	Top 3
Wood Village	Public safety (53.36%)	Administration and finance (12.11%)	Building (10.5%)
Lafayette	Administration (37.22%)	Law enforcement (21.21%)	Fire (17.92%)
Boardman	Public safety (21.57%)	Facility (3.95%)	General government (3.38%)
Myrtle Point	Police (38.59%)	Public works (6.32%)	Administration and finance (5.38%)
Lakeview	Town hall (59.39%)	Fire (26.83%)	Legal services (4.9%)

Note: This summary aims to enhance our understanding of the major public services provided by each city's general fund. Some information is drawn from their general fund for operating expenditures (Wood Village, Lafayette, Myrtle point); other information is drawn from their total general fund (Boardman, Lakeview). Every city uses a different budget definition, categorization, and structuring method. No consistent matrix in comparison is available.

population and the budgeting practices, and the forms of government and the budgeting practices. However, it is interesting to note that five of the six cities operate under the council-manager form of government.

Summary

This chapter aims to provide an overview of budgeting in small communities in Oregon. Their general fund operating budgets mostly come from property taxes and franchise taxes. Also, these cities invest in various public capital assets (e.g., water and sewer systems, parks) to provide public services, and at least some cities report that they aim to align these expenditures with their missions and goals.

These cities use line-item budgets, mainly focusing on expenditure controls. Given the budget format, it is little known how budgets are associated with outputs, outcomes, and plans. Comparing their practices is somewhat challenging as they use different categorization and reporting methods. Interestingly, most of these cities do not have a multi-year CIP. However, developing a CIP using a strategic prioritization process reflecting citizens' demands is critical to fairly allocate resources. To improve the vertical equity, CIPs should contain new construction, improvement, and preventive maintenance spending and fairly share the costs of using public capital assets between the current and future taxpayers.

State law plays a large role in the budgeting that happens in these small communities. All cities in this study develop their budgeting process and tools according to Oregon Local Budget Law. Typically, budgets are prepared by appointed budget officers, reviewed, and approved by budget committees, and adopted by city councils. While Oregon Local Budget Law requires public budget hearings, earlier citizen engagement in the budget preparation stage is critical so that citizen opinions are reflected in budget priorities. It is recommended that introducing citizen input into the budget process much earlier can enhance social equity and budget accountability and potentially improve service quality and citizen satisfaction.

References

Dluhy, M. J., & Kwon, M. (2006). Elected decision makers and budgeting practices in small towns and rural areas: Rational choice or the political imperative? http://people.uncw.edu/dluhym/documents/ElectedDecisionMakersandBudgetingPracticesinSmallTownsandRuralAreas.pdf

Jimenez, B. S. (2020). Municipal government form and budget outcomes: Political responsiveness, bureaucratic insulation, and the budgetary solvency of cities. *Journal of Public Administration Research and Theory, 30*(1), 161–177.

Key, V. O. (1940). The lack of a budgetary theory. *American Political Science Review, 34*(6), 1137–1144.

Kim, J., & Ebdon, C. (forthcoming). Capital asset reporting and information use in U.S. counties. *Municipal Finance Journal.*

Levine, C. H. (1978). Organizational decline and cutback management. *Public Administration Review, 38*(4), 316–325.

Lewis, V. B. (1952). Toward a theory of budgeting. *Public Administration Review, 12*(1), 42–54.

McCauley, M. (2021). City government. *Oregon Blue Book.* Available from https://sos.oregon.gov/blue-book/Pages/local/cities/about.aspx

Nelson, K. L., & Svara, J. H. (2012). Form of government still matters: Fostering innovation in U.S. municipal governments. *American Review of Public Administration, 42*(3), 257–281.

Oregon Department of Revenue (2012). *Oregon Local Budgeting Manual 150-504-420* (Rev. 05-12). Available at https://secureservercdn.net/198.71.233.111/23v.84f.myftpupload.com/wp-content/uploads/2022/04/local-budgeting-manual_504-420.pdf

Peterson, P. E. (1981). *City Limits.* University of Chicago Press.

Population Research Center (2021). *2021 Annual Oregon Population Report.* Portland State University. www.pdx.edu/population-research/sites/g/files/znldhr3261/files/2022-04/2021%20Annual%20Population%20Report%20Tables.pdf

Schick, A. (1966). The road to PPB: The stages of budget reform. *Public Administration Review, 26*(4), 243–58.

Sokolow, A. D., & Honadle, B. W. (1984). How rural local governments budget: The alternatives to executive preparation. *Public Administration Review, 44*(5), 373–383.

The City of Wood Village. (2015). Wood Village Charter. Available at https://woodvillage.municipal.codes/Charter

The City of Wood Village. (2021). *City of Wood Village, Oregon: Adopted Budget Fiscal Year 2021–22.* Available at www.woodvillageor.gov/wp-content/uploads/City-of-Wood-Village-Adopted-Budget-2021-22.pdf

The City of Wood Village. (2021). *Comprehensive Annual Financial Report Fiscal Year Ended June 30, 2021.* Available at www.woodvillageor.gov/wp-content/uploads/City-of-Wood-Village-2021-Issued-Audit.pdf

The City of Wood Village. (2020). *Wood Village Urban Renewal Agency Adopted Budget.* www.woodvillageor.gov/wp-content/uploads/City-of-Wood-Village-2021-Issued-Audit.pdf

The City of Lafayette. (2002). The city charter: 1984 Lafayette Charter. Available at www.ci.lafayette.or.us/index.asp?SEC=BEC86EA2-87A7-4231-962B-83AD860F9242&DE=92E20D3E-86C0-40F7-B099-0640522194D2

The City of Lafayette. (2021). *City of Lafayette Adopted Budget Fiscal Year 2021–22.* Available at www.ci.lafayette.or.us/vertical/sites/%7B43AAC4DA-ABAD-4F35-91B6-4D693AE69205%7D/uploads/2021-22_Budget_Adopted_YC(1).pdf

The City of Lafayette. (2022). *Recommended Budget in FY 2022–23.* Available at www.ci.lafayette.or.us/vertical/sites/%7B43AAC4DA-ABAD-4F35-91B6-4D693AE69205%7D/uploads/FY_2023_Recommended_Budget.pdf

The City of Boardman. (1985). City charter of 1985. Available at https://library. municode.com/or/boardman/codes/code_of_ordinances?nodeId=BOCH1985_ CHIIIFOGO_S9MA

The City of Boardman. (2021). *The City of Boardman, Oregon, 2021–22 Adopted Budget.* Available www.cityofboardman.com/sites/default/files/fileattachments/ finance/page/2321/2021-2022_city_of_boardman_budget_adopted.pdf

The City of Myrtle Point. (2022). Administration. Available at www.ci.myrtlepo int.or.us/general/page/administration

The City of Myrtle Point. (2021). *City of Myrtle Point 2021–22 Adopted Budget.* Available at www.ci.myrtlepoint.or.us/sites/default/files/fileattachments/general/ page/1855/adopted_budget_2021-2022.pdf

The City of Rogue River (2019). The City of Rogue River charter of 1982. Available at www.codepublishing.com/OR/RogueRiver/html/RogueRiverCH.html

The City of Rogue River. (2019). *The City's Proposed Budget Fiscal Year 2019–20.* Available at https://cityofrogueriver.org/images/public-notices/2019/2019-20%20LB1%20Budget%20Website.pdf

The League of Oregon Cities. (2020). Home rule and its limits. In *Oregon Municipal Handbook* (ch. 2). Available at www.orcities.org/application/files/3715/9917/ 4968/Handbook_-_Chapter_2_Home_Rule_and_Its_Limits.pdf

The Town of Lakeview. (2011). The charter for the Town of Lakeview, Lake County, Oregon. Available at https://secureservercdn.net/198.71.233.111/23v.84f.myft pupload.com/wp-content/uploads/2021/09/2011-Town-Charter.pdf

The Town of Lakeview. (2011). *Town of Lakeview 2021–2022 Budget.* Available at https://secureservercdn.net/198.71.233.111/23v.84f.myftpupload.com/wp-content/uploads/2022/04/21-22-BUDGET.pdf

Toukabri, A., & Medina, L. (2020). America: A nation of small towns. Available at www.census.gov/library/stories/2020/05/america-a-nation-of-small-towns.html

US Census Bureau. (2019). *From Municipalities to Special Districts, Official Count of Every Type of Local Government in 2017 Census of Governments.* Census Bureau. www.census.gov/library/publications/2019/econ/from_municipalities_t o_special_districts.html

US Census Bureau. (2005). *Finances of Municipal and Township Governments: 2002.* US Census Bureau. www2.census.gov/programs-surveys/govs/tables/gc024-4/ gc024x4.pdf

Wildavsky, A. (1961). Political implications of budgetary reform. *Public Administration Review, 21*(4), 183–190.

6

USING FINANCIAL STATEMENTS TO IMPROVE FISCAL STRENGTH AND MAKE POLICY DECISIONS

William C. Rivenbark

Local governments are required to produce financial statements to report on their financial position at the end of each fiscal year, providing information on the inflow and outflow of resources as shown on operating statements and the stock of resources (assets, liabilities, and equity) as shown on balance sheets. These financial statements are then subjected to an independent audit to obtain an unmodified audit opinion. This means that the statements were prepared in conformity with generally accepted accounting principles (GAAP), and the financial position of the respective local government is materially accurate. Smaller local governments often face more challenges than their larger counterparts with maintaining the internal financial expertise to produce annual financial statements, where the responsibility for data accuracy and fairness of presentation ultimately rests with management.

Prior research has explored this lack of expertise within smaller local governments along various financial dimensions. Patrick (2010), for example, reported much lower adoption rates among smaller local governments of the Governmental Accounting Standards Board (GASB) guidelines for improving financial accountability and transparency following the issuance of GASB Statement No. 34 (GASB, 1999). However, an even larger problem among smaller local governments that has received minimal attention in the literature relates to the ability to move from reporting on an organization's financial position to interpreting its financial condition. While an unmodified audit opinion is extremely important to local governments of all sizes, the significance of this audit designation is that it requires the statements to be prepared in conformity

DOI: 10.4324/9781003287766-12

with GAAP and assures the data are materially accurate; the designation does not reflect fiscal strength or stress. Local officials must interpret the data shown on the financial statements to determine the financial condition of their respective organizations, which requires another level of expertise (Gargan, 1987).

Focusing on the general fund and the water and sewer fund, this chapter provides smaller local governments with a methodology to move from relaying financial position to determining financial condition after the preparation and audit of annual financial statements. The chapter begins with a brief overview of financial condition and the need for financial context, before presenting several financial metrics that can be used to interpret and improve the financial condition of the general fund. The following section then introduces several financial metrics that can be used to interpret and improve the financial condition of the water and sewer fund, which often receives less attention than the general fund in smaller local governments. The chapter concludes with two cases that demonstrate how smaller local governments have used this information to make policy to improve both financial capacity and organizational stability.

Defining Financial Condition

The current definitions of financial condition found in the literature tend to be either too specific or too broad in scope (Wang et al., 2007). A specific approach would define financial condition as solvency, selecting a metric like fund balance as a percentage of expenditures to measure solvency. An advantage to this approach is the simplicity of using a single financial ratio when communicating financial condition, including the ability to compare it against the local government's fund balance policy. A major limitation to this approach is that a narrow definition of financial condition supported with a single financial ratio simply cannot capture the numerous financial dimensions of a local government across the multiple funds used to account for the multiple types of services provided.

One of the most cited definitions of financial condition comes from the International City/County Management Association (ICMA). It is much broader in scope and focuses on a government's ability to finance its services on a continuing basis and meet the demands of natural change over time (Nollenberger, 2003). This definition is supported with a methodology that includes over 40 financial and environmental indicators. A clear advantage of this definition is its similarity to how bond rating agencies measure financial condition and community risk. A major disadvantage is the internal capacity needed to calculate, interpret, and communicate the financial condition of a local government through the lens of these 40-plus metrics.

Any definition of financial condition in local government will have advantages and disadvantages. However, the two basic reasons local governments prepare annual financial statements provide a starting point for how to think about financial condition. First, financial statements report on the *flows* of resources during a given period (Berne & Schramm, 1986) using an operating statement that includes the organization's revenues and expenditures (expenses). Focusing on resource flow supports two financial reporting objectives—assessing whether the local government operated within its financial means and providing information about sources and uses of financial resources (GASB, 1987). Second, financial statements report on the *stocks* of resources at a given point (Berne & Schramm, 1986) using a balance sheet that lists assets, liabilities, and fund balance (net assets). Focusing on resource stock also supports a financial reporting objective—providing information to determine whether an organization's financial position improved or deteriorated because of resource flow (GASB, 1987).

The two purposes behind local government financial statements (Berne & Schramm, 1986) combined with the objectives of financial reporting (GASB, 1987) form the foundation of the following definition, which can guide the analysis of financial condition: *a local government's ability to meet its ongoing financial, service, and capital obligations based on the status of resource flow and stock as interpreted from annual financial statements* (Rivenbark et al., 2010). The next step toward determining financial condition is to select the financial dimensions and metrics that most closely align with resource flow and resource stock and that can be applied to the general fund and the water and sewer fund.

Financial Context

The financial metrics that can assist smaller local governments with the transition from financial position to financial condition must be presented in a financial context to be useful in interpreting results (Marlow et al., 2009). In other words, one data point in time provides only minimal context when addressing fiscal strength or stress along a selected financial dimension. The first type of context is trend analysis, which requires calculating at least a five-year trend for each financial metric. Using this context, the consumer of the information can determine whether the metric is improving or deteriorating over time. Figure 6.1, for example, contains the debt service ratio for the general fund, showing that the local government is improving its service flexibility by decreasing the amount of resources dedicated to annual debt service as a percentage of total expenditures.

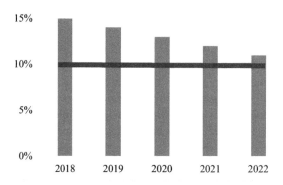

FIGURE 6.1   Debt Service Ratio: General Fund.

The second type of context is benchmarking, which requires comparing the respective metric against an identified benchmark. There are various approaches to identify the most appropriate benchmark for each financial metric. Some metrics have a natural benchmark—1.0 or above, for example. Other metrics require a benchmark from an internal policy decision, the average from selected benchmark peers (other local governments), or a professional standard from an organization like the Government Finance Officers Association (GFOA). Therefore, the consumer of the information can compare the internal trend, improving or deteriorating, against a predetermined benchmark for additional financial context. Figure 6.1 shows that the debt service ratio remains above the selected benchmark of 10 percent, which is a recognized professional standard for comparative analysis. One possible policy decision that might result from the interpretation of this ratio would be to refrain from issuing additional debt until the debt service ratio is less than the selected benchmark.

General Fund

Table 6.1 contains the financial metrics used for evaluating resource flow for the general fund, which are calculated from the statement of revenues, expenditures, and changes in fund balances that measures financial resources using the modified accrual basis of accounting (Rivenbark et al., 2009). These metrics can be used to analyze the financial condition of special revenue funds, debt service funds, capital projects funds, and permanent funds, given that their financial statements also measure financial resources using the modified accrual basis of accounting. While smaller local governments may not have these other fund types, all local

TABLE 6.1 General Fund Financial Metrics

Dimension	Description	Metric	Calculation	Interpretation
Resource Flow				
Service obligation	Addresses whether a government's annual revenues were sufficient to pay for annual operations	Operations ratio	Total revenues divided by total expenditures (plus transfers to the debt service fund and less proceeds from capital leases)	A ratio of 1 or higher indicates that a government lived within its annual revenues.
Dependency	Describes the extent to which a government is reliant on other governments for resources	Intergovernmental ratio	Intergovernmental revenue divided by total revenue	A high ratio may indicate that a government is too reliant on other governments.
Financing obligation	Provides feedback on service flexibility with the percentage of expenditures committed to annual debt service	Debt service ratio	Debt service (principal and interest payments on long-term debt, including transfers to the debt service fund) divided by total expenditures plus transfers to the debt service fund	Service flexibility decreases as more expenditures are committed to annual debt service.
Resource Stock				
Liquidity	Government's ability to address short-term obligations	Quick ratio	Cash and investments divided by current liabilities (minus deferred revenue)	A high ratio suggests a government can meet its short-term obligations.
Solvency	Government's ability to continue service provision	Fund balance as a percentage of expenditures	Available fund balance as a percentage of total expenditures (less proceeds from capital leases) plus transfers out	A high ratio suggests a government can continue to provide uninterrupted services.
Leverage	Extent to which a government relies on tax-supported debt	Debt as percent of assessed value	Tax-supported, long-term debt divided by assessed value	A high ratio suggests a government is overly reliant on debt.

governments have a general fund to account for all activities not included in another fund.

Service obligation represents the first financial dimension for evaluating the resource flow for governmental funds. The operations ratio is used to analyze this dimension, representing total revenues divided by total expenditures. This metric has a natural benchmark, with a ratio of 1.0 or above indicating that a government lived within its means. When the ratio is below 1.0 for a given fiscal year, the local government should examine why actual expenditures were more than actual revenues to prevent financial deterioration over time.

The financial dimension of dependency, which is measured with the intergovernmental ratio, determines the extent to which local governments are reliant on other governments for resources. The calculation is intergovernmental revenue divided by total revenue. Seeking and receiving financial resources from other funding entities are not inherently wrong, but public officials must understand the advantages and disadvantages of this type of policy decision. One advantage is extracting fewer resources from their communities. A disadvantage is that the local government assumes more financial risk, funding local services on the probability that the other entity will not change its funding formula.

The dimension of financing obligation provides feedback on service flexibility by using the debt service ratio to measure the resources committed to annual debt obligations. Service flexibility—the ability to increase current service levels—decreases over time as more resources are obligated to debt service payments. For this reason, some local governments adopt limits on this metric within their debt management policies. A common threshold is that the debt service ratio should not exceed 10 percent of total expenditures.

Table 6.1 also includes the financial metrics used for evaluating resource stock for the general fund. These metrics are calculated from the balance sheet that measures financial resources using the modified accrual basis of accounting. The financial dimension of liquidity is measured with the quick ratio, which is calculated by dividing cash and investments by current liabilities. The ratio helps to determine whether a local government can meet its short-term obligations. While the benchmark is normally 2.0, smaller local governments should maintain higher levels of liquidity for managing short-term liabilities over time.

The financial dimension of solvency is evaluated with one of the most recognized financial metrics in local government–fund balance as a percentage of expenditures. Smaller local governments typically carry higher percentages of fund balance than larger local governments. However, each local government must designate its own percentage threshold by adopting a fund balance policy based on historical trends, other local governments identified as benchmarking peers, or industry standards through professional organizations such as the GFOA.

The final financial dimension for evaluating resource stock for the general fund is leverage, which is supported with the financial indicator of tax-supported, long-term debt divided by assessed value. Without question, local governments rely on tax-supported debt to invest in much needed capital assets to advance their respective communities. However, they must understand the implications of this policy decision, which also impacts the financial metric of debt service ratio. Most states have laws governing the amount of tax-supported debt local governments may issue. For example, Section 159-55(c) of the North Carolina General Statutes does not allow net debt of a local government to exceed 8 percent of the assessed value of property subject to taxation.

Water and Sewer Fund

Table 6.2 contains the financial metrics for evaluating resource flow for the water and sewer fund (enterprise fund), which are calculated from the statement of revenues, expenses, and changes in fund net position that measures economic resources using the full accrual basis of accounting (Rivenbark et al., 2009). These metrics can be used to analyze all types of proprietary funds (enterprise funds and internal service funds). They also can be used to evaluate government-wide statements (governmental activities and business-type activities), given that these statements also measure economic resources using the full accrual basis of accounting.

The first dimension, interperiod equity, addresses whether a government lived within its means during the fiscal year. The total margin ratio evaluates this dimension, representing the total inflow of resources divided by the total outflow of resources for the water and sewer fund. This metric has a national benchmark parallel to the operations ratio of the general fund, where a ratio of 1.0 or above indicates that a government lived within its means. When the ratio is below 1.0 for a given fiscal year, local governments should examine why actual expenses exceeded actual revenues to prevent financial deterioration over time.

While the total margin ratio analyzes the relationship between total resources available and total resources consumed, the financial indicator of percent change in net assets used to evaluate the financial performance dimension provides feedback on how a government's net assets improved or deteriorated because of resource flow. In other words, a positive percent change indicates that a government's financial position improved because of the resource flow that occurred during the fiscal year. Periodic modest fluctuations are generally expected; significant fluctuations in either direction should be evaluated.

The financial dimension of self-sufficiency addresses the extent to which service charges were used by the government to cover total expenses. This dimension is especially important to the water and sewer fund, where the goal is to cover total expenses on a charge-for-service basis. The financial metric of charge-to-expense ratio is used to analyze this dimension. A ratio of 1.0 or above indicates the fund was self-sufficient. However, smaller local governments often are hesitant to raise water and sewer rates, which results in a charge-to-expense ratio of below 1.0. When this occurs, the local government progresses along one of two roads. First, the local government is using operating and nonoperating revenues to cover annual expenses as shown by the total margin ratio. Second, the local government is relying on current cash or interfund transfers to cover the annual shortfall. Both roads should be scrutinized from the standpoint of sustainability.

The final dimension for resource flow for the water and sewer fund is financing obligation, which is analyzed with the debt service ratio. The ratio is calculated by dividing annual debt service of principal and interest payments by total expenses *plus* principal. Because of their measurement focus, enterprise funds do *not* report principal repayments on debt as an expense. To achieve a proper calculation of this debt service ratio, the principal amounts must be included in both the numerator and denominator. The purpose of this ratio is to provide feedback on service flexibility, which decreases as more resources are committed to annual debt service. This line of thought parallels the debt service ratio of the general fund.

Table 6.2 also contains the financial metrics for evaluating resource stock for the water and sewer fund, which are calculated from the statement of net position that measures financial resources using the full accrual basis of accounting. An advantage of the stock indicators over the flow indicators is that stock indicators tend to be more recognizable in the profession because they are associated with the balance sheet, which is more frequently used to evaluate financial condition in the public and private sectors. In other words, balance sheets report on equity, or net position, at a given point in time.

Liquidity is the financial dimension that analyzes an organization's ability to meet its short-term obligations as calculated with the quick ratio, where cash and investments are divided by current liabilities. A high ratio suggests that the government is more likely to meet its short-term obligations. The benchmark for this financial metric is often cited as 2.0 or above, indicating that the water and sewer fund has more than double the cash and cash equivalents as compared to current liabilities. However,

TABLE 6.2 Water and Sewer Fund Financial Metrics

Dimension	Description	Metric	Calculation	Interpretation
Resource Flow				
Interperiod equity	Addresses whether a government lived within its financial means during the fiscal year	Total margin ratio	Total revenues divided by total expenses	A ratio of 1 or higher indicates that a government lived within its financial means.
Financial performance	Provides the magnitude of how a government's financial position improved or deteriorated because of resource flow	Percent change in net assets	Change in net assets divided by net assets, beginning	A positive percent change indicates that a government's financial position improved.
Self-sufficiency	Addresses the extent to which service charges and fees covered total expenses	Charge-to-expense-ratio	Charges for services divided by total expenses	A ratio of 1 or higher indicates that the service is self-supporting.
Financing obligation	Provides feedback on service flexibility with the percentage of resources committed to annual debt service	Debt service ratio	Debt service (principal and interest payments on long-term debt) divided by total expenses plus principal	Service flexibility decreases as more resources are committed to annual debt service.
Resource Stock				
Liquidity	Government's ability to address short-term obligations	Quick ratio	Cash and investments divided by current liabilities (minus deferred revenue)	A high ratio suggests a government can meet its short-term obligations.
Solvency	Government's ability to address long-term obligations	Net assets ratio	Unrestricted net assets divided by total liabilities	A high ratio suggests a government can meet its long-term obligations.

(Continued)

TABLE 6.2 (Continued)

Dimension	Description	Metric	Calculation	Interpretation
Leverage	Extent to which total assets are financed with long-term debt	Debt-to-assets ratio	Long-term debt divided by total assets	A high ratio suggests a government is overly reliant on debt for financing assets.
Capital	Condition of capital assets as defined as remaining useful life	Capital assets condition ratio	1 − (accumulated depreciation divided by capital assets being depreciated)	A high ratio suggests a government is investing in its capital assets.

each local government should adopt a financial policy for its utility fund stating the liquidity threshold, given the importance of this financial metric for monitoring financial condition.

Solvency is the financial dimension that analyzes an organization's ability to meet long-term obligations as calculated with the net assets ratio, where unrestricted net assets are divided by total liabilities. Like the quick ratio, a high ratio suggests that the government is more likely to meet its long-term obligations. Some research advocates using total assets as the denominator for this calculation rather than total liabilities (Wang et al., 2007). However, standardizing unrestricted net assets with total liabilities provides a stronger indication of an organization's ability to meet long-term obligations (Rivenbark et al., 2009).

The financial dimension of leverage provides feedback on the extent to which total assets are financed with long-term debt, which is measured by the debt-to-assets ratio. If a government becomes too reliant on debt financing for securing capital assets, service flexibility may be compromised as more resource flow is committed to annual debt service obligations. An overreliance on debt also may have unfavorable bond rating implications.

Capital represents the final financial dimension of resource stock for the water and sewer fund. This dimension analyzes the condition of capital assets as defined by their remaining useful life. The financial metric to measure this dimension is capital assets condition ratio. The data used for this calculation are in the capital assets section of the notes to financial statements. To calculate the indicator, accumulated depreciation is first divided by capital assets subject to depreciation. The resulting percentage is then subtracted from 1, which results in the remaining useful life of the total capital assets being depreciated. Local governments should benchmark themselves against other local governments on this metric, placing the policy decision of capital investment into an appropriate context.

Cases

The Village of Pinehurst

The Village of Pinehurst, North Carolina, is a destination community with a resident population between 10,000 and 15,000. Its elected officials and administrators value sound financial management, as evidenced by annual audits that receive unmodified audit opinions, adopted financial policies that include a fund balance policy, and a commitment to ongoing professional development. The village also is committed to financial condition analysis, using the financial ratio of fund balance as a percentage of expenditures to provide elected officials with annual feedback on the financial dimension of solvency. This approach is logical for several reasons. The village accounts for most of its services and activities in the general fund, it has a fund balance policy that states the required percentage (benchmark), and the fund balance ratio is arguably the most important ratio in local government (Rivenbark & Roenigk, 2011).

The finance director decided to use financial metrics associated with the general fund presented in this chapter to help elected officials meet their fiduciary responsibility of maintaining sound fiscal policy for the village. He also wanted to expand the utility of annual financial statements for decision-making, given the amount of time and effort needed to produce them. One of the first steps in this process was to identify benchmarking partners for comparative analysis. The village selected four local governments based on the criteria of population, service provision, and tax base. The service provision criterion was extremely important because the village wanted to compare itself to local governments that also accounted for most of their services and activities in the general fund; it did not want to select a local government with a utility fund like water and sewer, which can often change the dynamics of financial condition.

The finance officer calculated the five-year trend for each flow and stock indicator used to analyze the general fund, including the average benchmark from the four comparative local governments. The financial condition analysis presented to the elected officials showed that the village had lived within its financial means over the past five years (operations ratio) and was less reliant on intergovernmental revenue (intergovernmental ratio) than the benchmark communities. On the other hand, the village identified its concerns as limited cash liquidity (quick ratio) and fund balance reserves (fund balance as percentage of expenditures) as compared to the benchmark group.

Based on the reported analysis, the manager recommended that the fund balance policy be revised. The governing board decided not to change the fund balance policy given the current economic crisis. However, it directed the village manager to identify strategies to increase the liquidity and solvency of the general fund during the forthcoming budget process and to continue to monitor these financial dimensions as compared to the benchmark group. The financial condition report provided to the Pinehurst governing board prompted board members to ask more insightful questions about the annual audit of financial statements.

Camden County

Camden County, North Carolina, located contiguous to Chesapeake, Virginia, has a population between 10,000 and 15,000. The county manager asked the School of Government at the University of North Carolina at Chapel Hill to facilitate the county's annual commissioner retreat in preparation for the budget process and requested help with analyzing the county's financial condition. A faculty member agreed to facilitate the retreat, which included working with the county's finance director to calculate, analyze, and interpret the financial metrics presented in this chapter (Rivenbark & Roenigk, 2011).

Two dashboards were presented and explained to the county commissioners during the retreat. The first dashboard contained the three flow indicators and the three stock indicators for the general fund. The operations ratio revealed that annual revenues were sufficient to pay for annual operations, and the debt service ratio of 11 percent was within the county's policy of 15 percent. In addition to sufficient resource flow, the stock dimension of liquidity as revealed by the quick ratio was very strong and the county's fund balance as a percentage of expenditures used to analyze the stock dimension of solvency was well above the state average. The overall conclusion was that the financial condition of the general fund was robust at the end of the respective fiscal year.

The second dashboard presented to the county commissioners included the four flow indicators and the four stock indicators for the water and sewer fund. The first indicator discussed was the total margin ratio. It was approximately 1.0 for each of the past five fiscal years, representing a break-even trend. This resulted in the quick ratio never being above 1.0 and well below the industry standard of 2.0 or above. On the other hand, infrastructure assigned to the fund was relatively new, as revealed by the capital assets condition ratio of 84 percent. The outcome of this analysis was that the county commissioners made the policy decision to raise water and sewer rates for the following fiscal year to improve the liquidity of the water and sewer fund.

Conclusion

This chapter begins by discussing the bifurcation between financial position and financial condition in local government. The financial position is represented when annual financial statements receive an unmodified audit opinion, designating that the statements were prepared in conformity with GAAP and are materially accurate. However, management must interpret the financial data from these statements to determine whether the local government is financially strong or stressed. The move from financial position to condition can often be challenging for smaller local governments, given the internal capacity needed to make this transition.

In response to this challenge, this chapter presents a collection of financial metrics for the general fund and the water and sewer fund that can be used to analyze, interpret, and communicate the financial condition of the respective local government. The reason two sets of metrics are provided is that the financial statements for the general fund measure financial resources on the modified accrual basis of accounting and those for the water and sewer fund measure economic resources on the full accrual basis of accounting. The purpose remains the same, however, which is to calculate a series of metrics from the operating statements and balance sheets of these two critical funds to help local officials understand the financial condition of their respective local governments.

Two cases are then presented, including how a smaller municipality used the financial metrics to decide not to change its fund balance policy for the general fund and how a smaller county used them to decide to raise its water and sewer rates. These cases illustrate the ultimate outcome of moving from financial position to financial condition in local government by using specific metrics to make policy decisions to improve both financial capacity and organizational stability. This transition is becoming even more important in local governments facing the inherent challenges of growth and development (Clark, 2015) often found in smaller communities.

References

Berne, R., & Schramm, R. (1986). *The Financial Analysis of Governments.* Prentice-Hall.

Clark, B. (2015). Evaluating the validity and reliability of the financial condition index for local governments. *Public Budgeting and Finance, 35*(2), 66–88.

Gargan, J. (1987). Local government financial management capacity: A political perspective. *Public Administration Quarterly, 11*(3), 246–276.

Governmental Accounting Standards Board. (1987). *Objectives of Financial Reporting* (GASB Concept Statement No. 1). GASB,

Governmental Accounting Standards Board. (1999). *Basic Financial Statements— and Management's Discussion and Analysis—for State and Local Governments* (GASB Statement No. 34). GASB.

Marlow, J., Rivenbark, W. C., & Vogt, A. J. (2009). *Capital Budgeting and Finance* (2nd ed.). ICMA Press.

Nollenberger, K. (2003). *Evaluating Financial Condition* (4th ed.). ICMA Press.

Patrick, P. (2010). The adoption of GASB 34 in small, rural local governments. *Journal of Public Budgeting, Accounting & Financial Management, 22*(2), 227–249.

Rivenbark, W. C., & Roenigk, D. J. (2011). Implementation of financial condition analysis in local government. *Public Administration Quarterly, 35*(2), 238–264.

Rivenbark, W. C., Roenigk, D. J., & Allison, G. S. (2009). Communicating financial condition to elected officials in local government. *Popular Government*, 75(1), 4–13.

Rivenbark, W. C., Roenigk, D. J., & Allison, G. S. (2010). Conceptualizing financial condition in local government. *Journal of Public Budgeting, Accounting & Financial Management*, 22(2), 149–177.

Wang, X., Dennis, L., & Tu, Y. S. (2007). Measuring financial condition: A study of U.S. states. *Public Budgeting & Finance*, 27(2), 1–21.

7

SMALL TOWN REVENUES FOR BIG TIME PUBLIC SERVICES

Deborah A. Carroll

Introduction

Due in large part to data availability and the magnitude of impact of public policies and service delivery, much scholarly research on government revenue structures has focused on states and larger sub-state jurisdictions like counties and municipalities. Town governments—defined here as those with a traditional town meeting governance structure—are generally an understudied form of government with some exceptions in the extant literature. Yet, as the oldest form of local government in the US and the governance structure where nearly 20 percent of the US population resides, town governments are an important form of government that is inherently different from other forms of local government like counties, cities, and villages. Town governments are characterized as perhaps the truest form of democracy, as residents have direct input in government affairs and community governance through participation in the annual town meeting. However, town governments generally have an elected board of supervisors that handle the daily operations of the town. In addition, towns are often strictly guided by state constitutions and statutes and often operate under Dillon's rule (as opposed to home rule often granted to cities and villages), thereby providing towns with less fiscal autonomy and fewer options for generating revenue to finance the provision of public services.

Research has found that towns governed by town meetings have lower levels of diversification overall compared to states and other local governments. This lack of diversity is at least partially explained by the high reliance of towns on property taxation (partially due to the lack

DOI: 10.4324/9781003287766-13

of home rule) as well as the longstanding impact of the tax revolts and consequent widespread implementation of tax and expenditure limitations. In addition, towns are generally more susceptible to annexation by surrounding jurisdictions as well as fiscal stress resulting from economic downturns and population growth. On the other hand, the smaller geographical size and more homogeneous population of towns often prove to be beneficial and more efficient for serving the needs of community residents. These characteristics suggest that governance and administration in small towns—particularly with respect to the allocation of revenues—is inherently different from other forms of local government.

This chapter provides an evaluation of revenue diversification among town governments in an effort to draw comparisons between the recent state of revenue structures and prior decades and to offer potential explanations for overarching changes (or lack thereof) that have occurred. Many small governments across the US often lack professional expertise and therefore draw upon their knowledge of people and place as a compensatory approach to financial management. Ultimately, this chapter considers how social capital in these communities helps to solve collective action problems and the creation of collaborative governing institutions with respect to financial management of their revenue structures.

Town Governance and Administration

The defining characteristic of town governments—or townships, as they are sometimes referred to—is the annual town meeting, which allows for direct input from town residents regarding budgetary, governance, and other administrative decisions. Towns with a town meeting governing structure provide residents the abilities to directly influence revenues, expenditures, and public policy, which is a form of direct democracy that does not exist in other local governing structures (Helpap, 2017). Moreover, engagement in town meetings reflects a commitment from town residents to dedicate their time to solving community problems and administering its affairs that is inherently different from other forms of direct democracy like initiatives and referenda (DeSantis & Hill, 2004). Due to this unique feature, town governments have often been lauded as the truest form of democracy (Carroll & Johnson, 2010). Moreover, because of greater proximity and accessibility to residents and voters compared to larger jurisdictions, towns and townships are generally more responsive to community needs (NATaT, n.d.). Yet this form of local governance is not without its challenges.

Small towns are faced with the unique challenges of proximity to residents with particular interests and opinions on policy issues combined with apathy from other segments of the community who are unwilling to become involved (Trautman, 2016). Specifically, turnout in annual town meetings is generally much lower than that of elections, and special town meetings often have even lower turnout than the annual meeting (DeSantis & Hill, 2004). Since extant research shows a direct connection between socioeconomic status and civic participation, DeSantis and Hill (2004) surveyed a random sample of 375 Massachusetts residents in towns operating with a traditional town meeting to explore their political attitudes and behaviors and reveal the factors most correlated with town meeting participation. They found that individuals aged 18–25 had very low probabilities of attending all or some town meetings in the five years prior, while individuals aged 61 and older had rather high probabilities. Greater town meeting participation was also motivated by the extent to which individuals engaged in discussion with friends and family about community problems. Thus, age and community engagement were found to be the two main drivers of town meeting participation.

The smallness and homogeneity of towns has promulgated their unique governing structure, which has been described as consensual and dominated by personal relationships (Johnson & Ihrke, 2004). Small towns and their dynamics can be viewed and understood as dense, multiple networks of relationships with individuals often embodying multiple roles within the community (Catlaw & Stout, 2016). Such networks can help to maintain social norms, create community cohesion, and improve the flow of information among residents to encourage change (Catlaw & Stout, 2016). On the other hand, such dense and complex relationships can be exclusionary and constraining as social norms emphasizing civility often discourage direct confrontation and open conflict (Catlaw & Stout, 2016). For example, towns generally have little to no conflict on their town boards because of the homogeneous nature of town residents, the relatively small role of the government in delivering services and programs, and the values of residents in decision-making (Johnson & Ihrke, 2004).

In addition, towns in some states are limited to only those powers granted by the state and tend to be more susceptible to annexation from neighboring jurisdictions (Diaz & Green, 2001; Helpap, 2017). With more options for developers and realtors, as well as greater infrastructures, cities and villages often approach economic development from the perspective of promoting growth to spread the cost over a broader base of taxpayers (Diaz & Green, 2001). While this might exert more pressure on town governments, particularly towns facing fiscal stress, town governments generally have less capacity for managing development-related growth (Diaz & Green, 2001). "Rural small towns often lack the technical, managerial, and financial capacities needed to adequately provide the variety of expected public services" (Morton et al., 2008, p. 46). On the other hand, towns may not experience the negative consequences of growth compared to cities and villages, likely due to the more efficient size of towns (Diaz & Green, 2001).

Compensatory Approach to Financial Management

From a financial perspective, the unique governance structure of towns translates into an expectation that expenditures for public service provision in such communities should most closely reflect the desires of residents (Helpap, 2017; DeSantis & Hill, 2004; Maher & Johnson, 2008; Tiebout, 1956). Evidence of this can be seen by the fact that expenditures of some town governments focus on a small number of services, while expenditures of others are divided among a more diverse offering of services (Helpap, 2017). However, many small governments across the US lack professional expertise and therefore draw upon their knowledge of people and place as a compensatory approach to financial management. For example, Helpap (2017) examined variation in service provision among Wisconsin town governments and found that differences can be explained by community characteristics, location, and capacity; the presence of a professional administrator was not statistically significantly associated with more diverse service provision or per capita expenditures. Towns with higher populations, greater density, proximity to metropolitan areas, located within counties with less diverse service offerings, robust property values, and slightly older populations are more likely to provide a greater diversity of public services (Helpap, 2017).

Moreover, towns are more likely to use incrementalism than sophisticated techniques in fiscal policy planning due to their scale, the personalized nature of local politics, the lack of professional management capacity, and the individualized nature of the political subculture (Mattson, 1994). In addition, towns are more likely to use simpler non-regression-based methods of forecasting revenues, line-item budgets that limit administrative discretion, have less cash on hand for investments, and generate more revenues from user fees based upon the benefits received principle (Mattson, 1994). For example, Maher and Johnson (2008) surveyed more than 1,000 Wisconsin town board members and found that among five types of revenues—conditional grants, unconditional grants, property taxes, user charges and fees, and debt service—elected officials seeking another term in office have a greater tendency to support charges and fees over other revenue sources. However, there is little evidence to suggest that elected officials are manipulating revenue sources for political gain through fiscal illusion, as opposed to revenue structures primarily being influenced by socioeconomic factors like median household income, population shifts, and per capita property valuation (Maher & Johnson, 2008). As such, implementation of user fees might actually prove useful for these smaller jurisdictions, which tend to be less wealthy and more vulnerable to fiscal stress (Mattson, 1994).

While larger urban communities often have some flexibility in their tax bases, most small towns lack such flexibility that stems from diversity (Mattson, 1994). As a result of the lack of budgetary slack and array of services that enable tradeoffs in expenditure reductions or policy innovations during times of fiscal stress, small towns are more likely to implement drastic retrenchment approaches in response to decreasing revenues (Mattson, 1994). Evidence of this can be found in comparisons of expenditures among different forms of local governments. For example, French (2004) used survey data to examine 559 cities and towns throughout the US with populations between 2,500 and 25,000 and found that jurisdictions with council-manager forms of government maintain significantly higher per capita expenditures than those with other forms of government, particularly in the Southern and Western regions of the country. However, it is unclear whether these financial management practices of town governments, which are often seen as less innovative in terms of alleviation of fiscal stress, are the result of a more traditional-individualistic political culture or a lack of financial management skills of pertinent staff (Mattson, 1994).

Revenue Diversification in Town Governments

One of the more recent and comprehensive examinations of the revenue structures of town governments is provided by Carroll and Johnson (2010). Using data from the finance portion of the US Census Bureau's Census of Governments survey, the authors evaluate the levels of diversification among town governments located in the five states in which towns utilize the traditional annual town meeting governing structure (i.e., Connecticut, Maine, Minnesota, Vermont, and Wisconsin) while also grouping the states according to whether towns function under Dillon's rule with tax and expenditure limitations (TELs) (Wisconsin), Dillon's rule without TELs (Minnesota and Vermont), or home rule without TELs (Connecticut and Maine) as potential factors influencing the level of diversification among town governments in these states. The authors then calculated the mean and median levels of revenue diversification for all towns in each state by replicating the Hirschman-Herfindahl Index (HHI) formulas and time periods utilized by notable prior studies (i.e., Carroll, 2005; Carroll et al., 2003; Hendrick, 2002; Suyderhoud, 1994), which the authors claim provide the most consistent definitions and quantitative examinations of diversification among state and local governments, to provide for a strict comparison to town governments. Based upon this comparative analysis, Carroll and Johnson (2010) then provide a modified definition of revenue diversification that diverges from prior research but is more relevant and appropriate for town governments. Using their newly recommended HHI measure, the authors then evaluate trends in the level of revenue diversification among town governments for census years 1972–2002. Ultimately, the authors found lower levels of revenue diversification among town governments due to less reliance on sales taxation, differences in home rule status, and state-imposed tax and expenditure limitations.

Using the definition of revenue diversification for town governments developed by Carroll and Johnson (2010), this analysis offers an account of diversification among towns since 2002 and draws comparisons to the prior decades. To do so, data were collected from the finance portion of the US Census Bureau's Census of Governments survey for each full census year 2002–2017.[1] Figure 7.1 illustrates the number of towns and townships reported by the Census of Governments during this time period.

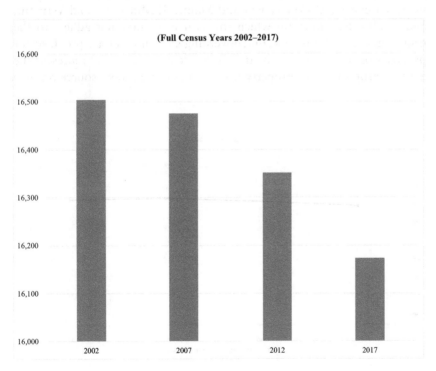

FIGURE 7.1   Number of Towns and Townships Reported by Census of Governments.

As can be seen in Figure 7.1, the number of towns and townships throughout the US has declined somewhat over the 15 years studied. In 2002, there were 16,504 towns and townships reported by the Census of Governments survey. This number declined to 16,475 in 2007 to 16,351 in 2012 to 16,173 in 2017, which amounts to a roughly 2 percent decline in town and township governments over the time period. Yet, the number of towns and townships in 2017 still reflects nearly 18 percent of the 90,075 total local government units throughout the US in that year. And this number hardly pales in comparison to the 19,495 municipal governments in the US in 2017, which is only a 0.34 percent increase in municipalities since the 2002 Census of Governments survey. Finally, the latest Census of Governments survey (2017) reported 18.6 percent of the total population residing in areas with township governments.

Looking more specifically at their revenue structures, Figure 7.2 illustrates trends in property tax reliance among towns for each census year from 2002 to 2017. For purposes of comparing the most recent trends in town revenue structures to prior decades as reported by Carroll and Johnson (2010), data are grouped and reported according to towns located in: 1) Wisconsin, 2) Connecticut and Maine, 3) Minnesota and Vermont, and 4) all other states (in which towns may or may not adhere to the traditional annual town meeting governing structure but are provided for purposes of comparison). The trends depicted in Figure 7.2 represent the average proportions of property tax revenue to total own source revenue

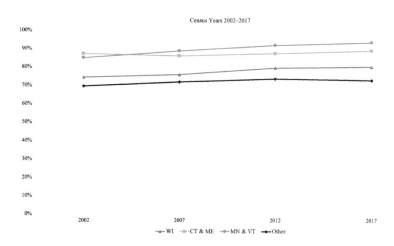

FIGURE 7.2 Property Tax Revenue as a Proportion of General Own Source Revenue.

for all towns within the states grouped into each category. Consistent with the earlier time trends reported by Carroll and Johnson (2010), Figure 7.2 shows a relatively high and rather stable reliance on property tax revenue over time with some noticeable differences between towns located in the states of Connecticut, Maine, Minnesota, and Vermont compared to those in Wisconsin and all other states.

According to Figure 7.2, towns located in Minnesota and Vermont are the most reliant on property taxation as they generated increasing proportions over time of 84.83 to 92.92 percent of their own source revenue from it. In a similar regard, towns in Connecticut and Maine decreased their reliance on property taxation slightly between 2002 and 2007—starting out above towns in Minnesota and Vermont at 86.94 percent of own source revenue and dropping below them to 85.85 percent—before steadily increasing reliance (albeit still remaining below towns in Minnesota and Vermont) to 88.55 percent of own source revenue by 2017. By comparison, towns located in Wisconsin and all other states exhibit noticeably lower reliance on property taxation, which is most likely a reflection of the tax and expenditure limitations imposed upon local governments in those states. In Wisconsin, town governments generated 74.18 percent of own source revenue from property taxation in 2002 and steadily increased that reliance over time to 79.87 percent by 2017. Towns in all other states—many of which operate more like cities and villages in terms of their governance structure—exhibit lower, but still increasing, reliance on property taxation ranging from 69.50 percent in 2002 to 72.59 percent of total own source revenue in 2017. Overall, these trends mimic those reported by Carroll and Johnson (2010), particularly with respect to the relatively stable but slightly increasing trends seen since the 1987 Census of Governments.

Figure 7.3 illustrates trends in the proportion of towns generating any amount of revenue from general charges for census years 2002–2017. As

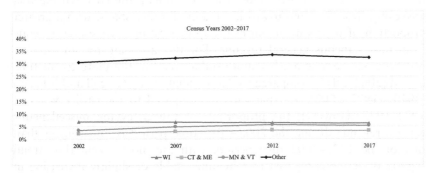

FIGURE 7.3 Proportion of Towns Generating Revenue From General Charges.

116 Deborah A. Carroll

can be seen, the proportion of towns utilizing this revenue source slightly increased between 2002 and 2012 before slightly decreasing between 2012 and 2017. However, there is a stark difference in the proportion of towns relying on this non-tax source between those located in the five states with traditional annual town meeting governing structures and those located in all other states; among the latter group, a considerably larger proportion of towns generate revenue from this alternate source. In states other than the five that utilize the traditional annual town meeting governing structure, the proportion of towns generating own source revenue from general charges ranges from 30.48 to 33.55 percent during the time period. By comparison, between 6.28 and 6.91 percent of Wisconsin towns generated own source revenue from general charges, while 3.42 to 5.68 percent of towns in Minnesota and Vermont levied general charges, and the lowest proportion of between 2.13 and 3.40 percent of towns in Connecticut and Maine generated own source revenue from general charges. These trends in the proportions of towns generating own source revenue from general charges are actually more stable during the 2002–2017 time period compared to the 1972–2002 trends highlighted by Carroll and Johnson (2010). In addition, the towns in Minnesota and Vermont surpass those located in Connecticut and Maine in terms of reliance on general charges revenue during the 2002 to 2017 time period, which is striking because towns in Connecticut and Maine exhibited heavier reliance on this alternate source in all prior census years dating back to 1972. Finally, these trends in reliance on general charges revenue are consistent to those of prior decades by showing a greater overall proportion of towns in Wisconsin with reliance on this nontax revenue source compared to towns in the other four states with a traditional annual meeting governing structure.

Figure 7.4 illustrates trends in the proportion of towns generating any amount of revenue from miscellaneous general revenue for census years 2002–2017. Again, we see a stark contrast in reliance on this revenue source between towns in the five states with traditional annual town meeting governing structures and towns located in all other states, with a greater proportion of towns in the latter group generating own source revenue from miscellaneous general revenue. For this alternate revenue source, however, we see a somewhat more stable trend in the more recent time period (2002–2017) compared to that highlighted by Carroll and Johnson (2010) (1972–2002), and particularly compared to the earlier years of 1972–1987. However, the proportion of towns levying miscellaneous general revenue during the 2002–2017 time period is much lower than that of the 1972–2002 time period, with the more recent time trend slightly declining compared to remaining stable or slightly increasing in the earlier time period. Specifically, the proportion of towns in states other

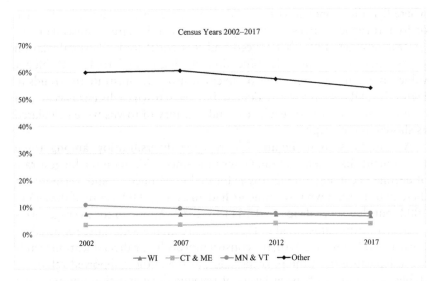

FIGURE 7.4 Proportion of Towns Generating Miscellaneous General Revenue.

than the five with a traditional annual town meeting governing structure with reliance on miscellaneous general revenue ranges from a high of 60.65 percent in 2007 to a low of 54.02 percent in 2017. By comparison, between 10.74 and 7.33 percent of towns in Minnesota and Vermont generated own source revenue from miscellaneous general revenue, while 7.58 to 6.42 percent of Wisconsin towns levied this alternate source, but only 3.74 and 3.33 percent of towns in Connecticut and Maine generated a portion of their own source revenue from miscellaneous general revenue sources during the 2002–2017 time period.

Finally, Figure 7.5 illustrates the trends in revenue diversification among town governments for census years between 2002 and 2017. Revenue diversification for towns is defined as: "A diversified revenue structure for town governments consists of relatively equal reliance on revenue generated from property taxes, general charges, miscellaneous general revenue, and other taxes" (Carroll & Johnson, 2010, p. 231). Based on this definition, the Hirschman-Herfindahl Index (HHI) measure of revenue diversification is calculated as:

$$HHI_{town} = \frac{1 - \sum_{i=1}^{n} R_i^2}{1 - (100\% / n)} \quad (1)$$

where R_i is the proportion of general own source revenue generated by each of four revenue sources—property taxes, general charges, miscellaneous general revenue, and other taxes—and n is equal to 4.[2] This calculation yields values of revenue diversification ranging from 0 to 1, with higher values indicating greater levels of diversification. To illustrate the trends in Figure 7.5, HHI scores were calculated for each town each census year, and then the mean values for each year and category of towns were calculated as shown in the graph.

As can be seen in Figure 7.5, revenue diversification among town governments has been declining over time since 2002 with the biggest rate of decline occurring among towns located in Minnesota and Vermont. In these two states, town governments had an average HHI score of 0.2945 in 2002, but that score drops to 0.1411 by 2017. Although the average levels of diversification illustrated in Figure 7.5 are in line with those reported by Carroll and Johnson (2010), the consistently declining diversification trends are a departure from the prior decades, as the authors reported relatively stable or slightly increasing levels of revenue diversification among town governments in the earlier census years (1972–2002). However, these more recent trends are unsurprising considering the relatively high and increasing

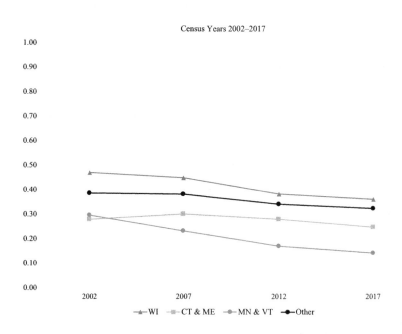

FIGURE 7.5   Towns Revenue Diversification Trends.

reliance of towns on property taxation as a proportion of general own source revenue as illustrated in Figure 7.2.

Another finding from Figure 7.5 that is consistent with the earlier findings reported by Carroll and Johnson (2010) is that town governments in Wisconsin maintain the highest average levels of revenue diversification among towns throughout the entire US, suggesting the continued importance of tax and expenditure limitations in the state. As shown in Figure 7.5, Wisconsin towns had an average HHI score ranging from 0.3590 to 0.4689 during the 2002–2017 time period. This compares to the highest average diversification score for towns in Minnesota and Vermont of 0.2945, in Connecticut and Maine of 0.2994, and in all other states of 0.3860. This higher average level of diversification is especially notable because, although Wisconsin towns are generally less reliant on property taxation than towns located in the other four states highlighted in this study, they are more reliant on property taxation than towns in all other states including those that do not maintain the traditional annual meeting governing structure.

Using Social Capital for Collaborative Governance

With relatively lower and declining levels of revenue diversification, there may be cause for concern about the financial viability of town governments. However, the governing structure of towns and townships might prove useful for overcoming this potential threat. Specifically, town governments are uniquely situated to leverage the social capital in their communities to help solve collective action problems and create collaborative governing institutions with respect to financial management of their revenue structures. "Social capital is defined as the relationships between people characterized by trust and norms of reciprocity that can be utilized for individual and collective goal achievement" (Besser, 2009, p. 185). Higher levels of trusting relationships among town residents are associated with greater voluntarism and civic involvement (Besser, 2009; Putnam, 2000). Such mobilization of town residents makes for more effective local government compared to other places (Rice, 2001), leading to economic and social benefits for the community (Besser, 1999; Knack & Keefer, 1997; Morton, 2003). Specifically, social capital theory implies that towns with trusting relationships will be more resilient to economic restructuring as high social capital towns are expected to have more civic engagement and higher levels of collective action aimed at the public good (Besser, 2009). Garnering greater public participation in the form of volunteering time, skills, and financial resources to solve public problems is based upon the notion that small communities are able to use their strong civic culture to extend limited public resources (Morton et al., 2008).

Morton (2003) examined the influence of individual-level social capital (i.e., an attribute of an individual's human relations characterized by personal norms of trust and reciprocity) and community-level civic structure (i.e., the dynamic relations among multiple networks characterized by norms of cooperation and community benefits), and found that civic structure helps to explain variation *between* communities while individual social capital helps to explain variation *within* communities, as high civic structure provides communities the capacity to meet the collective needs of town residents. "The civic structure of a community consists of normative expectations that multiple individual and group actions will lead to solving collective problems in the broad community interest" such as the allocation of public resources (Morton, 2003, p. 105). Ultimately, civic structure is important for resident perceptions of service quality, suggesting residents are engaged in solving community problems by investing personal and public resources, which might provide rural towns with a competitive advantage in retaining current residents and attracting new residents if public provision can maintain high satisfaction (Morton et al., 2008). In turn, this will help to ensure the continued financial viability of the community to meet the needs of its residents.

Notes

1 The US Census Bureau conducts a full census of governments finance survey every five years in each year that ends in two and seven, so 2017 is the most recent full census year of available data.
2 The other tax category comprises all non–property tax revenue, including general and selective sales, personal and corporate income, license, and any other miscellaneous taxes.

References

Besser, T. L. (2009). Changes in small town social capital and civic engagement. *Journal of Rural Studies*, 25, 185–193.

Besser, T. L. (1999). Community involvement and the perception of success among small business operators in small towns. *Journal of Small Business Management*, 37(4), 16–30.

Carroll, D. A. (2005). Are state governments prepared for fiscal crises? A look at revenue diversification during the 1990s. *Public Finance Review*, 33(5), 603–633.

Carroll, D. A., Eger III, R. J., & Marlowe, J. (2003). Managing local intergovernmental revenues: The imperative of diversification. *International Journal of Public Administration*, 26(13), 1495–1519.

Carroll, D. A., & Johnson, T. (2010). Examining small town revenues: To what extent are they diversified? *Public Administration Review*, 70(2), 223–235.

Catlaw, T. J., & Stout, M. (2016). Governing small-town American today: The promise and dilemma of dense networks. *Public Administration Review*, 76(2), 225–229.

DeSantis, V. S., & Hill, D. (2004). Citizen participation in local politics: Evidence from New England town meetings. *State and Local Government Review*, 36(3), 166–173.

Diaz, D., & Green, G. P. (2001). Fiscal stress and growth management effort in Wisconsin cities, villages, and towns. *State and Local Government Review*, 33(1), 7–22.

French, P. E. (2004). Form of government and per capita expenditures: An evaluation of small cities and towns. *Journal of Public Budgeting, Accounting & Financial Management*, 16(2), 193–209.

Helpap, D. J. (2017). Assessing public expenditures in small towns: Beyond roads and fire engines. *State and Local Government Review*, 49(2), 75–86.

Hendrick, R. (2002). Revenue diversification: Fiscal illusion or flexible financial management. *Public Budgeting & Finance*, 22(4), 52–72.

Johnson, T., & Ihrke, D. M. (2004). Determinants of conflict on Wisconsin town boards. *State and Local Government Review*, 36(2), 103–117.

Knack, S., & Keefer, P. (1997). Does social capital have an economic payoff? A cross country investigation. *Quarterly Journal of Economics*, 112(4), 1251–1288.

Maher, C. S., & Johnson, T. (2008). Testing for fiscal illusion in Wisconsin towns. *International Journal of Public Administration*, 31, 1138–1156.

Mattson, G. A. (1994). Retrenchment and fiscal policy planning: The political culture of small southern towns. *Public Productivity & Management Review*, 17(3), 265–279.

Morton, L. W. (2003). Small town services and facilities: The influence of social networks and civic structure on perceptions of quality. *City & Community*, 2(2), 101–120.

Morton, L. W., Chen, Y.-C., & Morse, R. S. (2008). Small town civic structure and interlocal collaboration for public services. *City & Community*, 7(1), 45–60.

National Association of Towns and Townships (NATaT). (n.d.) *Town and township government in the United States*. NATaT.

Putnam, R. (2000). *Bowling Alone: The Collapse and Revival of America's Civic Community*. Simon & Schuster.

Rice, T. W. (2001). Social capital and government performance in Iowa communities. *Journal of Urban Affairs*, 23, 375–390.

Suyderhoud, J. P. (1994). State-local revenue diversification, balance, and fiscal performance. *Public Finance Quarterly*, 22(2), 168–95.

Tiebout, C. M. (1956). A pure theory of local expenditures. *Journal of Political Economy*, 64(5), 416–424.

Trautman, R. R. (2016). Small-town policy makers. *Public Administration Review*, 76(2), 221–224.

CASE STUDY: CROWDFUNDING LOCAL GOVERNMENT: BELMONT'S BICYCLE SUNDAY PROGRAM

Martin K. Mayer and John C. Morris

The Wisdom of the Crowd

The "wisdom of the crowd" is the occurrence where a group comes together to create value and leverage collective resources for community betterment. Crowdsourcing, as it is often called, provides several potential benefits for the public sector. Crowdsourcing data and information is made possible by the growth of information technology and our increasingly connected and integrated society.

Crowdsourcing is a broad, encompassing term; crowdfunding, as a subset of crowdsourcing, is focused solely on connecting the financial resources of the crowd to a particular issue or need. Ultimately the success of the project is determined by the public's willingness to invest in it.

Civic Crowdfunding

Born out of the Great Recession in 2008, civic crowdfunding bridges private-sector resources with public-sector, or public-minded projects. In the simplest of terms, civic crowdfunding is the process of appealing to and leveraging the resources of the crowd for local government and community projects. The process itself is not new, as much as it is an updated model of giving that takes advantage of our digital environment and has the potential to augment traditional local government service delivery. Civic crowdfunding projects vary wildly by municipality; in some locales, they may be shovel-ready proposals that have yet to find a budget expenditure. In others, the proposals can be entirely citizen-driven, but

DOI: 10.4324/9781003287766-14

the common denominator in civic crowdfunding projects is the utilization of community resources for the realization of community goals. Civic crowdfunding projects often require little local government planning and funding, making them even more appealing for the capital and resources they can raise. This case provides a brief discussion of the strengths and weaknesses of civic crowdfunding in local government, an examination of a civic crowdfunding campaign, and the implications of civic crowdfunding for local government and the community.

Opportunity Environment

The digital age has changed the way we consume information and left organizations constantly trying to adapt to new technologies and information exchange mechanisms. Social media have made it easier to organize and rally individuals to support a cause than perhaps ever before. Yet, the public sector has been slow to fully realize and implement this technology for citizen input and information exchange.

Traditionally, much of the revenue of local government comes from property and sales tax. People increasingly demand more services but want to pay fewer taxes. Furthermore, the needs of a given district can vary greatly across and even within metropolitan areas and can be significantly impacted by size and structure of each municipal government, which in turn can have numerous adverse impacts on the quality of life of the citizenry.

One way in which to address this growing issue is to begin to rethink local government revenue sources and reimagine taxation and service. Crowdfunding is one such example, where an initiative must sell itself to the funding public. This is typically done through online platforms that specialize in advertising and marketing crowdfunding campaigns in exchange for a small commission. In most cases, the crowdfunding platforms are open-ended, allowing anyone to propose a project, anywhere in the country. In rare, but increasing instances, several municipalities have partnered directly with crowdfunding platforms to build out regionally dedicated databases. Each donation across the civic crowdfunding platforms serves as a barometer of public opinion and an indicator of preference revelation that allows citizens a more active and impactful voice in local government service delivery.

Crowdfunding in Action: Belmont's Bicycle Sundays

Belmont, California, is a small town about 20 miles south of San Francisco. Belmont has a population of approximately 27,000 people, and it prides itself on being a unique, accepting, small town from which the big cities of San Francisco and San Jose can be accessed with ease.

Over the last two decades in Belmont, the town has shut down roughly seven miles of scenic Canada Road every Sunday from 9:00 a.m. to 3:00 p.m. for recreational cycling and other non-motorized activities. Highly popular amongst experts and novices alike, bicycle Sundays have recently come under risk due to budget cuts and constraints within the local government. The annual cost to the town of roughly $36,000, which is necessary to pay three park rangers for their time and efforts in shutting down the road and ensuring a safe and welcoming environment for cyclists, has proven too much to bear. Initially, the town tried to institute volunteer programs to assist the rangers with their weekly duties, but the success of those programs was minimal. As future funding sources continued to be investigated, the town of Belmont decided to turn toward its citizens to prolong the program while additional resources were sought out.

With the help of the San Mateo parks department, local online news source the *Belmont Patch*, as well a network of dedicated technologically savvy constituents, the town of Belmont engaged in a crowdfunding campaign through Citizinvestor. As with nearly all campaigns of this nature, social media were vitally important. The campaign went live in September of 2013 and immediately the town and major stakeholders encouraged people not just to donate to the cause, but also to help by spreading the word on social media, as well as installing the crowdfunding wiki on their own websites. Longer than most crowdfunding initiatives, the bicycle Sunday's program ran for nearly five months and progress was slow.

With just over a week to go in the funding cycle, only a little over 60 percent of the requested amount had been raised. Somewhat remarkably, and with a strong push on social media and other platforms, the remaining funds were raised, bringing the weekly total nearly in line with the total funds raised over the prior 19 weeks. A total of 97 citizens, some donating multiple times, raised nearly $11,000 to help keep bicycle Sundays in Belmont, showcasing the power of community and what is possible when an issue resonates with the public.

Bicycle Sundays is a popular, uncontroversial program in which it is easy to see the public benefit. But still, project organizers must convince citizens to support and donate to the projects. Highlighting a community need or problem area is one way to create buy-in. In an effort to show why this program mattered in Belmont, the town pointed to unfortunate but highly effective accident reports. The region had been plagued over the last few years with numerous reports of vehicles colliding with pedestrians and cyclists throughout the area, causing serious injury or worse. Belmont appealed to the public by presenting Bicycle Sundays as a safe recreational opportunity for citizens both young and old, and a place for new riders as well as seasoned pros. By focusing on safety issues and highlighting the duties and work of the rangers, which includes stopping cars that inevitably drive around the weekly barriers, Belmont successfully identified a community need and empowered the citizens to take action to save it.

Projects like the bicycle Sunday program allow project conveners to fund their efforts through large-scale, micro-donations that, through the use of technology, have the ability to recruit large numbers of donors and alter the traditional local government finance and service delivery structure. Identifying a community need, highlighting the mutual benefit, and appealing to as many individuals as possible through various platforms and channels is critical to building community support and creating buy-in necessary to project success.

Implications and Conclusion

Civic crowdfunding has the potential to be a disruptive positive force due to its success as a non-traditional funding mechanism for local government. This early success and continued growth of projects around the country coupled with eased federal regulations have led to an increasing number of local governments turning to crowdfunding to solve local dilemmas. As civic crowdfunding projects become more prevalent and are employed on a wider scale, such projects have the potential to shake up local government by altering and impacting the traditional roles and boundaries between citizens and administrators.

Place and space matter in successfully funding civic crowdfunding campaigns. More affluent communities may have larger budgets and other resources at their disposal to fund the types of projects typically proposed through civic crowdfunding platforms; whereas the jurisdictions on the other end of the financial spectrum may lack the necessary resources to effectively initiate and support a crowdfunding project. The smaller, middle-class areas in many cases exhibit a greater sense of project need than more affluent proposing jurisdictions, but still retain enough collective resources to meet project and funding goals. This may be an avenue worth further exploration in small and rural communities.

Subsection: Healthcare, Parks and Recreation, and Wellness

8

RURAL COMMUNITIES AND ACCESS TO HEALTHCARE

Mary Ellen Travers and Sue M. Neal

Introduction

Access to healthcare is a dire and problematic need for many Americans, and can mean the difference between life and death. The challenge is particularly profound in less populated areas as the mortality rate for rural individuals tripled between 1999 and 2019 (Cross et al., 2021). In the United States, rural populations tend to be both poorer and sicker than those who live in urban areas (Dearinger, 2020; Leider et al., 2020). Unfortunately, the problem is magnified by the multiple barriers to healthcare that rural populations experience (Centers for Disease Control and Prevention, 2019). When considering how to address these challenges, it is important to acknowledge that the term *access to care* is broad and is impacted by many different factors (Cyr et al., 2019). For example, hospital closures in rural areas have provided a significant barrier to rural populations accessing care in general, including access to primary care providers and specialists (McCarthy et al., 2021; NACRHHS, 2020). However, access to care can involve more than just the physical location of a building.

While proximity to a physical clinic or office is critical, there may be a host of additional factors impacting a rural resident's access to healthcare, including workforce shortages in rural clinics, a lack of healthcare coverage, and mental health stigmas or a lack of literacy skills that prevent citizens from seeking care. This can impact both the convenience and the confidence of rural citizens, causing them to delay care and lose the opportunity to have improved health outcomes as a result (Rural Health

DOI: 10.4324/9781003287766-16

Information Hub, 2021). These additional barriers cannot be ignored as rural communities attempt to address healthcare disparities in their communities. This chapter will provide an overview of some of the terms and issues related to healthcare access in rural areas, and look more closely at the example of maternal healthcare to highlight specific needs and strategies for public leaders to consider.

An Overview of the Terms and Structures of Public Health in the United States

In order to understand the background of public health issues that can impact those living in rural communities, it can be helpful to look at the larger framework of public health issues in the United States. Barriers to healthcare are not just dire issues for those living outside of urban areas. Whitman et al. (2022) provide an overview of the various groups (including rural residents) that experience health inequities in our country, as noted below:

Despite significant investments to improve access to high-quality health care, health inequities in the United States persist by race, ethnicity, sexual orientation, gender identity, and disability, as well as by economic and community level factors such as geographic location, poverty status, and employment. Black, Latino*, American Indian and Alaska Native (AI/AN), Asian American, Native Hawaiian, and Pacific Islanders (AANHPI), and LGBTQ+, individuals, people who live in rural areas, and people with disabilities fare worse than their White, heterosexual, and urban counterparts and people without disabilities. These disparities exist for many health outcomes, including infant and maternal mortality, heart disease, diabetes, hypertension, chronic illness, disability, cancer, mental illness, substance use, and overall life expectancy.

(Whitman et al., 2022, p. 2)

Further, "the COVID-19 pandemic highlighted health disparities across groups based on social, racial, ethnic, economic and environmental characteristics" (National Conference of State Legislatures, 2021), and demonstrated that there can be no one set of policy solutions (National Conference of State Legislatures, 2021) to reduce these disparities and provide relief to those in need. There must be different approaches and collaborative measures taken to begin to eliminate the barriers to healthcare in the United States.

Federal-Level "Social Determinants of Health"

Since US healthcare needs are complex, they must involve collaboration between the public, private, and nonprofit sectors to be effective. From a federal perspective, the US Department of Health and Human Services (HHS) seeks to improve health conditions through five domains that can increase or decrease the Social Determinants of Health (SDOH) of individuals. SDOH are the conditions where people are born, live, learn, work, play, worship, and age that affect a wide range of health, functioning, and quality-of-life outcomes (Whitman et al., 2022, p. 2). The goal is to improve the factors that impact these domains in order to achieve increased health and wellbeing for all people. The five domains of Social Determinants of Health include economic stability, social and community context, education access and quality, healthcare access and quality, and neighborhood and the built environment (Office of Disease Prevention and Health Promotion, 2020).

HHS, through the Office of Disease Prevention and Health Promotion, has developed Healthy People, a list of objectives and goals that uses the Social Determinants of Health to measure progress towards these objectives (Office of Disease Prevention and Health Promotion, 2020). The five domains of Social Determinants of Health are explored, along with current programs that seek to improve access to care despite the barriers and limitations that can hinder these efforts. In one more specific example, we provide suggestions for the planning and implementation of effective, sustainable programs to deliver care to mothers within rural communities in order to highlight the role of local government in improving maternal health outcomes.

Maternal Health and Maternal Mortality in the United States

Understanding maternal mortality rate is important as it is generally used as an indicator of a population's overall health (Douthard et al., 2021). Maternal health is a great concern among all communities in the United States, as US maternal mortality rates are high compared to other developed countries (Cameron et al., 2020; Ahn et al., 2020). Within the United States, maternal mortality disproportionally affects Black and American Indian/Alaska Native women (NACRHHS, 2020). In 2016-2017, non-Hispanic Black women had maternal mortality rates 2.5 times higher than non-Hispanic White women (Joseph et al., 2021; MacDorman et al., 2021). This disproportion is even more heightened in rural Black communities, where there are higher odds of hospital closures (NACRHHS, 2020).

Compared to urban areas, women residing in rural areas have a higher risk of experiencing severe maternal morbidity and mortality (Kozhimannil et al., 2019). The longer a mother has to travel for obstetric care, the higher the risk of complications, the higher the cost, and the longer the length of stay (Kozhimannil et al., 2019;). Rural mothers also tend to have a higher rate of delayed prenatal care, due to rural counties hospital closures in general, but particularly hospitals with obstetric services. Now, rural residents are more likely to have births outside of a hospital, or in a hospital that does not have an obstetric unit, and less than half of women who are rural residents are within a 30-minute drive of a hospital with obstetric services (US Department of Health and Human Services, 2020, p. 10). There has been a significant decline in access to hospital based obstetric services from 2004–2018 in US rural counties, which may contribute to the aforementioned problems (i.e., higher rate of delayed prenatal care) (Kozhimannil et al., 2020). The decline of hospital based obstetric care has been found to be significantly associated with an increase in preterm births (Kozhimannil et al., 2018). This is particularly alarming when the most common reason for hospitalization in the United States is childbirth (Anderson et al., 2019).

A 2021 study by Armstrong-Mensah et al. focused on maternal mortality in the state of Georgia, which has the highest maternal mortality rate out of all 50 states. They identified five key SDOH contributing to the high maternal mortality rate in Georgia, which include geographic location of obstetric services, socioeconomic status, access to healthcare providers, racism, and discrimination (Armstrong-Mensah et al., 2021). In Georgia, many rural women are single mothers and do not have a family and/or partner supporting them, which highlights the need for social service programs to provide mothers with support (NACRHHS, 2020). Researchers also found that, in order to reduce the state's maternal mortality rate, there will need to be multiple interventions such as expanding Medicaid coverage, providing rural communities with access to maternal care, reducing maternal healthcare disparities, and training a culturally competent health workforce (Armstrong-Mensah et al., 2021). Social service programs that do provide care and address multiple SDOH (like the Maternal, Infant, and Child Home Visiting Program, Healthy Start, and Early Head Start programs) lack adequate resources and are underfunded in rural areas (NACRHHS, 2020).

Maternal mortality is a large problem in the United States, and in order to make data informed decisions, accurate, high-quality data are needed. Unfortunately, there have been data reporting and coding issues in the National Vital Statistics System (NVSS) (MacDorman & Declercq, 2018). The NVSS contains maternal mortality statistics, and estimates of US maternal mortality have been found to have inaccuracies (MacDorman & Declercq, 2018). In 2003, the US provided improvements to maternal death reporting by including a question asking about pregnancy to the standard death certificate, but this caused data issues such as overreporting due to pregnancy checkbox errors (MacDorman & Declercq, 2018). After recoding, the National Center for Health Statistics found that there was not a significant change in crude maternal mortality rates from 2002–2018, but there was a temporal decrease of 21% for age-adjusted maternal mortality rate, and racial disparities persist (Joseph et al., 2021). Even with these data issues, the maternal mortality rate in the US is too high. Accurate data are vital to effectively address ethnic and racial disparities, social determinants of health, and to implement successful programs (MacDorman & Declercq, 2018; Joseph et al., 2021).

Small town and rural leaders can improve this situation by being advocates for data collection in their regions. Partnering with primary care providers, obstetrics and gynecological specialists as well as local and regional hospitals could aid the local leader in developing a clearer picture of the challenges confronting their communities. One commonly used tool is a Community Needs Assessment. Community Needs Assessments aim to identify the specific needs of the community where they occur and examine potential gaps that exist in critical service areas. There are also new federal efforts aimed at improving rural access to care and specifically access to maternal health through research partnerships funded by the Patient Centered Outcome Research Institute (Hughes & Vohra, 2021). A number of other novel solutions exist that are important for rural and small town leaders to be aware of in order to meet key health needs in their communities.

Interventions and Programs

Successful solutions have already been proposed to try to address access to care challenges in rural communities. Certificates of Need, the Affordable Care Act, Medicaid, Community Health Centers, and Birth Centers exist and have been used in various ways to address rural access to care in the US. When analyzing the many options to meeting their community needs, local government leaders need to ask themselves a series of assessment questions which include: does the program meet the needs of their residents; is the community prepared to invest in programs that require community-level funding support; what funding sources (such as federal grants) might be available to support implementation; and do the programs have a track record of successful outcomes? Leaders who have done this type of research will be best positioned to evaluate the shortcomings and successes of the many programs in order to build and implement an effective, sustainable intervention tailored to their specific community's needs.

Certificates of Need

Certificates of Need (CON) laws are used by 35 states and Washington, DC, to approve large capital expenditures and projects for specific healthcare facilities and try to control healthcare costs by deciding if a capital expenditure meets a community need and reducing any services that may be duplicative (National Conference of State Legislatures, 2021). While CON programs vary from state to state, most CON laws regulate outpatient facilities, hospitals, and long-term care facilities (National Conference of State Legislatures, 2021). Researchers reviewing the cost effectiveness of CON laws have found some negatives. Rivers et al. found that they actually increase hospital costs by decreasing competition (2007). Another study stated that the costs of CON surpass any benefits, although the authors did note that more research is needed (Conover & Bailey, 2020).

Expanding Medicaid

The Affordable Care Act (ACA) allowed states to expand Medicaid eligibility to more people with low income, and by January 2018, Medicaid had been expanded in 32 states and Washington, DC (Cole et al., 2018). This expansion impacted community health centers (CHCs), providing opportunities both for CHC patients to have more access to care and CHCs to have more revenue per patient that can be invested into improving services (Cole et al., 2018). The first two years of Medicaid expansion in CHCs in rural areas was associated with several healthcare improvements for rural residents, an increase in insurance coverage, and an increase in visit volumes to CHCs (Cole et al., 2018). Healthcare improvements included an increase in blood pressure control, quality of care for asthma treatment, and in BMI assessments and follow-up (Cole et al., 2018).

Midwifery

Ensuring access to maternal healthcare involves access to more than one provider. It takes a team to deliver maternal care, from primary to specialty care providers, advanced practice nurses, nurses, community health workers, doulas, and midwives (Centers for Medicare & Medicaid Services, 2019). In this interprofessional collaboration, midwives play an especially important role in the rural community, attending over

30 percent of deliveries in rural hospitals compared to attending less than 10 percent of all births in the US (Centers for Medicare & Medicaid Services, 2019). Increasing midwives in rural areas could also provide a solution to rural women's limited access to care. Certified nurse-midwives who provide maternity care are a critical part of the rural hospital workforce (Kozhimannil et al., 2016). In the US, midwives have three professional titles: certified midwife (CM), certified nurse-midwife (CNM), and certified professional midwife (CPM) (Vedam et al., 2018). Increasing the midwifery workforce could also provide maternal health services to rural communities via birth centers led by midwives. Research showed that the birth center model of care delivered quality outcomes that surpassed national benchmarks, and researchers suggest that the US expand birth center models of care to rural communities in order to improve maternal health (Jolles et al., 2020).

Vedam et al. (2018) used a Midwifery Integration Scoring (MISS) system to depict how well midwives are integrated in each state, while also assessing regional access to high-quality maternity care. Researchers found that the higher integration scores were associated with less obstetric interventions, higher rates of physiologic birth, and lower adverse neonatal outcomes (Vedam et al., 2018). Interprofessional collaboration for decision-making and care coordination has been found to lower the amounts of intrapartum neonatal and maternal deaths during critical obstetric events, and improve safety and quality of care for women (Vedam et al., 2018; Cornthwaite et al., 2013). When government leaders facilitate collaboration among different professions, researchers have highlighted the importance of shared ethical standards that they strive to ensure these ethics align for a successful collaboration (Neal et al., 2021).

Complicating Factors and Specialized Solutions

Both urban and rural residents face the challenges, and have similar SDOH, but it is important to tailor policy and clinical interventions for rural settings, as rural residents face their own set of unique challenges (Kozhimannil et al., 2019). Determinants such as education, income, housing, food, social support, and transportation all play a role in how rural residents, including women, can access care (Centers for Medicare & Medicaid Services, 2019). Therefore, programs for these communities will need to include interventions to tackle various social determinants to provide better access to all healthcare and specifically maternal care. The Centers for Medicare & Medicaid Services describe the ideal maternal health system as one that would be equitable, accessible, affordable, high quality, risk appropriate, patient centered, innovative, and coordinated (Centers for Medicare & Medicaid Services, 2019).

There are successful programs aiming to achieve that ideal system. One case study approach was the Antenatal & Neonatal Guidelines and Education Learning System (ANGELS) program. This state-based program is located in Arkansas, and focuses on improving both the quality of and access to maternal health services in the state. It addresses barriers such as access to care, insurance coverage, hospital closures, quality, health disparities, and social determinants of health. A barrier it does not address is workforce supply and distribution. They have a call center for providers and patients who may be experiencing perinatal complications or emergencies that is open 24/7, teleconferencing, and are increasing the rural providers' readiness and capacity in the event of an obstetric emergency. The program is also implementing a training, AIM Disparities Safety Bundle, to address unconscious or conscious provider bias in order to improve equitable access to healthcare services for minority communities (Centers for Medicare & Medicaid Services, 2019).

Telehealth interventions to help reach rural women where there is broadband access available is another solution that has received increased attention over the last few years (Bathija, 2020). Educational apps and apps that provide text message reminders about important health topics have also been developed to provide access to care (Bathija, 2020). Another telehealth focus was the Health Resources & Services Administration's (HRSA) remote pregnancy monitoring challenge that is focused on helping provide quality care for those who are in rural or medically underserved areas, and have limited access to care (Ahn et al., 2020). HRSA also aids states' telehealth interventions via the Screening and Treatment for Maternal Depression and Related Behavioral Disorders program, which helps states provide care coordination support, psychiatric consultation, and training for healthcare providers in medically underserved and rural areas (Ahn et al., 2020). Since the COVID-19 pandemic, telehealth programs have increased, and reimbursements for these services by the Centers for Medicare and Medicaid Services have expanded (Hirko et al., 2020). It will be important to ensure third-party reimbursements continue after the pandemic, to ensure this type of intervention is sustainable (Hirko et al., 2020).

When considering a telehealth approach, reliable broadband internet access is critical. Telehealth video-based visits can be supported by at least 25 megabits per second of internet speed, but researchers found that within rural counties where there is inadequate access to care, there is also lower broadband internet access (Drake et al., 2019). With 33 percent of rural populations in the US not having access to broadband speeds of at least

25 mbps, it is important to be cautious of telehealth services widening this disparity for rural communities (Hirko et al., 2020).

There are also healthcare policies that aim to address the US's maternal mortality problem and support the use of care teams for maternal health. In 2018 the Preventing Maternal Deaths Act (HR 1318) was signed into law, providing funding for states to establish and sustain maternal mortality review committees, and there is also the Maternal Care Access and Reducing Emergencies (CARE) Act, the Mothers and Offspring Mortality and Morbidity (MOMMA) Act, and the Rural Maternal and Obstetric Modernization of Services (MOMS) Act which are in Congress (Collier & Molina, 2019). These bills work to address disparities in access to care for rural women, expand Medicaid through one year after delivery and provide reimbursement for doula services, and standardize data collection (Collier & Molina, 2019).

Federal Programs

There are numerous organizations that work to provide care to those with limited healthcare access, such as the National Health Service Corps, the Rural Maternity and Obstetrics Management Strategies (RMOMS) Program, and the National Rural Recruitment and Retention Network (3RNET). The National Advisory Committee on Rural Health and Human Services (NACRHHS, 2020) provided six policy recommendations for improving access to maternal care in rural communities:

Recommendation 1: ... encourage the adoption of comprehensive, integrative, and intensive case management within the Healthy Start, Early Head Start, and the Maternal, Infant, and Early Childhood Home Visiting Programs.

Recommendation 2: ... develop guidelines and implement safety and treatment protocols in rural hospitals and clinics, both with and without OB services, to respond to obstetric complications.

Recommendation 3: ... enhance CDC funding for both the CDC Levels of Care Assessment Tool program and the Enhancing Reviews and Surveillance to Eliminate Maternal Mortality program to ensure all states have standardized assessments of levels of maternal and neonatal care and Maternal Mortality Review Committees.

Recommendation 4: ... work with states to standardize scope of practice laws between and within maternal healthcare providers, and to expand the scope of practice for nurse midwives.

Recommendation 5: ... in support of the Administration's broader graduate medical education goals, include an expansion of the current statutory cap on Medicare-supported residencies that allows for support of new rural residencies in high-need areas like primary care and obstetrics. Recommendation 6: … address the obstetrical workforce shortage by working with Congress to increase support for the National Health Service Corps to expand the number of physicians, nurses and certified nurse midwives working in rural and underserved areas.

Barriers and Limitations to Programs and Interventions

While a number of solutions do exist, there are distinct barriers and limitations to these programs. As local leaders consider options for addressing access to care in their communities it will be necessary to consider the degree to which these potentially complicating factors may influence which solutions are most likely to succeed or what additional implementation steps may need to be taken to ensure success. Issues around social determinants of health and the limited access to broadband internet are two concerns that have already been discussed yet there are additional factors that should be taken into account.

Medical Mistrust

Along with the physical distance that acts as a barrier to accessing care in rural areas is an invisible distance between patients and healthcare. Researchers interviewed rural women and found that there is an "unwillingness" to access healthcare, which is made up of multiple factors and interpretation of barriers (Statz & Evers, 2020). The rural women interviewed in the study would either rather travel further physical distances to receive "better" care from a provider or health setting they trust, or avoid healthcare completely (Statz & Evers, 2020). It is important to learn the needs of the community rural women are in, and acknowledge that trusted social networks within these communities are important, as they have the power to promote mistrust in clinicians and healthcare systems (Statz & Evers, 2020). Therefore, programs and policies that only address physical rural distance would cause more medical distrust among rural women (Statz & Evers, 2020).

Health Literacy

Even if a program has all of the materials necessary to reach maternal mothers in rural areas and provide healthcare, information, and resources, if the receiving mothers do not understand the information and resources provided, the effects will be quite limited. In this way, health literacy for maternal women is critical for any program or intervention to be successful. Sociodemographic factors, such as age, gender, education, socioeconomic status, race and ethnicity, were found to have the greatest associations with health literacy in rural and urban areas (Aljassim & Ostini, 2020). While urban populations have higher health literacy than rural populations, rurality itself was found not to be a determinant of health literacy (Aljassim & Ostini, 2020). This highlights the need for programs to address the previously mentioned sociodemographic factors to ensure success. Programs for improving maternal health literacy through home visits by registered nurses have been found to be successful (Mobley et al., 2014).

Broader Access Issues in Rural America

Access to maternal healthcare is further complicated by some of the same overarching care access barriers that confront many in rural America. Not only does this add to the challenge of delivering care to mothers and infants in rural areas, it also is indicative of broader obstacles that can impact all members of rural communities regardless of sex or reproductive status. Rural hospitals are closing at alarming rates, with 182 closures of rural hospitals since January of 2005 according to the University of North Carolina Center for Health Services Research (Sheps Center, 2022). Rural hospitals confront challenges in remaining open due to low patient volumes, high numbers of patients with chronic/complicated care needs associated with an ageing population, and the uncertainties of operating in an unsure regulatory environment tied with a heavy reliance on government funded care (AHA, 2021). Rural hospitals are also confronted with catastrophic challenges of natural disasters and epidemics (both behavioral health and medical) (AHA, 2021).

The impacts of hospital closures are far reaching. At the most basic level, fewer hospitals in rural areas can mean that residents need to drive further for care and may not be able to receive prompt medical attention for more complicated care needs. Hospital closures in rural areas have been shown to have a disproportionate impact on patient outcomes (mortality) when compared to non-rural closures, which indicates a need to consider the ramification of rural hospital closures as uniquely damaging to surrounding resident wellness (Gujral and Basu, 2019). Outside of the medical impacts of rural hospital closures, there are also major economic consequences when a hospital, which may be the largest employer in a region, ceases to function. These closures can impact a number of economic measures including regional unemployment and per capita income in already struggling communities (Holmes et al. 2006; Manlove and Whitacre 2017).

While the trends related to generalized barriers to healthcare access in rural America are discouraging there are a number of solutions directed at this specific issue. The Rural Health Care Taskforce, for example, generated an extensive report of possible solutions released in May of 2021 (AHA, 2021). While not specific to maternal healthcare, a number of solutions advanced in this document overlap with solutions discussed previously in this chapter indicating significant opportunities to improve access for both maternal health challenges and general lack of access for all residents in rural communities. Solutions such as telehealth, greater use of strategic partnerships, increased use of broadband and mobile technologies are all ideas explored both previously in this chapter as related to maternal health but also within the Taskforce's Final Recommendation Report (AHA, 2021).

Conclusion

The research has shown that the US has a maternal health crisis, and rural communities are facing a crisis in access to maternal care. Multiple social determinants of health impact how successful these programs will be and must be considered along with physical access to care providers by government leaders in small and rural communities. It is evident that this is a major problem that will likely confront small town and rural government leaders. There are a number of federal programs, agencies, and organizations that exist with many different options to improve access in any community. Understanding the threats, needs, and opportunities that exist in a community were highlighted as important ways that local leaders could start selecting programs appropriate for their communities. Taking steps to assess the need and evaluate the strengths and weaknesses of the various programs are valuable ways to select programs that align with a specific community.

Disparities to care persist and they sit at the intersection of other major challenges that rural and small towns confront. Active governmental leadership in these areas will be important to ensure that everyone in a community has access to the healthcare they need. Infrastructure concerns including the location of physical care facilities and stable broadband access are two direct ways small town government leaders can be part of the solution to these complex problems. A number of programs exist that can assist local leaders in confronting these challenges. Future leaders in small and rural governments will be critical actors as the US takes steps to improve outcomes for maternal health, as well as many other healthcare concerns across the country.

References

AHA. (2021). *Final Recommendations on the Future of the Rural Health Care Task Force May 2021*. AHA. www.aha.org/system/files/media/file/2021/05/final-recommendations-future-of-rural-health-care-task-force-may-2021.pdf (September 8, 2022).

Ahn, R., Gonzalez, G. P., Anderson, B., Vladutiu, C. J., Fowler, E. R., & Manning, L. (2020). Initiatives to reduce maternal mortality and severe maternal morbidity in the United States. *Annals of Internal Medicine, 173*(11_Supplement), S3–S10. https://doi.org/10.7326/M19-3258

Aljassim, N., & Ostini, R. (2020). Health literacy in rural and urban populations: A systematic review. *Patient Education and Counseling, 103*(10), 2142–2154. https://doi.org/10.1016/j.pec.2020.06.007

Anderson, B., Gingery, A., McClellan, M., Rose, R., Schmitz, D., & Schou, P. (2019). NRHA policy paper: Access to rural maternity care. National Rural Health Association Policy Brief. Retrieved from www.ruralhealth.us/NRHA/media/Emerge_NRHA/Advocacy/Policy%20documents/2019-NRHA-Policy-Document-Access-to-Rural-Maternity-Care.pdf

Armstrong-Mensah, E., Dada, D., Bowers, A., Muhammad, A., & Nnoli, C. (2021). Geographic, health care access, racial discrimination, and socioeconomic determinants of maternal mortality in Georgia, United States. *International Journal of MCH and AIDS, 10*(2), 278–286. https://doi.org/10.21106/ijma.524

Bathija, P. (2020, November 17). Improving access to maternal care in rural communities. AHA. www.aha.org/news/blog/2020-11-17-improving-access-maternal-care-rural-communities

Cameron, N. A., Molsberry, R., Pierce, J. B., Perak, A. M., Grobman, W. A., Allen, N. B., Greenland, P., Lloyd-Jones, Donald M., & Khan, S. S. (2020). Pre-pregnancy hypertension among women in rural and urban areas of the United States. *Journal of the American College of Cardiology, 76*(22), 2611–2619. https://doi.org/10.1016/j.jacc.2020.09.601

Centers for Medicare & Medicaid Services. (2019). Rural maternal healthcare. CMS. www.cms.gov/About-CMS/Agency-Information/OMH/equity-initiatives/rural-health/rural-maternal-health

Cole, M. B., Wright, B., Wilson, I. B., Galarraga, O., & Trivedi, A. N. (2018). Medicaid expansion and community health centers: Care quality and service use increased for rural patients. *Health Affairs, 37*(6), 900–907.

Collier, A. Y., & Molina, R. L. (2019). Maternal mortality in the United States: Updates on trends, causes, and solutions. *NeoReviews, 20*(10), e561–e574. https://doi.org/10.1542/neo.20-10-e561

Conover, C. J., & Bailey, J. (2020). Certificate of need laws: A systematic review and cost-effectiveness analysis. *BMC Health Services Research, 20*, 748. https://doi.org/10.1186/s12913-020-05563-1

Cornthwaite, K., Edwards, S., & Siassakos, D. (2013). Reducing risk in maternity by optimising teamwork and leadership: An evidence-based approach to save mothers and babies. *Best Practice & Research: Clinical Obstetrics & Gynaecology, 27*(4), 571–581. https://doi.org/10.1016/j.bpobgyn.2013.04.004

Cross, S. H., Califf, R. M., & Warraich, H. J. (2021). Rural-urban disparity in mortality in the US from 1999 to 2019. *JAMA, 325*(22), 2312–2314. https://doi.org/10.1001/jama.2021.5334

Cyr, M. E., Etchin, A. G., Guthrie, B. J., & Benneyan, J. C. (2019). Access to specialty healthcare in urban versus rural US populations: A systematic literature review. *BMC Health Services Research, 19*(1), 1–17.

Dearinger, A.T. (2020). COVID-19 reveals emerging opportunities for rural public health. *American Journal of Public Health, 110*, 1277–1278. https://doi.org/10.2105/AJPH.2020.305864

Douthard, R. A., Martin, I. K., Chapple-McGruder, T., Langer, A., & Chang, S. (2021). U.S. maternal mortality within a global context: Historical trends, current state, and future directions. *Journal of Women's Health, 30*(2), 168–177. https://doi.org/10.1089/jwh.2020.8863

Douthit, N., Kiv, S., Dwolatzky, T., & Biswas, S. (2015). Exposing some important barriers to health care access in the rural USA. *Public Health, 129*(6), 611–620. https://doi.org/10.1016/j.puhe.2015.04.001

Drake, C., Zhang, Y., Chaiyachati, K. H., & Polsky, D. (2019). The limitations of poor broadband internet access for telemedicine use in rural America: An observational study. *Annals of Internal Medicine, 171*(5), 382–384. https://doi.org/10.7326/M19-0283

Green, B. N., & Johnson, C. D. (2015). Interprofessional collaboration in research, education, and clinical practice: working together for a better future. *Journal of Chiropractic Education, 29*(1), 1–10. https://doi.org/10.7899/JCE-14-36

Gujral, Kritee, and Basu, Anirban. (2019). Impact of rural and urban hospital closures on inpatient mortality. www.nber.org/papers/w26182 (accessed September 8, 2022).

Hirko, K. A., Kerver, J. M., Ford, S., Szafranski, C., Beckett, J., Kitchen, C., & Wendling A. L. (2020). Telehealth in response to the COVID-19 pandemic: Implications for rural health disparities. *Journal of the American Medical Informatics Association, 27*(11), 1816–1818. https://doi.org/10.1093/jamia/ocaa156

Holmes, G. M., Slifkin, R. T., Randolph, R. K., & Poley, S. (2006). The effect of rural hospital closures on community economic health. *Health Services Research, 41*(2), 467–485.

Hughes, L., & Vohra, S. (2021). Rural health care just got an advocate in Pa.'s Levine: Five ways she and Biden's team can help it thrive. Pennsylvania Capital-Star , March 26. www.penncapital-star.com/commentary/rural-health-care-just-got-an-advocate-in-pa-s-levine-five-ways-she-and-bidens-team-can-help-it-thrive-opinion/

Jolles, D., Stapleton, S., Wright, J., Alliman, J., Bauer, K., Townsend, C., & Hoehn-Velasco, L. (2020). Rural resilience: The role of birth centers in the United States. *Birth* (Berkeley, CA) *47*(4), 430–437. https://doi.org/10.1111/birt.12516

Joseph, K. S., Boutin, A., Lisonkova, S., Muraca, G. M., Razaz, N., John, S., Mehrabadi, A., Sabr, Y., Ananth, C. V., & Schisterman, E. (2021). Maternal mortality in the United States: Recent trends, current status, and future considerations. *Obstetrics and Gynecology, 137*(5), 763–771. https://doi.org/10.1097/AOG.0000000000004361

Kozhimannil, K. B., Henning-Smith, C., & Hung, P. (2016). The practice of midwifery in rural US hospitals. *Journal of Midwifery & Women's Health*, *61*(4), 411–418. https://doi.org/10.1111/jmwh.12474

Kozhimannil, K. B., Hung, P., Henning-Smith, C., Casey, M. M., & Prasad, S. (2018). Association between loss of hospital-based obstetric services and birth outcomes in rural counties in the United States. *JAMA, 319*(12), 1239–1247. https://doi.org/10.1001/jama.2018.1830

Kozhimannil, K. B., Interrante, J. D., Henning-Smith, C., & Admon, L. K. (2019). Rural-urban differences in severe maternal morbidity and mortality in the US, 2007–15. *Health Affairs, 38*(12), 2077–2085. https://doi.org/10.1377/hlth aff.2019.00805

Kozhimannil, K. B., Interrante, J. D., & Tuttle, M. S. (2020). *Loss of Hospital-based Obstetric Services in Rural Counties in the United States, 2004–2018*. University of Minnesota Rural Health Research Center. Retrieved March 11, 2022, from http://rhrc.umn.edu/publication/loss-of-hospital-based-obstetric-services-in-rural-counties-in-the-united-states-2004-2018/

Leider, J. P., Meit, M. J., McCullough, M., Resnick, B., Dekker, D., Alfonso, Y.N., & Bishai, D. (2020). The state of rural public health: Enduring needs in a new decade. *American Journal of Public Health, 110*, 1283–1290, https://doi.org/10.2105/AJPH.2020.305728

MacDorman, M. F., & Declercq, E. (2018). The failure of United States maternal mortality reporting and its impact on women's lives. *Birth* (Berkeley, CA), *45*(2), 105–108. https://doi.org/10.1111/birt.12333

MacDorman, M. F., Thoma, M., Declcerq, E., & Howell, E. A. (2021). Racial and ethnic disparities in maternal mortality in the United States using enhanced vital records, 2016-2017. *American Journal of Public Health, 111*(9), 1673–1681.

Manlove, J., and Whitacre, B., Eds. (2017). Short-term economic impact of rural hospital closures. (No. 1377-2016-109896). Selected paper prepared for presentation at the Southern Agricultural Economics Association's 2017 Annual Meeting, Mobile, Alabama, February 4–7, 2017. https://ageconsearch.umn.edu/record/252716/

McCarthy, S., Moore, D., Smedley, W. A., Crowley, B. M., Stephens, S. W., Griffin, R. L., Tanner, L. C., & Jansen, J. O. (2021). Impact of rural hospital closures on health-care access. *Journal of Surgical Research, 258*, 170–178. https://doi.org/10.1016/j.jss.2020.08.055

Mobley, S. C., Thomas, S. D., Sutherland, D. E., Hudgins, J., Ange, B. L., & Johnson, M. H. (2014). Maternal health literacy progression among rural perinatal women. *Maternal and Child Health Journal, 18*(8), 1881–1892. https://doi.org/10.1007/s10995-014-1432-0

National Advisory Committee on Rural Health and Human Services (NACRHHS). (2020). *Maternal and Obstetric Care Challenges in Rural America*. May. Retrieved March 11, 2022, from www.ruralhealthinfo.org/webinars/nacrhhs-maternal-care

National Conference of State Legislatures. (2021). Certificate of need (CON) state laws. Retrieved from www.ncsl.org/research/health/con-certificate-of-need-state-laws.aspx

Neal, S. M., Travers, M. E., & Brastow, I. (2021). When X shouldn't mark the spot: A crosswalk to a unified code of ethics for collaboration in the COVID-19 era. *Public Integrity,* 23(4), 349–368. https://doi.org/10.1080/10999 922.2020.1869407

Nicholas, G., Sharma, S., Walton, M., Hepi, M., & Hide, S. (2022). Critical collaboration model: An enhanced model to support public health collaboration. *Health Promotion International,* 37(1), daab075. https://doi.org/10.1093/hea pro/daab075

Office of Disease Prevention and Health Promotion. (2020). *Social Determinants of Health—Healthy People 2030.* Retrieved April 9, 2022, from https://health. gov/healthypeople/priority-areas/social-determinants-health

Rivers, P. A., Fottler, M. D., & Younis, M. Z. (2007). Does certificate of need really contain hospital costs in the United States? *Health Education Journal,* 66(3), 229–244. https://doi.org/10.1177/0017896907080127

Rural Health Information Hub. (2021). Telehealth use in rural healthcare overview. Retrieved March 11, 2022, from www.ruralhealthinfo.org/topics/ telehealth

Rural Obstetric Unit Closures and Maternal and Infant Health. (2021, February). www.ruralhealth.us/advocate/policy-documents

Sheps Center. (2022). Rural hospital closures. Sheps Center. www.shepscenter. unc.edu/programs-projects/rural-health/rural-hospital-closures/ (accessed September 8, 2022).

Simpson, J. B. (1985). State certificate-of-need programs: The current status. American *Journal of Public Health,* 75(10), 1225–1229. https://doi.org/ 10.2105/AJPH.75.10.1225

Statz, M., & Evers, K. (2020). Spatial barriers as moral failings: What rural distance can teach us about women's health and medical mistrust author names and affiliations. *Health & Place,* 64, 102396. https://doi.org/10.1016/j.healthpl ace.2020.102396

US Department of Health and Human Services. (2020). *Healthy Women, Healthy Pregnancies, Healthy Futures: Action Plan to Improve Maternal Health in America.* https://aspe.hhs.gov/system/files/aspe-files/264076/healthy-women- healthy-pregnancies-healthy-future-action-plan_0.pdf

Vedam, S., Stoll, K., MacDorman, M., Declercq, E., Cramer, R., Cheyney, M., ... & Powell Kennedy, H. (2018). Mapping integration of midwives across the United States: Impact on access, equity, and outcomes. *PloS One,* 13(2), e0192523.

Whitman, A., De Lew, N., Chappel, A., Aysola, V., Zuckerman, R., & Sommers, B. D. (2022). *Addressing social determinants of health: Examples of successful evidence-based strategies and current federal efforts.* US Department of Health and Human Services, Office of Health Policy.

CASE STUDY: MATERNAL HEALTH AND THE HEALTHY START PROGRAM

Mary Ellen Travers and Sue M. Neal

Introduction

Living in a rural area should not determine whether a pregnant mother will have a safe delivery free from complications and without risk to her life or her general health. Yet it appears to do just that. Rural mothers have been found to have a greater chance of severe maternal morbidity and maternal mortality than those living in urban areas (Kozhimannil et al., 2019). To provide for more equitable outcomes for mothers, programs need to be developed that are unique to the needs of each community in order to address place-based disparities and the social determinants of health that influence health outcomes.

One maternal health program, the Healthy Start Program, provides tailored community resources to mothers. The program was started in 1991 as a presidential initiative by George H. W. Bush, and was eventually authorized as part of the Children's Health Act of 2000 by Congress (National Healthy Start Association, 2022). There are currently over 100 federally funded Healthy Start Projects in the US and the program specializes in home visiting and outreach (National Healthy Start Association, 2021). This case study will review the Healthy Start Program and challenge readers to think through the successes and limitations of the program among rural mothers.

The Healthy Start Program has been proven to be successful in reducing infant mortality within communities, and provides many services to mothers and their family to improve health outcomes before, during, and after pregnancy (HRSA MCHB, 2022; Wilson et al., 2018). This program

DOI: 10.4324/9781003287766-17

has strengths that rural areas could benefit from, and could help provide care to rural mothers. Program planners should consider this program model when creating rural maternal health programs to provide more access to maternal care, but should also ensure factors specific to rural mothers are addressed.

Healthy Start Program Overview

The Healthy Start Program invests in communities where the infant mortality rates are at least 1.5 times higher than the US national average. The program has two primary aims: (1) to improve health outcomes before, during, and after pregnancy, and (2) to reduce racial and ethnic differences in rates of negative maternal health outcomes and infant deaths (HRSA MCHB, 2022). The common principles of the program include innovation in service delivery, public education, community commitment and involvement, personal responsibility demonstrated by expectant parents, multi-agency participation, increased access to care, and integration of health and social services (National Healthy Start Association, 2022). The Healthy Start Program also addresses multiple issues such as the provision of adequate prenatal care, promotion of positive prenatal health behaviors, meeting basic health needs, enabling client empowerment, reducing barriers to access, and advocating fatherhood and male involvement (National Healthy Start Association, 2022).

Healthy Start Program Strengths

One unique aspect of the Healthy Start Program is the degree to which the program integrates the voices and leadership of local community members. Every project develops a consortium of community members, also known as a Community Action Network or CAN. Members include neighborhood residents, medical providers, clients, social service agencies, businesses, and faith-based representatives (National Healthy Start Association, 2021). This approach exemplifies interprofessional collaboration and a "whole of community" approach to ensure that the community is engaged in the solution. This program not only provides parenting, health education, and care coordination for appointments for prenatal and postpartum care, but also provides depression screening referrals and follow-ups, infant and child health follow-ups, and fatherhood programs. The program also works with families before, during, and after pregnancy until the child is 18 months old (National Healthy Start Association, 2021).

The program's outreach workers and home visitors are made up of women who live in the community. This helps to address any potential mistrust by patients, especially if the home visitor or outreach worker is part of the community's trusted social network. The program also provides jobs to women (National Healthy Start Association, 2021). The health education portion of the program could also improve health literacy among participants, and there is continuity for the participant as the program doesn't just provide one point of care visit, but follows the mother throughout her pregnancy and afterwards. The Healthy Start Program appears to meet mothers and other family members where they are, and brings resources to them. This provides a much-needed approach to providing maternal care to the mothers who need it most.

Healthy Start Program Limitations

While there are Healthy Start Programs in over 35 states, there is no specific evaluation of how successful the Healthy Start Program is in rural settings. Abt Associates conducted a point-in-time evaluation of the Healthy Start Program of the third year in a fiveyear grant cycle (Hitchcock et al., 2020). Ninety-five program grantees were analyzed, with only 20 percent located in rural areas (Hitchcock et al., 2020). A strength of the Healthy Start Program is the interprofessional collaboration and community action network, yet it may be very difficult to establish this type of network when rural areas simply lack providers. An evaluation of the Healthy Start Program in rural communities would provide more insight into challenges and successes of the program in a rural setting. Additional research that explored how telemedicine, or other health technologies could be used to overcome the challenges of gaps in providers to serve on CANs.

Recommended Reading

On the Social Determinants of Health we recommend Office of Disease Prevention and Health Promotion (2020) and on the Healthy Start Program HRSA MCHB, (2022).

Discussion and Exercise

We have reviewed a maternal health program that has been used in the US and identified strengths, limitations, and provided recommendations for improvement. Now it's your turn.

Put yourself in the position of a local government administrator in a small, rural community. You have been tasked with creating a maternal health program. In this community, a hospital recently closed. The next closest hospital is over an hour away, and there are no sidewalks or bus routes. There are also no primary care physicians within the community, and no OB-GYN providers at the closest hospital. The population is low-income, most households do not have a car, and the ones who do only have one shared vehicle. The closest gas station is at least two miles away and gas prices have recently increased. Most community members have a high school degree, but few went to college. There was a local pop-up clinic 20 minutes away from the center of the community. However, after one of the community members had a poor experience, mistrust in the clinic spread, resulting in no one wanting to go, so it closed.

- Consider this community and identify what social determinants of health might be complicating the health outcomes for expectant mothers.
- Based on your understanding of the unique challenges that confront the provision of maternal care in small town and rural communities, does the Healthy Start Program have the potential to be an effective solution there?
- Consider a specific community and identify what questions a local leader would need to ask in order to determine if their community would benefit from the Healthy Start Program.
- Research the requirements for a community to participate in the Healthy Start Program. Based on your analysis, would this be a feasible program for most small or rural towns to participate in?
- What professionals would you want to include for interprofessional collaboration when planning and implementing your program?
- How will you evaluate your program to identify what is working and what is not working? After identifying any parts of the program that are not working, how will you address and improve them?

References

Health Resources and Services Administration Maternal & Child Health Bureau (HRSA MCHB). (2022). *Healthy Start.* https://mchb.hrsa.gov/programs-imp act/healthy-start

Hitchcock, S., Villalba, B., Etolue, J., Loeffler, A., & Flygare, C. (2020). Analysis of the national Healthy Start program of the Maternal and Child Health Bureau, Health Resources, and Services Administration. https://healthystartepic.org/wp-content/uploads/2021/07/HS-Evaluation-Final-Report_2.19.20-Final-NoWa termark.pdf

Kozhimannil, K. B., Interrante, J. D., Henning-Smith, C., & Admon, L. K. (2019). Rural-urban differences in severe maternal morbidity and mortality in the US, 2007–15. *Health Affairs, 38*(12), 2077–2085. https://doi.org/10.1377/hlth aff.2019.00805

National Healthy Start Association. (2021). *Healthy Start to the Rescue.* Retrieved from https://441563-2014355-raikfcquaxqncofqfm.stackpathdns.com/wp-cont ent/uploads/2021/06/Healthy-Start-to-the-Rescue-1.pdf

National Healthy Start Association. (2022). National Healthy Start Association. Retrieved April 15, 2022, from www.nationalhealthystart.org/healthy-start-ini tiative/

Office of Disease Prevention and Health Promotion. (2020). *Social Determinants of Health—Healthy People 2030.* Retrieved April 9, 2022, from https://health. gov/healthypeople/priority-areas/social-determinants-health

Wilson, R., Salihu, H., Salemi, J., Patel, P., Daas, R., & Berry, E. (2018). Effectiveness of a federal healthy start program in reducing infant mortality. *Journal of Health Disparities Research and Practice, 10*(3). https://digitalscho larship.unlv.edu/jhdrp/vol10/iss3/7

9

RURAL PARKS AND RECREATION

Understanding and Meeting the Needs

Clement Lau

Introduction

Rural areas have unique park and recreation needs and preferences due to demographics, location, topography, history, and other factors. The approaches and methods used to reach out to residents, collect their input, and analyze issues related to access to parks and recreational programming must be tailored and appropriate for the rural context. To better understand and address the park and recreation needs of rural communities, local governments need to continually invest time, funding, and other resources to engage and collaborate with residents, community-based organizations, and other partners, and implement a variety of creative solutions.

Role of Local Park and Recreation Agencies

Traditionally, local park and recreation agencies serve as direct providers of parks and recreational services. As such, park agencies develop, operate, and maintain parks, manage recreational facilities, operate programs, and deliver services using public funding and government employees. Park agencies may seek input from park users, the general public, and other stakeholders, but they are fully responsible for planning and providing a variety of park and recreation services to meet community needs.

This traditional model of direct service provision has become increasingly challenging, and even impractical, due to growing and diversified

DOI: 10.4324/9781003287766-18

community needs coupled with limited public funding. Thus, many park agencies are adopting creative approaches that focus on providing these services in new ways. Agencies are looking for opportunities to provide more and improved recreational services through multiple-use facilities and partnerships with other public agencies, community-based organizations, and other entities. In a rural context where residents tend to be more hands-on and self-sufficient than their urban counterparts, some residents volunteer to be actively involved in the construction of park amenities and provision of recreational programming rather than relying solely on public park agencies.

Benefits of Parks

Increasingly, parks are considered essential infrastructure (Lau, 2017). All parks, including those in rural areas, offer a variety of environmental, social, and economic benefits within and beyond park boundaries, as summarized below.

Environmental Benefits

- Improve air quality
- Capture and clean stormwater
- Mitigate heat and stabilize temperature

Social Benefits

- Improve public health
- Improve community safety
- Enhance community cohesion
- Improve walkability
- Reduce stress and improve academic performance

Economic Benefits

- Increase property values
- Create temporary and permanent jobs

Given these benefits, it makes sense for all local governments to invest in parks. To ensure that they are making strategic investment decisions that benefit all the residents and address community priorities, park agencies must first measure and understand park needs.

Measuring and Understanding Rural Park Needs

What are the unique park and recreation needs of rural areas and what are the best ways to address them? These are key questions for local park agencies to answer. To that end, the Los Angeles County Department of Parks and Recreation (DPR), for example, has conducted various park planning efforts to collect input from residents in rural communities throughout Los Angeles County.

One of these planning projects is the 2022 Parks Needs Assessment Plus (PNA+),[1] which is a focused update to the 2016 Los Angeles Countywide Parks Needs Assessment (PNA).[2] The PNA was a historic undertaking to engage all cities and the unincorporated areas in Los Angeles County in a collaborative process to identify and quantify park need and determine the potential cost of meeting that need (Lau, 2021a, 2021b). The PNA+ builds on the PNA by providing a more in-depth and nuanced understanding of regional and rural park needs. To address a motion passed by the Los Angeles County Board of Supervisors[3] in 2019, the PNA+ comprehensively identifies, analyzes, maps, and documents regional facilities and the park needs of rural communities (Lau, 2022).

Defining Rural Study Areas

As a first step of any park and recreation needs study, agencies should identify the rural areas. As part of the PNA+, 14 rural study areas are identified within Los Angeles County in the Antelope Valley, Santa Clarita Valley, Santa Monica Mountains, and on Santa Catalina Island. These areas are not homogeneous and each has unique demographics, location, topography, history, park and recreation needs, and community preferences.

Rural areas are often characterized by their vastness and the abundance of open space. The PNA+ reveals that the rural areas of Los Angeles County are home to a significant amount of parkland, including about 1,100 acres of local parks, 12,700 acres of regional recreation parks, and 636,000 acres of nature-based recreation areas.

Engaging Rural Communities

When seeking input from residents, it is critical to develop and implement a community engagement and outreach strategy that is tailored to the needs, sensitivities, comfort levels, and preferences of rural residents. This may require 1) meeting rural residents where they are, such as participating in community-led or organized events or gatherings such as festivals and fairs; and 2) hosting standalone meetings to engage the public specifically on rural park and recreation issues.

As part of the PNA+, we partnered with local community-based organizations to collect input from rural residents using a variety of methods, including key stakeholder interviews, surveys, public workshops, tables at community events, social media, and meetings with town councils formed specifically to represent the interests of unincorporated rural communities. We also coordinated with staff from the board of supervisor offices, various friends of park groups, and community-based organizations to ensure that we heard from as many residents as possible to gain a thorough understanding of rural park needs. Not all of these activities were in the original outreach plan; a few were added based on feedback received throughout the process. Flexibility is critical and park agencies should be prepared and willing to adjust or modify engagement and outreach methods and strategies as needed.

Land Rich, Amenities Poor

While rural areas are generally rich in parkland, they still have unmet park and recreation needs. The abundance of rural open space does not offset residents' need for additional rural parks, recreational amenities, and programming.

In Los Angeles County, for example, the PNA+ reveals that the Antelope Valley is lacking in certain amenities, especially water-based recreation facilities such as swimming pools and splash pads, shaded seating and play areas, and trails. Also, many of the existing local parks are old and have deferred maintenance and improvement needs. Another identified need is for more park facilities and amenities that serve local residents on Santa Catalina Island which is a popular tourist destination. In addition, residents in the Santa Monica Mountains, which is a national recreation area, pointed out the urgent need to acquire open space and natural areas to preserve habitats, protect watersheds, and facilitate wildlife movement.

Rural residents use their local parks for a variety of reasons. As part of the PNA+, rural residents in the county shared that they visited local parks because of:

- **Family Activities:** Parks provide space to spend time with family and friends, and opportunities for active recreation for all ages.
- **Affordability:** Parks are usually free and provide an opportunity for family time without the need to spend money.
- **Shade:** Some parks have shade which is hard to come by in desert communities.
- **Aquatic and Water Activities:** Some parks provide places for kids and families to cool off, including splash pads and pools, and access to activities like fishing.

- **Diversity:** Residents enjoy the diversity of people they see using parks.
- **Community Events:** Parks provide places for cultural celebrations, concerts and festivals, and many offer educational programs by park staff.
- **Cultural Pride:** Parks provide opportunities to learn about local history and honor the lands of Indigenous peoples and build a collective sense of stewardship and purpose.
- **Wildlife and Nature:** Parks offer opportunities for bird watching and other wildlife viewing, and local wildlife reserves and conservation areas capture the natural essence of the region.
- **Relaxation and Reflection:** Parks provide benefits to mental health, and spaces to spend time in nature away from technology and busyness of everyday life.

Population Vulnerability

Population density is often used as a primary metric to identify areas of high park need. While this makes sense for urban areas, it is less applicable as an indicator of need in rural areas. As part of the PNA+, we examined population vulnerability using data from the California Healthy Places Index (HPI) to help identify rural recreation priority areas. Specifically, four dimensions of population vulnerability are used for analysis in the PNA+, including: 1) social barriers like poverty and unemployment; 2) transportation barriers like limited access to public transit or automobile; 3) health vulnerability like reduced life expectancy at birth; and 4) environmental vulnerability like a high number of excessive heat days and limited tree canopy.

Rural residents face social and transportation barriers as well as health and environmental vulnerabilities that may differ from those experienced by urban dwellers. For example, the lack of public infrastructure such as sidewalks and bike lanes, limited community resources, and social isolation may impact the mental and physical health and wellbeing of rural residents. In addition to the four population vulnerability dimensions, we also considered proximity to rural recreation sites and proximity to recreational opportunity types, in terms of amenities.

A variety of challenges and barriers also prevent rural residents from using parks and recreational facilities. For example, residents of LA County's rural communities identified the following barriers:

- **Long Distance:** Some rural areas have few parks of any size, and many residents and families must travel long distances to parks and facilities.

- **Lack of Transit:** Public transit wait times to parks can be up to two hours or more and there are few options for carpooling or shuttles. Most rural residents have to drive to get to parks and facilities, but not everyone has access to a car.
- **Limited Parking:** There is not enough parking for cars or horse trailers, and the high cost of parking at facilities is a barrier for lower income residents.
- **Lack of Shade:** There are no shade structures in seating and play areas, and trails and paths in parks do not always have shade.
- **Limited Access to Water:** There is a lack of water facilities and features like fountains, pools, and splash pads to keep residents cool and hydrated in hot months.
- **Safety Concerns:** More lighting at parks is needed, especially after dark. Better trailhead maintenance and coordination among different types of trail users is needed to improve trail safety, especially for equestrians and hikers.
- **Lack of Information:** There is not enough information about events and facilities at local parks, or how to get there.
- **Inadequate Signage:** Signage is not maintained or provided in multiple languages.
- **Limited Americans with Disability Act (ADA) Accessibility:** Better wheelchair and disabled access is needed in parks and on trails.
- **Limited Native American and Tribal Access:** Tribal members do not have land access for ceremonial purposes and other practices and need privacy during gatherings and activities.

Measuring Rural Park Access

Park access is often measured in terms of the percentage of residents in a community living within a half-mile of a park. This metric has been made popular by the ten-minute walk campaign which is a national initiative to ensure that everyone in a city has safe, easy access to a quality park within a ten-minute walk of home by 2050. While this metric makes sense in urban areas, it is less applicable in rural areas where residents are less able and/or less likely to walk to a park due to the spread-out nature of rural areas, safety issues associated with the lack of pedestrian infrastructure (like sidewalks, street trees), challenging weather conditions (like excessive heat, strong winds), and other factors. On average, only 19 percent of rural residents in Los Angeles County live within a half-mile walk of a rural recreation site. In comparison, the 2016 PNA reported that 49 per cent of residents countywide lived within a half-mile walk of a local park.

Thus, in addition to walkability, the PNA+ also examines park access via other travel modes, including driving, bicycling, and taking public transit. An average of 90 percent of rural residents live within a five-mile drive of a rural recreation site. However, there are communities along the northern Los Angeles County line in the Antelope Valley and in the western reaches of the Santa Clarita Valley that are located beyond ten miles from any rural recreation site. Rural residents also overwhelmingly lack public transit access to rural recreation sites, with only 2 percent of such sites being served by public transit; this is defined as being located within a half-mile walk of a public transit stop.

Meeting Rural Park Needs and Improving Rural Park Access

Rural residents should be considered experts on their own park needs and consulted for ideas on how best to address those needs. Rural residents in LA County, for example, offered the following suggestions to increase and improve visits to rural parks and recreational facilities:

- **Expanded Transit Options:** Improved and more frequent public transit service, carpools, and shuttle options to parks.
- **Increased Parking:** Affordable parking options with ample space for horse trailers and electric car charging stations.
- **More Shade:** Shaded seating, play areas, and walking trails, and shaded greenbelts between and around parks.
- **More Access to Water:** More hydration stations for people and animals, and additional water facilities and features like pools and splash pads to keep residents cool in hot months and provide swimming lessons.
- **Enhanced Safety Measures:** Improved lighting at parks, more desert walking paths, and better maintenance of trailheads.
- **Better Access to Information:** More information about events at local parks, public transit to parks, and walking and hiking opportunities at wildlife sanctuaries. More publicity about community workshops and other opportunities to provide feedback.
- **Enhanced Signage:** Signage maintained and provided in multiple languages, as well as additional interpretive and wildlife identification signage needed along trails.
- **Improved ADA Accessibility:** Trails and parks with better wheelchair and disabled access, and playground equipment that is accessible.
- **Expanded Native American and Tribal Access:** Privacy for ancestral practice, and land access for gatherings and events.
- **More Cultural Events and Activities:** More community events like art shows and concerts.

- **Improved Maintenance and Infrastructure:** Better upkeep of restroom facilities, improved lighting on streets and paths, trash and vegetation overgrowth removal in parks and on trails.
- **Enhanced Trails and Trail Safety:** Protected and safe bike trails to connect users to parks, and conflicts between trail users addressed to ensure trails are safe for horses, riders, and other users.
- **More Facilities for Equestrian Use:** Staging areas for horses and trailers at trailheads with trees, water, and picnic tables, and a place to host horse shows and equestrian events.
- **Additional Programs:** More park activities and programs available to people of all ages.
- **Expanded Recreation Facilities:** More tennis and pickleball courts, and swimming facilities.

Given budget, labor, and other constraints, park agencies must be creative and bold in how they meet the diverse and growing recreational needs of rural communities. Just as no single agency can do it all, no single solution will be adequate. There are a variety of ways to address the rural park needs and improve rural park access. Highlighted below are examples of key strategies which may be implemented depending on the characteristics of a community as well as the availability of funding, staffing, and other resources:

- **Provide Transportation to Regional and Rural Recreation Sites**
  Public transit service is often lacking in rural areas. One of the key issues identified through the PNA+ is the lack of public transit access to recreation sites. Examples of services that can be expanded to address this need include a bus service[4] which takes inland residents to beaches during the summer and an on-request micro-transit[5] which serves rural communities by connecting them with important destinations like parks and libraries.
- **Develop New Parks**
  Another strategy is to develop new parks in rural communities which lack such facilities. For example, DPR is pursuing funding to develop a new three-acre local park in the community of Littlerock in the Antelope Valley. Proposed park amenities include a restroom building, shaded picnic areas and children's play areas, an equestrian pen with tie-ups and water, shaded fitness area, art/interpretive elements, picnic tables, bike racks, a gazebo, and porch swings (Drake, 2020, 2021).
- **Improve and Expand Existing Parks**
  For those rural areas that already have parks, improving and/ or expanding them would be a logical and economical way to meet

community needs. DPR, for example, has developed a conceptual plan to expand the 9-acre Jackie Robinson Park[6] in the community of Sun Village, which is also located in the Antelope Valley. The proposed expansion includes the construction of a new splash pad, a community stage, a multi-purpose sports field, new walking paths, picnic tables, a new restroom, a new parking lot, new solar lighting, and drought-tolerant landscaping.

- **Replace Destroyed/Damaged Recreational Facilities**
  Due to natural disasters and other unforeseen circumstances, recreational facilities in rural areas may be destroyed or damaged. Thus, the replacement or renovation of these facilities is another way to address rural park needs. For example, DPR is working on plans to replace the nature center at Devil's Punchbowl,[7] a popular destination for locals and visitors and a unique 1,310-acre geological wonder which suffered extensive damage during the 2020 Bobcat Fire.[8] DPR will incorporate fire resilient architecture and best practices for building design, including the use of noncombustible materials for the building exterior. Additionally, the new nature center will include new interpretive and educational materials about fire safety, defensible space, fire ecology, and other related topics.

- **Acquire Open Space**
  It is also important to acquire open space parcels for conservation, especially in rural areas which are located within or adjacent to environmentally significant or sensitive areas. A recent example from Los Angeles County is the Mountains Recreation and Conservation Authority[9] (MRCA)'s acquisition of the final 150 acres of the 325-acre Triangle Ranch open space in the Santa Monica Mountains (Mountains Recreation and Conservation Authority, 2021). The area has long been identified as a crucial linkage for habitat preservation, watershed protection, and wildlife movement.

In addition to the above strategies, local park agencies may also explore other interventions that were originally developed within and for underserved urban communities. Some approaches that may work equally well in rural areas include the joint use of school facilities, mobile recreation, and temporary closure of streets for recreational purposes (Lau, 2012).

- **Pursue Joint or Share of School Facilities**
  Increasing access to recreational facilities that already exist at schools is one of the most effective ways to provide more opportunities for physical activity and play in rural areas. The Trust for Public Land (TPL), for example, is leading a national movement to transform schoolyards into

shared public parks as a cost-effective solution to address park equity issues. Renovated schoolyards can serve as vital green space for entire communities. A growing numbers of school districts are allowing local residents to use their school grounds after school and on weekends, giving not only students but people of all ages new access to parkland. According to TPL (2022), public schools across the US occupy about 2 million acres of land. By making schoolyards available to the public during non-school hours, school districts could provide park access for almost 20 million people, including 5.2 million children.

- **Offer Mobile Recreation**
  Given the success of mobile libraries, and the limited amount of funding to develop permanent parks, mobile recreation should be considered as a way to bring in outside resources to rural areas in need. As Loukaitou-Sideris (1995) states, "the ever-changing urban form and social ecology of neighborhoods calls for a flexible rather than rigid park design and for spatial layouts that can be easily changed in response to future needs . . . One can even think of mobile parks-spaces whose equipment and furniture can be transported to other parts of the city if the need arises." (p. 101)

Mobile recreation provides additional opportunities for residents, especially children, to play and exercise and are flexible in that they can be parked at any location where vehicles are allowed (Lau, 2020). DPR recently initiated Parks On The Move, which is a mobile recreation program that brings sports equipment, like basketball hoops, soccer balls and goals, and mobile skate ramps, to communities lacking in parks and recreational facilities.

- **Close Streets Temporarily for Recreation**
  Closing some rural streets for recreational activities temporarily is another way to create additional opportunities for recreation and physical activity. While this approach has been popular in urban areas where major streets are closed for biking, walking, and running, it can also be employed in rural areas to create more publicly accessible safe spaces for play and exercise and improve health outcomes. These "Play Streets" offer similar benefits as parks, including enhanced safety, improved health, more physical activity opportunities, better community relations, reduced traffic concerns due to street closures, and increased adult supervision (Physical Activity Research Center, 2019). Considering that main streets in small towns are often used for parades and festivals, the idea of closing these roads more regularly for the benefit of community members may be well-received.

Funding for Rural Parks

Local governments often have limited funding available to develop, operate, and maintain parks, and offer recreational programming. Some rural communities may be allocated a certain amount of parks funding based on the size of their population or on a per capita basis. However, due to small population size, the amount of funding for each rural community can be relatively low.

One way to address this limitation is for two or more rural communities to combine their funding resources. Some funding programs, like Los Angeles County's Measure A,[10] allow for this, recognizing that the sharing of annual allocation funds among multiple communities can benefit all the areas involved (Los Angeles Regional Park and Open Space District, 2022). Such pooling of resources explicitly addresses an issue discovered through the PNA+: numerous rural communities have similar requests or priorities.

While each rural community may have specific recreation preferences and needs, there are also overlaps. For example, stakeholders from several rural communities in the Antelope Valley requested more shade structures and water-based recreation facilities, especially swimming pools. Commonalities among recreation needs provide an opportunity for local park agencies to strategically locate parks and recreational facilities to address the needs of multiple communities at once, rather than try to provide each community with a separate facility, which is often infeasible due to budget, staffing, land use, and other constraints.

Some states also offer grants specifically for rural communities. The Rural Recreation and Tourism Program (RRT), for example, is a program created by the California Department of Parks and Recreation to generate new recreation opportunities within rural communities to support health-related and economic goals (California Department of Parks and Recreation, 2022). This program is funded by Proposition 68 (2018 Bond Act), which is found in Public Resources Code §80090(a)(b). Eligible projects and priorities include:

- Acquisition and development, or development of land to:
  - Create new recreational opportunities in rural communities that have a lack of outdoor recreation infrastructure. Projects that support both economic and health-related goals for residential recreation and attract out-of-town visitors are given priority.
- New opportunities are the creation of facilities that currently do not exist, and may include but are not limited to:
  - Accessible trails and bikeways for wildlife viewing or other significant draws

- Sports complexes that host travel ball tournaments and leagues
- Visitor centers that interpret a significant historic or natural resource
- Amphitheaters that support performing arts and other cultural recreation attractions
- Campgrounds
- Access to waterways
- Aquatic centers

The types of eligible projects listed above clearly address some the priorities identified by rural residents in Los Angeles County as well as other parts of the country. However, it also raises the issue of attracting out-of-town visitors and how they may impact rural areas. As part of the PNA+, some rural residents observed that use of local park facilities from out-of-town visitors increased during the COVID-19 pandemic. They also pointed out that outdoor recreation areas are needed not only to meet the needs of rural community members, but also serve visitors.

Concluding Thoughts

Rural areas certainly have unique park and recreation needs, as documented in studies like Los Angeles County's PNA+. It is important that park agencies take the time and employ appropriate methods to understand and capture the desires and priorities of rural residents. To address the identified needs and improve park access in rural communities, park agencies must continually engage and collaborate with residents, community-based organizations, and other public agencies, and pursue funding and other resources to implement solutions such as those described above.

Special thanks to rural residents of Los Angeles County for their input, community-based organizations for their assistance with outreach and engagement, and MIG for their work on the PNA+.

Notes

1 For more information, please visit this website: https://lacountyparkneeds.org/pnaplus-report/
2 For more information, please visit this website: https://lacountyparkneeds.org/pna-home/
3 The five-member Board of Supervisors, created by the state Legislature in 1852, is the governing body of the County of Los Angeles.
4 An example is the Beach Bus offered by the Los Angeles County Public Works: https://dpw.lacounty.gov/pdd/beach_bus/
5 An example is Metro Micro offered by the Los Angeles County Metropolitan Transportation Authority: https://micro.metro.net/

6 More information about Jackie Robinson Park is available at: https://parks. lacounty.gov/jackie-robinson-park/
7 More information about Devil's Punchbowl is available at: https://parks.lacou nty.gov/devils-punchbowl-natural-area-and-nature-center/
8 The Bobcat Fire was a fire that started on September 6, 2020. By December 18, 2020, it was fully contained and had burned 115,796 acres in the central San Gabriel Mountains, in and around the Angeles National Forest. It was one of the largest fires on record in Los Angeles County to date. For more information, please visit: https://en.wikipedia.org/wiki/Bobcat_Fire
9 The MRCA is local government public entity dedicated to the preservation and management of open space and parkland, watershed lands, trails, and wildlife habitat.
10 Measure A is a parks funding measured passed by Los Angeles County voters in November 2016 (with an approval rate of nearly 75%) and generates about $94 million in revenues annually.

References

10-Minute Walk. (2022). About 10-minute walk campaign. https://10minutewalk. org/#About
California Department of Parks and Recreation. (2022). *Rural Recreation and Tourism Program*. www.parks.ca.gov/?page_id=28439
Drake, J. (2020). Primmer Park grant options mulled. *Antelope Valley Press*, September 27. www.avpress.com/news/primmer-park-grant-options-mulled/ article_b6876d9a-006d-11eb-a756-171ffc07143f.html
Drake, J. (2021). Officials scale back Primmer Park plans. *Antelope Valley Press*. www.avpress.com/news/officials-scale-back-primmer-park-plans/article_79e17 84e-6db0-11eb-9bfe-53d6c527a354.html
Lau, C. (2012). Alternative approach to meet the recreational needs of underserved communities: The case of Florence-Firestone. *Public Works Management & Policy*, *17*(4), 388–402.
Lau, C. (2017). Nurturing neighborhoods. *Planning*, *83*(10), 20–25.
Lau, C. (2020). Mobile recreation for fun, health and wellness. *Parks & Recreation*, *55*(7), 24–25.
Lau, C. (2021a). Conducting a regional and rural parks needs assessment. Open Space. March 24. www.nrpa.org/blog/conducting-a-regional-and-rural-parks-needs-assessment/
Lau, C. (2021b). From plans to parks. *Parks & Recreation*, *56*(5), 40–45.
Lau, C. (2022). Rural parks and recreation. *Parks & Rec Business.*, October. www. parksandrecbusiness.com/articles/rural-parks-and-recreation
Los Angeles County Department of Parks and Recreation. (2016). *Los Angeles Countywide Comprehensive Parks and Recreation Needs Assessment Final Report*. https://lacountyparkneeds.org/final-report/
Los Angeles County Department of Parks and Recreation. (2022). *Parks Needs Assessment Plus*. https://lacountyparkneeds.org/pnaplus-report/
Los Angeles Regional Park and Open Space District. (2022). *Grants Administration Manual for Measure A*. https://rposd.lacounty.gov/measure-a-grants-adminis tration-manual/

Loukaitou-Sideris, A. (1995). Urban form and social context: Cultural differentiation in the uses of urban parks. *Journal of Planning Education and Research, 14(2)*, 89–102.

Mountains Recreation and Conservation Authority. (2021). Mountains Recreation and Conservation Authority completes acquisition of 325-acre Triangle Ranch at the gateway to the Santa Monica Mountains National Recreation Area. https://mrca.ca.gov/press/mountains-recreation-and-conservation-authority-completes-acquisition-of-325-acre-triangle-ranch-at-the-gateway-to-the-santa-monica-mountains-national-recreation-area/

Physical Activity Research Center. (2019). Implementing play streets in rural communities. www.baylor.edu/publichealth/index.php?id=961864

Trust for Public Land. (2022). *Community Schoolyards™ projects*. www.tpl.org/community-schoolyards

Subsection: Human Resources

10

HUMAN RESOURCES

Recruitment and Retention in Small Cities and Towns

Jaymes Vettraino and Sue M. Neal

Introduction

Government jobs were once highly sought after due to their stability, relatively high rates of pay, health insurance, and retirement benefits. Shifts in the attitude toward government and changing priorities of the "new" workforce have caused a crisis in the recruitment and retention of the next generation of local-level bureaucrats (Linos, 2018). Demographic swings are another pressure confronting small governments in need of staff. Individuals born between 1946 and 1964 (baby boomers) came of age during a time when government service was aspirational, longer term employment by a single employer was expected, and local government jobs offered both stability and excellent fringe benefits. In 2018, another generation, millennials (born between 1981 and 1996), was about to become America's largest (Fry, 2020) and the most sought-after demographic for employers, including local government. Unlike the prior generation, by 2018, employment in local government had become more transient and fringe benefits no longer outpaced those offered by the private sector.

Local jurisdictions are not immune from the broader trends in civil service hiring where outsourcing, efficiency pressures, and deregulation have lowered the per capita public workforce, while at the same time the overall workforce is increasing as populations increase (Berman et al., 2021). According to a 2019 survey by the Center for State and Local Government Excellence, hiring government employees at the local level will outpace state-level hiring with an anticipated increase of 7.4 percent in local government hiring in the years from 2016 to 2026 (Centre for

DOI: 10.4324/9781003287766-20

State and Local Government Excellence, 2019). This indicates that small towns may face stiff competition from larger cities for human resources as the decade moves forward. Small local governments may face particular difficulty recruiting for certain high-demand professionals such as those working in the field of information technology (Lan et al., 2005).

Nepotism and cronyism can be an issue in local government where elected officials have some appointment power to fill key positions that are outside of a merit hiring process. Small towns, especially in rural or isolated regions, face two distinct merit hiring challenges. First, familial and friend relationships create strong ties between people. When a member of a family or friend group is elected and has hiring power, he or she likely looks to those they know and trust. Second, a limited number of applicants results in a challenge in recruitment and retention of qualified employees. Nepotism and/or cronyism have been proposed to include a broad range of actions including favoritism in hiring or contracting between two individuals who have a relationship which may manifest as immediate or extended family, friendship, or shared organizational affiliation (club or professional) (Gyimah-Boadi, 2000). Research has indicated that nepotism in government is most prevalent when positions pay relatively higher amounts compared to other opportunities in the local job market (Chassamboulli & Gomes, 2021).

There is a distinct lack of research addressing the broad question of human resource recruitment and retention in small town government. Instead, we tie the benefits of working for small towns to the work motivations of the next generation of small town leaders and see these as unique opportunities for recruitment through specific tools such as social media. We then look at innovative approaches to both recruitment and retention being used in small towns and provide detailed best practices to guide the implementation of these selected strategies. We close by examining the role of higher education institutions as key partners in the development of the next generation of local government leaders.

The Benefits of Being Local

While small and rural governments may face significant challenges in the recruitment and retention of municipal employees, there are some distinct advantages for these employers. Government work offers the opportunity to help people (Frank & Lewis, 2004). The opportunity to have an immediate and meaningful impact on their community is something that may offer strong appeal to young professionals seeking civic employment and meaningful rewards in their employment (Suleman & Nelson, 2011). The desire to engage with their communities is not only a motivator for employees. Small town citizens prioritize civic engagement, which is found to be associated with increased public satisfaction in the provision of public services (Morton et al., 2008). While a low- to mid-level bureaucrat may be lost in the noise of a large city, in the small town everyone from the water billing clerk to the city manager has direct contact with the public and the real opportunity to directly impact individual citizens and have meaningful input on key community issues.

Small towns offer their own unique culture atmosphere that may appeal to the right candidate. Research around recruiting physicians to practice in smaller towns has indicated that those who are either rural-raised or are community-oriented were more likely to practice in small towns (Hancock et al., 2009). This implies that robust programs aimed at recruiting locally may yield long-term results in the small town. Programs that range from outreach and engagement with regional associations, development of Youth Councils, and formal internships are all key strategies aimed at the cultivation of local talent and are covered in detail later in this chapter. Small towns can also be incubators where innovation in public sector service delivery may flourish (Chase, 2021). The combination of a unique sense of place and the opportunity for innovation may create an attractive climate for the next generation of small town government employees.

Recruitment Strategies

Social media can be powerful tools to reach job candidates from a broad geographic and demographic pool. Social media outreach strategies should be intentional so that job opportunities rise to surface and quickly grab the attention of the desired candidate. Signals can be thought of as the key marketing message that reaches potential candidates. Research into what signals were effective at recruiting public service employees cutting through the "noise" of a robust hiring environment needed to be multi-dimensional and not focus only on aspects of public service motivation but instead focus on employment stability and reaching a gender-diverse audience (Keppeler & Papenfuß, 2021). This is far from a settled topic, however. Recruitment strategies that focus on the unique challenges of the job or the career benefits associated with the opportunity have been shown to be significantly more effective at recruiting public-sector employees (Linos, 2018). Yet research has indicated that brand signaling that rests solely on the value of making a societal impact was not effective in social media based recruiting for government employment (Keppeler & Papenfuß, 2021). Despite this research, the opportunity to make a positive difference in the world should be highlighted as an additional benefit, with the other benefits of competitive pay and employment stability.

In addition to the utilization of specific signals in social media, attention should be paid to the type of individuals being recruited. The identity of the small town in America is changing with demographic shifts. While many may still envision a homogeneous community of white, middle-class, agriculture workers (rural), or semi-skilled laborers (suburban), the face of small towns is becoming increasingly diverse (Slack & Jensen, 2020). Local governments should be intentional in their recruitment of individuals who might be underrepresented. Women also are underrepresented at all levels of local government (Holman, 2017). There are opportunities to deploy targeted recruitment on popular social media platforms. An example is LinkedIn. For low or no cost, local governments can use key search words to develop a diverse potential talent pool. Once these individuals are identified, the local government can reach out directly to market their community and employment opportunities. A distinct advantage of using tools like LinkedIn is that local governments can directly communicate with potential candidates, who may not even be looking for another job, and describe the benefits of working in their organization.

Post-military employment is another potential source of "home grown" talent in small town governance. Rural Americans make up a disproportionate number of military service employees and are also an integral part of our military. "Although rural residents account for 17% of the population, they make up 44% of the men and women who serve in uniform. In fact, approximately 6.1 million veterans currently live in rural communities" (The White House Office of the Press Secretary, 2011, p. 3). Recruitment of veterans has been a supported focus of the US government through the Transition Assistance Program (Faurer et al., 2014).

Intentional programs that engage state and regional associations to promote to college, high schools, and trade schools are one potential option for creative recruitment by small and rural governments. Small local governments may be limited in their recruiting capacity and thus narrow their reach. Active engagement with state and national associations can greatly increase that reach as well. Individually, local governments can partner with local educational institutions to create internships and youth council programs, but by design these are personalized and will focus on investing in expanding the interest of a relatively few students.

Local governments should look to their state or regional associations to develop more broad engagement and recruitment programs. Engaging with state or regional associations can take a number of forms. This could include actively sitting on committees where networking opportunities abound, advertising in association publications, or hosting events or conferences. Local government staff can directly engage in these outreach initiatives or encourage their local associations to provide greater engagement with state and regional associations. For example, Rochester Hills, Michigan, identified the Michigan Career Educator & Employer Alliance (MCEEA) and the National Association of Colleges and Employers (NACE) (Rochester Hills, 2018) as organizations to engage with to try to spread the message of local government employment opportunities. Through strategic engagement with organizations like these, local government associations can have meaningful conversations with a wide range of career counselors, with the goal of making public-service jobs/professions a priority for career counselors to promote to students.

Recruitment through Cultivating the Next Generation

Recruitment strategies can be operationalized that focus on early career cycle recruitment starting as early as high school. Programs aimed at students before they enter higher education can bring an awareness of career opportunities that exist within their own communities. This has the added benefit of keeping a local pool of potential municipal employees which may aid in retention because those students already have deep place-based ties. It also may help students see the opportunities available locally and reduce the "brain drain" that can occur in rural and small communities. Lastly, active recruitment can help governments avoid the common trap of operating only in a reactionary way (Jacobson & Sowa, 2016) and instead focus energy on proactive recruitment strategies.

The active engagement of high school students can be accomplished in a few different ways. High school students are often looking for ways to enhance their resume and be engaged in their community, which makes them a perfect match for local government service opportunities. Some cities partner with high schools to offer a "government day" to expose students to the types of job opportunities and work environments that exist in the public sector.

One unique way to engage students early on with municipal government is Youth Councils. In fact, both the students and city can benefit from a Youth Council (Rochester Hills, 2022). Youth Councils are bodies formally created by a city to represent and give voice to young people in a community. Through engaging students directly in the governance process, they become aware of the core functions of local government and may become more invested in their communities. The structure and scope of activities of Youth Councils is dynamic. Despite the advantages, they are not widely used (Collins et al., 2016).

Establishment of a Youth Council

Generally, a Youth Council is formed at the beginning of a school year, and it serves throughout that academic year. Practices to consider when developing a Youth Council program include:

1. Seats. The city should develop a specific number of Youth Council seats. A common number is to equal the number of elected officials (for example if the city has six council members and a mayor, there would be seven Youth Council seats available). The elected body enacts legislation officially recognizing the Youth Council and empowering it with specific rights and duties.
2. Applications. The Mayor or City Manager's office leads the development of a competitive and inclusive application process. Using social media and in-person messaging, the city should market the opportunity to local public, private, charter, and parochial high school students. Specific recruitment approaches that include non-traditional schools aid in building a more diverse Youth Council (Augsberger et al., 2018). The application process should engage department heads and elected officials and consider the students' interests, professional goals, demographic diversity, and community involvement. Appointments are recommended by the Mayor or City Manager, with the City Council voting to approve the appointments.
3. Meetings. The Youth Council should have consistent meetings at a cadence to match City Council meetings. During its meetings the Youth Council reviews matters to be considered by the City Council during its upcoming public meetings. If appropriate, the Youth Council drafts reports providing opinion on matters reviewed. Youth Council members attend all City Council meetings and are called upon by the elected officials to report as necessary.
4. Liaison. The city should appoint a staff member to be the liaison to the Youth Council, assisting the Youth Council in its duties and responsibilities. The liaison assures the Youth Council members receive all relevant information and delivers correspondence from the Youth Council to the elected officials and staff. Including students and young people in the decision-making process is important to aid in elevating Youth Councils. Too often, these groups are limited to the organization of recreational or leisure activities. While research has indicated that students find this type of work meaningful and engaging, it may limit the full development of the potential of the Youth Council (Nir & Perry-Hazan, 2016).
5. Involvement. In addition to the formal meeting of the Youth Council and City Council meetings, Youth Council members are invited to all

public city activities (i.e., State of the City, parades, ribbon cuttings) and may engage in as many, or as few, of these activities as they desire.

6. Continuing Education. Ongoing efforts that provide for training, skills development, opportunities to expand their social networks and providing ways to further engagement with the community can help to make sure that Youth Councils are cultivating social equality instead of reinforcing existing inequities (Augsberger et al., 2018).

Developing Formal Internship Programs

Internships are a more individualized and structured way to expose the next generation of workers than Youth Councils and usually focus on post-high school students. Organizational and interpersonal relationships that can influence people to choose to develop a career in local government can be fostered through internship programs offered within or outside of collaborative relationships with local or regional universities. Through formal and informal internships or mentorship programs local governments can develop talent for their organization and for the broader public sector.

There are a number of steps to consider when developing an effective internship program include:

1) Familiarize yourself with the Department of Labor rules around internships (for example see: www.dol.gov/agencies/whd/fact-sheets/71-flsa-internships). If internships are being offered without pay there are specific considerations that must be made under the Fair Labor Standards Act. Some key considerations include ensuring that an unpaid intern is not replacing a paid employee, directly connecting the intern's work responsibilities with their academic coursework, and having a staff person who can spend the time to directly oversee the work of the intern. This is not an exhaustive summary of the requirements.

2) Staff preparation for an intern. City department managers should develop a proposal, to be reviewed and approved by the chief administrative officer. The proposal should outline the specific objectives the department will assign to the intern. The objectives should include both independent project work and work with employees of the city. Once the chief administrative officer approves the plan the department can move forward with developing a brief position description for the internship (Troy, 2014).

3) Identification and outreach to potential candidates. A formal description of the internship opportunity should be drafted and include the required skills, any physical demands of the job, and the learning benefits an intern would expect to derive from the experience. Local

high schools, community colleges, undergraduate degree programs, masters degree programs, and individuals who desire a career change are all viable sources of interns.

4) Placement and oversight. Interns should be assigned to one city employee, who will serve as their formal connection to the organization. The intern–employee match should be based on the intern's interest and the employee's professional experience. The primary objectives of the internship will directly relate to the objectives outlined in step 2. In addition to the day-to-day internship objectives, interns should be included in departmental leadership meetings.

5) Cross-department shadowing. As part of an internship program, interns should have an opportunity to shadow department leaders outside of the department they are assigned to. Local government includes a wide diversity of professions. Students can gain a better understanding of the full operation of a city, and increase their awareness of the many professional options in local government when the internship program includes a formal shadow day with each department.

A specific example of a model student engagement program is the Pontiac (Michigan) Community Foundation's program to recruit Pontiac high schoolers to consider public administration careers with the city (Rochester University, 2022). The Foundation has partnered with a local university to coordinate generous scholarships to up to three high school students. The conditions of the scholarship include: (1) the students are selected by the Foundation based on their public administration interest, (2) the student must major in public administration or related field, (3) the student is placed with the city of Pontiac for an internship during their Junior year. This program serves as an excellent example that innovatively blends keeping talent local, high school engagement, college student recruitment, and formal internship.

Retention Strategies

Small governments are using a variety of tools to retain workers. In the previously cited survey, in-house training programs as well as tuition reimbursement schemes were two most popular strategies being employed by local governments to retain employees (Centre for State and Local Government Excellence, 2019). These programs may be difficult to put into place in a small town that has a tightly constrained human resource budget. City manager turnover is often high in any community but research identified a subset of city managers that had stayed in the position for more than 20 years and the similar characteristics of these managers was that they were located in small towns that were homogeneous and politically stable (Watson & Hassett, 2003). This is good news for these government agencies who can benefit from the rootedness of employees who have developed deep ties to their community.

Mentorship across Town

One creative way to invest in retention of employees is cross-city mentorship. Small local government organizations often only have two or three levels of management and a few individuals employed in each operational department, which may limit opportunities for upward mobility and skills-development for new employees. Further, combining direct day-to-day management and informal mentorship is not ideal, so within the flat structure of small local government, meaningful mentorship between experienced and junior employees can be extremely difficult to achieve. Local governments need to think about mentorship relationships beyond their own organizations, encouraging relationships between their employees and employees with other towns. Cross-city mentorships can provide the needed separation between direct day-to-day management, while providing younger employees with valuable informal relationships to build their technical, interpersonal, and public-sector skills. Mentoring is also a key tool to increase diversity and equity in the public sector. Small local governments can be geographically isolated from each other, making face-to-face mentorship difficult. In these cases, e-mentoring can be used (Neal et al., 2022). Mentoring through video chat tools can help bridge the gap between geographic distance and can create meaningful cross-city relationships.

Succession Planning and Compensation Studies

An additional key component in a rigorous retention plan is succession planning. Succession planning is more strategic than workforce development (Reeves, 2010). It involves the identification of the next generation of leadership but also the cultivation of those individuals so that they are prepared when it comes time to take over a higher position. The first step in succession planning is to inventory employee information including their career goals, skills, and level of commitment to the organization. The second step is for the city leaders to create an assessment of future leadership position needs, considering retirement and new positions that might be added. Using the results of the inventory and future leadership assessment, department leaders should create individualized training plans to prepare specific employees for the identified needs (Myers, 2021). While no future positions can be promised, leaders are encouraged to discuss openly with employees the training and success plans. Seeing that there are opportunities for growth and advancement may help to mitigate the brain drain that can occur if employees do not see a viable future for themselves within the local government structure. Succession planning is critical to overcome the challenges of a shrinking workforce and the evidenced link between planning and organizational effectiveness, yet it is often overlooked, particularly for senior-level government staff in local governments (Leland et al., 2012). Just as a community considers its Master Plan, Capital Plan, Budget Forecast, it should also consider adopting a Succession Plan. A formal succession plan is intended to identify employees who could fill key leadership positions.

Compensation

It is important for local governments to develop clear and appropriate compensation plans. Generally, compensation levels are considered public information and disclosed in the annual budget or may be requested through a freedom of information request. The publicness of compensation presents both a challenge and opportunity. The challenge is that communities must create a compensation plan that is clear and consistent across all levels of the organization. The opportunity is that communities can easily compare the competitiveness of the compensation they offer versus other similar communities.

An appropriate compensation plan will consider internal factors (classification) and external factors (comparable communities). Internal factors, or classifications, should be developed through a job evaluation of each position classification. The evaluations should consider factors such as skills required, responsibility level, and working conditions. The city can develop additional factors, but at a minimum these three factors comprise a basic classification review. A point system should be utilized to compare employees, with the higher level of skill, more responsible, and harder working conditions receiving a higher point level than employees with lower level of skill, less responsibility, and more comfortable working conditions. At the conclusion of this process, each employee classification can be ranked from highest to lowest point value. The second part of the compensation plan is an analysis of comparable communities. Several state associations keep compensation data for a wide variety of local government positions. Where public aggregate data are not available, the city should develop and distribute a compensation survey to similar cities. Factors to consider when determining similarity are population, revenue, proximity, and form of government. Through the review of the internal factors (the points system described above) and the external comparable community data, a local government can develop a transparent and appropriate compensation plan.

Succession planning can be combined with compensation studies to provide both a picture of where the organization is at in a competitive hiring market while also creating a road map for the future of the leadership staff.

The Role of Higher Education

Education is both a recruitment and retention strategy as partnerships with higher education institutions can be thought of as both a tool to recruit the next generation of leaders and also a key method to provide workforce development opportunities aimed at retaining the existing workforce. Small town governance is not a scaled back version of managing a large city. Instead, small and rural communities confront their own unique set of very complex challenges (Fitchen & Gittelman, 2019). Universities that have MPA programs should not overlook the unique needs and opportunities of local government employment. This may require examining the curricula and internship opportunities to align the needs of the local government workforce with the design of programs. Place-based educational and mentorship opportunities in small and rural towns may help students see first-hand the value, opportunity, and livability benefits associated with work in these areas (Hancock et al., 2009). Service learning by students enrolled in Masters of Public Administration programs has been advanced as one key way for future leaders to develop the emotional intelligence needed to navigate the uniquely engaged environment of small town governance (Catlaw & Stout, 2016).

When asked to look toward the future, state and local governments identified the recruitment of workers with the skills needed for success as one of the top three challenges they face in human resources (Centre for State and Local Government Excellence, 2019). Many of the skills they prioritize are the type of soft skills that can be challenging to assess in higher education including interpersonal skills, management skills, and written communication skills (Centre for State and Local Government Excellence, 2019). These soft skills were also enumerated as needed for other administrative professionals in rural towns such as police officers with characteristics of: integrity, service orientation, empathy, communication and human relations skills, self-control, team orientation, and problem-solving skills (Morison, n.d.).

Conclusion

The pandemic may have had significant impacts in the way and where people work. It has been theorized that the temporary shift toward remote working will stick for the longer term. The great resignation and move toward remote working means that more people may move from larger cities, which were once seen as the only opportunity for those seeking certain positions, to smaller communities for the improved quality of life. This has a number of potential impacts on the human resources of local government. Where the future will go is still undetermined but possible directions could include (1) greater pressure on local governments to provide the types of services and amenities that former city residents have grown to expect from their public service providers (both in the degree of services, the type of services, and the level of professionalism in their government workforce); (2) an increase pool of workers who may be spouses or dependents on the worker who is now able to work remotely; and (3) a decreased pool of workers because now people in small towns will have an increased diversity of remote-work professional opportunities that they did not have before.

Regardless of how future employment trends impact the recruitment and retention of small and rural government employees, it is clear that being positioned in an active—instead of reactive—position will be critical. Managers have a number of strategies that they can use that play off of the distinct advantages inherent in the small town such as the opportunity for innovation, the rewards of having an impact on the community, and the deep ties that individuals develop over years of service to small town government. By looking toward creative strategies that do not rely on a large budget, small towns can be well prepared for whatever the future brings.

References

Augsberger, A., Collins, M. E., Gecker, W., & Dougher, M. (2018). Youth civic engagement: Do youth councils reduce or reinforce social inequality? *Journal of Adolescent Research*, *33*(2), 187–208. https://doi.org/10.1177/074355841 6684957

Berman, E. M., Bowman, J. S., West, J. P., & Wart, M. R. V. (2021). Human Resource Management in *Public Service: Paradoxes, Processes, and Problems*. CQ Press.

Catlaw, T. J., & Stout, M. (2016). Governing small-town America today: The promise and dilemma of dense networks. *Public Administration Review*, *76*(2), 225–229. https://doi.org/10.1111/puar.12520

Centre for State and Local Government Excellence. (2019). *Survey Findings: State and Local Government Workforce*. Retrieved February 26, 2022, from www.slge.org/wp-content/uploads/2019/07/slge-workforce2019.pdf

Chase, S. (2021). Innovative lessons from our small and rural public libraries. *Journal of Library Administration. 61*(2), 237–243. Retrieved February 26, 2022, from www.tandfonline.com/doi/abs/10.1080/01930 826.2020.1853473

Chassamboulli, A., & Gomes, P. (2021). Jumping the queue: Nepotism and public-sector pay. *Review of Economic Dynamics, 39*, 344–366. https://doi.org/ 10.1016/j.red.2020.07.006

Collins, M. E., Augsberger, A., & Gecker, W. (2016). Youth councils in municipal government: Examination of activities, impact and barriers. *Children and Youth Services Review, 65*, 140–147. https://doi.org/10.1016/j.childyo uth.2016.04.007

Faurer, J., Rogers-Brodersen, A., & Bailie, P. (2014). Managing the re-employment of military veterans through the transition assistance program (TAP). *Journal of Business & Economics Research, 12*(1), 55–60. https://doi.org/10.19030/jber. v12i1.8378

Fitchen, J. M., & Gittelman, S. R. (2019). *Endangered Spaces, Enduring Places: Change, Identity, and Survival in Rural America.* Routledge. https://doi. org/10.4324/9780429033285

Frank, S. A., & Lewis, G. B. (2004). Government employees: Working hard or hardly working? *American Review of Public Administration, 34*(1), 36–51. https://doi.org/10.1177/0275074003258823

Fry, R. (2020). Millennials overtake Baby Boomers as America's largest generation. April 28. Pew Research Center. www.pewresearch.org/fact-tank/2020/04/28/ millennials-overtake-baby-boomers-as-americas-largest-generation/.

Gyimah-Boadi, E. (2000). Conflict of interest, nepotism, and cronyism. In *Confronting Corruption: The Elements of a National Integrity System* (ch. 21). https://bsahely.com/wp-content/uploads/2016/10/21.pdf

Hancock, C., Steinbach, A., Nesbitt, T. S., Adler, S. R., & Auerswald, C. L. (2009). Why doctors choose small towns: A developmental model of rural physician recruitment and retention. *Social Science & Medicine, 69*(9), 1368–1376. https://doi.org/10.1016/j.socscimed.2009.08.002

Holman, M. R. (2017). Women in local government: What we know and where we go from here. *State and Local Government Review, 49*(4), 285–296. https://doi. org/10.1177/0160323X17732608

Jacobson, W. S., & Sowa, J. E. (2016). Municipal human resource management: Challenges and innovative practices in turbulent times. *State and Local Government Review, 48*(2), 121–131. https://doi.org/10.1177/0160323X1 6658696

Keppeler, F., & Papenfuß, U. (2021). Employer branding and recruitment: Social media field experiments targeting future public employees. *Public Administration Review, 81*(4), 763–775. https://doi.org/10.1111/puar.13324

Lan, G. Z., Riley, L., & Cayer, N. J. (2005). How can local government become an employer of choice for technical professionals? Lessons and experiences from the city of Phoenix. *Review of Public Personnel Administration, 25*(3), 225–242. https://doi.org/10.1177/0734371X05276218

Leland, S. M., Carman, J. G., & Swartz, N. J. (2012). Understanding managerial succession planning at the local level: A study of the opportunities and challenges facing cities and counties. *National Civic Review, 101*(2), 44–51.

Linos, E. (2018). More than public service: A field experiment on job advertisements and diversity in the police. *Journal of Public Administration Research and Theory*, 28(1), 67–85. https://doi.org/10.1093/jopart/mux032

Morison, K. P. (2017). *Hiring for the 21st century law enforcement officer: Challenges, opportunities, and strategies for success*. Office of Community Oriented Policing Services.

Morton, L. W., Chen, Y., & Morse, R. S. (2008). Small town civic structure and interlocal collaboration for public services. *City & Community*, 7(1), 45–60. https://doi.org/10.1111/j.1540-6040.2007.00240.x

Myers, K. (2021). Preparing for the silver tsunami with succession planning. *PM Magazine*. https://icma.org/articles/pm-magazine/preparing-silver-tsunami-succession-planning#:~:text=This%20%E2%80%9Csilver%20tsunami%E2%80%9D%20will%20result,within%20city%20and%20county%20governments.&text=Once%20succession%20planning%20is%20fully,term%20success%20of%20the%20organization

Neal, S., Kline, A., Olejarski, A., & Gherardi, M. (2022). I'm only human: A new e-road to advancing social equity through a humanist approach to mentoring in public service. *Review of Public Personnel Administration*. https://doi.org/10.1177%2F0734371X211058180

Nir, T., & Perry-Hazan, L. (2016). The framed right to participate in municipal youth councils and its educational impact. *Children and Youth Services Review*, 69, 174–183. https://doi.org/10.1016/j.childyouth.2016.07.012

Reeves, T. Z. (2010). Mentoring programs in succession planning. *State and Local Government Review*, 42(1), 61–66. https://doi.org/10.1177/0160323X10368036

Rochester Hills, Michigan. (2018, March). *USCM/Wells Fargo Community WINS Grant Program Application*. Public document from the Office of the Mayor.

Rochester Hills, Michigan. (2022). Retrieved February 15, 2022, from www.rochesterhills.org/government/city_council/rhyouthcouncil.php

Rochester University, Rochester, Michigan, (2022, March). *Memorandum of Understanding, Rochester University and the Pontiac Community Foundation*. Document received via email from the Office of the Vice President for Admissions.

Slack, T., & Jensen, L. (2020). The changing demography of rural and small-town America. *Population Research and Policy Review*, 39(5), 775–783. https://doi.org/10.1007/s11113-020-09608-5

Suleman, R., & Nelson, B. (2011). Motivating the millennials: Tapping into the potential of the youngest generation. *Leader to Leader*, 2011(62), 39–44. https://doi.org/10.1002/ltl.491

Troy, Michigan. (2014, March). Next professional development program presentation. Public document received from the Office of the City Manager.

Watson, D. J., & Hassett, W. L. (2003). Long-serving city managers: Why do they stay? *Public Administration Review*, 63(1), 71–78.

The White House Office of the Press Secretary. (2011, August 12). White House Rural Council Delivers Report on Rural America – Jobs and Economic Security for Rural America (Press Release). https://obamawhitehouse.archives.gov/the-press-office/2011/08/12/white-house-rural-council-delivers-report-rural-america-jobs-and-economi

CASE STUDY: VOLUNTEER FIRE DEPARTMENTS IN SMALL TOWN AMERICA

Jonathan M. Westendorf

Background

The volunteer fire service which started as a call to duty of all able-bodied persons protecting their town from catastrophic fire damage now has to meet the community expectation of providing a modern-day all-hazards integrated approach to emergency preparedness, planning, response, and recovery system as prescribed by FEMA's National Response Framework (2019). The National Fire Protection Association reports that 67 percent of America's fire service are volunteers. Small towns with fewer than 10,000 residents are almost exclusively served by volunteer firefighters (Fahy et al., 2021), and this is part of a longstanding tradition of families serving in local emergency services from one generation to the next throughout the United States (National Fire Association, 2007). Interestingly, only 9 percent of all the fire departments in the United States are solely staffed by career firefighters. However, over time the number of volunteer firefighters has decreased and they are getting older. Individuals who are willing to volunteer their time and service to fire departments have decreased from a high of 8.05 per 1,000 people in 1987 to a low of 5.8 per 1,000 in 2017 (Fahy et al., 2021). In addition, more than half of the nation's existing firefighters are over the age of 40 (Firerescue1, 2017).

Fire departments provide services which extend well beyond structural firefighting duties. Firefighters are commonly called to rescue individuals from a variety of hazards resulting from crises and disasters that are both intentional and unintentional in nature. Fires occur in structures and wildland settings; they can occur as the result of natural events such as

DOI: 10.4324/9781003287766-21

lightning strikes or failure to properly maintain mechanical equipment. Motor vehicle crashes, hazardous chemical spills or leaks, people who are trapped by crumbling infrastructure or by thrill-seeking activities in nature—both above and below ground. Mass casualty incidents include tornadoes, hurricanes, and earthquakes or acts of terror like active shooting events. Regardless of the reason for the call, firefighters are among the first to arrive on the scene and begin to rescue, disentangle, medically treat, and/or transport the sick and injured in the wake of heartbreak and grief. Sometimes the call to duty may last a few minutes, while other emergencies may last hours, days, weeks, months, or longer.

The Challenge

The recruitment and retention of firefighters in rural areas has been a struggle for the last several decades (Maruka, 2020). "Calls have increased threefold, while volunteer numbers are either stagnant or dropping" (Maruka, 2020). Are we as society asking for too much from a group of volunteer firefighters? Volunteer means unpaid as opposed to those firefighters who serve in such roles as their full-time career. Yet the physical and psychological risks to fire service professionals are equally as dangerous to all of them. Fires burn just as hot in communities that have full-time career fire departments as they do in suburban or rural areas whose first responders are leaving their family dinner tables or places of full-time employment to provide aid to their neighbors during a crisis for little to no financial compensation. The technical competence necessary to address a hazardous materials incident is no less complicated or specialized in rural America than what is needed to safely mitigate a chemical spill within an industrialized metropolitan area. Local government leaders must reconcile the cost savings with the challenge of recruiting and retaining volunteer fire departments.

Determining the Value of Volunteerism

Volunteer firefighters have the same duty and responsibility as their career counterparts. Firefighters in every state are trained and certified based on national qualification standards based on classroom performance and practical evolutions. Not once has the pay status of career firefighters been referred to as "professional." Volunteer firefighters are in no way an amateur version of the former. Rather, volunteer firefighters can (and absolutely do) display outstanding professional characteristics that meet or exceed those of career members of the profession.

Professionalism is determined upon characteristics such as skill, competence, reliability, exacting standards, and an ethical pursuit of excellence whereby services are delivered with care and compassion for others. Such attributes are not dependent upon pay status, but rather the intrinsic humanistic value of life and wellbeing for those in need. One does not need to look far to find examples of lapses of sound judgment by career firefighters who easily take for granted the gift of operating within a well-resourced and fully funded operation.

The time donated by the volunteer fire service saves local governments and taxpayers across the United States $47 billion annually (Zhuang et al., 2017). This estimate may be low. "While volunteer firefighters and emergency workers provide a tremendous contribution to our country, they are often under-funded and ill-equipped" (Gary & Buckman, 2004, p. 5). Small and mid-sized communities and those in rural areas often rely heavily on volunteer firefighters. The demands placed on volunteer organizations are high. Increasing training requirements and growing call volumes require greater amounts of time from volunteer departments that are already struggling to address a variety of recruitment and retention challenges.

The Problem

The challenges and risks to volunteer first responders in small and rural towns may be even greater than their urban counterparts as those agencies often have far less funding, equipment, and training available to address the same hazards that big city departments utilize in responding with personnel who have chosen to dedicate their entire career to learning and perfecting their craft. Of the 102 total firefighter fatalities that occurred in 2020, 44 volunteers died in the line of duty compared to 49 lives lost of those who served in a career firefighting role (US Fire Administration, 2022). This data do not yet contemplate the impact of the COVID-19 pandemic that will surely disproportionately impact the volunteer fire service. "Departments already suffering from shrinking membership and growing demand for services have been crippled further by an inability to hold fundraisers or recruit and retain new members during the current emergency" (Roman, 2020). Despite all of the challenges, the volunteer fire service continues to respond to calls for help placed by neighbors, friends, and complete strangers.

Intergovernmental Assistance

Despite the looming crisis that stands to cripple volunteer first responders, there are federal and state funds that may provide some degree of relief by the provision of equipment and other needed resources. For example, the US Department of Interior appropriates funding annually to the Rural Fire Assistance (RFA) program which provides grants of up to $20,000 to Rural Fire Departments (RFDs). These grants can help RFDs meet training and equipment standards needed to respond effectively (FRAMES, n.d.). In Minnesota, the Minnesota Department of Natural Resources collaborated with the US Department of Defense and the Forest Service through the Federal Excess Property Program (FEPP) to acquire a wide range of equipment that can be distributed throughout RFDs in the state (Haugen and Beauregard, 2015). It was noted in this example that "the more flexible a fire department is with its request or desired outcome, the better its chances that the equipment will soon become available" (Haugen and Beauregard, 2015).

Concluding Thoughts

One can effectively argue that the passion of a volunteer firefighter is even greater than that of a career member because the volunteer is freely giving their own time and energy, sacrificing time from family and friends without receiving pay. Not only that, but many often forgo pay that could be earned elsewhere (lost opportunity cost) but instead choose to pursue increasing demands for training and education to build upon the necessary experience to safety and effectively fulfill the essential functions of the position. Further, many volunteer fire departments are often forced to run bake sales and other fundraisers so the volunteer organization can afford to buy new equipment and vehicles. It is the same spirit and drive that demonstrates service to others, no matter the personal cost which has cemented the volunteer firefighter into the favor of public opinion so strongly. Yet small town and rural volunteer fire departments struggle mightily to recruit and retain the volunteers needed to protect the public safety in these communities (Yoon, 2014).

What Do you Think?

There are many examples of entire volunteer fire departments walking off the job, leaving small towns with no emergency personnel. Locate an example of this and determine what led to the resignation and how government leaders could have prevented the crisis.

The health and wellbeing of the individual serving their community demand that first responders are physically capable of fulfilling the stringent demands of the job. Does the fire department have a responsibility to screen volunteer firefighters to assure the candidates have the physical strength and stamina to function in that role, or should the department simply fill all available roster spots and do the best with what they have?

Have society's needs and expectations of the local fire department unreasonably exceeded the ability of volunteers to perform the necessary duties of serving the local community, despite the community pride and identity that is often associated with such benefactory gifts of service and sacrifice?

References

Fahy, R., Evarts, B., & Stein, G. (2021). U.S. fire department profile 2019. December, 7. www.nfpa.org/News-and-Research/Data-research-and-tools/Emergency-Responders/US-fire-department-profile

Firerescue1. (2017). Officials; most volunteer firefighters are over age 40. www.fire rescue1.com/recruitment/articles/officials-most-volunteer-firefighters-are-over-age-40-oWK7o2epaXKc8zoz/

FRAMES. (n.d.) Rural fire assistance program. *Resource Catalog.* www.fra mes.gov/catalog/81#:~:text=RFA%20is%20intended%20to%20increase,att ack%20at%20the%20local%20level.

Gary, S., & Buckman, J. (2004). *A Call for Action: The Blue Ribbon Report: Preserving and Improving the Future of the Volunteer Fire Service.* www.iafc.org/topics-and-tools/resources/resource/vcos-ribbon-reports

Haugen, B. & Beauregard, J. (2015). Rural fire departments receive new equipment. *Fire Management Today,* 74(2), 27–28. www.frames.gov/documents/usfs/fmt/fmt_74-2.pdf

Homeland Security. (2019). National Response Framework. www.fema.gov/sites/default/files/2020-04/NRF_FINALApproved_2011028.pdf

Maruka, J. V. (2020). The rural community crisis: Small-town fire departments face unique recruiting issues. www.firehouse.com/volunteer-firefighter/article/21125920/nvfc-national-volunteer-fire-council-the-rural-community-volunteer-firefighter-crisis

Roman, J. (2020). "We're in disaster mode" Will lessons from the pandemic change emergency response forever? *NFPA Journal.* www.nfpa.org/News-and-Research/Publications-and-media/NFPA-Journal/2020/May-June-2020/Featu res/COVID/Responders

US Fire Administration. (2007). *Retention and Recruitment for the Volunteer Emergency Services: Challenges and Solutions.* May 2007. chrome-extension://efaidnbmnnnibpcajpcglclefindmkaj/ www.usfa.fema.gov/downloads/pdf/publi cations/fa-310.pdf

US Fire Administration. (2022). Firefighter fatalities in the United States. www.nfpa.org/research/reports-and-statistics/the-fire-service/fatalities-and-injuries/firefighter-fatalities-in-the-united-states

Yoon, D. K., Jensen, J., and Youngs, George A. (2014) Volunteer fire chiefs' perceptions of retention and recruitment challenges in rural fire departments: The case of North Dakota, USA. *Journal of Homeland Security and Emergency Management,* 11(3), 393–413. https://doi.org/10.1515/jhsem-2013-0103

Zhuang, J., Payyappalli, V. M., Behrendt, A., & Lukasiewicz, K. (2017). *Total Cost of Fire in the United States.* Fire Protection Research Foundation.

Subsection: Infrastructure and Highway Services

11

GATEWAY TOWNS

Loving our Rural Communities to Death

Roger R Carter

Introduction with a Mini-Case

It was always with some sadness that Mary Smith looked over the last remaining tourists having breakfast at her cafe. Having owned this restaurant for several decades and being a multi-generational resident of the community, she knew that this day would inevitably come each year. Growing up in the small town of Smithfield, she knew that she would never leave this small rural community located in a beautiful part of her state. Smithfield was situated in a remote area of Utah, adjacent to a national park and other federal lands; it attracted tourists worldwide because of its hiking and natural beauty. Over the past couple of decades, visitors from around the world have discovered the place that Mary calls home. They flock in by the thousands during the warmer summer weather. The town has also grown in population. As a small business owner in a tourist community, Mary constantly needs to balance the seasonal nature of her business to survive.

Today, as she watches the last few tourists finish up their meals, pay, and depart, her mind is not on her little restaurant but on the town council meeting she will preside over this evening. Mary was elected mayor a few years ago and tasked with the challenge of finding revenues sufficient to meet the demands of the small community. Balancing the town budget and having enough revenues to provide for the community's infrastructure needs seems to become more challenging each year. The tens of thousands of tourists who descend upon the community each year have a significant impact on the community's facilities and infrastructure. The roads have

DOI: 10.4324/9781003287766-23

potholes and are worn-out due to the volume of tourist traffic. The water system can barely keep up with the high demand of the summer months and runs dangerously low in pressure.

Although these visitors do sustain the primary economy in her community of gift shops and restaurants, the taxes generated from these businesses usually can't provide sufficient revenue for the community's needs. Historically, the community was established on farming, grazing, mining, and other land-based industries, but because the community is landlocked with federally owned lands, these uses have been restricted, and there is little option to diversify their economic base beyond tourism.

The relationship between the residents and the federal government has always been tenuous. There has never been a feeling of partnership between the two. The federal government manages and promotes the public lands and other tourism-related activities in the area but does not adequately provide for the impact of those uses, nor does the federal government allow the community to determine its own economic future.

Despite promises by congressional representatives, Mary has no confidence that Washington, DC, can help her solve the problems she faces as a mayor. The growing demand the tourists place on her small community's services, the dwindling revenue-sharing the community receives from the federal and state government, and her inability to diversify her own economy are the difficult realities she faces. As on so many other nights, Mary removes her apron, hands the keys to her sister who oversees the evening shift, and walks to city hall, pondering the many questions the city council will face in providing for her residents and ensuring their bright future.

Introduction

This fictional story of Mary Smith would simply be intriguing if not for the accuracy of the situation that many small communities, like hers, are facing across the country. Out of 3,143 counties in the United States, 1,889 are considered rural by the US Census Bureau (n.d.). Although rural communities have always struggled with adequate infrastructure and maintaining a solid economic base, the situation is additionally complicated in areas that experience large amounts of transient population and limited land-use options.

Although Congress has recently taken action to address the nation's ageing infrastructure, this need has compounded over many years, resulting in a backlog of decaying roads, bridges, and critical infrastructure. Even when a spending package is finally approved, time and effort will be needed to disburse funds to areas that need it the most. And for many rural communities, their lack of political influence may mean the much-needed funds may never come.

For many rural communities, tourism is the leading economic driver. With limited economic development options, small towns look to capitalize on adjacent natural scenic sites or historical and culturally significant places, but even if these didn't exist, it wouldn't stop other communities from building the largest mall or showcasing the biggest ball of twine; all for the opportunity to capture revenue from one of the few commercial markets that may exist. Aggregated domestic and non-domestic tourism benefits are well documented and often trumpeted as the saving industry for small town America, with little discussion regarding a tourism-based economy's cost, impact, and sustainability. When President Theodore Roosevelt created the national park system, it was with a desire to preserve and share these natural beauties. From this beginning, this branch of the federal government has grown to include oversight over vast acres of public lands, primarily located in the western United States. In the spirit of President Roosevelt's vision, these agencies are commissioned to preserve these lands and capitalize on these geographic treasures for the country's economic benefit as a whole. In many cases, this latter mission has driven visitors to these lands to unprecedented and possibly unsustainable levels.

While many rural towns in the United States can plan and develop their own community character, including their growth and economic development preferences, many other communities, mainly found in the western United States, are landlocked. During the great westward expansion, as states West of the Rocky Mountains entered the union, the federal government retained large amounts of land within its control. 45 percent of federally owned land exists within the 11 western states (GIS Geography, 2021). Unlike eastern communities, many rural western communities have been required to consider, consult, and comply with policies and directives from their far-flung land-use partner in Washington, DC. These western communities have never experienced the complete autonomy of their eastern counterparts or been fully allowed to determine their destiny; they have become "gateway communities" to federal lands. These gateway communities, which are often located near nationally recognized tourist sites as well as other federally controlled lands, are hit with a double-edged sword. Their community infrastructure and services are negatively impacted by visitation to these national sites, while at the same time, their ability to diversify their economic options is limited by these same neighboring federal landowners.

One such state is Utah. In a recent survey conducted by Southern Utah University, county leaders identified the top challenges facing their rural communities. These include infrastructure funding, federal revenue-sharing, and their relationship with federal and state officials. This chapter will identify the present infrastructure needs in our rural towns, the impact of a transient tourist population, federal land restrictions on revenue diversification, and revenue sharing.

Infrastructure Needs

In a recent report, the American Society of Civil gave an overall grade average of C- to our nation's infrastructure, the lowest in 20 years (American Society of Civil Engineers, 2021). Mckinsey & Company has estimated that an investment of $150 billion is needed annually until 2030 to address the infrastructure challenges within the United States (Woetzel et al., 2020). Compared to other industrialized nations, the United States ranks 13th in spending and public infrastructure (McBride & Siripurapu, 2021) due mainly to the complicated revenue-sharing between levels of government. From a high of 38 percent in 1977, today, the federal government only provides 25 percent of US infrastructure funding, with much of that gap not being made up by additional state funding (McNichol, 2019). This trickle-down economic model finds less and less revenue going to less politically influential and densely populated areas, which primarily consists of our rural communities. Regarding infrastructure, while 19 percent of the US population lives in rural areas, almost 68 percent of the lane miles exist within rural settings. For every 1,052 lane miles per 100,000 residents in an urban area, the rural areas of equal residential population must maintain 9,818 lane miles (Bureau of Transportation Statistics, 2022).

This infrastructure condition is additionally complicated in areas that experience a large amount of transient population, such as these gateway communities to national parks, monuments, and public lands. Beyond roads and highways, the transient population also demands that gateway communities improve water, sewer, power, gas, broadband, and other services to accommodate this peak population surge. These peak demands on service may only occur a few months a year along with its local revenue boost but leave the long-term payment residual to the resident population.

While some may argue that the transient or tourist traffic provides a sufficiently robust economy needed to address these impacts, tourism-related spending is highly elastic, can be unsustainable, and provides for low-wage, service industry jobs.

Tourism Revenue

Tourism represents a significant portion of the US GDP. In 2019, pre-COVID international and domestic travelers spent $1.2 trillion in the

United States. Despite this significant investment into the economy, tourism revenue can be fickle and subject to the smallest of market influences, such as fuel prices, currency value, and world conflict. As a result, small changes in tourism dollars can have significant ripple effects on communities that rely on this market as their primary revenue source. In particular, large market events—like a global pandemic—can devastate the financial viability of communities for years and even decades. For example, from a high of $1.2 trillion spent on tourism in 2019, the pandemic reduced this spending to $680 billion, a 56 per cent decrease (US Travel Association, 2021). For locations whose sole industry is tourism, the loss of even one year of revenue can have devastating effects on its ability to fund and finance infrastructure within the community for many years.

Consider the state of Utah. Utah is considered the 15th most visited state in the United States. This is due primarily to the fact that Utah is home to five national parks and nine national places, not to mention numerous state parks and vast open land. Most of the communities in Utah are rural by definition and often rely upon tourism as their primary economic driver. Between the years 2019 and 2020, total tourism-related spending in Utah declined by 29.8 percent to $7.07 billion. These $7 billion generated and supported over 119,000 direct and indirect jobs (Leaver, 2021). When tourism dries up, it has a "double-edged" impact. It eliminates the sole source of income for small businesses and reduces or eliminates the employment revenue of the local residents. Between 2019 and 2020, employment in tourism-related businesses dropped by 13.5 percent statewide. This decline affected a greater percentage of employees in the rural areas due to their proximity to natural attractions than in the urban areas. Most rural communities in the state declined in tourism employment by anywhere between 14 and 34 percent (Leaver, 2021).

The intersection of business loss and personal income can best be observed in the reduction of local tax collection. There are a variety of taxes that produce revenue for tourist and gateway communities. These include sales tax, transient room tax, resort tax, and other boutique taxes. While tourist-related taxes are a way for local governments to recoup some revenue from the transient population, local option sales tax can better indicate how changes in tourism spending affect the business income and the personal expenditure patterns of business owners. In 2020 there was a statewide decrease in local option sales tax by 17.9 percent. Several rural counties that are home to gateway communities reported losses upwards of 33.1 percent (Leaver, 2021). This decrease amounts to millions of dollars in unrealized revenues that communities now need to improve upon declining infrastructure or pay the debt service on previously constructed facilities.

Unfortunately, tourism is a fluctuating revenue source, while debt and infrastructure expenses are characteristically flat or growing.

Some would argue that there is proportionality in infrastructure needs with the number of tourists visiting. There would be less concern with the transient population paying their equitable share of infrastructure impact if this were correct. However, the nature of this economic model is such that expensive, long-term investments in infrastructure are not fully compatible with highly elastic tourism dollars. Since it is estimated that only about 5–10 percent of tourism dollars remain in the visited destination, there is a constant need to grow by demanding more tourists and visitor dollars (Mullis, 2017).

Accepting the premise that it is unhealthy for any economy to be based upon a single revenue driver, it makes sense that these communities should diversify their economic base. For gateway communities located in the western United States, this creates an additional challenge since most of the adjacent land is owned by the federal government which provides little or no option for local economies to exercise their own "manifest destiny."

Federal Land Ownership

Since a majority of land in the western states is federally owned and contains some of the most-visited national parks, monuments, and public lands, the gateway communities feel hamstrung. Due to the economic benefits noted, federal and state governments expend enormous amounts of money promoting visitation to the national parks, monuments, forests, and public lands, while at the same time pigeonholing local governments into a single revenue source. Consider the town of Springdale, Utah. This community sits as the western gate of Zion National Park. In 2020, Zion National Park received 5 million visitors (US Department of the Interior, n.d.), the majority of which came through this community. This town of 346 permanent residents struggles to provide the utility infrastructure necessary for thousands of visitors a night, well beyond what would be needed to provide for the resident population. The town of Springdale is a quaint community with hotels, restaurants, and gift shops lining the highway that runs through it. The tourism trade can be robust during travel season to the park, but since all lands adjacent to the community are federally controlled, there is little chance that Springdale will have any other revenue development option than tourism. This challenge can be additionally concerning to local officials as the visitor numbers to these parks have tended to trend lower each year (Leaver, 2021), not to mention the devastating impact of a significant disruption to travel, such as a pandemic, can have on their community and its residents.

The federal government has acknowledged the burden that untaxable federal land can pose upon a community and has made efforts to address this over the past several decades. US Code 31 creates a mechanism by which local governments can receive compensation for federally owned lands. This Act is known as the "Payment in Lieu of Taxes" (PILT) program.

This Act passed in 1976 is a formula-driven payment plan based upon the acreage of land that the government has legal permission to develop and use for specific purposes. PILT payments are paid "on public lands including state parks and forest, scientific and natural areas, wildlife management areas, school trust lands, consolidated conservation lands, and county-managed tax forfeit lands" (US Department of the Interior, 2022).

PILT payments are provided to local governments in lieu of their ability to collect property taxes. Payments are determined by multiplying the number of acres of qualified federal by an established rate, minus deductions for other land revenue-sharing income, such as Forest Service funds, Secure Rural Schools funds, and mineral-lease funds. Alternatively, these payments can be calculated at a lower amount with no deduction of other revenues. In addition, for newly acquired federal lands, there can be additional compensation equal to 1 percent of the value of that land. Five variables are used to calculate PILT payment, including total number of acres, population, prior year revenue-sharing amounts, inflation adjustment, and total appropriated program funds.

Katie Hoover (2017) acknowledged several concerns associated with PILT calculation or distribution. These concerns include the acreage and population caps, overlapping revenue-sharing deductions, and the historic discretionary funding of the program. Although well-intended, the acreage and population caps can create inequitable disbursements among parties. A case in point is while Garfield County, Utah, includes 300,000 more federally owned acres, they receive approximately $200,000 less in PILT revenue than their adjacent county, Kane County, Utah. Additionally, until Congress enacted a six-year mandatory spending requirement for PILT funds, the distributions were considered discretionary and annually calculated by the Secretary of the Department of the Interior, resulting in underfunding of the program. Local governments have long acknowledged these concerns.

Federal lands in Utah make up 63.1 percent of the total acreage of the state (Congressional Research Service, 2020). These 33,267,621 acres adjoin and surround the vast majority of rural communities throughout the state. While historically, these communities relied upon farming, ranching, timber harvesting, and mining as their economic livelihood, these lifestyles have diminished due to changes in the global economy or by restriction of these uses due to environmental pressure and government restrictions.

Additionally, as the federal government has reduced the amount of land available for non-tourism, the gateway communities are left with no other options than to increase their dependence on federal assistance, like PILT payments. Reliance on these revenue-sharing programs has been shown to slow economic transition and increase community risk (Godby et al., 2020).

A New Partnership

As indicated, the challenge facing these gateway communities' infrastructure needs is both a supply and demand problem. It is a supply problem because the revenue sources that local governments rely upon are both limited and unreliable. It is a demand problem because these communities are marketed in such a way that large impacts from tourism are inevitable. We are simply "loving these communities to death!"

This challenge can be more prevalent when there are overlapping governmental jurisdictions. Challenges will exist when decision-makers and impacted parties are so distinct in their goals and objectives, not to mention their distance and dialogue. How then can gateway community sustainability be adequately addressed? One suggestion is a change to the historical relationship between local governments and federal agencies and stakeholders. A new partnership between federal, state, and local officials will be needed to address the problems identified and other areas of disagreement on rural, public lands.

In a report produced by the University of Utah, the University of Montana, and the Consensus Building Institute (Fields et al., 2017) titled the *Future of Federal Public Land and Resources: A Need Assessment*, the authors identify potential reasons for the challenges in public lands management. These concerns include the historically corrosive political environment between federal and local officials; the myriad of rules, policies, and directives that create contention and confusion; a resistance to change by all stakeholders; and a lack of resources by all parties. The authors noted that, before anything else, however, there needs to be a resolution to the paradox of conflict and collaboration between all stakeholders.

Each of the characteristics identified in their report has led to the current environment where rural communities, particularly those in the west, face an unstable and volatile economic climate. A new partnership, working with an awareness of this challenge, can create a new paradigm where these communities can maintain and even improve the quality of life for their citizens while at the same time enhancing the intergovernmental relationship needed for long-term sustainability.

To address the financial challenges these particular rural communities face, this new partnership should consider the following:

1. Congress should strengthen infrastructure appropriation language to ensure that rural communities do not lose the capital funds needed due to their lack of political influence.
2. Congress should revise the PILT language to address the inequities associated with acreage, population, and shared-revenue deductions.
3. Congress should consider revising the PILT payment formula to align with the marketable value of federally restricted land, thereby creating a more fair value for local communities for unrealized development.
4. Congress should make PILT payments mandatory instead of a discretionary appropriation.
5. Congress should increase public investment in federal public land and resource management to the public value and benefit the lands produce. Enact new funding tools and streams that allow national parks, monuments, and other public lands to be more market-driven in controlling demand. Allow these new or enhanced revenue sources to be shared with impacted communities. And reform the budget process by moving from a resource-based, line-item budget to a more holistic, regional, eco-system budget.
6. Congress and federal agencies should provide a fair voice to impacted users as well as new users of public lands.
7. State governments should enable rural communities, especially tourist and gateway communities, with the necessary taxing and fee structure to capture an appropriate amount of transient market impacting their community.
8. All levels of government should develop leadership structures that encourage and allow for management across boundaries.

Although not exhaustive, these recommendations can bring both attention and solutions to these challenged, rural climates; potential solutions in which all parties share some responsibility for the present difficulties but will collectively work together towards a bright future for their citizens and visitors.

Conclusion

Due to the changing economic climate, the lack of political capital, and insufficient resources, our gateway communities have struggled to provide for their citizens' basic facilities and needs. Yet these communities contain and maintain some of our nation's most valuable treasures; our parks, monuments, and public lands. Due to the national benefit of these locations, the gateway communities are being asked to host millions of visitors, often at the expense of local citizens and services. While these communities do their best to take advantage of their national and international appeal, they have been forced to create and become dependent on a single and often unreliable market economy. For these communities, their adjacency to federal lands has restricted their ability to diversify their economy to provide for their citizens and visiting guests.

Although our "vacation-laden" memories of these quaint little communities make it easy to dismiss any challenges they might be facing, we must acknowledge the impact that our visit has upon them and their quality of life and work alongside them in a way that brings value to their communities long after we have left.

References

American Society of Civil Engineers. (2021). America's infrastructure report card 2021. In *GPA: C-. 2021 Report Card for American Infrastructure*. Retrieved March 15, 2022, from https://infrastructurereportcard.org/wp-content/uploads/2020/12/2021-IRC-Executive-Summary.pdf

Bureau of Transportation Statistics. (2022, March 31). Rural transportation statistics. Retrieved April 11, 2022, from www.bts.gov/rural

Congressional Research Service. (2020, February 21). Federal land ownership: Overview and data. Retrieved April 11, 2022, from https://sgp.fas.org/crs/misc/R42346.pdf

Field, P., Keiter, R., & Mckinney, M. (2017, November). *The Future of Federal Public Land and Resources*. Natural Resource Policy. Retrieved April 9, 2022, from https://naturalresourcespolicy.org/docs/Federal-Public-Land-Needs-Assessment-Final-20171.pdf

GIS Geography. (2021, November 2). Federal lands of the United States map. Retrieved April 7, 2022, from https://gisgeography.com/federal-lands-united-states-map/

Godby, R., Haggerty, M., & Coupal, R. (2020, March 4). The overlooked importance of federal public land fiscal policy. Headwaters Economics. Retrieved April 7, 2022, from https://headwaterseconomics.org/public-lands/papl-godby/

Hoover, K. (2017). *PILT (Payments in Lieu of Taxes): Somewhat Simplified* (Report 7-5700). Congressional Research Service. https://sgp.fas.org/crs/misc/RL31392.pdf

Leaver, J., Ed. (2021, December). *The State of Utah's Travel and Tourism 2020*. Retrieved April 7, 2022, from https://gardner.utah.edu/wp-content/uploads/TravelTourism-Dec2021.pdf?x71849

Leaver, J., Ed. (2020, September). *The State of Utah's Travel and Tourism Industry, 2019*. Retrieved April 7, 2022, from https://gardner.utah.edu/wp-content/uploads/TravTourReport-Sep2020.pdf?x71849

McBride, J., & Siripurapu, A. (2021, November 8). The state of U.S. infrastructure. Retrieved April 11, 2022, from www.cfr.org/backgrounder/state-us-infrast ructure

McNichol, E. (2019, March 19). It's time for states to invest in infrastructure. Retrieved April 11, 2022, from www.cbpp.org/research/state-budget-and-tax/ its-time-for-states-to-invest-in-infrastructure

Mullis, B. (2017, August 10). The growth paradox: Can tourism ever be sustainable? Retrieved April 11, 2022, from www.weforum.org/agenda/2017/ 08/the-growth-paradox-can-tourism-ever-be-sustainable/

US Census Bureau. (n.d.). Story map series. mtgis. Retrieved April 7, 2022, from https://mtgis-portal.geo.census.gov/arcgis/apps/MapSeries/index.html?appid= 49cd4bc9c8eb444ab51218c1d5001ef6

US Department of the Interior. (2022, March 14). Payments in lieu of taxes. Retrieved April 11, 2022, from www.doi.gov/pilt

US Department of the Interior. (n.d.). NPS Stats. National Parks Service. Retrieved April 9, 2022, from https://irma.nps.gov/STATS/Reports/Park/ZION

US Travel Association. (2021, November 15). Travel forecast fall 2021. Retrieved April 9, 2022, from www.ustravel.org/system/files/media_root/document/Rese arch_Travel-Forecast_Summary-Table.pdf?MvBriefArticleId=6249

Woetzel, J., Garemo, N., Mischke, J., Hjerpe, M., & Palter, R. (2020, October 20). *Bridging Global Infrastructure Gaps*. McKinsey & Co. Retrieved April 7, 2022 www.mckinsey.com/business-functions/operations/our-insights/bridging-global-infrastructure-gaps

Subsection: Nonprofits and Social Services

12

NONPROFIT ORGANIZATIONS AND ARTS EDUCATION IN A RURAL COMMUNITY

Elise Lael Kieffer

The connection between public administration and nonprofit administration has been in existence for centuries, when individual volunteers (the predecessors of a formal nonprofit sector) met humanitarian needs to which the government was unwilling or unable to attend. Addams (1910) formalized this intersecting relationship during her time working in Chicago's slums with refugees. Pandey and Johnson (2019) drew connections between public administration, public policy, and nonprofit management. They concluded that discoveries in one of those domains should necessarily be applied to the others. They advised that continued research should draw explicit connections across those sectors and highlighted examples of the many intersections between the three.

Nonprofit organizations play a particularly active and critical role in rural communities across the US. They often serve as a gap-filling mechanism to meet demands unmet by government entities stretched thin across sparsely populated areas (Walters, 2020; Kieffer, 2020). In addition to limited federal and state resources, nonprofit organizations in rural communities operate in a complicated local political environment wherein they are often perceived as competitors for limited local resources. This political climate is made additionally problematic by the reality of small town interpersonal relationship dynamics and multi-generational family histories that permeate the local population. To a greater extent than their urban counterparts, nonprofit practitioners in rural communities contend with outsider status, local perceptions, and persistent lack of funding.

This chapter explores these challenges through the founding and growth of one nonprofit interdisciplinary arts education organization

DOI: 10.4324/9781003287766-25

in a rural Appalachian community by examining the opportunities and challenges confronting nonprofit organizations in rural communities. The chapter concludes with a strong case for the essential value that nonprofit organizations bring to rural communities.

What we Know So Far

Rural communities face a diversity of challenges that are influenced by and in turn influence crime, poverty, education, health, and more. To confront these challenges, rural municipalities rely heavily on nonprofit organizations. Walters (2020) studied the organizational capacity of rural nonprofits that communities depend upon. Harrington (1962) published *The Other America*, a text largely credited with initiating the War on Poverty, a focused priority of US policy-makers in the late twentieth century. That book illuminated the realities of generational poverty prevalent in rural communities across the United States. Four decades later, a 2003 edition lamented that, in much of rural America, the characteristics of poverty remain unchanged (Sarnoff, 2003; Kieffer, 2020).

Intersection of Sectors

Nonprofit organizations are uniquely important in the US. They do not exist independently, but rather in an interconnected, interdependent relationship with the public and private sectors of our society (Berman, 2002). Where local governments cannot or will not step in to meet community needs, nonprofits become pivotal players, confronting societal challenges and improving quality of life for local residents (Berman, 2002). There is a dedicated space for services provided by federal, state, and local governments. Those are the services that will help the most people by expending the fewest, or most reasonable, expenditure of taxpayer resources. Those services are often restricted to those most in need, leaving a population of citizens ineligible for support somewhere in the middle of great and moderate need. The private, or for-profit sector, identifies niches both within and without their own circle to provide services. However, unlike public services, those private services are only available to those with the independent economic resources to pay. The nonprofit sector then fills the gaps in service that are not provided for by the business (for-profit) and government (public) sectors. Nonprofit organizations focus their missions on servicing unmet needs, and unreached populations. When nonprofit organizations find their missions or programs to be redundant, they necessarily shift to become unique service providers again.

Nonprofit organizations' influence and effect on communities "is so far-reaching – touching on every aspect of our lives and every level of institutions" (Renz, 2010, p. 4). Nonprofit organizations accomplish the fulfillment of their missions through creative partnerships, collaborations, programming, and outreach (Salamon, 2014). As noted by Berman (2002), "Increasingly, the nation is calling upon its nonprofit companies to take on some of the country's most pressing social welfare and educational needs" (p. 8). This is not a new phenomenon.

Jane Addams and the History of Nonprofit Organizations

There is much to learn about the history and evolution of the nonprofit sector within the US, but that is not the focus of this chapter. However, one important piece of historical context is critical to the understanding of what follows. The work of Jane Addams existed in the very space referenced above, where public services were not allocated, and private services were unattainable, The Hull House was founded to meet and serve the myriad needs of a particular population.

Widely acknowledged as the founder of modern social work, and a predecessor of the nonprofit movement, Jane Addams worked with immigrant communities in Chicago in the late nineteenth and early twentieth centuries. Addams devoted her work toward solving "wicked problems," those challenges that remain unaddressed or under-addressed by currently available programs. Wicked problems are not so-called because of moral importance, but rather because they perpetuate, despite myriad efforts directed toward their amelioration.

Addams approached her work with impoverished immigrant populations in Chicago by including their voices in the strategies directed at helping them. Her work was unique because, unlike many of her contemporaries, she sought the voices of those she served, including and incorporating them into their own solutions. Further, she did not duplicate services. She identified a gap in the available opportunities for a specific population of individuals and she worked with those individuals to fill that gap (Lake, 2014).

Addams recognized that government institutions, created by the people, should be the embodiment of those people. When government is not meeting the needs of the people, it is failing. Perhaps government alone cannot do this great task, but it can support those organizations working alongside it toward that end (Addams, 1910). People are resourceful and when their institutions fail them, they will creatively work to solve their own problems. It is in this context that the modern nonprofit sector still operates.

Into Modern Rural Life

Despite the essential services provided to rural communities by nonprofit organizations, rural communities are generally awarded less than 6 percent of federal grant funding (Arneal, 2015). Rural donors also give less frequently and lower amounts than their urban counterparts (Center on Philanthropy, 2010). Additionally, the Rural Philanthropic Analysis project suggested that "only seven percent of donor dollars are designated to rural areas" (Walters, 2020, p. 66; Campbell University, 2018). In addition to this lack of financial resources, rural nonprofit organizations also contend with their geographic isolation as a major hurdle. "On average, rural nonprofits are charged with serving over 49 square miles, compared to half of a square mile of urban organizations and about five square miles of suburban organizations" (Walters, 2020, p. 67; Fanburg, 2011).

Rural Arts Accessibility

For the sake of this chapter, one specialization in nonprofit service provision will be highlighted. As with other areas of nonprofit service, the arts and culture sector faces resource and accessibility challenges when operating in rural communities. Sidford (2011) noted that, despite the increasing engagement of rural populations in community-based arts programs, less than 2 percent of foundation funding for the arts goes to rural communities. "The arts provide unique value to rural communities … Arts-based development facilitates growth and a sense of community within rural areas. Collaborating on arts initiatives helps build community capacity" (Kieffer, 2020, p. 30).

Specific Rural Context

The organization at the heart of this study is Burkesville Academy of Fine Arts (BAFA), an interdisciplinary arts education organization founded in Burkesville, Kentucky (Cumberland County), in 2012. To understand the intricacies of this case, it is first necessary to understand the geographic isolation of the community.

When railroads were introduced to the Appalachian region, communities were revitalized, revived, and connected to one another and the broader world as many had never before been (Barker, 1991, Kieffer, 2019, 2020). This connection brought a renaissance of Appalachian folk arts and culture into the broader mainstream consciousness. In those communities, traditional Appalachian arts and crafts still thrive and support Appalachian artists, driving the economy and tourism in their communities (Kieffer, 2020). However, the community at their heart of this study rejected the railroad and the accompanying benefits.

Nestled in the center of seven contiguous counties, untouched by railway access, Cumberland County remains one of the most isolated counties in the Commonwealth (Wooten, 1992; Kieffer; 2020). Within that collection of counties, K-12 public schools struggle to maintain the inclusion of any arts curriculum within their schools (Graff, 2012; Kieffer, 2020). "The most isolated communities are so economically depressed that they have lost pride in their cultural heritage, making the need to preserve their artistic traditions and promote artistic innovation more necessary" (Kieffer, 2020, p. 34). That gap in available public arts education creates an environment wherein the impact of nonprofit arts organizations is even greater. Again, the nonprofit sector identified a gap in public services and private opportunities, and an organization was born.

Burkesville Academy of Fine Arts

After two years of unofficial community activities, Burkesville Academy of Fine Arts (BAFA) was officially founded and incorporated in 2012. It was first conceived and planned as a summer program for local children. It would be an interdisciplinary camp, offering exposure to all aspects of the arts. The founder was a transplant from outside the community, but she worked to recruit local artists from various fields of specialty to teach a range of classes in music, theatre, dance, and visual arts. Those artist-instructors were a combination of native residents and transplants. BAFA found ways to interact and collaborate with the community, increasing effectiveness, impact, and access to services.

In a small, rural community in Appalachia, success is driven by relationships. The growth and impact BAFA experienced were only possible through the deliberate and strategic cultivation of interpersonal relationships and collaboration between BAFA and community stakeholders. BAFA representatives utilized the most effective communication strategies in their small town: local radio interviews, school assemblies, and the start of a weekly arts column in the newspaper. Through collaborations with the city and county government, the public library, the public school district, the University of Kentucky Extension Office, and other nonprofit organizations, BAFA grew into a vibrant and integral part of the community. Its growth and presence in the community bring unique opportunities to local residents.

City Support

Almost immediately, the opportunity arose for the local government to reject or support the BAFA initiative. Qualified instructors were willing and available to teach, but where could the organization actually hold the camp? The town's mayor and city council saw the benefit of the program for local children and immediately offered the city's park facilities as the location for BAFA's first summer camp. This partnership held for the first three years of BAFA camp. Dance, photography, and stage make-up classes were held in the agriculture building. Music and art classes happened in the historic log cabin, a preserved one-room schoolhouse. Theatre was taught on the stage of our outdoor amphitheater, and anything else that didn't have a location met under the picnic pavilion. Although BAFA did provide hand soap and toilet paper, the camp also relied on the city's restroom facilities.

It is impossible to overstate the value of this connection between BAFA and the city government. Without cooperation from the municipality and support of city services, no matter how stellar the arts programming, it never would have happened. The city never supported BAFA with actual funding, but with the sharing of spaces, and the accompanying utility costs of using those spaces, the city facilitated the birth and growth of BAFA as an independent nonprofit organization.

School District

Cumberland County, Kentucky has one school district containing three schools. There is a K-fifth grade elementary school, a sixth–eighth grade middle school, and a ninth–twelfth grade high school. The Cumberland County school district has no vocal music programs, no dance programs, one art teacher at the high school, and one band director (also at the high school). Private instruction is equally unavailable. Students who come from families with substantial resources might travel up to two hours multiple times weekly for dance or music instruction. This commitment is prohibitive for those whose financial limitations, work schedules, or personal inclinations do not allow for that level of travel and that commitment of time.

Knowing the limitations of their own resources, educators and administrators within the Cumberland County School District quickly latched on to the value of BAFA's mission. Before the second summer of programming, BAFA was identified as an officially sponsored summer opportunity for local youth. Scholarships to attend were made available through twenty-first-century grant funding, the camp was promoted and endorsed through the schools, and registrations doubled. A week of camp for pre-school-aged children was also added to BAFA's programming.

Desirous of taking the program further, and further increasing local opportunities, district teachers and administrators worked with BAFA to plan a more ambitious project. BAFA partnered with the schools to produce the musical, *The Wizard of Oz*, in the fall of 2013. It is impossible to overstate what a big commitment this was from the schools, and how outside of the box the thinking was that brought it to pass. The best district performance space was at the middle school, attached to the gymnasium. For many years that stage-space had been unused for its intended purpose. It was, instead, functioning as a catch-all storage space. To even use the stage as a stage, substantial inconvenience and effort was required. Its location in the gym also meant that, in order for BAFA to use the space, basketball practices would be affected. Either BAFA would be on stage behind the curtain rehearsing to the accompaniment of bouncing basketballs and coaches' whistles, or everyone would have to compromise. BAFA learned quickly that no one messes with Kentucky basketball.

Regular communication occurred between school administrators, individual instructors, coaches, and BAFA personnel. An uneasy understanding was reached to accommodate the needs of all groups. The final show, featuring a cast of over 60 performers ranging from 5–17 years old, produced the first full-length musical production that anyone in local memory could recall in their own town. Although highly successful, this particular partnership would not be repeated. This production proved to stretch the stakeholders too far, and future BAFA performances were held elsewhere. However, the district and administrative support of this endeavor, the community-wide visibility it provided, and the sheer number of performers included, moved BAFA's programming to another level.

By the third summer, BAFA's camp enrollment had tripled and they were able to purchase their own property to be renovated and outfitted to include private spaces for music lessons, a dance studio, and a classroom space for visual arts instruction. The first year of camp BAFA had five full-time paid staff—all instructors with no assistants on hand. By the third year, in partnership with the city, and the local school district, BAFA had 12 full-time paid staff. Six of those staff were instructors and every instructor had a dedicated classroom assistant. With the purchase and renovation of their own building, BAFA evolved from a summer program into a full-time community arts center with year-round educational opportunities in the arts.

The collaboration between BAFA and the school district was mutual. In addition to the support from the district toward BAFA's offerings, BAFA provided on-site opportunities at each of the school campuses. BAFA instructors brought dance and music classes to the elementary and middle schools. BAFA instructors facilitated "Arts Days" at the middle school. These were formated like a one-day BAFA camp, during which students could explore dance, visual arts, drama, and music. BAFA instructors worked with the high school also, supporting classroom activities that included arts initiatives. This brought BAFA representatives in front of every student in the school district, providing exposure to the arts for every public-school student in Cumberland County, regardless of whether they ever attended an external BAFA event.

Fischel (2006) highlighted the influence of public schools not only on the students receiving direct education services, but also on the adult community that interacts with and through the schools. I would argue that, by networking and sharing resources with the schools in the community, BAFA found community support much more readily than they would have done if they had tried to operate independently. Because BAFA invested in the local schools, the community invested in BAFA. The social capital engendered through this one collaboration cannot be overstated.

Library and Other Nonprofit Organizations

One challenge of operating a nonprofit organization in a rural community is the increased competition with other organizations for funding from a smaller pool of donors. The donor pool is limited by both a lack of population density, affecting available donors, and a generally lower socioeconomic capacity of the locality. To mitigate these challenges, BAFA found ways to support other local initiatives. In so doing, it was able to establish its place in a community that is otherwise skeptical of newness and of "the arts" as a nonprofit endeavor in a sector that is more often perceived to be populated by charity organizations. Student participants and instructors in BAFA's many programs provided entertainment for other nonprofit organization's fundraising and community engagement events. Being present and showing support for other charitable initiatives gave BAFA a unique opportunity to create relevance for its activities that expanded beyond the arts and culture sector. BAFA students and instructors demonstrated that BAFA could support other local issues of concern, including Relay for Life events, other small local human service nonprofits, the library, the Chamber of Commerce, the Farmer's Market, and more.

Cross-sector and inter-sector collaborations like those utilized at BAFA serve to meet the needs of rural communities. Through their increased capacity, these partnerships then create more effective solutions and more impactful programming. Improved opportunities emerge for residents in rural communities when sectors collaborate, rather than compete (Walters, 2020).

Growth

By year four, BAFA had purchased and moved into its own building where began implementing year-round programming, including music, dance, and art lessons, in addition to full-length theatrical productions. In six years, BAFA went from two weeks of full-capacity summer programming in 2012 to six weeks of arts-based camps in 2017 and multiple full-length stage productions each year. BAFA is still serving an identified community need. The local government placed value on that service, and facilitated the first steps of the organization. The lives of local children are richer for it.

No one in the county fiscal court or city council was asking themselves how they could increase arts programming in the community. That was not a need they had identified. However, they showed great forward thinking when the founder stepped forward with an idea, and a plan. They supported and endorsed the program in the ways they were able. In due course, that program would provide increased summer traffic to the community, with campers and families coming from counties across central Kentucky and Tennessee, as well as several states.

Obstacles and Opportunities

As previously suggested, it was BAFA's willingness and eagerness to actively participate in the community that enabled the founder, instructors, and organization as a whole to establish trust within the community. Local residents in rural areas are often wary of outsiders who enter into their close-knit, multi-generational communities (Kieffer, 2019, 2020; Walters, 2020). To a greater extent than their urban counterparts, nonprofit practitioners in rural communities contend with outsider status, local expectations, and persistent lack of funding.

Outsider Status

Communication between organizations and sectors are central to BAFA's success, however these very things were also a challenge. The initial perception of local residents was that BAFA was a business, rather than a nonprofit organization. This perception was fueled by the lack of previous exposure to the arts, the otherwise social service-dominated local nonprofit sector, and the founder's status as a transplant into the community (outsider status).

Rural communities are often skeptical of nonprofit organizations. This mistrust is fed by a consistent expectation that people come into their community with an outside agenda, and they come to take and use local resources, leaving less for the residents. While these attitudes are somewhat based on historical misdeeds, they are also fed by the perpetuation of rural stereotypes in popular culture (Kieffer, 2020; Walters, 2021). These attitudes serve to discourage external nonprofit organizations from entering into some communities, which then perpetuates the lack of services available to those populations.

External funding sources often require collaboration between entities, and the hesitancy to enter into collaborative partnerships then further disadvantages organizations operating in small towns. Additionally, the lack of external support not only decreases service capacity, but also quality of service. With no external review or standard of care, organizations can offer diminished quality of services, at further detriment to the community.

While cooperation among local entities has been found effective and should be encouraged as a mechanism for maximizing resources, there is often a lack of local advocacy in support of such cooperation. This absence of support for collaborative efforts is additionally fueled by a feeling of competition for resources (despite the reality that collaboration maximizes resource effectiveness), and suspicion of others with alternative interests and agendas (Lackey et al., 2002). This mistrust and skepticism are present in collaborations between various nonprofit organizations and between nonprofits and local governments, as well.

Local Expectations

Lichter and Crowley (2002) noted that within the US many poorer populations feel entitled to public support. That mindset of entitlement has contributed to the perpetuation of poverty within rural, impoverished communities. Exacerbated by the rejection of new people and opportunities, rural residents tend to prefer the status quo. This includes embracing their socioeconomic status, as well as the opportunities currently available, rather than welcoming new developments. They will both receive and accept what has always been available, but might be hesitant to accept something new, no matter how beneficial the offering. Activities like the aforementioned newspaper column served to promote BAFA's activities by educating the community. Columns such as "Why do theatre tickets cost so much?" brought awareness to the community about the nature of the organization as a nonprofit.

When the problem of underexposure to opportunities is generational, as is so often the case in rural towns, parents place less value on opportunities that were unavailable to them as children. After all, what they had, or didn't have, as children was good enough for them, so it is also good enough now for their own children (DeYoung, 1992; Kieffer, 2019). DeYoung (1995) also found that rural school administrators intentionally model and teach their own perceptions of normative behavior and expectations. This perpetuates what was before into what still is now. What was familiar and normal to them as children continues to be promoted as normal for their students (Kieffer, 2019). In addition, King (2012) credited not only the unfamiliarity of opportunities but also the perceived necessity. Those living in generational poverty come to process opportunities on the basis of survival. As stated by Lichter and Crowley (2002) "Poverty often begets more poverty" (p. 24). This results in a nonprofit sector identifying gaps in service but a population sometimes unwilling to accept the offered solutions.

Persistent Lack of Funding

There is a relatively well-known and understood vastness of need in rural communities, yet there remains a perpetual underfunding and underinvestment therein. Even in an environment where philanthropic giving rises, funding to rural initiatives remains depressed (Cohen, 2011). Rural communities account for approximately 18 percent of the US population but only 8 percent of foundation funding. Per capita, the rural nonprofit sector is only about 30 percent the size of the sector in urban areas. Nonprofit organizations in rural communities lack both actual financial resources, and also the capacity to pursue them (Neuhoff & Dunckelman, 2011).

Conclusion

Nonprofit organizations serving rural communities face economic struggles differently than their urban counterparts. Persistent poverty in rural areas results in the perpetual demand of serving more individuals with less resources. In rural communities, public and private funding is consistently under-invested. Rural nonprofits receive both less federal funding and less private support. The private support they do receive from local residents is often insufficient to meet organizational demands. This creates an atmosphere in which nonprofit organizations have to be innovative to meet local needs and fulfill their missions. These creative approaches include partnerships with other nonprofit organizations and across sectors (Walters, 2021).

Despite the obstacles in their way, nonprofit organizations continue enhancing rural life in communities across the US. The essential value that nonprofit organizations bring to rural communities needs more research attention, but the ultimate goal of nonprofit practice, whatever the service area, is to improve the quality of life in communities (Long, 2001). Meanwhile, nonprofit practitioners often find that interactions with local government are awkward, because government officials undervalue or misunderstand the work of the organization (Walters, 2021).

Rural communities are often defined by persistent poverty and lack of access to experiences and services more readily available in urban communities. They need improved healthcare access, infrastructure improvements, and, as in the case of BAFA, access to public funding for the arts (Kieffer, 2020). Every dollar is hard-earned and hard to come by. We squander those dollars when we do not strategically work together, across sectors, to support our constituents. Every dollar must be spent wisely. If local governments and their local nonprofit organizations could communicate more effectively, and collaborate more willingly, they might stretch those dollars further.

Nonprofit organizations are critical to the building of healthy communities. They provide important services that support economic growth, educational opportunities, and improved outcomes in all areas of life. As Jane Addams pioneered, nonprofit organizations continue to serve as spokespeople for their special populations, advocating for otherwise unseen or underserved individuals. Government alone cannot meet every need for every citizen. However, it can support the efforts of those organizations striving to do just that.

Local governments can support their nonprofit sectors by including them in policy-making discussions and solutions. Nonprofit organizations in direct service to the community should be at the table when that community is being considered. A strong nonprofit sector contributes to a stronger community with a higher quality of life.

References

Addams, J. (1910). Charity and social justice. *The North American Review*, *192*(656), 68–81.

Arneal, L. (2015). *Report: Rural-Based Organizations Receive Fewer Grants than Urban NPOs*. Retrieved from http://nonprofithub.org/grant-writing/report-rural-based-organizations-receive-fewer-grants-than-urban-npos/

Barker, C. (1991). *The Handcraft Revival in Southern Appalachia, 1930–1990*. Knoxville, TN: University of Tennessee Press.

Berman, H. J. (2002). Doing "good" vs. doing "well": The role of nonprofits in society. *Inquiry*, *39*(1), 5–11. doi:10.5034/inquiryjrnl_39.1.5

Campbell University. (2018). About rural philanthropy. Retrieved from www. campbell.edu/about/research/rural-philanthropic-analysis/about-rural-phila nthropy/

Cohen, R. (2011). No surprises, rural philanthropy still lags behind. *Nonprofit Quarterly*, Retrieved June 14, 2022 from www.nonprofitquarterly.org/index. php?option=com_content&view=article&id=9876:rural-   philanthropy-still-lags-behind-no-surprise-here&catid=149:rick-cohen&Itemid=991

DeYoung, A. J. (1992). At risk children and the reform of rural schools: economic and cultural dimensions. White paper sponsored by the American Institutes for Research in the Behavioral Sciences. https://files.eric.ed.gov/fulltext/ED361 153.pdf

DeYoung, A. J. (1995). Constructing and staffing the cultural bridge: The school as change agent in rural Appalachia. *Anthropology & Education Quarterly, 2*, 168–192.

Fanburg, S. (2011). Rural nonprofits lag on revenue, access. *The Nonprofit Times*. Retrieved from www.thenonprofittimes.com/news-articles/rural-nonprofits-lag-on-revenue-access/

Fischel, W. (2006). Why voters veto vouchers: Public schools and community-specific social capital. *Economics of Governance, 7*(2), 109–132. https://doi.org/10.1007/s10101-005-0005-5

Graff, E. R. (2012). Preserving traditional culture in the Cumberland Gap Region. *Journal of Appalachian Studies, 18*(1), 234–243.

Harrington, M. (1962). *The Other America: Poverty in the United States*. Macmillan.

Kieffer, E. L. (2020). *Exploring Relationships between Arts Administrators in Appalachian Kentucky and Tennessee and their State Arts Agencies: A Qualitative Narrative Inquiry*. ProQuest Dissertations Publishing.

Kieffer, E. L. (2019). I landed a U.F.O. on Main Street: An autoethnography of the founding of an arts education organization in Appalachian Kentucky. *International Journal of Social, Political and Community Agendas in the Arts, 14*(1), 3–15.

King, C. S. (2012). What's a girl like you doing in a place like this? *Journal of Public Affairs, Education, 18*(1), 51–66.

Lackey, S. B., Freshwater, D., & Rupasingha, A. (2002). Factors influencing local government cooperation in rural areas: Evidence from the Tennessee Valley. *Economic Development Quarterly, 16*(2), 138–154. https://doi.org/10.1177/0891242402016002004

Lake, D. (2014). Jane Addams and wicked problems: Putting the pragmatic method to use. *The Pluralist, 9*(3), 77–94.

Lichter, D. T. & Crowley, M. L. (2002). American attitudes about poverty and the poor. *Population Bulletin, 57*(2). Retrieved June 13, 2022 from www.prb.org/resources/poverty-in-america-beyond-welfare-reform/

Long. R. (2001). Building bridges between practice and knowledge in nonprofit management education: An initiative that is unleashing resources for the common good [Confidential programming update], p. 3. Robert Long Papers, personal collection, Murray, Kentucky.

Neuhoff, A., & Dunckelman, A. (2011). *Small But Tough: Nonprofits in Rural America*. Bridgespan Group.

Pandey, S. K., & Johnson, J. M. (2019). Nonprofit management, public administration, and public policy: Separate, subset, or intersectional domains of inquiry? *Public Performance & Management Review*, 42(1), 1–10.

Renz, D. (2010). *The Jossey-Bass Handbook of Nonprofit Leadership and Management* (3rd ed.). Jossey-Bass.

Salamon, L. M. (2014). *The Resilient Sector Revisited: The New Challenge to Nonprofit America*. Brookings Institution Press.

Sarnoff, S. (2003). Central Appalachia—Still the *Other* America. *Journal of Poverty*, 1/2, 123– 139.

Sidford, H. (2011). Fusing arts, culture and social change: Philanthropy at its best. National Committee for Responsive Philanthropy. www.ncrp.org/wp-content/uploads/2016/11/Fusing_Arts_Culture_and_Social_Change-1.pdf

Venture Pragmatist. (2010). Introducing the L3C. http://venturepragmatist.com/2010/09/introducing-the-l3c/

Walters, J. E. (2020). Organizational capacity of nonprofit organizations in rural areas of the United States: A scoping review. *Human Service Organizations: Management, Leadership & Governance*, 44(1), 63–91. doi: 10.1080/23303131.2019.1696909

Walters, J. E. (2021). More than meets the eye: Organizational capacity of nonprofits in the poor, rural South. *Journal of Rural Studies*, 86, 497–507. doi:10.1016/j.jrurstud.2021.07.017

Wooten, R. (1992). *Cumberland County, Kentucky, Yesterday and Today*. Dallas, TX: Curtis Media Corporation.

13

GUTHRIE KY AND CIVIC ENGAGEMENT

How Small Groups of People Make a Difference

Stephanie L. Bellar

Along I-24 and on Highway 41 there are signs for Guthrie KY; at the bottom of the sign is the additional marker "Home of Robert Penn Warren." It is a sign that draws tourists to the community and reminds us of the power of civic engagement. The story of Guthrie is similar to many rural areas and lessons can be distilled from their recent experiences. There was a cadre of people who wanted to ensure the legacy of America's first Poet Laureate and only winner of the Pulitzer Prize for both poetry (1958 and 1979) and fiction (1947) was anchored in Guthrie by saving his birth home and having it placed on the national registry of historic homes. They worked, sometimes in opposition to the interests of surrounding larger communities, to purchase and refurbish the home and more recently in cooperation with the same institutions they had earlier had some disagreement with.

The purpose of this chapter is to examine the impact of nonprofits in Guthrie to assess their civic contributions. Verba and Nie (1972) showed that citizens who live in a bonded community where interactions were communitarian had a citizenry more engaged in civic life. Not all small towns are bonded. Therefore, it is important to examine how different groups and their members promote mission-driven goals and collaboration with other groups. The chapter is presented in three sections. The first section provides an overarching review of the city from 1950–present, setting a context for how and why people perceive certain issues as problems. This time limit was set because it corresponds to the timeline of when some of the participants who established the groups moved to the community which informs their recollections and aspirations for

DOI: 10.4324/9781003287766-26

their legacy. Furthermore, it also encompasses the timelines of the three generations (Boomers, Generation X, and Millennials) who are engaged in the nonprofit organizations. The second section describes the groups, their origin, mission, and activities. The third section distills lessons. The methodology is qualitative and participant observation. Data are taken from a larger project that includes city officials and business owners. Quotes and attributions used in this chapter are taken from public utterances at public events.

Context

During the 1950s Guthrie was a thriving community hosting a motel, a general department store, a ladies clothing store, a hardware store, a furniture store, a pharmacy, two grocery stores, a dime store, two service stations, a bank, restaurants, a funeral home, a physician, and a dentist. The local school contained first through twelfth grades. There were three churches with congregations of well over 150 and several smaller congregations of 100 or so. Institutions for honing engagement thrived.

Less than a mile away was a business area comprised of a major truck stop, two restaurants, and a motel. The area benefitted from being on Highway 41 which traverses from Michigan to Florida. Even as the interstate system was developed, travelers and long-distance haulers still had to use 41 to connect from a west–east direction. Between the truckers and the tourists there was additional traffic to help support the businesses of the community.

In addition to the benefits of sitting along a major travel route, Guthrie benefitted from being on a railroad line that provided passenger service. It was an easy rail trip from Guthrie to Nashville, TN, or Louisville, KY, on the L&N line. The rail brought opportunity for access to larger towns and brought business to the community. One long-term company in the community, Koppers, is a creosote company that supplies railroad ties and utility poles to railroads.

Then, there were shifts. In 1963 the county consolidated the high schools and that anchor of community engagement shifted. Later on, in 1988, the elementary schools were consolidated and the community aspect of school functions was lost to the towns. The community was beginning to feel the effects of the brain and brawn drain. The physician relocated to the county seat. People had to drive to see the doctor. Passenger trains were fading out, although freight still moved through town. For some local businesses, there was no one to carry on the business at the owner's retirement. Moreover, there was less and less need for a local source of shopping because it was becoming easier to drive to the larger towns for a wider range of items to purchase and activities to enjoy. The decline was slow and community leaders worked to stop the exodus of opportunity. There was limited success in that regard. A new factory was built and for a time that provided employment opportunities with decent wages. Housing developed with a new sub-division. Closing family businesses did not signal rapid decline. Shifts were occurring but they were manageable. However, the growth and maintenance of long-term economic stability was cyclical. Factories came in with smaller workforce requirements and closed within a 10–15 year period.

The shift that proved to be seismic was when I-24 was completed. In 1980 the Midwest to Southeast connector officially opened, and Highway 41 began the steady decline from being a significant business route to becoming a scenic route. Seven miles away, along the intersection of I-24 and Highway 79, there was a booming business corridor. Residents of Guthrie benefitted from the economic engine Hopkinsville, Nashville, and Clarksville, TN, but the town of Guthrie lost both business and revenue.

Nevertheless, there is reason to be optimistic about the future. A new aluminum plant, Novelis, has been built, with guaranteed hiring of people who reside in Kentucky. The plant opened and in January 2022 announced plans for expansion adding an additional 140 jobs (Kentucky Council of Economic Development, 2022). This will be a significant change because Guthrie sits on the Kentucky/Tennessee state line. Tennessee does not have an income tax and the area around Guthrie has seen a housing surge with higher end homes. The ability of Guthrie to attract those residents hinges on the work of the city leaders and nonprofits. Housing stock will be in demand for Guthrie to bring the workers into the city as residents. Moreover, the city will need to imagine a mixed economy honoring the agricultural base while preparing for a more commerce and technology adaptable future. The community is showing success, being led by persons engaged in the nonprofits.

Nonprofits: Who and Mission

Of the nonprofits that operate in the city of Guthrie, four of them stand out for having a sustained, positive effect on the city: Interfaith Council, Senior Citizen Council, Robert Penn Warren Committee, and Main Street. There is overlapping membership among these groups, but each keeps its own mission intact.

The Interfaith Council is a constellation of faith-based organizations. It includes all local congregations except one which chooses not to participate. The group is made up of ministers and volunteers. It operates on donations from the different congregations generally collected during the community-wide worship services. These activities are also notable because of the opportunity they provide in bringing different race-segregated congregations together for joint worship. Originally the Council was served by a group of ministers upon whom people traveling through Guthrie could call for assistance. The financial burden of buying a new tire, putting a family up in the local hotel, and providing food would not fall on the congregation most visible from the road. Likewise, ministers were trusted to know who in town was recovering from an adverse event, be it a house fire, accident or illness, that could cause a family to lose housing. The idea was that those families could be helped without fanfare.

During the last 20 years, the mission has shifted to the management of the local Food Pantry. This food pantry is not a member of Second Harvest, the nation's food bank network; all food and monetary donations are gathered and distributed at the local level. Two days a week volunteers open the Food Pantry for food distribution. Almost to a person the volunteers are culled from the congregations that support the pantry. There is a core of people who serve as the regular staffers for the pantry. Volunteers have said they are motivated by their deep commitment to the community along with their own faith journey in a commitment to serve their neighbors. Neighborliness *as a vehicle for building social capital is a concept well developed in* Putnam's *Bowling Alone* (2000), and Rosenblum's *Good Neighbors* (2016) makes a powerful argument for the importance of neighbor relations in how democracy is negotiated.

The second nonprofit is the Senior Citizen Center. The name is somewhat misleading in that the Center has become a community event venue that serves the community through programming and the building can be rented for private occasions. While in the building it is easy to do a walk-through of the history of Guthrie, photographs of significant events ring the room, including a visit by T. Roosevelt, prior to his becoming president. Their programming has been a constant in bringing people to town. For a long period of time, the Center was the most active group in the community. On Monday evenings the group hosts a dance. That event gives people who live in the region a chance to gather for social time and recreation. These events promote "thick trust" described by Putnam (2000) as trust embedded in personal relationships and experiences that are strong, frequent, and rooted in broader social networks.

For those who attend regularly it is a chance to see friends and share conversations. They offer other recreational events as feasible, such as chair exercise classes designed for those with limited mobility and calisthenics for those who can engage more vigorously. Moreover, this group of volunteers has instituted a monthly series of luncheon events. The cost is minimal; food is prepared by board members and volunteers. It is a drop-in event and recently it has been sold out early. These lunches help bridge groups who may not have the chance to see one another during a typical day. Farmers, business owners, managers from the new plant, and retired people attend. People from surrounding committees come as well. It has the feel of a family reunion affording people the opportunity to ask about one another's wellbeing. These events provide an opportunity to discuss common concerns in a more relaxed environment.

It is worth noting the Senior Citizen Center, which is nonsectarian, relies heavily on volunteers culled from church-based friendships. The overlapping memberships are noticeable. Furthermore, it was first organized by local nuns who saw the need in the community for a place where people could gather apart from a religious institution. The Center building has been used for health clinics, holiday bazaars, and cooperates with the city in being available for activities related to Heritage Days. While the Center itself is not aligned with a faith group, the reality is it shows the impact of faith organizations on honing organizational skill sets. Much has been written about the role of church for African American people (Greenberg, 2000; Harris, 1994; Vedlitz et al., 1980); it is also true in rural committees, regardless of race. People learn agenda-setting skills, event management, Robert's Rules of Order, and the like. Furthermore, some people learn to trust the skills that translate to civic engagement.

The next nonprofit is different in that the founding was not linked to a wider organization. The Robert Penn Warren Committee (RPW Committee) developed in reaction to what some people saw as an aggressive act by a regional university: Western Kentucky University. The university plan had been to move Warren's birth home to their campus for the purpose of building a writer's center. Two women talked and decided they wanted to explore options for the city to buy and maintain the home; the Robert Penn Warren Committee started with a core membership of eight people. Interest in the work of the Committee grew quickly. There were a number of community members who joined later or who served in an advisory or benefactor capacity. Within the community there was a feeling of the need to protect and own the prominence of having a person of Warren's stature honored.

In April 2005, the US Postal Service released a stamp in the Literary Arts series: it seemed the whole town turned out for the celebration. Robert Penn Warren's children attended the event and were stunned by the enthusiasm of the community. Representatives from the postal service publicly stated they had never seen such a crowd to attend the issuance of a stamp. In 2018 the Kentucky Humanities Council selected Warren's *All the King's Men* novel for the Kentucky reads program. The launch of the program was held in Guthrie, albeit to a much smaller crowd.

The coalitions they built were different in kind from the organizational nexus of the previously discussed groups. The RPW Committee members were active in reaching out to arts councils, state government officials, US House of Representative staff, and other institutions including area universities. They developed relationships with the academic circle who study Warren's writings and hosted group events when they came to the area for annual meetings.

Their fundraising efforts were prodigious. They asked for donations, wrote grants, and held a variety of events from book sales and hosted card parties at the house. When charitable gambling was made legal in Kentucky they made money in that venue, monitoring bingo games at the local bingo hall. They bought the house and have kept it in good repair. The furnishings are mostly donated, even some of the animals from the collection represented in Circus in the Attic were gifted on loan. Later the committee members bought a small plot across the street from the house to develop a park with an area for reading and reflection. This park was named for one of the early members who was a stalwart worker on behalf of the committee. The committee members further extended their work to buy and refurbish a caboose to serve as a tourist attraction. Committee leaders were able to secure funding from various grants and kept the house open for tours. The current RPW committee members continue the legacy of working with the academic group that continues to come to Guthrie for part of their annual meeting. Furthermore, they have spent a considerable amount of time and resources on additional repairs and improvements to the structure of the house. The committee has also supported the city in hosting Heritage Days by having some of the members of the RPW Circle engage in readings at the house of Warren's work.

The last non-profit is Main Street, accredited by the Kentucky Main Street Program and the National Main Street Program. The local Main Street group has been phenomenally successful and has changed the dynamics of the town.

To date, Main Street has led two major improvements. The first is reclaiming a dilapidated building with a long-term plan of developing it into a railroad museum. The group's partnership with Pennyrile Area Development resulted in refurbishing the building which has already been used for community-related events such as Heritage Days. When the new plant was being built, operations were temporarily located in this building.

The second venue the Main Street group improved is Longhurst Park, a pocket park named in honor of a resident who was a strong supporter of Main Street, a business owner, and a second-generation resident of the town. This park is a focal part of town. Throughout the summer there are live bands and food trucks. The main road is shut down and people gather to hear music and enjoy themselves. Main Street leadership is purposeful in keeping a variety of music available so that most people get to hear their preferred music at least once during the season. These events are supported by several local businesses, but it is Main Street that organizes and manages the events. The organization has recently built restrooms adjacent to the park. They are in the process of restoring another building that will serve as their office space and provide room for a small business incubator. One of their partnerships was with the South Guthrie Improvement Association to improve the community center in that area which sits just inside the Tennessee state line, but it feels like a part of Guthrie proper.

Main Street also engages in town beatification and upkeep. They have provided streetscape grants for new sidewalks and lamps. Their members have workdays and have cleaned up much of the abandoned and neglected property throughout the downtown area, making it more attractive. Members of their board of directors sweep the streets on clean-up day, then use power washers to clean the sidewalks. They sponsor an event at Halloween for children. During the growing season, the executive committee maintains the flowerpots placed throughout town. Main Street is a paid membership organization; they can accept financial and in-kind donations. Just as the RPW Committee did at one time, Main Street is using charitable gambling to provide financial support for their work.

Lessons Moving Forward

Taken together these four organizations tell a story of commitment, shared values, and desire to fulfill the goal of, paraphrasing RPW, making Guthrie a place to come to. They have followed the advice of community builders to "use what they have." This advice is sage for those who want to lift their communities. All too often people see success in one community and believe that the same program can be replicated in their town. There is an upper limit on the number of antique malls that can be economically viable and in the number of museums. Making use of what you have is seen in the South Pittsburg, TN, community that, like Guthrie, was left only miles away from I-24 but Kimball, TN, was adjacent to the interstate. South Pittsburg was shriveling up and Kimball was growing. Civic leaders in South Pittsburg joked they had to work with what they had and what they had was the Lodge cast-iron factory. South Pittsburg is now an envy of communities who seek to develop community festivals as revenue-producing endeavors. South Pittsburg hosts the National Cornbread Festival, often drawing crowds in excess of 10,000 people each day. The festival is a ticketed event as are many of the activities.

Another lesson the volunteers have learned is that cooperation is vital. Putnam (2000) reminds us that thick trust has a downside. While there may not be even an awareness of a closed system, the perception is there. As decision-makers have appointment power or suggest members there should be a more concentrated effort to include people with diverse backgrounds. The awareness of bringing everyone to the table often sits with race and that is important. Nevertheless, diversity reminds us there are many different groups of people to invite to participate. For example, a constituent group in the diversity conversation too often ignored is young people. One of the reasons Main Street has been successful is that they have young people in their membership. As the city expands due to the new plant, leaders of all four of the nonprofits will need to be mindful of the fresh perspectives people can bring to deliberations.

The idea of rural brain drain has become an accepted and documented fact (Artz, 2003; Carr & Kefalas, 2009). Rural America has hollowed out and Carr and Kefalas sounded the alarm arguing "hollowing out has repercussions far beyond the boundaries of the small towns it affects. ... it can be ground zero for the green economy and sustainable agriculture ... and it sends more than its fair share of young men and women to fight for this country" (2009). The question is "Is hollowing out inevitable?"

Waldorf (2007) provides a provocative argument that in-migration often brings persons with higher educational attainment than those in the area or those who were lost. She notes the impact is greater for urban areas than rural ones, but the result exists even in rural areas. Given recent behavior by states and regional agencies, the trend may be expanded in rural or more isolated areas. Alabama has an incentive program to pay qualified remote, tech, workers to move to the northern region. Communities like Bentonville, AR, are seeking to buy "top remote working talent" by offering incentives of $10,000 cash and a bike to get workers with the capacity to work remotely to move to the area. While Bentonville is not a small town nor is it lacking in amenities, it is geographically isolated. Rural states like Maine and Vermont offer incentives to have people relocate there. The impact of this type of in-migration may not reach small towns but it can be instructive. Civic leaders, elected and volunteer, need to take hard stock to ask—why would someone want to live here? A city like Guthrie will not have the resources of Bentonville to entice residents of a certain educational level, but they can rethink some of their programming.

For example, the members of the Robert Penn Warren Committee, through their relationship with the RPW Circle, have access to professors in English, Folklore, American Studies, History, and the like. As an extension of their work in promoting the work of Warren, they could run a film series of movies made from his novels, engage in a deep analysis of how race was depicted in his works and how his view(s) on race evolved, or use his poetry to teach more about language and imaginary in his work.

For Generation X and Millennials, knowing that the community supported serious inquiry into hard topics may be a factor in favor of a smaller, rural community. Millennials and older Generation Z persons say they want to see authenticity in leadership. The leaders of these groups can provide them the opportunity to engage in meaningful activity by promoting study circles that tackle hard conversations.

Redlin et al. (2010) tackle this question from a different perspective. They ask if small communities are "hotbeds of democracy" (p. 9) built on the idea that deep rural communities afford opportunity for widespread participation. Their work further allows them to examine the roles of place and culture from an asset perspective rather than the deficiency model of drain. Their results are mixed but they are instructive in demonstrating that economic development alone cannot ensure the persistence of rural communities (p. 16). Specifically, they argue "rural leaders and activists should further develop systems that invest in human capital, build on existing social networks and enlarge opportunities for citizens to practice deliberative problem-solving" (p. 16). Guthrie is being served by the nonprofits as they train members of the respective executive committee/board of directors. The give and take of idea development and negotiation is honed, while volunteers develop programs and learn how to hold people accountable for their work.

Situating the argument a bit differently, Crabtree (2016) shows how rural America can tackle problems with imagination. She cites an example from Cody, NE, where students rallied when the only grocery store in town closed. Students took the initiative to develop and launch a community-owned store, run in part by students. In another Nebraska town, the school lunch program was redesigned by high school students, in consultation with the school nurse. Meals are made from scratch using local ingredients. In yet a third example Crabtree points to the work of Latino immigrants who formed a committee to help meet the needs of the immigrant community in their area. They serve as a bridge between the Spanish-speaking persons and the English-speaking community. They volunteer to serve on boards and other community agency committees to help address barriers. These examples are illustrative of how people who are underutilized can bring more inclusion to programming options and decision-making. While there is no guarantee diversity will lift civic engagement, it is a reality that a lack of diversity will depress civic life.

Finally, McMahon (2017) reminds us that every community will have its naysayers. However, they cannot drive the conversation. While their points of view should be heard, and if instructive incorporated into plans, the reality is that there needs to be more willingness to say yes. Volunteers in Guthrie have done that. They said yes to helping people who are having a difficult time with food security. They said yes to the challenges of having a place where people could gather at the senior citizen center and at Longhurst Park. In this way, Guthrie has opened the door to place. Pride of place is evident when people gather in these venues to enjoy the company of friends and music. Dancing in the park is a hashtag people can use as an affirmation of their community. These good feelings spill over to support a vision of Guthrie as a vibrant town.

The community is, however, at a juncture where there is opportunity to be deliberative. Newcomers, people from out-of-town, have bought property because they see the potential. A new restaurant is being developed, an old home has been restored to make it an event venue, and the old home that has a storied history is being redone as a tavern. There is a historical connection at that location as an old stagecoach inn. These people can see what naysayers cannot see. Nashville, TN, is a scant 50 miles along I-24. There are already a number of people who live in Guthrie and make the drive. With the change in work patterns that number could balloon if the city can demonstrate they have the technical infrastructure to support hybrid work. Likewise, the city should become a model in supporting more green technology.

Leaders in the city remind people that Guthrie has its roots in agriculture, and they are correct. But agriculture is changing. While it would be mission creep for any of the nonprofits detailed in this essay to take on the work of helping farmers, the skills they have developed could be used in a different endeavor. Collaboration with the appropriate agencies is possible. There are grants at the state level that can help farmers and small business owners incorporate more solar energy in their farming practices. Increasingly farming is becoming a technology-using industry. Farmers use drones to check on crops. Every farmer uses weather forecasts dependent on satellite technology, just as they use software to track their yields and market conditions. Communication technologies are vital when farm owners and managers are miles away in different fields. Demonstration events could be held at Longhurst Park to show farmers how they can better use familiar technology and learn more about software or even the basics of programming for their specific needs.

One group not yet mentioned is forming and they have the capacity to broaden the vision of the city. This group is composed of retired schoolteachers who have stocked and keep open a local library. There is a county public library but it is in a different town with limited hours. The bookmobile comes to town but, again, hours are limited. The mayor provided space in city hall for the library which makes it accessible during business hours. The vision was articulated, developed, and implemented by this group of dedicated teachers. The model of committed individuals making a difference in their hometowns was seen in their action. The work they did built on and extended the efforts of the nonprofits detailed here: citizens see a need, organize, and work with the city to produce an acceptable solution.

Guthrie has been made better off by the nonprofits that exist in the community. There are more opportunities for engagement. Of the four groups discussed, it is the Robert Penn Warren Committee that has the broadest mission and therefore the capability to revise their agenda. Their work in keeping the house on its original site was accomplished so that Warren's writings would be celebrated in the community. The hope was that school children and adults would be given a place and opportunity to learn more about Warren and the power of language. The leadership of the RPW committee is stepping into the opportunities of the future by collaborating with both the city and the Robert Penn Warren Circle in the celebration of Warren's birthday. The balance for Guthrie and so many small towns is how to maintain the special feature of the town while building the structures that will allow it to grow and sustain into the future.

Acknowledgments

I would like to thank Al DeCiccio who read a rough draft of this chapter and provided feedback.

References

Artz, G. (2003). Rural area brain drain: Is it a reality? *Choices: The Magazine of Food Farm and Resource Issues, 2003*(4), 11–15.

Carr, P. J., & Kefalas, M. J. (2009). The rural brain drain. *The Chronicle of Higher Education*, September 21.

Crabtree, J. (2016). A different path for rural America. *American Journal of Economics and Sociology, 75*(3), 605–622.

Greenberg, A. (2000). The Church and the revitalization of politics and community. *Political Science Quarterly, 115*(3), 377–394.

Harris, F. C. (1994). Something within: Religion as a mobilizer of African-American political activism. *Journal of Politics, 56*(1), 42–68.

Kentucky Council of Economic Development. (2022, January 11). https://ced.ky.gov/Newsroom/NewsPage/20220111_Novelis

McMahon, E. (2017). Why some places thrive and others fail: The new formula for community revitalization. *Virginia Town & City*, January/February, 21–25.

Putnam, R. D. (2000). *Bowling Alone: The Collapse and Revival of American Community*. Simon & Schuster.

Redlin, M., Aguiar, G., Langelett, G., and Warmann, G. (2010). Why are you still out there? Persistence among deep rural communities in the Northern Plains. *Online Journal of Rural Research and Policy* 5(5), 1–22. https://newprairiepr ess.org/ojrrp/vol5/iss5/

Rosenblum, N. L. (2016). *Good Neighbors: The Democracy of Everyday Life in America*. Princeton University Press.

Vedlitz, A., Alston, J., & Pinkele, C. (1980). Politics and the Black church in a Southern community. *Journal of Black Studies*, 10(3), 367–375.

Verba, S., & Nie. N. (1972). *Participation in America: Political Democracy and Social Equality*. University of Chicago Press.

Waldorf, B. (2007). Brain drain in rural America. Paper presented at Annual Meeting American Agricultural Economics Association, Portland, OR, July 28–30.

Subsection: Technology, Internet, and Broadband Availability

14

THE WHERE OF SMALL-TOWN GOVERNANCE

Charting the Path from Technocracy to Democracy

Sue M. Neal and Jaymes Vettraino

Introduction

Governments of all sizes face a wide variety of challenges as they make decisions, implement policies, and manage their workforces. These functions rest not only on the management and interpretation of vast amounts of data but also the generation of additional location-specific data. These data can be generated from the direct workflow of employees, information about the environment, planning information, and population data. Managing and making use of high volumes of data have been identified as a major concern of cities as they move into the future (Barnaghi et al., 2015). Generally, a technocracy is a term used to describe a form of governance where government officials use their technical skills (or access to employees with those skills); this may be seen as a form of 'elite" policy-making based on the limited expertise and access used to make decisions and manage government policies and operations.

Small rural towns may be disadvantaged when it comes to working with these large volumes of data. Management and interpretation of data requires information technology systems that may be costly to acquire and maintain. Further, staff that have the technical knowledge and ability to curate these data systems may be out of reach. Small governments may also be at an increased risk of data security breaches due to both cost and personnel. This is problematic because small governments stand to gain a tremendous amount when given access to the deep insights that can be generated from so-called big data. Increases in operational efficiencies of municipal support functions and improved employee workflows that allow

DOI: 10.4324/9781003287766-28

a limited staff to accomplish more work as well as the increased ability to engage the public with the work of government are all key gains that could be very beneficial for small and rural local governments. Much of the data used by governments can be spatially associated. Data that are either spatial in nature or can be logically associated with physical points or spatial areas lend themselves to organization and interpretation within a Geographic Information System (hereafter GIS). GIS is a term used to describe the set of things that make up the system or the science/ profession of using and applying said system (Cox & Gifford, 1997). When considered as a system, GIS incorporates the people, software, and data that are combined to create a framework to generate, manage, and analyze information (ESRI, 2020).

GIS is used by governments to manage, improve, and monitor public services as well as generate input and public engagement. Particularly in small towns and rural communities where IT infrastructure is costly and expert staff may not be available, significant barriers are faced in the adoption and application of this powerful approach to information management.

Overview of GIS in Governance

Mapping is used as a way to visually identify and understand patterns in data. The classic example of using maps to advance the public good dates back to 1854 when epidemiologist John Snow mapped cases of cholera in London. By analyzing spatial patterns evident from the maps, Snow was able to identify water as the source for the outbreak. The development of GIS itself gained traction in the 1960s when Roger Thompson, considered the father of GIS, pioneered the creation of the Canadian Geographic System which used a layered approach to relating numerous independent pieces of geographic data. In the US, around the same time, Howard Johnson was advancing the computing software at the Harvard Laboratory for Computer Graphics (ESRI, n.d. b). An employee of this laboratory, Jack Dangermond, subsequently founded in 1969 what would become the leading GIS software and development in the world, the Earth Science Research Institute (hereafter ESRI) (ESRI, n.d. b). In the 1970s the US Census started digitizing information such as geographic boundaries and roadways (GIS Geography, 2015). ESRI held its first conference in 1981 (GIS Geography, 2015), the same year the company released the first commercial GIS product (ESRI, n.d. b).

GIS has a long history of use in government operations, policy, and planning (Göçmen & Ventura, 2010; Greene, 2000; Halpern & Troupp, 2013; O'Sullivan, 2006). GIS can be used to understand and explore policy areas such as education, health/safety, public services, environment, social services, and international (Greene, 2000). A leading site for public policy related data layers includes categories of social equity and health, economic opportunity, transportation/infrastructure, resilience and sustainability, environment and natural resources, and public safety (ESRI, n.d. a).

GIS is a powerful tool to provide insight into complex data sets surrounding environmental issues and policy alternatives (Requia et al., 2019). GIS can also be used to evaluate the impacts of a policy post implementation by helping policy-makers consider problems from a systems perspective (Hadian, 2013). This type of policy evaluation helps to inform policy modifications. As an example, Saultz et al. (2015) used GIS to take a quantitative exploration of which spatially linked factors were important for charter schools in New York City. The authors refer to the school choice policy as a policy lever to improve overall school performance.

The need for policies to satisfy divergent stakeholder goals and priorities is another policy challenge where GIS can be useful. Absent from previous examples of GIS are the individual stakeholders in the community—a key voice in governance (Duvernoy, 2018; Phillips et al., 2012; White & Bourne, 2007). Brill (2009) used GIS to evaluate stakeholder objectives in public policy, an important example of how GIS can be used by policy-makers to integrate the public's voice into policy debates.

GIS and Governance Paradigms

GIS and Performance Management

GIS offers a way to improve government service provision through the tracking and evaluation of special data. For example, in 2020 Utah developed a guide for rural towns across the state to more effectively use GIS to aid the management of tangible assets and to facilitate communication and collaboration (*St George News*, 2020). According to a press release, GIS is being promoted in small town Utah in order to accomplish the following key priorities: "Manage community infrastructure and assets; estimate future growth demands, optimize public safety information and reporting, expand public engagement opportunities and platforms; share, collect, and analyze critical physical and cultural municipal data" (Utah Workforce Services, 2020).

New Public Management (NPM) has become a driving force in the way that governments are managed. Growing out of the scientific management movement in the private sector, NPM holds many of the same core values (Barberis, 1998). The focus on the collection of data to inform decisions, the use of performance measures, and an eye toward customer service are all defining themes of NPM (Barberis, 1998; Head & Alford, 2015; Virtanen et al., 2018). With this focus on the tracking and reporting of data, NPM may well be one of the driving forces behind the adoption of GIS within government. In an ESRI published book on using GIS to improve government services, the authors highlight the connection between four tenets of performance management and use of GIS. These tenets include (1) widely sharing accurate/timely information, (2) quick response to resource needs, (3) utilization of effective operations, and (4) continual iteration (O'Malley, 2019).

GIS and Public Service Values

NPM has been criticized in the years since it was introduced for privileging scientific data over the softer customer service orientation of governance. In response to these criticisms, the newer conceptualization of the New Public Service (NPS) operates from a set of values including democracy and citizenship (Denhardt & Denhardt, 2015a, 2015b). NPS envisions the public administrator as one who *serves* the public, in contrast to the traditional role of *steering* the government (Denhardt & Denhardt, 2015a, 2015b). While GIS is a scientific approach, this does not necessarily limit its uses to an NPM paradigm.

The International City/County Management Association (ICMA) has identified GIS as a way to enhance the public service paradigm in a number of critical ways. These include using GIS to communicate transit information to facilitate the expedited travel within congested areas, to manage the relationship between government agencies and citizenry (such as tracking complaints or requests for services), to develop citizen volunteered information (identifying areas of concern or crowdsourced data), and to allow citizens to actively engage in planning and decision-making (Ganapati, 2010).

Public participation GIS (PPGIS) and Critical GIS are two excellent examples of how GIS could be used to support the NPS paradigm of governance and the public-service values that sit at the heart of contemporary public administration. PPGIS is marked by a few key characteristics: its inclusion of full complexities and "messiness" of human geography, arguing that traditional GIS is an oversimplification (Dunn, 2007). Under this conceptualization, PPGIS aims to incorporate local and indigenous knowledge to advance a participatory governance paradigm (Brown & Brabyn, 2012; Brown & Kyttä, 2018; Ghose, 2013). Public participation, as it relates to the concept of PPGIS, ranges from manipulative/passive to self-initiated/mobilized (Dunn, 2007). These manifest through examples ranging from the construction of 3D maps made of inexpensive and locally available materials to the inclusion of photos, videos, and oral histories alongside more traditional spatial data (Dunn, 2007). Issues of accuracy, legitimacy, and role of the web as a way to upscale PGIS are all potential challenges to the operationalization of PPGIS as a democratizing force (Brown & Kyttä, 2018; Dunn, 2007; Ghose, 2013).

E-governance has been conceptualized as a third way that sits between the data-driven focus of NPM while also striving for maximum customer service as in NPS (Sá et al., 2016). Both e-governance and PPGIS share a similar goal of increasing democratic participation in government and GIS has been advanced as one of the key technologies for facilitating e-governance (Ganapati, 2011). Ganapati (2011) points to applications of PPGIS within the public administrative functions of traffic, transit, and improved relations with the public and volunteered spatial data. The reasons that PPGIS has not become more widely adopted as a decision-making tool rests with institutional constraints (Radil & Anderson, 2019). Radil & Anderson (2019) argue that PPGIS has also fallen far short of incorporating marginalized voices because it is de-political and has continued to operate within the existing institutional framework (Radil & Anderson, 2019).

Ganapati (2011) uses the classical Arnstein's ladder measurement of public participation hierarchy arguing that PPGIS has largely fallen on the lower rungs of participation (information provision and feedback) as opposed to higher level participation (involvement, collaboration, and empowerment). Arnstein's ladder of public participation in decision-making is a widely used way of conceptualizing the success of tools within e-governance for advancing public engagement with government (Ianniello et al., 2019; Karner et al., 2019; Vulfovich, 2017; Slotterback & Lauria, 2019).

Barriers to Wider Adoption

With so much evidence discussing how GIS is used within government and governance, it is tempting to assume that it is ubiquitous in the public sector, yet a number of barriers to wider adoption persist. Writing on potential challenges for the future, an article appearing in the *Journal of Public Administration Review* takes a theory-based approach to examining key questions in the use of GIS at the intersection of government and the public. The authors present a central concern of whether GIS will become technocratizing or democratizing force due to inequities in access and mode of operationalization and urge that GIS experts recognize the paradox of this impact (Haque, 2001).

The concerns introduced by Haque (2001) are not the only issue in implementation barriers. In one sweeping review of the question, the authors begin by putting forward the argument that there are factors limiting the adoption of GIS more broadly in the field of government/public administration. The primary issues discussed include the lack of technical expertise and access to software (Caldeweyher et al., 2006). Unlike Haque (2001), the authors provide an alternate solution looking to the OpenGIS project as a potential remedy to these issues. They advance the idea of a simple, inexpensive solution that could be implemented to increase access to GIS and use it to empower grassroots initiatives (Caldeweyher et al., 2006). Gieseking (2018) echoes the opinion of Caldeweyher et al. (2006) by calling for robust open source software to reduce barriers to GIS, yet points to issues in cost of access to ESRI products as a barrier. This is reinforced by others who call for open source software to break down barriers to GIS use (Caldeweyher et al., 2006). Ganapati (2011) identifies barriers shared from the broader field of e-governance, citing the asymmetries of political relationships with stakeholders, the general culture of public agencies, and the self-selective nature of access to technology (still present despite the evolution of GIS).

Continuing to update the review of challenges to implementation, a web survey was completed in 2007 with follow-up interviews of planning professionals in Wisconsin in 2008 (Göçmen & Ventura, 2010). The main limitation is that it provides more of a historical perspective than a current view (given the vintage of the research) and is limited to the state of Wisconsin which may result in challenges generalizing the findings. However, the research identified several technological, organizational, and institutional barriers in implementing a GIS that could be present in local, especially small local governments. The barriers that emerged as the most significant included: training, funding and data reliability/validity issues (Göçmen & Ventura, 2010). The authors conclude that this means organizational and institutional barriers are more prevalent than technological issues (Göçmen & Ventura, 2010). Several of their findings align with those in Ye et al. (2014). One notable divergence is that the latter identifies issues of software usability as more of a barrier than a lack of data (Ye et al., 2014). Their literature review is also helpful as it shows a similarity but not identical findings in past research. Lastly, the authors conclude that practitioners are not necessarily even aware of the "full potential of GIS."

Recent research has also identified some of the potential ethical pitfalls that can occur when attempts are made to operationalize GIS for data communication. Neal et al. (2021) found a number of potential ethics violations in the dashboard and maps that were widely used to communicate data during the early days of the COVID-19 pandemic. Probably more than ever before, the pandemic was a test in how tools such as ESRI and other powerful software tools such as PowerBI and Tableau could be used to share and take action on large amounts of local data. While the power of these tools is very promising, government administrators must develop and adhere to stringent ethical, confidentiality, and data accuracy principles.

Conclusion: Democratizing the Technocracy—a Path Forward

The need for leaders in small towns to have an understanding of data has possibly never been more critical. City managers and government leaders of rural communities face a number of obstacles to adoption that remain problematic. Ongoing changes by the commercial GIS industry will enable greater penetration of GIS to small and rural community governments.

The academy needs to recognize the importance of training students in the basic use of GIS as part of the curriculum in undergraduate Public Policy and Masters of Public Administration programs (Obermeyer et al., 2016). This could provide future small town managers with the background to understand how GIS could be used in their towns to accomplish important local policy goals and objectives. Just as many students are trained in basic research and data analysis techniques, a foundational understanding of GIS is critical for the modern administrator. GIS could be integrated into existing methodology courses or offered as a stand-alone course within the program or in partnership with a geography department (Obermeyer et al., 2016). The academy could also take the lead to establish a consortium across public interest, private interest, and the academy to help close the gap between the haves and have nots of GIS (Haque, 2001) and encourage theoretical approaches that envisage the goal to work with people in the community on issues the community identifies as important instead of a more "top down" approach more typical of the traditional city planning process (Duvernoy, 2018; Gieseking, 2018; Liu et al., 2016).

GIS support is available from professional organizations. An excellent example of this is a partnership between ESRI and the ICMA. The partnership has generated a report that outlines the many ways that GIS is used in local governance both from an operational and a decision-making perspective. The report is part of the Smart Communities Movement (ICMA & ESRI, 2018). Some key topics include how GIS can be used to engage the public through dashboard and issue reporting tools, workflow management and maintenance of key infrastructure projects, open data, storymapping, and dashboards. Further collaboration that creates pathways for practitioners to gain skills in GIS management would benefit smaller towns that do not have staff capability.

Industry changes are also improving the access that small rural towns have to GIS. ESRI has migrated many of its services to the cloud where they can be purchased under a software-as-a-service (SaaS) model. Not having to manage desktop clients means employees have easy access to updated software at any time and computing intensive geospatial analysis runs on ESRI servers. This greatly reduces the need for IT specialists to maintain the system. Additionally, ESRI has been proactive in the curation of data layers specific to public policy and government use. Through its online platform, these layers are easily accessed and users can quickly identify useful layers. The online platform also allows for simple integration of complex workflows to manage geodatabases, collect additional data in the field, and provide access for a number of user types to maintain the integrity of underlying data.

Cloud-based solutions empower the vertical sharing of GIS resources that allows wider adoption of GIS by small towns (Harvey & Tulloch, 2006). This can include access to a cost shared cloud SaaS, sharing of data with the higher level of government taking the charge for curating the data, sharing expert staff, and provision of training opportunities. Oakland County, Michigan, is a prime example of how this can work. The county-funded GIS program actively assists every village, city, and township by providing access to ESRI's ArcGIS Online, a premier cloud-based GIS platform. Oakland County develops its own GIS data layers, pulls in layers from regional, state, and national data sets, and authenticates data from local government users, making hundreds of layers of data available across its 62 units of government. This use of a web-based, centrally maintained, GIS system is a model for how larger governments (counties or states) can work cooperatively to provide smaller units of government access to GIS technology, while also enhancing the larger government's data by pulling in otherwise not available smaller governments' data.

While these solutions make the future of GIS in small and local government increasingly accessible, it will be important to continue to address the challenges of how GIS can be used as a force to increase public participation across the full range of public sphere decision-making and creatively applied with a critical lens to give voice to historically marginalized knowledge. The various barriers that have been identified through this chapter also point to important challenges that the industry will face moving forward in the public sector use of GIS. While the challenges are many, the future appears to be bright as government and academics push the boundaries of the role of GIS in the public sector. There appears a clear path that will allow use of GIS across communities of all sizes to remediate the conflict of technocracy and instead provide a forward force to grow democracy between and within communities.

References

Barberis, P. (1998). The new public management and a new accountability. *Public Administration*, 76(3), 451–470. https://doi.org/10.1111/1467-9299.00111

Barnaghi, P., Bermudez-Edo, M., & Tönjes, R. (2015). Challenges for quality of data in smart cities. *Journal of Data and Information Quality*, 6(2–3), 6:1–6:4. https://doi.org/10.1145/2747881

Brill, C. W. (2009). Using GIS to contrast perceived versus preferred priorities for brownfield redevelopment in Worcester, Massachusetts. *Journal of the Urban & Regional Information Systems Association*, 21(2), 49–57.

Brown, G., & Brabyn, L. (2012). An analysis of the relationships between multiple values and physical landscapes at a regional scale using public participation GIS and landscape character classification. *Landscape & Urban Planning*, 107(3), 317–331. https://doi.org/10.1016/j.landurbplan.2012.06.007

Brown, G., & Kyttä, M. (2018). Key issues and priorities in participatory mapping: Toward integration or increased specialization? *Applied Geography*, 95, 1–8. https://doi.org/10.1016/j.apgeog.2018.04.002

Caldeweyher, D., Zhang, J., & Pham, B. (2006). OpenCIS—Open Source GIS-based web community information system. *International Journal of Geographical Information Science*, 20(8), 885–898. https://doi.org/10.1080/1365881060 0711378

Cox, A. B., & Gifford, F. (1997). An overview to geographic information systems. *Journal of Academic Librarianship*, 23(6), 449. https://doi.org/10.1016/ S0099-1333(97)90169-5

Denhardt, J. V., & Denhardt, R. B. (2015a). The new public service revisited. *Public Administration Review*, 75(5), 664–672. https://doi.org/10.1111/ puar.12347

Denhardt, J. V., & Denhardt, R. B. (2015b). *The New Public Service: Serving, Not Steering* (4th ed.). Routledge/Taylor & Francis Group.

Dunn, C. E. (2007). Participatory GIS: A people's GIS? *Progress in Human Geography*, 31(5), 616–637. https://doi.org/10.1177/0309132507081493

Duvernoy, I. (2018). Alternative voices in building a local food policy: Forms of cooperation between civil society organizations and public authorities in and around Toulouse. *Land Use Policy*, 75, 612–619. https://doi.org/10.1016/j.lan dusepol.2018.01.019

ESRI. (n.d. a). Esri Maps for Public Policy. Retrieved June 26, 2023, from https:// livingatlas.arcgis.com/policy/browse/?col=null&hs=0&viz=196df855fd954 22e9e5c5d6210209d5a&loc=-97.419,38.054,4

ESRI. (n.d. b). History of GIS: Timeline of early history & the future of GIS. Retrieved April 2, 2022, from www.esri.com/en-us/what-is-gis/history-of-gis

ESRI. (2020). What is GIS? Geographic information system mapping technology. (n.d.). Retrieved December 5, 2020, from www.esri.com/en-us/what-is-gis/ overview

Ganapati, S. (2010). *Using Geographic Information Systems to Increase Citizen Engagement.* IBM Center for the Business of Government. Retrieved 4/2/2021 from https://icma.org/sites/default/files/301388_GIS.pdf

Ganapati, S. (2011). Uses of public participation geographic information systems applications in e-government. *Public Administration Review, 71*(3), 425–434. https://doi.org/10.1111/j.1540-6210.2011.02226.x

Ghose, R. (2013). Defining public participation GIS. *Reference Module in Earth Systems and Environmental Sciences.* https://doi.org/10.1016/B978-0-12-409 548-9.09630-5

Gieseking, J. J. (2018). Operating anew: Queering GIS with good enough software. *Canadian Geographer, 62*(1), 55–66. https://doi.org/10.1111/cag.12397

GIS Geography. (2015, October 12). The remarkable history of GIS. https://gisge ography.com/history-of-gis/

Göçmen, Z. A., & Ventura, S. J. (2010). Barriers to GIS use in planning. *Journal of the American Planning Association, 76*(2), 172–183. https://doi.org/10.1080/ 01944360903585060

Greene, R. W. (2000). *GIS in Public Policy: Using Geographic Information for More Effective Government.* ESRI Press.

Hadian, S. (2013). *A Systems Approach to Sustainable Energy Portfolio Development.* https://search.ebscohost.com/login.aspx?direct=true&AuthT ype=sso&db=ddu&AN=8F8A859F4B57D2A7&site=eds-live&scope=site&cus tid=s3916018

Halpern, A., & Troupp, M., Eds. (2013). *Federal Geospatial Information: Management and Coordination.* Nova Science; Gazelle [distributor].

Haque, A. (2001). GIS, public service, and the issue of democratic governance. *Public Administration Review, 61*(3), 259–265. https://doi.org/10.1111/ 0033-3352.00028

Harvey, F., & Tulloch, D. (2006). Local-government data sharing: Evaluating the foundations of spatial data infrastructures. *International Journal of Geographical Information Science, 20*(7), 743–768. https://doi.org/10.1080/ 13658810600661607

Head, B. W., & Alford, J. (2015). Wicked problems: Implications for public policy and management. *Administration & Society, 47*(6), 711–739. https://doi.org/ 10.1177/0095399713481601

Ianniello, M., Iacuzzi, S., Fedele, P., & Brusati, L. (2019). Obstacles and solutions on the ladder of citizen participation: A systematic review. *Public Management Review, 21*(1), 21–46. https://doi.org/10.1080/14719037.2018.1438499

International City/County Management Association and ESRI. (2018). *A Guide for Smart Communities: Using GIS Technology for Local Government Management.* Retrieved November 4, 2020, from https://icma.org/sites/default/ files/18-137%20GIS%20e-Primer%20Report_final.pdf

Karner, A., Brower Brown, K., Marcantonio, R., & Alcorn, L. G. (2019). The view from the top of Arnstein's ladder: Participatory budgeting and the promise of community control. *Journal of the American Planning Association, 85*(3), 236–254. https://doi.org/10.1080/01944363.2019.1617767

Liu, H., Silva, E. A., & Wang, Q. (2016). Incorporating GIS data into an agent-based model to support planning policy making for the development of creative industries. *Journal of Geographical Systems*, *18*(3), 205–228.

Neal, S. M., Travers, M. E., & Brastow, I. (2021). When X shouldn't mark the spot: A crosswalk to a unified code of ethics for collaboration in the COVID-19 era. *Public Integrity*, *23*(4), 349–368. https://doi.org/10.1080/10999 922.2020.1869407

Obermeyer, N. J., Ramasubramanian, L., & Warnecke, L. (2016). GIS education in U.S. public administration programs: Preparing the next generation of public servants. *Journal of Public Affairs Education*, *22*(2), 249–266.

O'Malley, M. (2019). *Smarter Government: How to Govern for Results in the Information Age*. Esri Press.

O'Sullivan, D. (2006). Geographical information science: Critical GIS. *Progress in Human Geography*, *30*(6), 783–791. https://doi.org/10.1177/030913250 6071528

Phillips, L., Carvalho, A., & Doyle, J. (2012). Citizen *Voices: Performing Public Participation* in Science and *Environment Communication*. Intellect Books. https://search.ebscohost.com/login.aspx?direct=true&AuthType=sso&db=e000 xna&AN=1135651&site=eds-live&scope=site&custid=s3916018

Radil, S. M., & Anderson, M. B. (2019). Rethinking PGIS: Participatory or (post) political GIS? *Progress in Human Geography*, *43*(2), 195–213. https://doi.org/ 10.1177/0309132517750774

Requia, W. J., Roig, H. L., Koutrakis, P., & Rossi, M. S. (2016). Mapping alternatives for public policy decision making related to human exposures from air pollution sources in the Federal District, Brazil. *Land Use Policy*, *59*, 375–385. https://doi.org/10.1016/j.landusepol.2016.09.017

Sá, F., Rocha, Á., & Pérez Cota, M. (2016). From the quality of traditional services to the quality of local e-Government online services: A literature review. *Government Information Quarterly*, *33*(1), 149–160. https://doi.org/10.1016/ j.giq.2015.07.004

Saultz, A., Fitzpatrick, D., & Jacobsen, R. (2015). Exploring the supply side: Factors related to charter school openings in NYC. *Journal of School Choice*, *9*(3), 446–466. https://doi.org/10.1080/15582159.2015.1028829

Slotterback, C. S., & Lauria, M. (2019). Building a foundation for public engagement in planning: 50 years of impact, interpretation, and inspiration from Arnstein's Ladder. *Journal of the American Planning Association*, *85*(3), 183–187. https://doi.org/10.1080/01944363.2019.1616985

St George News. (2020). Utah gives rural towns big city planning power with new digital tool. St George News, December 27. Retrieved April 2, 2022, from www.stgeorgeutah.com/news/archive/2020/12/27/dld-new-gis-guide-helps-rural-towns-unravel-community-assets/#.YkimHejMK2F

Utah Workforce Services. (2020). Press release. November 25. Retrieved April 2, 2022, from https://jobs.utah.gov/department/press/2020/112520.html

Virtanen, P., Stenvall, J., Kinder, T., & Hatam, O. (2018). Do accountabilities change when public organisations transform to service systems: A new conceptual approach. *Financial Accountability & Management*, 34(2), 166–180. https://doi.org/10.1111/faam.12149

Vulfovich, R. (2017). Participatory budgeting as an instrument of collaboration in public policy. *IMS2017: Proceedings of the Conference*, IMS-2017, 237–242. https://doi.org/10.1145/3143699.3143724

White, L., & Bourne, H. (2007). Voices and values: Linking values with participation in OR/MS in public policy making. *Omega*, 35(5), 588–603. https://doi.org/10.1016/j.omega.2005.11.002

Ye, H., Brown, M., & Harding, J. (2014). GIS for all: Exploring the barriers and opportunities for underexploited GIS applications. *OSGeo Journal*, 13(1), 19–28.

15

BROADBAND AVAILABILITY AND ADOPTION IN RURAL AMERICA

Simone Silva and Narine Badasyan

Introduction

The internet has become more and more intertwined with our daily lives and broadband is behind some of the most significant transformations in our social relationships, business activities, and government services. There is a general consensus in the literature on the positive impacts of broadband access on economic indicators, including GDP (Koutroumpis, 2009), productivity (Czernich et al., 2011; Gallardo et al., 2021), employment (Lehr et al., 2006; Shideler et al., 2007; Holt et al., 2009; Kolko, 2012), establishment growth (Conroy et al., 2022; Shideler et al., 2012), and entrepreneurship (Kim & Orazem, 2016).

More recently, attention has been focused on rural–urban (Prieger, 2013; Silva et al., 2018; Hollman et al., 2021), racial, and economic disparities (Reddick et al., 2020) in broadband access and on the effects of broadband speed (Lobo et al., 2020; Ford, 2018) on the broader economy. Rural areas have fewer high-speed fixed and mobile providers but greater lower speed fixed broadband availability (Prieger, 2013). Persistently poor counties, with 20 percent or more of the population living at or below federal poverty levels, are more racially and ethnically diverse in rural areas and have lower access to high-speed broadband (Dobis et al., 2021).

The literature on the effects of broadband speed on economic indicators is mixed. Lobo et al. (2020) examine the impact of broadband availability on unemployment rates over the period 2011–2015 in Tennessee. Their findings suggest that high-speed broadband significantly affects county-level unemployment rates. Additionally, the benefits of better-quality

DOI: 10.4324/9781003287766-29

broadband are disproportionately greater in rural areas. Ford (2018) argues that, accounting for the differences between counties, there is no effect on economic outcomes from higher broadband speeds from 2013 through 2015. Abrardi *et al.* (2019) survey the existing literature on ultra-fast, fiber-based broadband. They conclude that "There is still a very scant literature that addresses the impact of fiber investment on economic growth and assesses the differentiated effect (if any) of speed on national or local growth".

This study examines broadband availability and adoption by speed tiers in rural areas utilizing NTIA and FCC census tract-level data from 2011 through 2019. The results show that, while the broadband availability gap between urban and rural areas remains, it has gotten much smaller over the years in the overall US. However, state-to-state results vary considerably. The FCC reports adoption data for fixed broadband connections with at least 10Mbps download and 1Mbps upload speeds. The data indicate that, even though minimum 10Mbps download and 1Mbps upload speeds were available to all rural households by 2015, only at most 63 percent of rural vs 85 percent of urban households had subscriptions to those speeds in 2018. Adoption of high-speed broadband has been slow, which may partially explain the lack of consensus on the impacts of high-speed broadband on economic outcomes since most studies use availability data.

Our findings are based on the pre-COVID-19 pandemic data. Low demand and the cost of subscriptions have been cited as the top reasons for not having high-speed internet at home (Pew Research Center, 2019, 2021). The demand for high-speed broadband is likely to have changed over the past few years. During the pandemic, homes turned into offices, classrooms, private movie theaters, and shopping malls (Dobis et al. 2021). "Workplaces were on the path to becoming more technology-enabled before the pandemic. The COVID-19 pandemic has not only accelerated the pace and intensified the need for digital workplace transformation," but it also "shows that digital connectivity is critical to societal resilience and business continuity in times of crisis" (Acoba et al., 2021; Strusani et al., 2020). As a result, company operations in the months and years following the pandemic have accelerated digital workplace transformations, further increasing the demand for high-speed internet. However, since affordability is a critical adoption obstacle, the pandemic has likely widened the preexisting digital divide. To mitigate the digital divide, local governments should focus their efforts on making high-speed broadband more affordable.

Broadband Availability

The present analysis utilizes broadband availability data collected by the National Telecommunications and Information Administration (NTIA) for years 2011 through 2013 (NTIA, 2014) and the Federal Communications Commission's (FCC) Form 477 data for 2014 through 2019 (FCC, 2021a). The data provide the number of broadband service providers with a maximum advertised downstream and upstream speeds in each census block. Except for mobile, it includes all types of technologies used to offer broadband service such as DSL, cable, electric power line, satellite, and fiber.

The Federal Communication Commission's current benchmark for broadband internet access (updated in 2015) is an always-on connection with 25Mbps downstream and 3Mbps upstream speeds. However, nowadays 100Mbps download speed is needed to stream a high definition or 4K video on multiple devices or participate in online gaming. A number of internet service providers most recently have boosted their internet speeds on their lower-tier plans (Comcast, Charter, Cable One, Mediacom, Cox Communications), offering 100Mbps download speeds (Gouvaerts, 2022). Following USDA's categorization of broadband availability, we will use "moderate-speed" for download speeds in Tier 10 and "high-speed" for download speeds in Tier 11 (Dobis et al., 2021).

The data have several observations per census block, one per service provider. Since the census block is the most granular geographical level defined by the US Census, we made the assumption that, if a certain speed is available in a block by at least one service provider, then that speed is available to all households in that block. We acknowledge that this assumption may overstate the availability of higher speed broadband services in some areas. Still the census blocks are the smallest geographical units for which census data are tabulated and half of the census blocks are smaller than a tenth of a square mile. We used the 2010 Decennial Census to obtain the number of households per block. Then we determined the household weighted average speed in each census tract. Using USDA's Rural-Urban Commuting Area (RUCA) classification codes (USDA ERS, 2019), which utilize population density, urbanization, and commuting pattern, census tracts are grouped into two categories: "urban" (RUCA Codes 1–3) and "rural" (RUCA Codes 4–10). Urban areas include metropolitan areas while Rural consists of all non-metropolitan areas.

The data shows that, in 2011, 10 percent of households in rural areas did not have any access to broadband, 19 percent of rural households had access to at least 100Mbps downstream, and 20 percent had access to at least 10Mbps upstream speeds. By contrast, 49 percent of urban households had access to at least 100 Mbps downstream speed and 59 percent had access to at least 10Mbps upstream speed in 2011 (data on urban households are not shown). By 2015 rural households had access to at least 10 Mbps downstream and 1.5 Mbps upstream speeds; 50 percent of rural and 80 percent of urban households had access to moderate or high download speeds in 2015. By 2019 those numbers increased to 86 percent for rural and 98 percent for urban households. While the availability gap between urban and rural remains, it has gotten much smaller over the years in the overall US.

However, the rural–urban availability gap varies among states. In Massachusetts and New Jersey, for example, over 90 percent of rural and 96 percent of urban households have access to at least moderate download speeds, so the rural–urban gap is smaller in those states. In other states, the rural–urban gap is larger; 70 percent of rural and 94 percent of urban households in Idaho and 80 percent of rural and 95 percent of urban households in Kansas have at least moderate download speeds.

Nevertheless, interestingly, only 12 percent of urban and 3 percent of rural households in Massachusetts and 1 percent of urban and 0 percent of rural households in New Jersey could access download speeds 1Gbps or higher in 2019. By contrast, 87 percent of urban and 57 percent of rural households in Kansas, and 77 percent of urban and 46 percent of rural households in Idaho could access download speeds 1Gbps or higher in 2019. While there is a large rural–urban availability gap in those states, a much higher percentage of rural households in Idaho and Kansas can access better downstream speeds than even urban households in Massachusetts and New Jersey. So some states may have less rural–urban availability gap but they lack access to higher speeds, while other states may have a larger rural–urban availability gap, but the quality of access for rural households may be better. Nowadays, households' media consumption is increasingly driven by streaming. It is essential for policy-makers in each state to implement policies targeting not only the rural–urban availability gap, but also the overall quality of access to broadband.

Broadband Adoption

This study uses FCC's Form 477 census tract data on residential fixed connections to determine state-level adoption rates in urban and rural areas. The FCC determines the adoption rates as the ratio of residential subscriptions of fixed broadband services of at least the designated speed (over 200kbps or 10Mbps downstream and over 200kbps or 1Mbps upstream) to the total number of households in each census tract (FCC, 2021b). We use the subscription data with at least 10Mbps downstream and 1Mbps upstream speed levels since those are the highest adoption speed levels available at the census tract level.

Since the data on actual subscription rates are not available, we determined the minimum and the maximum subscription rates in rural census tracts which are aggregated for each state. Our calculations include a range for adoption rates because the data on subscriptions are available by tiers. The overall adoption rate in the US was between 62 and 82 percent in 2018. The FCC reported a 73.3 percent adoption rate for the overall US in 2018, 78.1 percent for "Urban-Core" areas, and 67.4 percent for "Non-Urban Core" areas.[1] However, in our study, urban areas include all metropolitan areas, while all non-metropolitan areas are designated as rural. This is similar to the classification used by the USDA ERS (Dobi et al., 2021).

In 2015 as few as 28 percent and as many as 48 percent of rural households had subscriptions of at least 10Mbps download and 1Mbps upload speeds. By 2018 those numbers increased to as few as 43 percent and as many as 63 percent. There is a larger rural–urban adoption gap than an availability gap in the US. Even looking at the maximum adoption rates, 86 percent of urban households vs 63 percent of rural households had subscriptions to at least 10Mbps download and 1Mbs upload speeds in 2018. State differences are much more prominent. In Arkansas, Idaho, Louisiana, Minnesota, Missouri, New Mexico, Oklahoma, and Virginia as few as over 30 percent and at most 54 percent of rural households had subscriptions, while in states such as Connecticut, Delaware, and New Jersey, the adoption rates were between 70 and 90 percent.

Note that 10Mbps download and 1Mbps upload speeds were available to all rural households by 2015, according to the availability data, while only at most 63 percent of rural households had subscriptions to those speeds in 2018. There are several possible reasons for the low adoption rates in rural areas. Low demand for high-speed home connections, partially due to smartphone capabilities, has been cited as a reason for not having high-speed access at home (Pew Research Center, 2019). However, this may have changed over the past few years, especially since the COVID-19 pandemic. Though the restrictions due to the pandemic eased, they reshaped the workplace. Work lives of many white-collar workers have changed, and the changes may be here to stay. Workplace flexibility and virtual meetings are becoming more and more mainstream, which is likely to shift the demand for high-speed access.

Financial barriers may be why some Americans don't have home subscriptions. In the 2021 survey conducted by Pew Research Center, 45 percent of non-broadband users cited the high monthly cost of subscription for not having high-speed internet at home (Pew Research Center, 2021). As high-speed broadband availability increased, service providers' lower-tier speeds have increased as well. A rise in access quality may have contributed to higher prices for high-speed connections.

Conclusion

The importance of broadband for economic development has been recognized for decades. Recent evidence indicates that better quality broadband has a disproportionately greater impact on rural economies (Lobo et al., 2020). This study examines broadband availability and adoption by speed tiers in rural areas utilizing NTIA and FCC census tract level data over the period 2011 through 2019. The findings indicate that, although a broadband availability gap between urban and rural remains, it has gotten much smaller over the years in the overall US. Yet, state-to-state results vary considerably. The results also show that there is a sizeable rural–urban broadband adoption gap. The COVID-19 pandemic has accelerated digital workplace transformation and the need for high-speed connectivity. According to Pew Research Center (2021), the cost of subscription was the top reason for not having high-speed internet at home in 2021. Thus, it is important for policy-makers to intensify their efforts to make broadband more affordable.

A number of government funding initiatives have targeted rural–urban and socioeconomic disparities in broadband access. The Rural Digital Opportunity Fund (2019) aims to direct up to $20.4 billion to expand broadband in unserved rural areas (FCC, 2021c). The Connect America Fund Phase II reverse auction in 2018 allocated $1.49 billion to expand broadband to more than 700,000 rural locations in 45 states. Most recently, as part of the Infrastructure Investment and Jobs Act of 2021, $42.45 billion was allocated for the Broadband Equity, Access and Deployment (BEAD) program for deployments in unserved and underserved areas (offering less than 25Mbps downstream and 3Mbps upstream speeds) and $14.2 billion for an Affordable Connectivity Broadband subsidy program that provides discounts for internet service for eligible households. These programs will help lower the digital divide. Extra efforts raising awareness about these programs can help make high-speed broadband more affordable, especially among rural and socioeconomically disadvantaged communities.

Note

1 See FCC (2021c), figure 11. FCC designates a census tract as "Urban-Core" if it has a land area less than three square miles and a population density of at least 1,000 people per square mile. All other areas are designated as "Non-Urban Core."

References

Abrardi, L. & Cambini, C. (2019). Ultra-fast broadband investment and adoption: A survey. *Telecommunications Policy, 43*, 183–198.

Acoba, F. & Chulick, J. (2021). How lessons learned in 2020 are accelerating the workplace of the future. Ernst & Young. Retrieved March 26, 2022. www.ey.com/en_us/real-estate-hospitality-construction/accelerate-digital-workplace-transformation

Conroy, T., & Low, S. A. (2022). Entrepreneurship, broadband, and gender: Evidence from establishment births in rural America. *International Regional Science Review, 45*(1). https://doi.org/10.1177/01600176211018749

Czernich, N., Falck, O., Kretschmer, T., & Woessmann, L. (2011). Broadband infrastructure and economic growth. *Economic Journal, 121*(552), 505–532.

Dobis, E., Krumel, T., Cromartie, J., Conley, K., Sanders, A., & Ortiz, R. (2021). Rural America at a glance. USDA Economic Research Service. www.ers.usda.gov/publications/pub-details/?pubid=102575

FCC (2021a). Fixed Broadband Deployment Data from FCC Form 477. [Data set]. FCC. www.fcc.gov/general/broadband-deployment-data-fcc-form-477

FCC (2021b). Form 477 Census Tract Data on Internet Access Services. [Data set]. FCC. www.fcc.gov/form-477-census-tract-data-internet-access-services

FCC (2021c). Fourteenth Broadband Deployment Report. FCC. www.fcc.gov/reports-research/reports/broadband-progress-reports/fourteenth-broadband-deployment-report

Ford, G. (2018). Is faster better? Quantifying the relationship between broadband speed and economic growth. *Telecommunications Policy, 42*, 766–777.

Gallardo, R., Whitacre, B., Kumar, I., & Upendram, S. (2021). Broadband metrics and job productivity: A look at county-level data. *Annals of Regional Science, 66*(1), 161–184.

Goovaerts, D. (2022, March 14). Mediacom bumps up internet speeds for more than 80% of customers. *Fierce Telecom.* Retrieved March 21, 2022, from www.fiercetelecom.com/broadband/mediacom-bumps-internet-speeds-more-80-customers

Hollman, A., Obermier, T. & Burger, P. (2021). Rural measures: Quantitative study of the rural digital divide. *Journal of Information Policy, 11*, 176–201.

Holt, L., & Jamison, M. (2009) Broadband and contributions to economic growth: Lessons from the US experience. *Telecommunications Policy, 33*(10–11), 575–581.

Kim, Y., & Orazem, P. F. (2016). Broadband internet and new firm location decisions in rural areas. *American Journal of Agricultural Economics, 99*(1), 285–302.

Kolko J (2012) Broadband and local growth. *Journal of Urban Economics, 71*(1), 100–113.

Koutroumpis, P. (2009). The economic impact of broadband on growth: A simultaneous approach. *Telecommunications Policy, 33*, 471–485.

Lehr, W. H., Osorio, C., Gillett, S. E., & Sirbu, M. A. (2006). Measuring broadband's economic impact. Retrieved from https://dspace.mit.edu/handle/1721.1/102779

Lobo, B. J., Alam, M. R., & Whitacre, B. E. (2020). Broadband speed and unemployment rates: Data and measurement issues. *Telecommunications Policy, 44*(1), 101829.

NTIA (2014). National Broadband Map Datasets. [Data set]. NTIA. www2.ntia. doc.gov/broadband-data

Pew Research Center (2019, June 13). *Mobile Technology and Home Broadband 2019*. Pew Research Center. Retrieved March 22, 2022, from www.pewresea rch.org/internet/2019/06/13/mobile-technology-and-home-broadband-2019/

Pew Research Center (2021, June 3). *Mobile Technology and Home Broadband 2021*. Pew Research Center. Retrieved March 22, 2022, from www.pewresea rch.org/internet/2021/06/03/mobile-technology-and-home-broadband-2021/

Prieger, J. (2013). The broadband digital divide and the economic benefits of mobile broadband for rural areas. *Telecommunications Policy, 37*, 483–502.

Reddick, C., Enriquez, R., Harris, R. & Sharma, B. (2020). Determinants of broadband access and affordability: An analysis of a community survey on the digital divide. *Cities, 106*, 102904.

Silva, S., Badasyan, N., & Busby, M. (2018). Diversity and digital divide: Using the national broadband map to identify the non-adopters of broadband. *Telecommunications Policy, 42*(5), 361–373.

Shideler, D., Badasyan, N., & Taylor, L. (2007). The economic impact of broadband deployment in Kentucky. *Federal Reserve Bank of St. Louis Regional Economic Development, 3*(2), 88–118.

Shideler, D., & Badasyan, N. (2012). Broadband impact on small business growth in Kentucky. *Journal of Small Business and Enterprise Development. 19*(4), 589-606.

Strusani, D., & Houngbonon, G. (2020). *What COVID-19 Means for Digital Infrastructure in Emerging Markets*. EMCompass, 83. International Finance Corporation. https://openknowledge.worldbank.org/handle/10986/34306

USDA ERS (2019). *Rural-Urban Commuting Area Codes*. www.ers.usda.gov/data-products/rural-urban-commuting-area-codes/

Subsection: Public Safety and Emergency Management

16

PUBLIC SAFETY IN RURAL AND SMALL TOWN AMERICA

James C. Clinger

Protection of the public's safety and health is considered the most fundamental purpose of any government. For small towns and rural communities, these tasks can be difficult, since financial resources may be scarce and many professionals in law enforcement, firefighting, and EMS services may prefer to live and work in larger cities. Personnel in these services may, however, benefit from a knowledge of the people and the places that they serve, even if their functional capacity may leave something to be desired.

Public safety agencies, including police and firefighter departments and emergency medical service agencies, have increasingly professionalized over the last several decades. The credentials, training, and education required to work in these positions and the resources in terms of budget and staffing have increased dramatically. More and more agencies have achieved some form of programmatic certification, and fewer and fewer departments fail to employ professionally trained leaders. Nevertheless, smaller communities continue to rely heavily upon less professionally trained personnel, and the vast majority of rural firefighters are volunteers. How this is done, and how successful these efforts are, is the focus of this chapter.

The Nature of Public Safety in Rural Communities

Public safety is a local government service that involves several agencies. Law enforcement, firefighters, and emergency medical services are all integrally involved. State agencies such as court systems and probation

DOI: 10.4324/9781003287766-31

and parole offices as well as emergency preparedness and response agencies are also highly involved, but they are affiliated primarily with state rather than local government, so we will not dwell on them here.

The various local public safety agencies are highly collaborative, working with other government agencies but also with private-sector organizations. In fact, there may be substantial line blurring between public and private sectors (Brunet, 2008). For example, many public safety officers in rural areas work second jobs, and many agencies in law enforcement, EMS, and firefighting make use of volunteers for at least some functions (Wolf et al., 2016). Therefore, at the individual level at least, public safety personnel move in and out of governmental as well as private circles. Their contacts in each sphere may prove beneficial in performing their community service. But some of these interconnections can also limit the access to new ideas and innovation that successful agencies need.

Public safety operations in rural and small town governments share many of the attributes of their urban and suburban counterparts, although a few distinctive features of smaller communities deserve some discussion. Generally, those distinctive features are thought to pose significant problems for small community public safety providers, but the truth may not be so clear-cut.

Rural areas and small town public safety operations typically deal with greater distances between service providers and those they serve. Population densities in rural areas are lower than in urban areas, resulting in much longer response times once a call for assistance is made. First responders may also have to wait longer for assistance or back-up if they find that an incident requires more than one officer, team, or crew to handle. With fewer officers in a given agency, there may not be much opportunity for responders to fraternize or vent frustrations with colleagues (Oliver & Meier, 2004).

These agencies may not only have a small staff, they usually have a much smaller budget than urban agencies would, even after adjusting for the population size of their jurisdiction and the number of employees on the payrolls. These agencies may lack the equipment, training, and particularly new technology that other departments elsewhere may have. Cell phone service and broadband access may be sketchy in sparsely populated rural areas, no matter what resource capacity the local jurisdictions may have (Saunders et al., 2016).

Many of these agencies may appear to be lacking in professionalism. Volunteers may be used for many positions, and even paid professionals may not have the certifications or other paper credentials that may be common in their fields. Many agencies lack accreditation, which may hinder recruitment of new personnel and could increase the difficulty in qualifying for intergovernmental aid.

All of these features may be thought to pose enormous problems for public safety agencies in small communities, and, consequently, for the safety of the public that lives in those areas. Nonetheless, in some respects public safety appears to be greater in small towns and rural communities than in urban and suburban areas. For example, crime rates are generally much lower than in urban areas (National Criminal Justice Reference Series, 2017; Greenblatt, 2018), although there is quite a bit of variation among regions, with the Great Plains and Northeast communities having much less crime than in the southeast and west coast (Statista, 2021). Certain types of crime, such as robbery, are much higher in urban areas than in rural areas. Domestic violence and crimes against family and children are reportedly higher in rural areas than in suburban or urban locations (Weisheit et al., 2006). These differences could, of course, be attributable to the demographic makeup of these jurisdictions, rather than to the quality of the work of public safety personnel. Interestingly, the crime clearance rate is much higher in rural localities, despite their alleged lack of resources and professional capacity (Weisheit et al., 2006, pp. 127–129). Fire losses and ambulance response times are much greater in rural areas compared to urban areas, but this may be almost entirely because of the dispersal of the population and the distance between the incident locations and the locations of the first responders. Public satisfaction with rural firefighting and emergency medical services seems to be reasonably high in rural areas, despite the longer response time (see, e.g., Bogomolova et al., 2016).

Law enforcement in America is primarily a local function, although states have their state police and the federal government has various law enforcement agencies that focus on federal crimes. Most law enforcement officers are municipal police or county-level sheriff's department officers, normally styled deputies. Almost all municipal police departments are headed by an appointed official who normally has considerable professional training and experience. Sheriffs are elected in almost all parts of the country (see DeHart, 2020). They may or may not be professionally trained in law enforcement. They may also have other duties in addition to traditional law enforcement, such as serving subpoenas, collecting taxes, and managing jails. Despite their elected status, sheriffs often seem to have more job security than police chiefs, who have higher rates of turnover (Zoorob, 2019). In any case, the more overtly political position of sheriffs has caused many observers to examine their operations very critically. Since sheriffs' jurisdictions usually include the entire county, while police departments' jurisdictions are often limited by municipal boundaries, the work of sheriffs is considered particularly relevant for rural citizens who live in unincorporated areas. The large area covered in a sheriff's jurisdiction has often been said to lead to stress among deputies, because response times are slower and back-up from other officers when an incident gets out of hand may not be prompt or possibly not available at all (Oliver & Meier, 2004).

Sheriff's departments are less likely to be accredited by the Commission on Accreditation for Law Enforcement Agencies (CALEA) than are police forces. The significance of accreditation is not entirely clear, however, and it is not obvious that accredited agencies have higher performance (see Johnson, 2015), nor is there much evidence that minimum education requirements (e.g., requiring a college degree) has substantial impact upon police behavior (Worden, 1990). Sheriff's departments usually require deputies to reside within their jurisdictions, presumably to increase the personal connection between law enforcement and the community and also to diminish the time needed to respond to emergencies when an officer is off-duty.

Research on small town and rural law enforcement agencies reveal that in many ways they operate in the same manner as law enforcement in larger communities (see Liederbach & Frank, 2003; Saunders et al., 2016; Weisheit et al., 2006). Peace officers actually spend a great deal of their time and effort on non-law-enforcement, service-related activities. However, in smaller communities, non-law-enforcement activities constitute an even greater share of the work of police and sheriff's deputies. Possibly, these non-crime-fighting actions actually help in both preventing and investigating crimes. In any case, small town and rural officers appear less likely to enforce laws stringently and smaller communities have gained a reputation for being more willing to let private citizens work out disputes voluntarily (Ellickson, 1986).

Fire protection and firefighting in rural areas and small towns is another essential public safety function. Less scholarly research has been done on these services than on law enforcement, but some important distinctives can be drawn from the literature. Some firefighting in small towns and rural areas is the legal responsibility of a general-purpose government, such as a municipality. In rural areas, this function is often carried out by a single-purpose government, generally called a fire protection district. These districts are often led by an elected board, sometimes chosen solely by property owners in the district, meaning that residents living in rental properties may not vote in the elections and non-resident property owners can. This is an anomalous voting arrangement that has been noted in the legal literature regarding election qualifications (see Bauroth, 2007).

Generally speaking, rural and small town firefighting is carried out by volunteers, not by professional firefighters. Training and certification efforts are made by each governing jurisdiction, but rarely do the firefighters get the skills, equipment, and experience that their counterparts in traditional professional departments enjoy. Firefighting is a dangerous activity, and volunteers make up a large fraction of those killed in the line of duty each year (see NFPA, 2021). Recruiting and retaining volunteers is one of the most critical tasks for rural and small town departments (Henderson & Sowa, 2018). Volunteers are often recruited from among long-term community residents with high public service motivation and working-class backgrounds (Simpson, 1996). The fraternity of the firehouse, more than material incentives, seems to motivate behavior (Schmidthuber & Hilgers, 2019). Some volunteers are paid small amounts of money for their service, often on an incident-response basis.

Fires in rural areas tend to differ from fires in more urban areas. Heating systems are the leading causes of residential structure fires in the countryside, while cooking causes most fires in urban areas. Lack of maintenance of stationary heating units and creosote buildup in chimneys and flues are the source of many fires. Inadequate or absent smoke detectors are a significant problem in rural areas compared to urban areas. Furthermore, rural fires generally burn longer before they are detected and firefighters often must travel farther to arrive at the scene. Many volunteer firefighting units do not have personnel at the firehouse at all hours, so more time passes between the moment the alarm is sounded and the assembly of a fire crew at the station (FEMA, 1997).

Emergency medical services are chiefly provided by emergency medical technicians (EMTs) and ambulance personnel. These service providers may be employed by general-purpose governments, private firms, or hospitals. Hospitals may be government run or managed by for-profit or nonprofit organizations. In rural areas and small towns, hospitals will primarily be affiliated with local governments, which could be a general-purpose government such as a municipality or county or a special district or public authority. If a public authority is involved, the hospital would usually be governed by a board that is made up of individuals appointed by general-purpose governments.

He largest challenge for emergency medical services in small towns and rural areas is the response time caused by the low population densities and great distances faced by service providers. Helicopter life-flight services may lessen these problems, but it is a very expensive approach that many communities simply cannot afford.

A large number of rural and small town law enforcement officers, firefighters, and EMS personnel are also military reservists or National

Guard members. In the event that they are activated, local public safety organizations may be short-handed (Loughray et al., 2006). In fact, many volunteer firefighters also work as EMS staff, and some law enforcement officers serve as volunteer firefighters. The personal interconnectedness of public safety personnel may encourage collaboration among units, but it also may mean that problems within one functional unit may spill over into others.

The intersecting roles, personal connections, and overlapping responsibilities of public safety personnel and organizations in small towns and rural areas almost certainly create opportunities for collaboration among different units. These collaborations can be very fruitful, possibly compensating for some of the resource scarcity these agencies face (Brunet & Chandler, 2009). But considerable danger lies in the close-knit nature of some of the rural public safety networks. As noted by Maranto and Wolf (2013) in their discussion of local policing and education, disruptive yet useful reforms and innovations may be resisted when a local, cohesive, change-resistant establishment unites in opposition. If the interconnected public safety network within a small community is not receptive to new ideas, those innovations may never be adopted. Following Teodoro's work (2009, 2012), we may doubt whether many jurisdictions will accept innovations if there is little influx of new outside professionals into the local workforce. Perhaps, as Kim Wallace suggests in her case study, participation in conferences and state-wide professional associations can introduce novel ideas that would not naturally be considered in close-knit, somewhat isolated and insulated rural communities.

References

Bauroth, N. (2007). The effect of limiting participation in special district elections to property owners: A research note. *Public Budgeting & Finance*, 27(3), 71–88. https://doi-org.ezproxy.waterfield.murraystate.edu/10.1111/j.1540-5850.2007.00883.x

Bogomolova, S., Tan, P. J., Dunn, S. P., & Bizjak-Mikic, M. (2016). Understanding the factors that influence patient satisfaction with ambulance services. *Health Marketing Quarterly*, 33(2), 163–180. https://doi-org.ezproxy.waterfield.murraystate.edu/10.1080/07359683.2016.1166864

Brunet, J. R. (2008). Blurring the line between public and private sectors: The case of police officers' off-duty employment. *Public Personnel Management*, 37(2), 161–174. https://doi-org.ezproxy.waterfield.murraystate.edu/10.1177/009102600803700202

Brunet, J. R., & Chandler, W. C. (2009). Intersectoral police collaboration: An exploratory view from the states. *International Journal of Public Administration*, 32(2), 79–96. https://doi-org.ezproxy.waterfield.murraystate.edu/10.1080/01900690802434412

DeHart, C. (2020). The rise (and fall) of elected sheriffs. *APSA Preprints.* doi:10.33774/apsa-2020-gr1cm

Ellickson, R. C. (1986). Of coase and cattle: Dispute resolution among neighbors in Shasta County. *Stanford Law Review, 38,* 623–687. https://openyls.law. yale.edu/bitstream/handle/20.500.13051/4171/Of_Coase_and_Cattle___ Dispute_Resolution_Among_Neighbors_in_Shasta_County.pdf?sequence= 2&isAllowed=y

Federal Emergency Management Agency. (1997). *The Rural Fire Problem in the United States.* United States Fire Administration. www.usfa.fema.gov/downlo ads/pdf/statistics/rural.pdf

Greenblatt, A . (2018). In rural America, violent crime reaches highest level in a decade. Governing. www.governing.com/archive/gov-crime-rural-urban-cit ies.html

Henderson, A. C., & Sowa, J. E. (2018). Retaining critical human capital: Volunteer firefighters in the Commonwealth of Pennsylvania. *Voluntas: International Journal of Voluntary & Nonprofit Organizations, 29*(1), 43–58. https://doi-org. ezproxy.waterfield.murraystate.edu/10.1007/s11266-017-9831-7

Johnson, R. (2015). Examining the effects of agency accreditation on police officer behavior. *Public Organization Review, 15*(1), 139–155. https://doi-org.ezpr oxy.waterfield.murraystate.edu/10.1007/s11115-013-0265-4

Liederbach, J., & Frank, J. (2003). Policing Mayberry: The work routines of small-town and rural officers. *American Journal of Criminal Justice, 28,* 53–72. https://doi.org/10.1007/BF02885752

Maranto, R., & Wolf, P. J. (2013). Cops, teachers, and the art of the impossible: Explaining the lack of diffusion of innovations that make impossible jobs possible. *Public Administration Review, 73*(2), 230–40. doi:10.1111/ j.1540-6210.2012.02626.x.

National Criminal Justice Reference Service. (2017). Urban and rural victimization: Fact sheet. www.ncjrs.gov/ovc_archives/ncvrw/2017/images/ en_artwork/Fact_Sheets/2017NCVRW_UrbanRural_508.pdf

National Fire Protection Association. (2021). www.nfpa.org/News-and-Resea rch/Publications-and-media/NFPA-Journal/2021/Winter-2021/Reports/FF-Dea ths-2020

Oliver, W. M., & Meier, C. (2004). Stress in small town and rural law enforcement: Testing the assumptions. *American Journal of Criminal Justice, 29*(1), 37–56. https://doi.org/10.1007/BF02885703

Saunders, J., Cahill, M., Morral, A., Leuschner, K., Midgette, G., Hollywood, J., Matsuda, M., Wagner, L., & Taylor, J. (2016). The Justice Innovation Center: Identifying the Needs and Challenges of Criminal Justice Agencies in Small, Rural, Tribal, and Border Areas. RAND Corporation. Retrieved June 20, 2022 from: www.rand.org/pubs/research_reports/RR1479.html

Schmidthuber, L., & Hilgers, D. (2019). From fellowship to stewardship? Explaining extra-role behavior of volunteer firefighters. *Voluntas: International Journal of Voluntary & Nonprofit Organizations, 30*(1), 175–192. https://doi-org.ezproxy.waterfield.murraystate.edu/10.1007/s11266-018-0035-6

Simpson, C. R. (1996). A fraternity of danger. *American Journal of Economics & Sociology, 55*(1), 17–34. https://doi-org.ezproxy.waterfield.murraystate.edu/ 10.1111/j.1536-7150.1996.tb02705.x

Statista. (2021). Reported violent crime in the United States in 2020. www.statista.com/statistics/200445/reported-violent-crime-rate-in-the-us-states/

Teodoro, M. P. (2009). Bureaucratic job mobility and the diffusion of innovations. *American Journal of Political Science*, 53(1), 175–189. https://doi-org.ezproxy.waterfield.murraystate.edu/10.1111/j.1540-5907.2008.00364.x

Teodoro, M. P. (2012). Bureaucratic Ambition: Careers, Motives, and the Innovative Administrator. Johns Hopkins Studies in Governance and Public Management.

Weisheit, R., Falcone, D., & Wells, L. (2006). *Crime and Policing in Rural and Small Town America*. Waveland Press.

Wolf, R., Holmes, S. T., & Jones, C. (2016). Utilization and satisfaction of volunteer law enforcement officers in the office of the American sheriff: An exploratory nationwide study. *Police Practice and Research, 17*, 448–462.

Worden, R. (1990). A badge and a baccalaureate: Policies, hypotheses, and further evidence. *Justice Quarterly, 7*(3), 565–592.

Zoorob, M. (2019, November 12). *There's (Rarely) a New Sheriff in Town: The Incumbency Advantage for County Sheriffs*. Available at SSRN: https://ssrn.com/abstract=3485700 or http://dx.doi.org/10.2139/ssrn.3485700

CASE STUDY: PERSONAL REFLECTIONS ON SMALL TOWN POLICING

Kim Wallace

Local law enforcement agencies of 30 or fewer officers comprise 85 percent of the law enforcement agencies in the US. While policing in a small town can be challenging, it can also be a rewarding experience. Below is a perspective of police operations from a law enforcement professional serving a small town in Tennessee. The focus is on the distinctive features of policing in a small town and the impact of that rural setting on the officer.

I was born and raised in Stewart County, Tennessee, which has Dover as its county seat. This area is about 60 miles northwest of Nashville. According to the US Census, Dover's population in 2010 was 1,417. In 2020, it was 1,591.

While many officers come from a longstanding police family tradition, that was not my situation. I became interested in law enforcement at a young age and, unlike many officers, did not have a family member working in law enforcement. With an associate's degree in Police Science in hand, I was first hired as a dispatcher in 1988. After being turned down as a sheriff's deputy several times, I applied to the Dover police force in 1991 and became the city's first female police officer.

During my first year working in Dover, I attended the state law enforcement academy and completed DARE training. In Dover, I worked in patrol and in the school system for ten years. My education, community involvement, loyalty to the city, and longevity in the department prepared me to eventually serve as chief of police there.

Being a female chief in a predominantly male law enforcement profession in rural Tennessee presented me with many challenges. Some officers gave

DOI: 10.4324/9781003287766-32

me nicknames (some that should not be put in print), and I was teased about whether I had my bullet in one of my pockets, like deputy Barney Fife on "The Andy Griffith Show." However, I persisted. This was my dream job and my passion.

To be successful as a small town leader in law enforcement, a deep-seated commitment to both the people and place cannot be understated. At the time I was chosen to serve as police chief, I was involved in multiple civic groups (e.g., Kiwanis, Jaycees, church) and became even more involved in the community after becoming chief. These strong civic and community connections paid untold dividends for me professionally.

As a police chief of a small rural area, I was reluctant to join the Tennessee Association of Chiefs of Police (TACP). However, becoming a member of the TACP in 2000 ended up being one of the best decisions of my police career. Not only did I find professional colleagues, but I made friends for life. If I needed advice, I could pick up the phone and call any one of them. In 2007, they selected me as the first female president of the TACP.

Years later, when the city administrator left suddenly, I served in a dual role as both Dover city administrator and police chief. This dual post lasted seven years. Before I accepted the assignment, a former police chief advised me that there were three sets of people that I needed to keep happy to survive: employees, citizens, and the city council. I never forgot that.

In my experience, at least half of rural law enforcement is devoted to general service to the community rather than responding to criminal behavior. Serving the citizens is a priority. While this may mean that the officers are not spending most of their time on the narrow definition of law enforcement, community relationships help prevent crime or solve crimes when they occur. As I consider my work in rural law enforcement, a number of key ideas come to mind.

Hiring Hardships

At one time in rural America, the hiring process for police officers was simple and depended heavily on who you knew. While this is still true in some places, the process has changed considerably over the years. Thirty years ago, it would not be unusual for an applicant to talk freely with local council members, the chief, the mayor, or the city manager about their interest in the job. Those personal or political connections paid dividends. Through the years, however, the hiring process has transitioned to one that is more unbiased and fair.

One challenge that persists in police departments of small town America is the limited applicant pool. Many police recruits seek out the excitement that comes from being a part of a police force in a midsize or big city police force. To many qualified officers, rural America is simply not appealing in terms of their career or the salaries that are offered.

Rural communities are generally unable to offer salaries that attract large numbers of high-qualified applicants. Small departments generally cannot compete with salaries offered by large departments. As a result, small agencies must settle for candidates that are not as competitive. This can lead to an increase in turnover due to disciplinary action.

When large law enforcement agencies experience a shortage of officers, they aggressively recruit officers with the promise of an impressive benefit package and even incentives. This, of course, decreases the applicant pool for departments in smaller towns.

These challenges are not lost on rural departments. In response, many smaller departments are relaxing regulations and changing policies to compete with larger departments. Such changes include 12-hour shifts with every other weekend off, allowing tattoos that do not have to be covered up by long sleeves, and grooming policies that allow beards, and neatly groomed facial hair. Basic job qualifications are also relaxed. While large police departments often require applicants to have a college degree, many smaller departments do not have as stringent educational requirements.

While formal law enforcement training is critical, I have found that connections within the community are particularly important to the success of rural law enforcement officers. For that reason, some of the key skills we look for in new hires are people skills and common sense.

Onboarding new officers is another challenge for rural departments. Under Tennessee law, all new hire officers are required to attend the state police academy regardless of the size of the department. This requirement often puts a hardship on small police departments because the department is shorthanded for ten to twelve weeks while the newly hired officer is away at the academy.

On-the-job training looks different in rural police departments. After an officer graduates the state police academy, large departments generally have a field training officer (FTO) ride with the new officer for approximately three to six months. This is not the case with rural departments. While smaller departments value this kind of training, it generally occurs for a much shorter time, usually 30 days or less due to the limited number of officers on the force.

Small, rural police departments are also challenged with limited opportunities for career advancement. Typically, when someone reaches an administrative/rank position, they remain in that position for many years. While there is often substantial turnover in rural patrol divisions, this is generally not the case in supervisory positions. Furthermore, officer turnover in rural departments makes succession planning for leadership positions difficult.

Training Trials

Ongoing police training is another area where large and small departments differ. For example, the state of Tennessee requires a minimum of 40 hours of in-service training per year for an officer to receive an annual pay supplement and maintain his/her certification. Additional training beyond these 40 hours is strongly encouraged. Rural departments often seek out free training, district training, or online training provided by third-party vendors to minimize an officer's time away from the office, travel expenses, and overtime for existing personnel who cover for others who are away at training. As mentioned, the downside for rural communities is that, over time, their well-trained officers are increasingly more competitive job candidates for larger departments.

Rural public safety leaders must constantly fight against the mindset that "nothing bad happens here." This notion is commonly pervasive among small town residents, but can also be seen in officers. For their own safety, law enforcement officers must remain vigilant and not become complacent. Ongoing training is a large part of keeping officers alert and cautious for their own safety.

Officer Health and Safety

Due to the nationwide uptick in legal cases alleging officer misconduct, a mistrust toward law enforcement has occurred. Rural communities are not immune from this national trend. This shift has resulted not only in a decrease in those interested in pursuing law enforcement as a career, but also an increase in officer stress, sometimes manifesting in unhealthy lifestyles and health problems related to stress.

Officers today are more conscious of their personal safety than in the past, even in small departments. This is particularly true in rural communities where officers know that their only back-up is 15–30 minutes away. For this reason, the availability and quality of equipment used and worn by officers is critical. For example, officer body armor must be replaced every five years. Tasers, chemical spray, firearms, and other weapons carried by the officer require routine inspection and maintenance. Maintenance of equipment is not only a safety issue, but also a risk liability. Unlike larger municipal police operations, small rural departments struggle to provide officers with proper equipment due to limited funding. At times, grant money is the only option to address these safety concerns.

Personal Reflections on Rural Policing

As I look back, I feel a sense of satisfaction in the fact that I had a rewarding career in the town where I was born and raised. Serving those in my small town was like working with an extended family. In spite of the challenges that face rural public safety agencies today, career opportunities in law enforcement are bright. Rural America offers a valuable and fulfilling path for law enforcement professionals as they pursue their calling to protect and serve.

17
CHALLENGES IN RURAL EMERGENCY MANAGEMENT

Clinton McNair and Scott E. Robinson

Introduction

On December 10, 2021, the United States saw an unusual outbreak of tornadoes across Arkansas, Missouri, Tennessee, and Kentucky. While tornadoes are most commonly associated with the Texas panhandle, Oklahoma, and Kansas, the loosely defined "tornado alley" seems to be creeping east into the areas affected in this storm. Complicating the preparedness for these storms is the relative difficulty with emergency management activities in rural communities like Western Kentucky, Northeast Arkansas, and the "bootheel" region of Missouri. As weather patterns change, many areas – notably including rural areas– must begin preparing for new hazards and disasters.

This chapter will review the basics of emergency management followed by a discussion of the particular challenges facing public managers in rural areas. After the introduction of the underlying theoretical approach that defines contemporary emergency management, this chapter will focus on the four core phases of emergency management: mitigation, preparedness, response, and recovery. The chapter then explores the challenges within each of these four phases of emergency management within rural settings. The discussion concludes with a consideration of the major challenges looking forward for both scholarship and practice in rural emergency management.

DOI: 10.4324/9781003287766-33

An Introduction to Emergency Management

Emergency management has emerged as an interdisciplinary field of practice that aspires to reduce the damage done by a variety of hazards including natural hazards (e.g. tornadoes, hurricanes, earthquakes, floods), technological hazards (e.g. chemical spills, nuclear meltdown, widespread power loss), and intentional hazards (mass shootings, terrorism). At the core of this interdisciplinary field is the central dogma of emergency management:

HAZARD X VULNERABILITY → DISASTER (1)

This symbolic equation requires some explanation. The first important element of the central dogma is that a disaster is not merely the product of a specific hazard. For example, a tornado is a hazard but may, or may not, become a disaster. If the tornado strikes an entirely unpopulated area (say a deserted island), it will not become a disaster. Similarly, vulnerability in the absence of a hazard is not a disaster (which is not to say that it is not a problem). It is only when a hazard connects with a source of vulnerability that an event can become a disaster. The major implication of this central dogma is that the management of disasters requires the understanding of both hazards and vulnerability. This is why emergency management is inherently interdisciplinary. Emergency managers need to be familiar with the dynamics of specific hazards (e.g., how do winds develop during a hurricane?) as well as the vulnerabilities within their communities (e.g. who is most vulnerable to housing damage or an upcoming heat wave?). This requires a robust array of scholarship from meteorology, civil engineering, urban planning, geography, sociology, and public administration.

Within public administration, there is an additional central proposition related to the embeddedness of local governments within the US federal political system. The central dogma speaks to the general potential for an event to escalate into a hazard. Within the US federal system, the term "disaster" is reserved for an event that exceeds the capacity for local resources to address needs. One can think of this as starting at the household level. An event that may affect a household but does not disrupt their operations is not a disaster at all. The lack of household vulnerability prevented the hazards from escalating to a disaster. If the household cannot handle the hazard without significant disruption, the event can be a household-level disaster but is not a community-level disaster if the community can handle the disruption with its own resources (e.g., the fire department, local Red Cross housing assistance). Only if the community cannot address the disruption at the community level and has to appeal to the state for assistance is the event a local disaster. The event is only a state-level disaster if the state has to ask for outside assistance to address the disruption within its boundaries. Federal resources only become available when a state certifies that the event within its boundaries has exceeded its capacity to respond. This process represents the escalation logic of disaster to complement the central dogma of emergency management.

The last major concept in emergency management we need to understand in this chapter is the emergency management cycle—a sequence of four phases to help simplify and categorize the activities inherent in emergency management. These phases will serve as the basis for the discussion of the specific challenges faced in rural emergency management once we introduce each in general.

The Emergency Management Cycle

Although disasters are considered spontaneous, some natural disasters are seasonal or roughly predictable, such as hurricanes, tornadoes, or floods. These seasonal events force decision-makers to prepare communities for looming and unforeseen threats. Pragmatically, no plan is perfect and unexpected circumstances are guaranteed to happen in each event. However, the chance to predict the dynamics of natural hazards allows the community to prepare vulnerable areas to save lives and minimize damage (Khan & Khan, 2008). To help to create more effective plans and collaborate with other organizations, decision-makers and practitioners use the disaster cycle as a tool (Warfield, 2008). Although each disaster is different and no community is the same, the disaster cycle is a critical organizing principle for community efforts in emergency management.

The disaster cycle consists of four phases: mitigation, preparedness, response, and recovery.

Mitigation

The mitigation phase reduces the probability of damage within disasters. Examples of mitigation include land-use management, large construction projects like dams, and the use of construction code; all seek to reduce vulnerability. In addition, the mitigation phase looks at long-term activity to help reduce the effects caused by recurrent disasters, making it an important step in the disaster cycle. In 2000, Congress passed the Disaster Mitigation Act (DMA) to prioritize planning and help distribute disaster funds more effectively. The DMA works to help lessen the financial impacts of disasters and act as a more proactive approach (Nolon, 2009). The central goal of the mitigation phase is to create the hazard mitigation plan, which is the collection of data on vulnerable communities and identifying the potential dangers in the community. The completion of this plan allows communities to become eligible for pre- and post-disaster funding and the Hazard Mitigation Grant Program (Berke et al., 2012; Birkland, 2006; Burby et al., 1999; FEMA, 2008; Godschalk et al., 1999, 2009; Mileti, 1999; Smith, 2008).

Preparedness

The preparedness phase includes the effort of governments, organizations, and individuals to implement plans to save lives and minimize damage. Preparedness is the combination of planning, training, and exercising to design a system to help in an emergency (Quarantelli, 1999). Examples of preparedness would be creating stockpiles of food, medical supplies, organizing groups, testing the current emergency systems, and performing exercises and training with departments that assist with disaster response (Khan & Khan, 2008; Thorvaldsdóttirand Sigbjörnsson, 2014). The community's preparedness is key to coping with the impacts of a disaster and concerns the household and community levels. At the household level, preparedness includes securing supplies, developing evacuation strategies, and purchasing insurance. At the community level, being prepared consists of creating and testing warning systems to help the community become aware of oncoming danger (Comfort et al., 2004; Pinkowski, 2008; Prizzia, 2008).

As governments prepare for the unexpected, decision-makers must learn from past failures and successes. To do this, government and community organizations must look at how past events impact population density and vulnerable communities to help identify what resources impacted areas will need. Research suggests that effectively collaborating in the preparedness phase can offset the damage of spontaneous disasters and help distribute resources (Comfort et al., 2004; Pinkowski, 2008; Prizzia, 2008). Furthermore, the sophistication of each collaboration depends on the community network and their planning methods for each event. The more organized each network is, the more effectively the community can respond and help the community during and after the disasters (Jerolleman, 2020).

It is easy to confuse preparedness and mitigation efforts. Both phases involve pre-event activities to reduce vulnerability. The key difference is in scale. Mitigation efforts typically include large-scale operations at the community-level (sometimes at the county level—often larger units). While these units also prepare by developing plans, only larger communities are able to marshal the resources needed to build large mitigation-oriented projects like flood mitigation dams or to regulate building on a large scale as a mitigation effort.

Disaster Response

The third phase, response, involves emergency assistance for casualties of a disaster and the work of practitioners to help minimize further damage. This phase begins in the immediate aftermath of a hazard. The state or local leaders coordinate the response phase to implement rescues, provide shelter or medical aid during and after the storm (Jerolleman, 2020). Researchers and practitioners have found that each disaster has adverse effects on the most vulnerable groups in every community (Jerolleman, 2020). These vulnerable groups are children, the elderly, disabled, impoverished residents, or those in poor health. In a disaster, the community must work together to plan, respond, recover, help protect all community residents, and provide extra attention to the vulnerable community (Thorvaldsdóttirand Sigbjörnsson, 2014).

The disaster response phase relies on emergency response professionals' previous experience and technical knowledge. Although a significant amount of planning takes place, the response phase depends on local, state, and federal departments' ability to partner with NGOs to help response efforts. Essentially the success of this phase depends on the community's network of response teams and the strength of their collaboration. If the response to a disaster is not adequate, research has found that decisions made during the response stage affect the overall success of the recovery (Thorvaldsdóttirand Sigbjörnsson, 2014).

Disaster Recovery

The goal of the recovery phase is to restore housing, transportation, and public services, restart economic activity, and foster long-term community redevelopment and improvements. The recovery phase absorbs the majority of financial resources in the disaster cycle. (Orabi et al., 2009) The recovery process overlaps with the response stage and mitigation stage. After disaster response, recovery implements long-term efforts to rebuild and repair the community close to its pre-disaster form. The long-term recovery works into the mitigation phase to minimize future similar damages in another disaster. The immediate and long-term recovery stages need to be successful for an effective recovery phase.

Common terms used to define recovery include reconstruction, restoration, rehabilitation, and restitution (Quarantelli, 1999). All the terms work to bring communities back to the original form, but the emphasis on social relationships differs in each term. The term reconstruction focuses on the post-impact rebuilding of physical structures destroyed by disasters (Rouhanizadeh & Kermanshachi, 2020). Reconstruction is often the primary method decision-makers and operational personnel use to rebuild buildings and material infrastructures impacted by disasters. The term restoration attempts to bring a community's social relationships and physical structure back to pre-impact conditions (Fussell, 2015; Quarantelli, 1999; Rouhanizadeh & Kermanshachi, 2020). However, success is difficult to define due to the social response to the recovery efforts.

In post-disaster community rehabilitation, research finds the work focuses on rebuilding social connections with the community more than physical structures. However, rehabilitation's overall goal is to improve conditions relative to pre-disaster conditions. Of particular emphasis, community rehabilitation seeks to reduce vulnerability relative to the pre-disaster state. The final term, restitution, is the compensation provided to owners who experienced damage from the disaster (Quarantelli, 1999; Rouhanizadeh & Kermanshachi, 2020). It is the legal action for owners to come close to financial stability. An example of restitution would be insurance reimbursements or government buy-out programs. Although these terms can be considered analogous with recovery, the terms present a different outcome for individuals.

Immediate recovery efforts include restoring power, debris removal, or providing temporary shelter. At this step, local governments work to save lives and restore the community to normality. In addition, the local government will work to restore power and water within the impacted communities. Although the efforts for immediate recovery depend on the event's severity, the time for immediate recovery can be from one to six months (Fussell, 2015; Rouhanizadeh & Kermanshachi, 2020).

After removing debris, the local government begins the process of long-term recovery. According to FEMA, long-term recovery is the need to re-establish a healthy, functioning community that will sustain itself over time. In this stage of recovery, the time to bring communities back can take years. The examples of long-term recovery are to provide disaster-resistant housing units, offer low-interest loans to post-storm building improvements, provide buy-out programs for flooded areas, or infrastructure improvements (Frailing & Harper, 2015; Fussell, 2015; Rouhanizadeh & Kermanshachi, 2020). FEMA suggests that long-term recovery effort is community-driven to help decision-makers focus on the community's actual needs, so the work often falls on local organizations, NGOs, local and federal governments.

The Complications of Rurality

The general framework of emergency management (the central dogma, escalation logic, and phases of activities) reveals particular challenges one is likely to face in rural communities. This section will discuss some of the distinctive elements of rural communities that can influence the operations of emergency management. Of course, these challenges are not uniform across rural communities—there are many competing definitions of rurality that prevent such consistency. However, the discussed challenges have a particular relevance to rural emergency management.

The most familiar characteristic of rurality is low population density. The contrast between the isolated home on a large plot of land and the image of crowded cities is clear. The low population density has a variety of consequences for emergency management. A later section will discuss the implication for each phase of the emergency management cycle. However, the general consequences are related to the inability of communities with low population density to generate financial resources from taxes, the difficulty of supporting many organizations (e.g., charities, highly specialized government offices), and the difficulty of spontaneous organization at the neighborhood level. While sparse populations may indicate less concentration of vulnerability, they also indicate fewer resources to address the vulnerabilities that are present.

A second familiar characteristic is the geographic distance between rural households and larger cities. With many societal resources housed in large urban communities, access to some of these resources is limited within rural communities. A simple example can suffice. If one is forced to vacate a home damaged by a tornado, the stock of available temporary housing is quite limited. It is likely the case that the closest temporary housing is miles away—possibly in the nearest urban community.

A final general characteristic of relevance across the disaster cycle is the prevalence of emergency management professionals who serve in multiple roles. While larger communities can afford to hire a full-time emergency manager (or support an entire office of emergency management), rural communities often lack the resources to hire a full-time emergency management director. Instead, rural communities often rely on people serving in multiple roles simultaneously to reduce personnel costs. For example, emergency management responsibilities may fall to a local fire protection manager or, even, the county judge (who may not have any relevant training before assuming this role).

These three complications illustrate the general conditions of rural emergency management (though these issues have implications well beyond emergency management). The next sections will discuss how these and other elements define the context of rural emergency management.

Rural Mitigation

Rural communities have complex relationships with mitigation efforts. On the one hand, many large projects that help with mitigation and preparedness are located outside of urban areas. For example, flood mitigation dams are typically placed in sparsely populated rural communities. However, these facilities are placed in rural communities due to the relatively low costs of buying land for large projects. These facilities are not generally built to serve the rural communities in which they are placed—they reduce vulnerability for distant urban and suburban communities. It makes financial sense to build large projects in rural areas to reduce vulnerability in urban areas (lowering construction costs while serving a dense population).

Other issues arise in rural mitigation efforts: the comparison of building codes and regulations is yet more stark. The relatively low population levels and rarity of major building projects make building codes less relevant for rural communities than urban ones. Building hazard resilient structures is less of a concern in communities where there are fewer large structures overall. Further, the responsibility for vulnerability reductions within rural communities usually falls to individual households and businesses because there are fewer community resources available. Finally, rural communities often find themselves as the site of mitigation projects intended to reduce vulnerability in distant or neighboring communities. These additional issues and concerns regarding the challenges of rural mitigation planning have motivated various efforts to empower and inform rural emergency managers ().

Research into rural mitigation practices illustrates some of these tensions. A focused study of rural communities in central Florida revealed that there were significant needs for inter-organizational coordination for actors within these communities. This follows from the relatively low population density and consequently, low organizational density. Capacities and resources are spread more thinly across the organizations in rural communities. Only through coordination are these resources capable of supporting mitigation efforts (Kapucu, 2014).

Broader studies of the southeastern regions provide some contrasting—though not entirely contradictory—images of rural mitigation efforts. Jennifer Horney and her colleagues have conducted two studies of hazard mitigation plans across several southeastern states. In these communities, they found that there was more inter-organizational collaboration and better monitoring efforts within the rural counties than their comparable urban counterparts. However, the urban counties had more components in their plans related to goals and policies (Horney et al., 2013, 2015). Given the greater need for coordination in rural environments, which is the focus of the Kapucu et al. article referenced above, it is unclear whether the greater level of coordination in rural counties is yet sufficient to meet their needs in the absence of the concentration of resources (and vulnerability) in urban communities.

Rural Planning

Rural planning efforts overlap a great deal with mitigation efforts—as in their urban counterparts. The challenges of rural emergency planning are also similar. While the literature on rural mitigation emphasized the importance of inter-organizational coordination to overcome the challenges presented by low population density, the literature on planning emphasizes the limited access to specialized planning expertise in rural emergency management organizations.

In many ways, the limitations of planning expertise are the personnel counterpart to the resource challenges in rural mitigation. Rural communities typically lack the resources to hire teams of trained emergency management professionals and rely, instead, on generalists and people who occupy several organizational roles. A consequence of this challenge is that some scholars have developed indices and other analytical tools to help rural emergency managers to conduct risk assessments and other planning tasks without access to the teams and resources that more population dense communities may employ (Hoard et al., 2005; Cox & Hamlin, 2015). A good example of this is the Rural Resilience Index (RRI) (e.g., Cox & Hamlin, 2015). The RRI is built to be easy to use for planners with little emergency management training but still empower careful and important vulnerability and risk identification.

Similar research identifies the challenges of planning within hospitals, specifically. A national survey of rural hospitals provides a snapshot of how the challenges in rural hospitals mirror the challenges of rural emergency management generally. Hospitals, they note, have to adapt to circumstances in which they have limited resources to improve surge capacity to handle a large influx of patients related to a disaster. The solution they propose is to reframe hospital planning as a community-wide effort. This matches the previous recommendations to emphasize inter-organizational collaboration (Manley et al., 2006).

Rural Response

As the hazard arrives in a community, the focus shifts from planning and mitigation to issues of response and recovery. Like mitigation and preparedness, the boundaries between response and recovery can be blurry. Response activities typically involve immediate risks related to a hazard and the return of the community to basic functionality. Of course, response involves moving people out of immediate risks related to the hazard, directly or unrelated. Basic functionality also includes the provision of basic services like utilities (power, water, access to roadways) and the support for basic activities like groceries and healthcare.

Both removing people from harm's way and restoring community functions have a different tenor in a rural environment. The key element of rural response activities is the geographical isolation implied in most rural settings. It was low population density that cast the longest shadow over mitigation and planning efforts. For response, the actual physical environment plays a major role. Some rural environments are relatively accessible throughout their territory.

Consider an event in rural areas of Kansas. The victims of the disaster may be removed a great distance from emergency management resources. A household could be hours away, by car, from a hospital or law enforcement office. Access to faster resources like a medical helicopter may also be quite limited. Distance, itself, can present a challenge to responding to hazards that affect rural areas including areas far removed from emergency management resources. Rural areas are also more likely to include treacherous terrain that can complicate response activities. One is more likely to encounter areas that are mountainous or otherwise inaccessible in rural communities than in urban communities. Events affecting rural communities can include regions that are difficult to reach with emergency vehicles, for example. If one cannot drive an ambulance to an affected area, the ability to extend medical protection is limited. It is also likely the case in these situations that the factors that make getting an ambulance in difficulty will also make it difficult to get people out of the region for medical care.

The challenges of terrain have motivated the development of drone technologies for rural emergency management, though this work is still largely a focus of engineering development as a potential option in the future. Drones (more technically, unmanned aerial vehicles) present a key opportunity to extend emergency management services into challenging terrain (Bennett et al. 2017). The potential for drones extends beyond the visual surveillance they can obviously provide, though this can be important. Bennett et al. (2017) situate their analysis of the use of drones within a broader discussion of technological achievements in accessibility. Drones may also extend communication technologies and other forms of interactivity into spaces where there is no existing communication infrastructure. This could transform emergency management in the most challenging rural environments.

Like with planning, collaboration may be a barrier to a successful response. If organizations in the community work as individuals and not as a team, the potential for losing life increases, or the community can miss the opportunity to gain resources to help (Jerolleman, 2020). Often these areas are identified as smaller or rural communities where resources are minimal, and teams lack in-depth knowledge of disaster recovery. This is an example of the potential for all-hazards (and all phase) improvements made possible with investments in general emergency management capacities—particularly in rural areas.

Rural Recovery

The final phase of the emergency management process is recovery. This phase is difficult to distinguish from response. The focus here is not merely on the return to community operations. The focus of recovery is to either restore the community to its previous state, to restore the community to what it would have been but for the disaster, or to restore the community to its pre-event state but with reduced vulnerability. These efforts take on a particular tenor within rural environments.

It is important to note that many rural communities are struggling without being victims of hazards and disasters. Rural communities likely possess more limited economic bases than their urban counterparts. This creates specific complications for rural disaster recovery. A more limited resource base and/or a more focused reliance on a single industry or company can make disaster recovery much more challenging in rural environments.

In addition, many of the factors related to successful rural disaster recovery are similar to those of the other phases. A major factor, as in other phases, is the ability of a rural community to catalyze collaborative partnerships. To a great extent, a successful disaster recovery process depends on strong collaborative efforts between all levels of government. However, the need to understand who is in control can often be convoluted when working with multiple governments. In addition, the success of the recovery process can be affected by other factors, such as defined goals, level of recovery, community size, community opinion of recovery, and the ripple effects of disasters.

The most significant barrier to recovery is the size of the unit impacted by the community. For example, although a disaster impacted a whole city, only a small portion of the community experienced damage. The smaller unit size will experience more damage, and research has found that smaller, more rural communities will have greater difficulty with an overall recovery (Rouhanizadeh & Kermanshachi, 2020; Quarantelli, 1999). In addition, after each natural disaster, resources become scarce, and the most vulnerable/disadvantaged communities face difficulties receiving funds or repairs. If these communities encounter multiple disasters, recovery becomes a daunting task and hinders mitigation for future storms. Another barrier is whether communities should perform a rebuild or a restoration. Although the recovery method is at the operational level, the overall community's ability to recover from a disaster will depend on the disaster type and the preexisting condition of an area. In addition, the recovery is affected by the community's preparation for the disaster, combined with their ability to gain access to economic resources combined with effective leadership. Finally, researchers find that the need to repair the social and psychological effects within the community is just as critical, and these are considered the ripple effects of storms (Cochrane, 2004).

Conclusion

Many communities struggle to prepare for and respond to the diverse array of irregular but significant disasters they face. These struggles are all the more challenging in rural environments. For this reason, rural officials need to take particular care in emergency management—whether they are an emergency management official or being brought into emergency management efforts based on some other position.

A general concern across the phases of emergency management is the need for collaborative efforts connecting people across organizations and sectors. It is often the role of designated emergency management offices to serve as coordinators and conveners for such collaboration. However, it is rare for rural areas to have full-time emergency managers, much less entire, dedicated emergency management offices. Instead, people with other primary positions (planners, judges, etc.) may have to step into this role and will—even more than in urban settings—have to rely on coordination and collaboration to cover for the lack of resources dedicated to emergency management.

The two other, more obvious, concerns for rural emergency management are developing strategies to address regions with low population density and, possibly, difficult terrain. Communication strategies, for example, have to differ in rural environments because of the mixture of the demographics more common in rural areas and the still problematic digital divide (Robinson et al., 2022). There is reason for optimism amid these concerns. Rural regions avoid some of the thornier problems in urban environments related to particularly dense populations. What is most essential is that rural administrators understand the demands of emergency management (and the problems invited by the failing to prepare for hazards) and the needs of their particular communities.

References

Bennett, S., Agostinho, S., & Lockyer, L. (2017). The process of designing for learning: Understanding university teachers' design work. *Educational Technology Research and Development*, 65(1), 125–145. https://doi.org/10.1007/s11423-016-9469-y

Berke, P., Smith, G., & Lyles, W. (2012). Planning for resiliency: Evaluation of state hazard mitigation plans under the disaster mitigation act. *Natural Hazards Review*, 13(2), 139–149.

Birkland, T. A. (2006). *Lessons of Disaster: Policy Change After Catastrophic Events*. Georgetown University Press.

Burby, R. J., Beatley, T., Berke, P. R., Deyle, R. E., French, S. P., Godschalk, D. R., … & Platt, R. H. (1999). Unleashing the power of planning to create disaster-resistant communities. *Journal of the American Planning Association*, 65(3), 247–258.

Cochrane, H. C. (2004). Indirect losses from natural disasters: Measurement and myth. In *Modeling Spatial and Economic Impacts of Disasters*. In Y. Okuyama & S E. Chang (Eds.)), *Modeling Spatial and Economic Impacts of Disasters*. Springer Science & Business Media. 37–52.

Comfort, L. K., Ko, K., & Zagorecki, A. (2004). Coordination in rapidly evolving disaster response systems: The role of information. *American Behavioral Scientist*, 48(3), 295–313.

Cox, R. S., & Hamlin, M. (2014). Community disaster resilience and the rural resilience index. *American Behavioral Scientist*, 59(2), 220–237.

FEMA. (2008). *Local Multi-Hazard Mitigation Planning Guidance Under the Disaster Mitigation Act of 2000* (Blue Book). FEMA.

Frailing, K., & Harper Jr., D. W. (2015). Through the lens of Katrina: Long-term disaster recovery in the United States. *American Behavioral Scientist*, 59(10), 1207–1213.

Fussell, E., Haney, T. J., Elliott, J. R., Barber, K., Belkhir, J. A., Hite, A. B., … & Van Brown, B. L. (2015). *Rethinking Disaster Recovery: A Hurricane Katrina Retrospective*. Lexington Books.

Gebre, T., & Gebremedhin, B. (2019). The mutual benefits of promoting rural-urban interdependence through linked ecosystem services. *Global Ecology and Conservation*, 20, e00707.

Godschalk, D., Bohl, C. C., Beatley, T., Berke, P., Brower, D., & Kaiser, E. J. (1999). *Natural Hazard Mitigation: Recasting Disaster Policy and Planning*. Island Press.

Godschalk, D. R., Rose, A., Mittler, E., Porter, K., & West, C. T. (2009). Estimating the value of foresight: Aggregate analysis of natural hazard mitigation benefits and costs. *Journal of Environmental Planning and Management*, 52(6), 739–756.

Hoard, M., Homer, J., Manley, W., Furbee, P., Haque, A., & Helmkamp, J. (2005). Systems modeling in support of evidence-based disaster planning for rural areas. *International Journal of Hygiene and Environmental Health*, 208(1–2), 117–125.

Horney, J. A., Nguyen, M., Cooper, J., Simon, M., Ricchetti-Masterson, K., Grabich, S., … & Berke, P. (2013). Accounting for vulnerable populations in rural hazard mitigation plans: Results of a survey of emergency managers. *Journal of Emergency Management, 11*(3), 205–211.

Horney, J., Simon, M., Grabich, S., & Berke, P. (2015). Measuring participation by socially vulnerable groups in hazard mitigation planning, Bertie County, North Carolina. *Journal of Environmental Planning and Management, 58*(5), 802–818.

Jerolleman, A. (2020). Challenges of post-disaster recovery in rural areas. In S. Laska (Ed.), *Louisiana's Response to Extreme Weather*. Springer Open Series, 285–310. www.springer.com/series/15334

Kapucu, N. (2014). Collaborative governance and disaster recovery: The National Disaster Recovery Framework (NDRF) in the US. In R. Shaw (Ed.), *Disaster Recovery*. Springer Open Series, 41–59.

Khan, H., Vasilescu, L. G., & Khan, A. (2008). Disaster management cycle: A theoretical approach. *Journal of Management and Marketing, 6*(1), 43–50.

Kim, K. Y., Manley, D. G., & Yang, H. (2006). Ontology-based assembly design and information sharing for collaborative product development. *Computer-Aided Design, 38*(12), 1233–1250.

Mileti, D. (1999). *Disasters by Design: A Reassessment of Natural Hazards in the United States*. Joseph Henry Press.

Nolon, J. R. (2009). Climate change and sustainable development: The quest for green communities—Part II. *Planning & Environmental Law, 61*(11), 3–15.

Orabi, W., El-Rayes, K., Senouci, A. B., & Al-Derham, H. (2009). Optimizing postdisaster reconstruction planning for damaged transportation networks. *Journal of Construction Engineering and Management, 135*(10), 1039–1048.

Paton, D., Smith, L., Daly, M., & Johnston, D. (2008). Risk perception and volcanic hazard mitigation: Individual and social perspectives. *Journal of Volcanology and Geothermal Research, 172*(3–4), 179–188.

Pinkowski, J., Ed. (2008). *Disaster Management Handbook*. CRC Press.

Prizzia, R. (2008). *The Role of Coordination in Disaster Management*. Taylor & Francis.

Quarantelli, E. L. (1999). *The Disaster Recovery Process: What we Know and do Not Know from Research*. University of Delaware, Disaster Research Center.

Robinson, S., Bidwell, N. J., Cibin, R., Linehan, C., Maye, L., Mccarthy, J., ... & Teli, M. (2021). Rural islandness as a lens for (rural) HCI. *ACM Transactions on Computer-Human Interaction (TOCHI), 28*(3), 1–32.

Rouhanizadeh, B., & Kermanshachi, S. (2020). Post-disaster reconstruction of transportation infrastructures: Lessons learned. *Sustainable Cities and Society, 63*, 102505.

Thorvaldsdóttir, S., & Sigbjörnsson, R. (2014). Disaster-function management: Basic principles. *Natural Hazards Review, 15*(1), 48–57.

Warfield, C. (2008). *The Disaster Management Cycle: Disaster Mitigation and Management*. Retrieved October 17, 2012 from: www.gdrc.org/uem/disasters/1-dm_cycle.html

PART III

Partnerships

18

ENHANCING RURAL CAPACITY AND PUBLIC SERVICE VALUES THROUGH INTERGOVERNMENTAL AND INTERSECTORAL COLLABORATION

Jeremy L. Hall and Donna M. Handley

As we consider the environment within which local governments operate, it is critical to look at the other levels of government within the US federal system—the federal government and the states. Operating within the structure of federalism laid out in the US Constitution, whereby the federal government shares power with the sovereign states, the interactions that occur between and across these various levels of government is commonly called "intergovernmental relations" (IGR). If federalism is the structure, IGR is the pattern of day-to-day interactions among governments at all levels—federal, state, local, regional, and even quasi-nongovernmental organizations (QUANGOs)—that consists of the policy relationships, communications, and the redistribution of funding to provide public services across the nation. As the era of government transitioned into one characterized by governance, IGR is increasingly characterized by intersectoral relations, with private firms, nonprofit organizations, and, through coproduction, even citizens playing direct and influential roles. Hall and Battaglio (2018) have called this trend "reduced-boundary governance." While the boundaries are less clear, what remains clear is that various actors, formal and informal, play essential roles in governance, and governmental actors at all levels play key roles in bringing about policy results. Moreover, wicked problems have forced governments to be more and more creative in finding ways to collaborate, internally and externally, to bring about results (Christensen & Lægreid 2007). Over the years, the relationship between the national and state governments has remained in a near-constant state of flux, shaping and reshaping domestic public policies, expanding government programs, and redistributing fiscal

DOI: 10.4324/9781003287766-35

resources to states, counties, and cities in need. This chapter will discuss these relationships, elaborate on the importance of intergovernmental relations, and highlight key areas in which rural cities and towns are impacted by these relationships.

Overview and History of Intergovernmental Relations

The structure of US government as a federal republic institutionalized shared power between the federal and state governments. Over time, the relationship has shifted, with notable inequalities from state to state. Inequalities are more pronounced at the local level, where even vast regions, like Appalachia or the Mississippi Delta experience economic and social disparities from their urban counterparts. "The term *intergovernmental relations* originated in the United States in the 1930s, but it remains a relatively obscure and poorly understood phrase" (Wright, 1988, p. 3). Wright calls the timeframe prior to the 1930s the "conflict phase" of IGR (1988, p. 66), as there was an emphasis on identifying which roles and jurisdictions each level of government would oversee. Just as the Constitution outlines the powers of the federal government and the rights granted to states, Dillon's Rule was the 1868 ruling that maintained that local governments exist at the discretion and oversight of state governments. That is, while states are sovereign entities, local governments are their creatures; they exist at the pleasure of the state and are subject to state regulation. However, most states have chosen to reverse the bias against local autonomy by establishing home rule status for some local governments.

As the complexities of government grew along with the population of the United States, it became clear that maintaining strict boundaries and the concept of "layer cake federalism" (Grodzins 1960) would not solve the problems that were emerging with public infrastructure, education, finances, and healthcare. The "marble cake" version of federalism (Grodzins 1960) became a more appropriate symbol to describe the relationships between governments and their partners to ensure a more efficient delivery of public services, without separate layers and with a more intermingled existence.

The respective roles of state and federal governments have shifted drastically over time. From the founding, the states were the primary governmental units. Starting as colonies, and organizing through the Articles of Confederation after declaring independence from Great Britain, states had resources that the poorly organized nascent federal government did not. The constitution solidified the national government and its authority, though it was limited with a carefully worded 10th Amendment that reserved powers not delegated to the federal government for the states and the people. It was not until the Civil War, and the following period of reconstruction, that the powers of the federal government began to supersede those of the states. The role of the federal government has been in a state of increase over most of our nation's history, right up to the present. Significant events turned focus toward the federal government and fueled it with resources. The 16th Amendment, ratified in 1913, was a game changer by allowing the federal government to levy taxes on incomes. World Wars I and II required a centralized national response to global concerns. And Roosevelt's New Deal saw a massive involvement by the federal government at the community level, providing projects that fueled employment, income, and ultimately the infrastructure necessary for economic development. This growth in power was not without checks, though. Ronald Reagan swept into power with a message of smaller government, by which some discretion was restored to the states. Following the events of 9/11/2001, the federal government again found itself in the position to respond to common issues of global concern. Federal power is never absolute; there is a constant give and take, where the law is tested for the appropriateness of any action. The latest threat to unchecked federal authority is the US Supreme Court, which has begun a process of restoring policy powers to the states in decisions like *Dobbs v. Jackson Women's Health Organization.*

Through all of these ebbs and flows, the federal tax structure has been more productive than that of the states, which tend to be based on less progressive property tax bases. And the United States federal government has the ability to print currency and carry debt, which the states do not. Consequently, hard times have seen the federal government come to the rescue when states and localities are unable to do so themselves. Disaster relief is one example. Over time, the groundwork was laid for a partnership to develop; while the federal government was better equipped to raise revenue, it lacked the capacity and experience on the ground to be able to effectively use that revenue to address problems. The solution— a happy amalgamation of policy strengths—was the birth of fiscal federalism, whereby the federal government passes its funds back to state and local governments for their use in providing governance in its many forms. General Revenue Sharing was the unfettered, no strings attached, formulaic passing of federal funds to states and local governments for their use. Such open-ended transfers were eliminated in the 1980s. Over time, federal fiscal transfers became more task-specific. Block grants are, as the name implies, chunks of funding designated for particular purposes, such as the Community Development Block Grant (CDBG), which has a special set aside of money for small cities, with the money distributed by state governments.

Categorical grants are funding for specific projects that are offered on a competitive basis. As with the general trends in federalism, the federal government began to be more constructive in its use of grant conditions to effect federal priorities in local programs. Through these policy "strings"' and matching requirements, federal agencies have been able to leverage local investment while forcing local adherence to a host of federal policy requirements that range from labor rates to environmental review (Hall, 2009).

A new form of government was born in the 1960s to provide a mechanism for governmental coordination between federal, state, and local entities. Regional councils of government provide a mechanism for intergovernmental coordination, while also building the capacity necessary to facilitate local government success in competing for federal dollars (Hall, 2008a, Hall 2008b). Ronald Reagan attempted to use these regional councils to give states a voice in federal grant activities within their borders through Executive Order 12372 (Hall, 2008c). They have played a very important role in narrowing the capacity gap, and thereby giving rural and underprivileged communities a fair shot at federal grant revenue (Hall, 2010).

The several decades following WWII saw tremendous growth in federal grants-in-aid to states and local governments to help provide essential funding to serve communities' needs. This led to the involvement of additional sectors and groups and led to the "all join in" conclusion stated by Lovell:

Very few functions performed by any level of government are performed by that level of government alone. Almost all functions are shared by all levels of government, with each level contributing some portion or with all levels involved at all portions, depending on the function.

(Lovell, 1979, p. 14)

The competition for federal dollars is characterized by a fragmented, chaotic structure of grant funding and awards. Some funds are granted based on formulas, calculated based on certain demographic factors to provide a more equitable distribution of funding, while other grants were more specific based on the types of projects, such as infrastructure grants, focusing on highways, or water and sewer projects (Hall, 2009). As revenue sharing declined, there was a simultaneous movement to "block together" groups of categorical grant programs into broader block grant programs. These proved a popular alternative approach in the effort to provide funding to a state or local government and let them decide how to best use the monies, within broad parameters. Block grants have weaker restrictions on fund use, which helped to shift decision-making to lower levels of government, and coordinated with the changes in the federal budgeting process, as planning and measuring performance became important strategies for success.

A bit of a paradox has been at work over the last half century, with the federal government devolving policy responsibility to the states in some cases, while increasing strings and building federal control in others. Within the context of devolution writ large, IGR has witnessed a patchwork reversal of the longstanding trend of increasing federal government power to one that returns discretion to the states. Gradually policy decisions have been reformulated at the state level. In some instances, this authority trickled down to local governments, particularly through home rule legislation, in order to give these government leaders and even citizens more access to the policy process and the decisions impacting projects and funding in their states and communities.

Whatever the specific form of government grants, the shared responsibility between levels of government has been instrumental in bringing about results efficiently. As tensions rise among groups, including political parties—factions, to use Madison's terminology from Federalist 10—it is less clear that this shared service delivery relationship will be sustainable in the long term. In particular, party control now comes with visceral differences in policy priorities and approaches, and a willingness to execute those priorities through any means necessary. When a single party controls both the legislative and executive branches of federal government, the ground is laid for major policy shifts, some of which run contrary to state values. The federal system works well, so long as there is mutual respect among each level of government for the sovereign rights of the other. At such time as one level uses its leverage, financial or regulatory, to usurp another, conflict enters the arena and tension will result. For this reason, it is important to reflect on both the purposes and the politics of IGR.

Purposes and Politics of IGR

There are two primary purposes of the system of intergovernmental relations in the United States. They include the functions of redistributive policy and regulatory policy:

1. To redistribute funding from the federal government to both state and local levels in order to more efficiently provide public services while respecting contextual differences from place to place; and
2. To devolve policy decisions to the subnational levels of government in order to better target specific needs and financially support those

needs as deemed appropriate by the elected representatives in those jurisdictions.

While cooperation is a critical component of these relationships, it is also important to note that the politics of the IGR relationship can impact states and local governments in ways that promote competition and conflict. As Stephens and Wikstrom suggest, "the national government has the revenue sources of the nation at its disposal, whereas state and local governments are mostly limited to the resources within their respective political jurisdictions. As a result, the national government has used its ability to spend money to influence the activities of state and local governments using grants in aid. Some would say the spending authority has been to persuade, bribe, cajole, and affect what the state and local governments do" (2006, p. 27). It must be noted in this context that the politics of policy-making, and for setting guidelines for how and when funding can be spent at other levels of government, do inevitably play a role in maintaining federal supremacy in the IGR relationship.

Over the last century, there has been significant disagreement over how much discretion and autonomy subnational governments should have and where a uniform, national standard is needed. Often the consideration of how government functions are to be distributed relies upon some version of the *subsidiarity principle*. The subsidiarity principle refers to the proper allocation of responsibility and authority for decisions within a society. It can pertain to decisions located within any collection of units and civic associations nested within one another in any society. This doctrine largely asserts that responsibility and authority for decisions should be located at the lowest, most disaggregated level that is feasible to protect the dignity and autonomy of human beings. Centralized authority presumably is justified in protecting those abused in local communities by those empowered there, and centralized authority is justified in redistributing resources to those parts of society that suffer great poverty and want and should protect one community that is harmed by spillover effects from another. In these respects, the subsidiarity doctrine suggests standards comparable to those standards suggested by the fiscal federalism literature. That literature largely suggests that policy problems that have significant externalities or spillover effects, either beneficial or harmful, should be handled by higher levels of government.

Some policies are beyond the purview of local control because a decisive coalition at the national level believes that a uniform standard is morally required. Much of the controversy turns on disputes about where and when policy uniformity is required. In a diverse society, federalism allows considerable variation in which policies are adopted and implemented within different jurisdictions. Some states' constituents that have different preferences and values will adopt policies that differ from the policies of other states. More common is when one or more states refuse federal funding because with it comes interference with those local values. One of the most notable examples of this was Louisiana's reluctance to accept federal highway funds because the US Congress tied it to a minimum drinking age of 21, whereas Louisiana, until the cost became too great, had observed a legal drinking age of 18. Some states refused available federal dollars for various parts of the COVID-19 relief packages that were made available, while others even prohibited their local governments from drawing on those funds. Even within a state, preferences may differ substantially—especially from urban centers to rural hinterlands where government has traditionally played a more limited role.

For the purpose of this book, it is notable that the preferences that characterize small towns and rural areas differ from those of big city residents and suburbanites. At the risk of stereotyping or overgeneralizations, rural people and small town residents are more politically conservative, more religiously observant, and less cosmopolitan than the rest of the people in their state. They prefer limited government, low taxes, and only essential government services. In Kentucky, for example, there are county-level constitutional offices that fulfill those basic services: a sheriff for tax collection and, later, law enforcement, constables for law enforcement, county clerks for record keeping of marriages and land transfers, coroners for the obvious tasks associated with that position. As time wore on, demand for other services grew; some have been provided directly by those general-purpose governments, such as road maintenance and animal control, while others have been relegated to special districts that can carry debt and operate more efficiently as an enterprise, as is the case for utilities such as water and sewerage.

In addition to conditions of aid, higher levels of government can intervene in the policy affairs of lower levels of government through a mechanism known as *preemption*. In US law, preemption refers to "the principle that a federal law supersedes state law (and a state law supersedes local law) where both governments have made laws on the same subject and the laws conflict." (Nolo, 2022). This doctrine is derived from the supremacy clause of Article VI, paragraph 2, of the Constitution which provides that "This Constitution and the Laws of the United States which shall be made in Pursuance thereof, and all Treaties made, or which shall be made, under the Authority of the United States, shall be the supreme Law of the Land, and the Judges in every State shall be bound thereby, any Thing in the Constitution or Laws of any State to the Contrary notwithstanding." Preemption has been an important concern throughout American history, and some observers have claimed that preemption of state regulatory authority by national law is "the central federalism issue of our time" (Gardbaum, 1994, p. 768). As it pertains to local governments, it is helpful to note that from the twentieth century to the present, regulation at both the federal and state levels has increased dramatically. In many cases, we find that both the state and federal governments can share overlapping, concurrent regulatory authority in many policy areas (Gardbaum, 1997). With this overlapping of policy, authority conflicts between state and federal laws have become more common. The courts and legal scholars, over time, have developed theories of preemption to offer guidance regarding when federal law would supersede that of the states.

It is within this tension that policy is tested and tried, largely in the courts, to determine where federal government has overreached, and which powers truly do reside with the states. Where the federal government cannot pay for its priorities directly, it regulates them. Where they can't be bought, a combination of regulatory pressure and financial incentives are applied as leverage to shift state thinking. Still, states have proven time and again that there are areas in which they maintain and exercise considerable policy discretion. Were the field of values uniform and homogeneous, such distinctions would be without differences; however, values are varied, and organized through political processes, parties, and elections, creating the foundation for such tension and conflict. The nation was founded on the values of self-determination and liberty, and such values are closely held in many rural areas across the fruited plain; consequently, states continue to leverage considerable authority in many policy domains.

IGR Impacts on Rural Cities and Towns

Federal Support

Although the majority of federal government funding is distributed to larger cities across the nation, it is helpful here to consider the rural communities by the numbers. The US Census states that about 60 million people, or one in five Americans, live in rural America (2017). Geographically, 97 percent of the United States land mass is considered rural but only 19.3 percent of the population lives there (US Census, 2017). Conversely, urban areas make up only 3 percent of the nation's land mass, but over 80 percent of the population lives there (US Census, 2017). There are just over 3,000 counties in the United States, of varied size and composition; of those, 702 are completely rural. Like their urban counterparts, small towns and rural communities across the United States want to boost their economies and improve the quality of life for those who live there. Local leaders also want access and influence over policy decisions that will impact their constituents' lives.

Rural economies are characterized by primary economic activities: agriculture, fishing, mining, and extractive industries such as timber. Agriculture and the farming economy have historically been the primary source of employment and revenues for rural communities across the nation, where small family farms were once commonplace. The federal government has typically led efforts to address rural needs through its redistributive function. During the Lincoln administration, Congress established the US Department of Agriculture (USDA) in 1862 to provide leadership on food, agriculture, natural resources, and development efforts for Americans. Over 100 years later, the Rural Development Act of 1972 (RDA) directed the Secretary of Agriculture to establish a nationwide rural development partnership with states and local governments, and the National Rural Development Partnership (NRDP) emerged from the RDA. In the 1980s, a strategic effort was made to incorporate networks between the government, private, and nonprofit sectors to address rural needs and require annual updates on progress made (USDAg, n.d.).

Some large redistributive efforts have taken on a regional focus. The most notable is the Appalachian Regional Commission, which funnels federal monies for economic development into the 423 Appalachian counties of 13 states. ARC was established in 1965. The Mississippi Delta Regional Authority is a second example of targeted federal assistance to rural, underdeveloped regions, founded in 1988.

In 1990, the President's Initiative on Rural America presented several initiatives, including the formation of the President's Council on Rural America, with members drawn from farmers, state and local governments, rural businesses, and high-technology industries to advise the federal government on improving federal rural development policy (US Department of Agriculture, n.d.). A second initiative was for each state to establish a Rural Development Council to coordinate Federal Rural Development programs in its region, and as a result over 40 states developed rural development councils (USDA, n.d.). A hallmark of these changes was the establishment of highly targeted federal programs to invest in local economies in the most impoverished areas of the country, such as the federal empowerment zones program.

In 2009, the Obama administration launched the Partnership for Sustainable Communities to better coordinate policies, programs, and funding for rural areas across the various federal departments that support rural areas. The federal partnership included the US Department of Housing and Urban Development (HUD), the US Department of Transportation

(DOT), and the US Environmental Protection Agency (EPA)—along with the USDA—to ensure that priorities, spending, and programs were coordinated in ways that would help rural communities thrive for current and future generations (Partnership for Sustainable Communities, 2012). The impact of funding in support of programs for rural areas is vast, indicating a number of areas in which funding and technical assistance are available to help sustain rural areas (see Table 18.1).

TABLE 18.1 Federal Resources for Sustainable Rural Communities (US Departments and Programs)

US Department of Housing and Urban Development
   Community Planning & Development (Small Cities Program)
   Public Housing
   Multifamily and Single Family Housing
   Fair Housing
   Tribes
   Supportive Housing for Target Populations
   Healthy Homes
US Department of Transportation
   Planning & Capacity Building
   Multimodal Transportation
   Public Transit
   Streets & Highways
   Tribes
   Supportive Services for Target Populations
US Environmental Protection Agency
   Community Planning
   Brownfields Cleanup and Redevelopment
   Water Infrastructure & Water Quality
   Tribes
   Environmental Justice
   Healthy Buildings
   Energy Efficiency
US Department of Agriculture
   Community and Economic Development
   Business Development
   Single Family Housing (Rural Development mortgages)
   Multifamily Housing
   Agriculture and Food
   Land Conservation
   Utilities and Energy Efficiency

Note: A more detailed guide to programs, eligible applicants, and descriptions of the assistance programs can be found in a Summary Matrix at www.epa.gov/sites/default/files/documents/federal_resources_rural.pdf

State Support and Resources

Currently, the USDA is the lead federal agency helping to promote growth and prosperity in rural communities, providing technical assistance, loans, and grants to build critical infrastructure such as broadband, water systems, and hospitals (USDA, 2020). Their programs expand access to "e-connectivity, electric, and transportation infrastructure, and support business growth, healthcare, education, housing, and other community services" (USDA, 2020). They support multiple area offices in each state, and rural residents can access assistance through local cooperatives as well as cooperative extensions that are part of state land grant universities.

Most states engage in rural development and provide support for rural governance through a web of agencies and programs. Because, historically, agencies were developed as functional silos that address one specific duty (e.g., transportation, law enforcement, education), no single agency has sufficient span of control or resources to address all rural concerns. In an era characterized by wicked problems, governance rather than government, and whole-of-government solutions that disregard traditional silo-style management, budgets and capacity continue to exist within such silos. Consequently, the most coordinated approaches require considerable cooperation, planning, and interagency collaboration to address rural problems. For example, Kentucky has a dedicated Department for Local Government which provides technical assistance to local governments with basic functions like budgeting, but also offers grants and loans to finance local government projects. The Kentucky Transportation Cabinet assesses traffic volume, plans for road development, expansion, and improvement, and provides the necessary road capacity for communities to develop and thrive. The Kentucky Cabinet for Economic Development works to create and retain jobs by stimulating employment opportunities across the state. The Kentucky Department of Agriculture supports farms and agricultural businesses. The list goes on and on, as each agency tackles a small part of the comprehensive problem of rural underdevelopment and/or economic decline.

Even without formal coordinating agencies, many local officials are quite aware of the interconnectedness of grant programs across different policy areas. The Medicaid program provides substantial amounts of money for local transit authorities to transport Medicaid patients to doctors' appointments and hospital procedures. Reimbursement under Medicaid is relatively high, so the reimbursements effectively subsidize other, non-Medicaid passengers. The Department of Agriculture provides money for free and reduced cost school lunches and breakfasts. Even though USDA is not thought of as an education agency, and public schools are not often regarded as involved in nutrition, the reality is that they are each directly involved in more than one programmatic area.

The organization of executive agencies differs considerably from state to state, though the primary functions are usually found in common. To solve—or reduce—rural problems in any given state requires leadership in navigating this complex intergovernmental network of agencies at all levels. It usually begins with a firm understanding of the organization of state government as a source of capacity to address local concerns. Of course, all local leaders feel that their concerns merit attention, so state agencies, just like federal and local ones, face the constraint of scarce resources, which leads to targeting efforts in the areas of greatest need.

States have become more and more attentive to rural development, in part because of the significant brain drain that rural communities face. Many rural counties are experiencing population decline and increasing average population age as young generations flee to urban areas and the opportunities they present. The effect is a declining market, and a reduced draw for professionals and service industries to locate in those areas, perpetuating a vicious cycle of decline.

Regional Support

Thanks in large part to the efforts of the federal government to create regional planning councils in the 1960s, which carry various names such as regional planning commissions, regional councils of government, area development districts, and so on, regional governments now exist across the states to organize local government and to encourage a cooperative development style. These organizations provide much needed capacity for governance that is beyond the economy of scale for small rural governments to utilize independently. An exemplary list of services in which such organizations assist includes:

- Local & Regional Planning
- Transportation
- Workforce Development
- Programs for Senior Citizens
- Develop & Administer Grants
- Data Centers
- Community Development
- Business Loans
- GIS Mapping
- Economic Development
- Water Quality (Bluegrass Area Development District, n.d.)

When regional governments come to the table, they are able to prioritize local needs, and coordinate resources to plan for, and address, local problems. Because they are governed by elected officials from the areas they represent, these entities support and encourage coordination on projects that would typically be beyond the capacity of the individual local governments to address on their own.

The competitive mindset remains common among local officials, as economic development continues to be perceived as a zero-sum, winner-take-all, game. It is increasingly challenging to find common ground in encouraging economic development. While some projects may benefit residents of multiple counties, the benefits don't always accrue equally. For example, an industrial park might be located in the center of a county, near the urban core (even though that core is relatively small, say 15,000 residents). That provides the prospective industries with a labor market within the county, but they also compete with existing firms for such labor. Locating the park near the county line exposes prospective industries to a larger labor pool drawn from both county cores. The benefits, though, would be shared as income flows to the neighboring county and circulates therein. Meanwhile, the host county reaps the benefits of the corporate taxes, if any, and they may well be able to benefit from the income of all employees through an occupational tax. Such externalities can be controlled through cooperation. Cooperation has taken the form of collaborative parks, with shared investment from multiple governments, either across counties, or between county and city governments. There are many approaches to share costs and benefits when the motivation exists to do so.

Economic development is not the only function where local governments struggle for capacity. Another is rural transportation, especially for those with disabilities. There is insufficient economy of scale to operate bus routes or regular transit services in such areas, especially for trips to locations outside the county. A solution has been to subsidize regional transportation through scheduled-trip services often referred to as paratransit. The structure of such enterprises must ensure that trips are weighted in value to overcome moral hazards such as cherry-picking or route avoidance. An innovative approach has been tested in Kentucky, where sixteen regional brokers are responsible for allocating transportation services (University of Kentucky human Development Institute, 2020).

Shared services agreements provide another mechanism for capacity sharing. In such arrangements one municipality or county might decide it more economical to rely on the expertise and established capacity of a larger county to provide services for a fee. So, for example, a county of 10,000 population might utilize its $100,000 police budget to hire two deputies and a dispatcher, or it might choose to pay a neighboring county the same amount (or sometimes even a lesser amount) to respond to calls for police assistance on their behalf. The advantage comes not only in hiring more experienced and well-managed officers, but also in the indirect cost savings of operating the office, managing the associated human resources, and so on. Such arrangements have been made for policing, snow removal, garbage collection, and beyond. By increasing the economy of scale, they make service provision more efficient for local governments.

In like fashion, state and local governments seldom build or repave their own roads today. Rather, they monitor and provide urgent maintenance repairs. Larger upgrades are contracted out. Where an adequate number of bidders exists to prevent collusion, contracting such services to private firms enables those contractors the advantage of scale as they bid on more jobs, enabling them to reduce their unit prices. Ultimately, the local government is the beneficiary because they no longer have to maintain staff, equipment, or supplies necessary to build roads.

Leasing as opposed to purchasing has also enabled local governments to maintain capacity at lower cost. For example, a fleet of trucks for a road department (or cruisers for a police department) comes with a fixed purchase cost. However, to maintain those vehicles over their useful life requires a maintenance garage with qualified mechanics on staff. Leasing the vehicles for two-year increments, however, allows the government the ability to keep state-of-the-art equipment that requires little or no maintenance, most of which might be included in the lease agreement. Involving the private sector as a partner comes with numerous potential advantages for government agencies; it enables government to specialize in contracting (while service providers specialize in their respective areas of expertise) rather than providing a broad array of government services at a lower level of performance.

Other Rural Partners and Cooperative networks

Contemporary Challenges for Intergovernmental Cooperation

Thanks to the rapid rise of social media, and to the market segmentation of media and information outlets more broadly, we are all equipped with electronic devices that selectively feed us, or withhold from us, news and information based on our preferences. Information travels rapidly, and the matters facing society have been nationalized in many ways. That is to say, a poignant problem in one city or state can be rapidly pulled up into the internet and shared widely. The result is that people everywhere— even places those problems don't affect—develop attitudes, opinions, and positions based on the information they receive. Local problems in a small town may not even be noticed by local residents, while the whole country becomes aware of a localized problem like water quality in Flint, Michigan. We now operate in an environment characterized by information selectivity, where the most salacious stories are circulated broadly. This leads to tension, as it forces us to evaluate our values and choose sides on various issues. Moreover, it encourages action by a level of government. As the news is nationalized, it artificially turns the focus toward federal policy-makers to address.

This can be seen in recent years in the controversy over illegal border crossings along the Mexican border. Under the Trump administration, attention was drawn to illegal immigration and the externalities it brought about. While the direct costs of the problem were fairly localized, it became a rallying cry for conservatives all over the country. Under the Biden administration, though, border enforcement has been relaxed significantly, and absent national media attention, the problem rapidly worsened for those border states that lacked the ability or capacity to address the rapid influx of migrants. Taking the challenge to task, the governor of Texas began busing migrants to liberal cities, including New York City and Washington, DC—a move that has garnered new media attention and adjusted the policy focus. Perhaps of greatest intrigue here, is that immigration is, by definition, a federal policy concern, though the implementation of that policy affects some states more than others. This example reveals how federalism ebbs and flows, with political preferences often shaping opportunities for actors to become involved. In this case, federal abdication of its responsibility to defend the border, or to regulate it effectively, led states to engage the policy area in response to federal inaction.

Even absent structural differences, there are vast differences between places that are urban centers, those that are suburban in character, and the rural remainder. Value differences translate into policy differences, and considerable differences in the intensity of government (Hall, 2022a). Moreover, the current political environment is filled with vitriol and contentious bickering (Hall, 2022b), leading states to engage with one another in a far less cooperative manner.

Values differ widely from place to place, as do contextual factors and the problems they bring about. Intergovernmental relations provide an efficient mechanism for redistributing resources, so long as those value propositions are not so varied that they create conflict. Policy and regulatory conflict will continue unabated in those areas where questions are political—what to do—versus instrumental—how to do it (Jennings and Hall, 2012).

Conclusions

A recent editorial in *Public Administration Review* called for greater attention to rural concerns in public administration education and research (Hall, 2022a). It echoed many concerns from earlier research that calls for greater attention to county governments as the key service delivery agent for state services (Benton, 2005; Menzel et al., 1992). What we know is that rural administration is different, and that it largely operates at a deficit. Not a financial deficit, but a capacity deficit characterized by fewer resources, a less-educated workforce, and diseconomy of scale. While the intergovernmental framework is structurally the same in urban areas as rural ones, the informal structure of governance is not. Rural places have smaller populations, provide fewer services, and do so at much lower tax rates. There are fewer potential partners—private or nonprofit—and to undertake major improvements to local infrastructure may require cooperation, such as purchasing treated water from a nearby municipality, or intergovernmental assistance through grants, loans, or other forms of technical support.

Professional training programs, such as the Master of Public Administration, are not always available to rural residents, and when available, they suffer from the limitations of a curriculum oriented around larger governments—federal, state, and urban municipalities. More must be done to understand rural governments, to educate and train their leaders, and to better integrate them into the network of intergovernmental and intersectoral governance that exists today.

Funding support for local governments in rural places is in place and has been for quite some time; unfortunately, crises such as COVID-19 provide opportunity to invest in more pressing needs, such as health and income relief. The problem is now, as it has always been, whether policy supports structural attempts to organize the funding and implement it to the advantage of rural areas with greater need vis-a-vis urban areas with larger populations. Now that we have moved into the information age, new opportunities for connecting places and building partnerships exist. However, doing so requires investment in new forms of infrastructure; fiber optic cable is the backbone of the new economy, and the devices that rely on it to operate allow local governments in the most distant places to participate in the rapid interchange of information, providing them with power and more equal standing with their urban counterparts.

While we endeavor to support these communities, it is also important to remember why our government is structured as a federal republic—to better permit it to serve people and communities with unique values and contexts. While it may be easy to stereotype American rural areas as a collective, each is very unique with its own culture, values, and politics—its own way of doing things.

References

Benton, J. Edwin. (2005). An assessment of research on American counties. *Public Administration Review*, 65, 462–474. https://doi.org/10.1111/j.1540-6210.2005.00472.x

Bluegrass Area Development District. (n.d.). What is an "ADD"? https://bgadd.org/what-is-an-add/

Christensen, T., and Lægreid, P. (2007). The whole-of-government approach to public sector reform. *Public Administration Review*, 67(6), 1059–1066.

Gardbaum, S. (1994). The nature of preemption, *Cornell Law Review*, 79(4), 767–815.

Gardbaum, S. (1997). New deal constitutionalism and the unshackling of the states. *University of Chicago Law Review*, 64(2), 483–566. https://doi.org/10.2307/1600289

Grodzins, M. (1960). The federal system. In M. D. Irish (Ed.), *Goals for Americans: The Report of the President's Commission on National Goals and Chapters Submitted for the Consideration of the Commission*. Prentice-Hall, published for the American Assembly of Columbia University, 265–282.

Hall, J. L., and Battaglio, R. P. (2018). Reduced-boundary governance: The advantages of working together. *Public Administration Review*, 78, 499–501. https://doi.org/10.1111/puar.12965

Hall, J. L. (2008a). The forgotten regional organizations: Creating capacity for economic development. *Public Administration Review*, 68, 110–125. https://doi.org/10.1111/j.1540-6210.2007.00841.x

Hall, J. L. (2008b). Assessing local capacity for federal grant-getting. *American Review of Public Administration*, 38(4), 463–479. doi:10.1177/0275074007311385

Hall, J. L. (2008c). Moderating local capacity: Exploring EO 12372's intergovernmental review effects on federal grant awards. *Policy Studies Journal*, 36, 593–613. https://doi.org/10.1111/j.1541-0072.2008.00285.x

Hall, J. L. (2009). *Grant Management: Funding for Public and Nonprofit Programs*. Jones & Bartlett Publishers.

Hall, J. L. (2010). Giving and taking away: Exploring federal grants' differential burden on metropolitan and nonmetropolitan regions. Publius: *The Journal of Federalism*, 40(2), 257–274, https://doi.org/10.1093/publius/pjp046

Hall, J. L. (2022a). Public administration for a new season: Reflecting on neglected rural concerns. *Public Administration Review*, 82, 613–618. https://doi.org/10.1111/puar.13536

Hall, J. L. (2022b). Raising expectations: The war we must fight to prevent one. *Public Administration Review*, 82, 789–794. https://doi.org/10.1111/puar.13544

Jennings, Jr., E. T., & Hall, J. L. (2012). Evidence-based practice and the use of information in state agency decision making. *Journal of Public Administration Research and Theory*, 22(2), 245–266, https://doi.org/10.1093/jopart/mur040

Lovell, C. H. (1979). Where we are in intergovernmental relations and some of the implications. *Southern Review of Public Administration*, *3* (June), 13–14.

McLean, J. E. (1952). *Politics is What you Make it* (pamphlet). Public Affairs Committee.

Menzel, D. C., Marando, V. L., Parks, R. B., Waugh, Jr., W. L., Cigler, B. A., Svara, J. H., Reeves, M. M., Benton, J. E., Thomas, R. D., Streib, G., Schneider, M., & Salant, T. J. (1992). Setting a research agenda for the study of the American county. *Public Administration Review*, 52(2), 173–182.

Nolo (2022). Preemption defined. www.nolo.com/dictionary/preemption-term. html (accessed October 30, 2022).

Partnership for Sustainable Communities. (2012). *Federal Resources for Sustainable Rural Communities*. www.epa.gov/sites/default/files/documents/federal_reso urces_rural.pdf (accessed July 2, 2022).

Stephens, G. R., & Wikstrom, N. (2006). *American Intergovernmental Relations: A Fragmented Political Polity*. Oxford University Press.

University of Kentucky Human Development Institute. (2020). *Kentucky's Regional Transportation Brokers*. https://transportation.hdiuky.org/wp-content/uploads/2020/03/Regional-Transportation-Brokers.pdf

US Census. (2017). One in five Americans live in rural areas. www.census.gov/libr ary/stories/2017/08/rural-america.html (accessed July 2, 2022).

US Department of Agriculture. (n.d.) *National Rural Development Partnership*. https://www.rd.usda.gov/files/USDARD-NRDP.pdf (accessed July 2, 2022).

US Department of Agriculture (2020). USDA rural development summary of major programs: Together, America prospers. https://www.usda.gov/sites/default/files/documents/usda-rural-development-summary-major-programs.pdf

Wright, D. S. (1988). *Understanding Intergovernmental Relations* (3rd ed.). Wadsworth, Inc.

CASE STUDY: PERSONAL DIPLOMACY AND THE IMPORTANCE OF LOCAL MAYOR NETWORKING

Matthew L. Howell

Small towns make do under intense resource constraints. Lacking population and revenue, small towns lack administrative capacity to do the things expected of larger governments. Cleverness and going without are key solutions to the resource shortages, but in theory, intergovernmental agreements should be a way to relieve that constraint (Chen & Thurmaier, 2009). Whether seeking information, money, efficiency, or political support, there are many benefits from interlocal cooperation. It is reasonable to expect small towns to be heavy users of interlocal agreements and contracts—yet such agreements are more commonly seen in larger, richer jurisdictions (Thurmaier & Wood, 2016, p. 116). Agranoff and McGuire (2003) and Adrian (1961) noted that small towns often exist to maintain their independence and so do not desire entanglements with their neighbors, which may explain the reticence to cooperate or even communicate among smaller towns, but there is more to the calculation.

With the help of the Kentucky League of Cities, the mayors of member cities were surveyed in 2011, 2015, and 2019 about how they communicated with each other and how the League could facilitate cooperation. Most respondents were from smaller suburbs, or independent towns outside the major metros of Louisville, Lexington, and Cincinnati. Many mayors were excited about cooperating with their neighbors, but the amount of communication varied from one town to another. While the mean number of contacts was 13 in the 2015 survey (choosing from a list of member mayors), several cities reported no contacts, and the modal number was only one to two. In 2019 (having to produce contact lists from

DOI: 10.4324/9781003287766-36

memory) the mean number of contacts dropped to four, and the modal number was zero.

The mayors who rated networking as a high priority did so because they believed problems that plagued their city have—nine times out of ten, according to one mayor—been handled by older and more experienced officials in neighboring cities. Others noted that they would love to work with their neighbors, but have so many of their own problems they cannot keep track of their neighboring communities to even know who might be a good partner.

They also report reasons for not networking. Very small towns have fears of becoming dependent on another government, either because such dependence could be leveraged to take over the town, or because without a long-term guarantee, the town could be hurt later when shared resources are no longer available. The limited capacity of the towns largely prevented them from effective communication if they desired it, and a substantial subset did not see the value at all—small town problems are so idiosyncratic according to one mayor surveyed in 2019 that there is no point to sharing them.

Finally, there were mayors who not only reported being very interested in communicating and cooperating and who also were super-networkers. A very small and select group of mayors (members of the KLC executive board) would regularly communicate with 30, 40, even 50 different mayors every year. Clearly, there are many ways to run an intergovernmental communications network.

How to Network Mayors

Mayors of small towns are busy. Even if they are full-time officials, they have many administrative tasks to occupy their minds. Part-time officials often have another job. Networking is time-consuming, with even the weakest relationships still requiring occasional contact to maintain. For those who like to network, this is not always a problem. Occasional contact can maintain a "weak" tie, which is often a wonderful conduit for new information (Granovetter, 1973). Weak ties can tie an entire state together and help move information, one mayor at a time, from one side of the state to another—especially if one of the super-networked KLC board members acts as a clearinghouse of information. No mayor has to know everyone—hey only have to talk to someone who talks to someone who knows the right people.

For getting more than information, though, stronger ties are needed—and that requires more time and support, and it requires repeated interactions to build and maintain the relationship. Small towns run up against their time constraints and so cannot just go see other mayors. However, county governments, state government, the League, and regional organizations (Area Development Districts, ADDs in Kentucky) can make introductions or provide forums for interaction (Obstfeld, 2005). These social focuses (Feld, 1981) are not primarily networking events—the ADDs have regular meetings to discuss economic development, the biweekly County Fiscal Court meeting is a business meeting—but the events provide an opportunity for officials to interact with each other. By doubling up mayors with both a networking and a business focus, it allows officials to develop and maintain relationships over time.

A focus, though, is only useful if people can attend it, and the capacity issues of small towns often cause the smallest town mayors to miss the meetings—they require travel during the day when the mayors are at their day jobs, or when they lack staff who can watch City Hall. Nonetheless, having staff who can take up the slack, or using an intergovernmental organization (the Kentucky League of Cities) that hosts meetings off hours can allow even those officials to network with their colleagues.

Using Multiple Regression Quadratic Assignment Protocol (MRQAP)— a method of doing regression analysis on social networks—the 2011 and 2015 surveys were compared (2019 data was structured differently to allow for staff responses, and so was not included). Cities which were connected in 2011 were 41 percent more likely to communicate in 2015 than cities that were not connected in 2011. This was true even if the mayors were not re-elected in the intervening four years (though both mayors being still in office did raise the likelihood another 2 percenr). There were smaller effects for two mayors attending meetings together in 2011 or 2015 and the shared intergovernmental environment also increased the likelihood of networking—sharing a county increased the likelihood 7 percent. Similarly, a city manager made a city 2.5 percent more likely to network with another city, and mayors who served as KLC executives were 4 percent more likely to network. Geographic proximity did not increase likelihood of two cities communicating after the intergovernmental context was controlled.

Clearly, the best time for mayors to network is four years ago. Creating new networks is a slow process of accretion. Nonetheless, if a mayor wants or needs to build up their network, there is a lot of benefit from face-to-face meetings with other officials, participating in intergovernmental organizations, and having a professional city manager.

Benefits of the Network

Maintaining a network is hard—even with outside support—but there are benefits. In Kentucky, growing communication between cities of the

Second Class (populations between 20,000 and 100,000) led to a quarterly meeting where they shared best practices on a range of policies—from festival districts to tax collection. Ideas and policies spread across the state from this group. The same cities also cultivated a friendly relationship with the Third Class cities (8,000 to 19,999) to jointly lobby for a change to tax policy—which they had previously been at odds over. The tax did not change, but they did get changes to the home rule laws that governed their charters.

If the capacity is there, networking and communication can provide a wealth of information and opportunities for cooperation. If the desire is there, but not the capacity, intergovernmental organizations can provide an important service and forum for small towns. And the most wonderful thing about networking relative to interlocal agreements is that, if a town doesn't want to do it, they don't have to. Networking provides options to the small town, but it is up to the community what they want to do.

References

Adrian, C. R. (1961). Metropology: Folklore and field research. *Public Administration Review*, 21(3), 148–157.

Agranoff, R., & McGuire, M. (2003). *Collaborative Public Management: New Strategies for Local Government*. Georgetown University Press.

Chen, Y. & Thurmaier, K. (2009). Political agreements as collaborations: An empirical investigation of the impetuses, norms, and success. *American Review of Public Administration*, 39(5), 536–552.

Feld, S. (1981). The focused organization of social ties. *American Journal of Sociology*, 86, 1015–1035.

Granovetter, M. (1973) The strength of weak ties. *American Journal of Sociology*, 76, 1360–1380.

Obstfeld, D. (2005). Social networks, the tertius iungens orientation, and the involvement in innovation. *Administrative Sciences Quarterly*, 50, 100–130.

Thurmaier, K., & Wood, C. (2016). Interlocal agreements as an alternative to consolidation. In Jered B. Carr and Richard C. Feiock (Eds.), *City-County Consolidation and its Alternatives: Reshaping the Local Government Landscape*. Routledge, 113–130.

19

SOLUTION OR TROUBLE?

Privatization and Rural Governments

Martin K. Mayer and John C. Morris

One of the most common governance tools (Salamon, 2002) in use in the United States is privatization, most often in the form of contracting. Studies cited by Savas (2000) suggest that nearly all municipal governments and counties in the US engage in some form of contracting. The pervasiveness of the use of contracting is not a new phenomenon, although its use grew substantially in the US in the latter half of the twentieth century (Kettl, 1993). Privatization continues to be a viable form of service delivery, and its use remains common at the local level of government. However, privatization is not necessarily the "best" solution to issues of service delivery; this chapter explores the strengths and weaknesses of privatization in its different forms as alternatives to more traditional means of the provision, production, and delivery of government services. We then offer a case study to illustrate these strengths and weaknesses.

Some Definitional Issues

While the term "privatization" has become synonymous with "contracting" in common usage in the United States, the term "privatization" is more accurately thought of as a collection of arrangements that in some way alter the traditional role of government in service delivery. Savas (2000) offers a total of nine alternative arrangements that can be considered by local government, including contracting, franchises, government service, government vending, and self-service, among others. Each of these arrangements represents certain roles for government, the private-sector actor, and the citizen regarding who arranges for the services, who pays,

DOI: 10.4324/9781003287766-37

and who delivers the service. For example, in a contracted arrangement, government arranges and pays for the service with a private company, while the benefits flow to citizens (who pay government in the form of taxes). On the other hand, in a franchised arrangement, government arranges for a private company to provide the good or service, but citizens pay for the service directly to the private company, and the private company delivers the service directly to the citizen. The classic example of this arrangement is cable TV service. A company is awarded a franchise by a local government to provide cable TV service to citizens in a community. Citizens arrange for service at their individual residences, and pay the cable company directly for the service.

One arrangement not discussed in detail by Savas (2000) is "load-shedding," which involves the divestment of government-owned assets. This form of privatization is what comes to mind for people in many other nations around the world when the term "privatization" is used. For example, under the Thatcher government in Great Britain during the 1980s, the government sold its rail system, drinking water system, auto industry, and numerous other government-owned utilities and enterprises to private-sector companies. One reason that policy-makers in the US do not equate "privatization" with "load-shedding" is that US governments own comparatively little in the way of assets, and thus have little to sell off. The exception to this statement at the local level is utilities; many municipalities own and operate drinking water and wastewater systems. Other municipalities operate stand-alone electric utilities or electric cooperatives, or other forms of infrastructure. At the national level, the one asset controlled in abundance by government is land, especially in the western states. The national government does not often sell this land outright, but it does lease grazing rights, mineral extraction rights, and water rights.

The most prevalent privatization arrangement in use in the US is contracting. While exact figures are difficult to obtain, estimates suggest that nearly all municipal governments in the US engage in some form of contracting arrangement (Savas, 2000, p. 72). Some of the more commonly contracted services in smaller municipalities include garbage collection, legal services, and human services. These services are often awarded to private-sector firms, although nonprofit firms tend to be more dominant in social services and arts and culture.

For the purposes of this chapter, we will use the term "privatization" in a general sense to refer to a governance arrangement that engages either the private or nonprofit sector in the provision, production, or delivery of a traditional government good or service. When describing specific kinds of arrangements, such as contracting or load-shedding, we will use terms that refer to the specific arrangement in question.

A Privatization Primer

A common typology in the field of political economy is to identify two different mechanisms for the allocation of goods and services in society: government and the market. Each of these institutions has inherent strengths and weaknesses, and neither institution is without inherent flaws (Weimer & Vining, 1999). While a complete discussion of the strengths and weaknesses is beyond the scope of this chapter, the salient point is that policy debates around questions of privatization tend to focus on the relative importance (or impact) of these strengths and weaknesses (see Morris, 2007). Advocates for privatization point to the inherent limitations of government, and argue that the potential advantages of the market can overcome weaknesses in government; those opposed to privatization tend to argue the opposite point of view.

Advocates of privatization generally view the free market as a superior allocation mechanism for goods and services in society (Savas, 2000). These advocates typically point to specific features of a free market that, in a perfect market, should lead to higher quality at a lower cost. These features include the profit motive, competition, innovation, and a lack of regulatory constraints. A market unfettered by government control, in which buyers and sellers are free to make informed choices, will always produce goods and services of superior quality. Moreover, competition keeps prices low and quality high. This model of the free market makes certain assumptions about the nature of the market; for our purposes, two of the more important assumptions are the presence of competition and perfect information about a good or service.

In order to have market competition, two elements must be true. First, there must be multiple sellers of the same good or service, so that buyers have clear choices from a range of undifferentiated (that is, effectively the same) goods. If there is only one firm offering a particular good or service, there is no competition on the "seller" side and an effective monopoly exists. Second, there must be multiple buyers interested in purchasing the good or service; if there are few (or no) buyers, there is no incentive to produce the good. Buyers compete against one another to create demand for the good or service. An example of a market that functions well in this regard is the market for soft drinks. A trip to a local grocery store reveals multiple companies offering soft drinks for sale; judging by the contents of grocery carts, buyers are choosing products from a range of producers, and prices for most products are competitive.

On the other hand, consider the market for nuclear-powered aircraft carriers. In the US there is only one buyer for nuclear-powered carriers: the US government. Likewise, there is only one shipyard capable of producing these ships: Newport News Shipbuilding, operated by Huntington Ingalls. In this case, there is no competition in the market. At the local level, it is not uncommon for a rural local government to issue a request for proposals (RFP) to contract for solid waste collection, only to receive one, and sometimes no, bids. In this case, there is little competition on the seller side, and likely very little on the buyer side as well. Morris (2007) documented a case in Mississippi in which the state sought partners to build and operate three prisons. Only two companies and one local authority responded to the RFP; each bidder was ultimately awarded a contract for one prison in what was a largely uncompetitive process.

Traditional market theory also assumes that both buyer and seller have perfect information about the good or service in question. In contracting for services, this typically involves the party offering the contract to carry out "due diligence" by delving into the background of the awardee to ensure that the firm is able to deliver the good or service as promised. However, even if the buyer knows to do this, the costs associated with effective due diligence investigation can be prohibitively expensive. The result is asymmetric information, in which the seller knows much more about the good or service than the buyer. In a famous example of asymmetric information in the auto industry, Ford Motor Company sold a compact car called the Pinto in the early 1970s. There was a flaw in the design that caused the fuel tank to rupture in a rear-end accident. Ford knew this, but did not disclose this flaw to buyers. As a result, more than 500 people were burned to death in relatively minor collisions before the US government required Ford to recall all 1.5 million Pintos to modify the fuel system to prevent the fires (tortmuseum.org, 2022). It is safe to assume that, had Ford told buyers about the flaw in the Pinto, they would not have sold 1.5 million defective cars!

A common argument in favor of privatization is that government may lack the capacity to provide, produce, or deliver (Johnson & Watson, 1991) a good or service. This can be especially problematic in the case of infrastructure, which can require significant amounts of both money and specialized expertise to maintain (see Heilman & Johnson, 1992). Faced with a lack of resources, local governments may seek to divest ownership of critical infrastructure as a strategy to move the costs of operation and maintenance off-budget. Infrastructure maintenance can be very expensive, but the results (or benefits) of the expenditures are rarely visible to the public. On the other hand, when critical infrastructure is not available, citizens can be merciless in their criticism of government officials. By relinquishing ownership or control over infrastructure to a third party, government can save both money and aggravation.

However, to attract private investment, the private sector must have a clear path to a profit stream as a result of ownership. In the case of infrastructure such as roads, bridges, drinking water, or water treatment plants, this revenue stream is the result of user fees paid by citizens. In essence, citizens pay not only the costs of operation, but also the profit, through increased user fees. A case in point is the Downtown Tunnel between the cities of Norfolk and Portsmouth, Virginia. The Downtown Tunnel consists of two two-lane tunnels sunk beneath the Elizabeth River to connect the two cities. Faced with mounting maintenance costs, the state of Virginia elected to cede control of the tunnels to a private company. In exchange for maintenance and upkeep, the company was given the right to charge tolls for every vehicle passing through the tunnel. More ominously, the company was allowed to raise the toll amount up to 3.5 percent every year for the entire 50-year term of the contract (13News Now, 2022). Backlash from motorists was swift. As a short-term solution, the state of Virginia stepped in and made a deal with the company to freeze toll increases to motorists for two years, during which time the state would make up the difference in revenue (Ley, 2017). The state also sponsors a toll relief program, which helps offset the cost of tolls for low-income residents of the region (dotrelief.com, 2022).

Relatedly, governments can choose to sell infrastructure (load-shedding) as a mechanism to raise cash for other projects or needs. As noted earlier, governments generally do not own much in the way of assets; the exception to this is land owned by the national government, which is especially important in the western United States. For local governments, infrastructure is the most commonly owned asset—water treatment plants, roads and bridges, municipal buildings, and public parks are common assets. Municipally owned infrastructure does not generate any property tax revenue, but it does take money to maintain. A cash-strapped government might see benefit in the sale of assets as a means to raise cash and reduce budgetary expenditures. However, if the infrastructure generates an income stream, this income will be redirected to the new owners of the asset.

Finally, efficiency arguments are commonly voiced in privatization debates (see Kettl, 1993; Savas, 2000). The underlying belief is that competitive forces in the free market will force companies to be more efficient, which will result in higher quality goods or services at a lower cost. Because government ownership typically creates a government-owned monopoly, there can be no competition, and thus no incentive for efficiency. The process of privatization will cause companies to be efficient in order to outbid their competitors. The resulting efficiencies are passed on to consumers.

However, as Morris (2007) has pointed out, the efficiency gains are illusory, and selling off ownership or control of public assets can lead to "pathologies" of privatization. In a study of private prisons in Mississippi, Morris (2007) notes that, prior to the first private prison in Mississippi, all prisons were government-owned. In other words, there was a clear government monopoly for prison services. The state issued an RFP to build and operate three 1,000-bed medium-security prisons. Only three bidders responded, and the state awarded one contract to each of the three companies. The contracts were for build-own-operate arrangements for a period of 20 years, a time period driven by the federal tax laws regarding the tax depreciation of corporate assets. Each contract specified that the state would ensure that each prison was at maximum capacity each day, or the state would still pay for the unused beds. In other words, the companies did not compete for the initial contracts, nor did they need to compete to fill prison beds. In the process of relinquishing a public monopoly on prisons, the state effectively created 20-year private-sector monopolies.

In sum, privatization can result in several benefits for governments, including lower expenses, increased government capacity, cost savings, and increased property tax revenues, among others. However, the benefits of privatization are not automatic and, if both the process and arrangements are not carefully considered, privatization can result in a loss of public control, higher costs to citizens, and greater citizen dissatisfaction. In order to realize the benefits of privatization, policy-makers need to consider carefully the goals of privatization, the conditions under which the goods or services will be used, the prevailing market conditions, and the potential downsides of divestiture.

Contracting "On the Ground": The Case of Cape Charles, Virginia

Cape Charles, Virginia, is a small town of fewer than 1,000 year-round residents, situated on the shores of the Chesapeake Bay in Northampton County, on Virginia's Eastern Shore. A planned community, Cape Charles was designed to be the southern terminus of the New York, Philadelphia, and Norfolk railroad in the late 1800s. In the span of a decade, the town went from farmland to a bustling center of commerce, with four trains a day running from New York, and several passenger and industrial ferries traveling across the bay to Norfolk daily. For a time, Northampton County was one of the wealthiest rural counties per capita in the country. All this began to change around the conclusion of World War II. A combination of increasing automobile travel, the ferry terminal moving out of town, and finally the construction of the Chesapeake Bay Bridge Tunnel all but ended what was nearly half a century of growth.

The vast majority of the infrastructure in town was built during this period of industry when more than one million people would travel to and through Cape Charles on an annual basis. After the bridge tunnel was built and the ferry closed, tourism and industry dried up. The town fell mostly into disrepair throughout the latter half of the twentieth century, until recently experiencing a rebirth as a family-friendly vacation destination. People visit for the charm, the old houses, and the warm shallow water, but herein lies the problem from a local government infrastructure perspective. Despite the recent influx of people and money fixing up old homes and opening new businesses, many of the residences, the commercial district, the municipal building and other infrastructure, date back to the 1920s.

The most recent growth explosion has happened so rapidly the town has not been able to keep up, county assessments have not risen accordingly, and long abused, underfunded, and outdated infrastructure has come under increasing strain. This confluence of events has led the current town administration and leadership to explore the privatization of many of the community's most valuable assets including the town harbor. The harbor in Cape Charles is manmade, relatively large and sheltered, but with maintained deep water due to the presence of an important Coast Guard station, meaning it can accommodate larger vessels safely. In fact, the harbor at Cape Charles is the largest harbor on the Eastern Shore between Norfolk, Virginia (25 miles to the south), and Crisfield, Maryland (75 miles to the north).

Cape Charles Town Harbor

For more than one hundred years the town harbor was managed and operated by town employees, until September 2020. In the few decades prior, through a combination of grants and other assistance, the town's harbor experienced a massive facelift and business and traffic improved—never really to the point of making much money, but it has always been a working harbor, shared by a concrete plant to the south and commercial fishing everywhere else, all of whom depended on harbor access for their livelihood. But in recent years the town was having a difficult time keeping staff in place; there was repeated management turnover; and with limited upkeep, the facilities began to show their age. The renewed interest in town had not yet translated to the harbor and town leadership, tired of the turnover, frequent citizen complaints, and an expensive price tag that went along with maintaining and upgrading harbor facilities, began to explore the possibility of a potential sale. Everything was on the table, from outsourcing management to the outright sale of the harbor. The process dragged on for more than a year and was highly contentious, with the greatest outcry coming from the local commercial fishermen, who seemingly had the most to lose as heavily subsidized ratepayers.

Eventually, the town decided to issue a request for proposal for the management of the harbor. Three competitive bids were received, with the proposals coming from companies in Florida, Maryland, and Maine. A firm in Maine had previously acquired the Cape Charles Yacht Center (CCYC), which had years prior carved out a small private portion of the harbor. The local name seemingly made this option more palatable, despite the CCYC being owned and operated by a corporation far from Virginia.

Buoyed by promises to turn Cape Charles into the mid-Atlantic's "mega-yacht center," town leadership, by unanimous vote, entered into a three year renewable management agreement with the CCYC. To date, results have been mixed. Facilities, maintenance, and upkeep have improved by all accounts. It can be argued that the private sector has better managed and marketed the facility, with the 2021 season seeing record numbers of transient slip rentals. But the agreement has caused consternation between the CCYC and the town due to the management strategy of the CCYC. The CCYC and the town harbor continue to operate independently of each other, sharing staff, facilities, and management. The primary issue is the manner in which the CCYC has managed the harbor, effectively keeping the existing CCYC property and running it separately from the managed town harbor. This has allowed the CCYC to prioritize reservations toward their property before using the town harbor for what amounts to "spillover traffic."

The Cape Charles Water and Wastewater Facilities

About the time Cape Charles was finalizing the management agreement for the harbor, the town received an unsolicited bid to purchase the town water and wastewater infrastructure. Interviews with local officials highlighted the surprise and excitement that a private company would be interested in relieving the town's debt obligation, upgrading infrastructure, and improving water quality. Soon after, a call for proposals to purchase the town water and wastewater infrastructure went out, and three private water utilities responded.

Unlike much of the rest of the town, the water and wastewater infrastructure in Cape Charles is relatively young in its lifespan. The water plant was built in 1985 and the wastewater facility in 2012. The wastewater facility was funded by public grants and a 20-year, zero-interest loan of roughly $5 million. The town is approximately halfway through paying off the zero-interest debt service. Much like the case in the harbor, the common complaint from town administrators was that they simply do not have the capacity or ability to properly staff and maintain these facilities. The location of town is part of this, with storm surge, hurricanes, salt water intrusion, and century-old pipes buried on top of each other throughout town. In addition, there are incessant citizen complaints regarding the taste and smell of the drinking water. All fingers eventually point back to the capacity and ability of town operations staff. In addition to capacity issues and citizen complaints, water and wastewater infrastructure maintenance has been exceedingly costly. Factor in regional issues related to storm surge and saltwater intrusion and town infrastructure tends to degrade prematurely, specifically filtration and pumphouse components and facilities.

The complaints over the town's water and the mandatory minimum water utility bill, even for unoccupied second homes, have been a point of contention for more than a decade since the new wastewater plant was built. Yet, there had been no formal discussion to privatize any aspect of the service until the town received an unsolicited bid to purchase the water and wastewater plant from Aqua Virginia Water. The decision was soon made to accept the solicitation and open a request for bids for the potential sale of the town's water infrastructure.

Not long after, two additional proposals were received, and after months of additional RFPs for consultants, and mostly confidential, proprietary reports, the decision was made in a closed session council meeting to move to the negotiation stage with Virginia American Water (VAW). Virginia American has promised to assume the town's outstanding wastewater facility debt while also including an extra $2 million in the sale price. VAW has also pledged to invest $10 million into future infrastructure upgrades while agreeing to lock rate increases over the next three years. Town leadership has discussed this as an opportunity to relieve itself of debt, bring in additional capital, improve water quality, and relieve the city budget of future maintenance costs. The merit of each of these points is, however, questionable. The current debt is interest free and will be paid off in ten years, at which time existing rates/consumers will provide a surplus of nearly half a million dollars a year (in today's dollars), in addition to future expansion. In terms of water quality, there have never been any legal or regulatory issues with the safety of the town's drinking water, although the taste is a frequent citizen complaint.

As of this writing, the town has agreed to enter into the contract negotiation phase with Virginia American Water in an effort to better understand the specific concessions being offered.

Discussion

While the general trend in the US has been toward more privatization, it is important to note that local governments also recognize the inherent limitations and drawbacks to privatization as a governance choice. In one of the more famous examples available, the City of Phoenix, Arizona, contracted for many services, but eventually allowed city departments to enter competitive bids for those services. In a 2013 survey of local governments, 18 percent of respondents reported they brought services they had previously privatized back in-house (Saywitz, 2013).

Our case studies illustrate both the incentives for, and pitfalls resulting from, privatization for small, rural communities. In the case of Cape Charles, the city was not in financial distress, and the assets it had at its disposal were providing service and value to both government and citizens. In the case of the town docks, the city was clearly facing management issues, driven (at least in part) by the gentrification of the town and the difficulties of finding qualified staff to work in a profession not known for its high salaries. Still, since the town owned the facilities, which were in good repair, all of the revenue from enterprise came to the town budget. By entering into a management contract, much of that revenue has been diverted to the private management company. However, since the town still owns the infrastructure, it is the town that will bear the cost of any needed repairs.

The water and wastewater facilities illustrate a different kind of pitfall, but one that is common in rural locations. In spite of operating a well-run service with very low debt, the receipt of an unsolicited bid to transfer ownership to the private sector essentially created a policy issue where there had been no real issue. Much of the town's drinking water infrastructure was in need of replacement, yet current programs such as the Drinking Water State Revolving Loan Fund (DWSRF) have significant set asides to offer small and financially disadvantaged communities very low-cost loans to address infrastructure needs. Indeed, the $1.2 trillion Infrastructure Investment and Jobs Act, signed into law in 2021, includes billions of dollars in set asides (including grants) to serve the needs of small, rural communities. In short, this was not a case in which the town had pressing needs and no other way to raise money to meet those needs.

Also striking in this case was the lack of transparency in the decision process. The water infrastructure and town harbor are the two largest, and most valuable, elements of the town's assets, and a process that determines the future ownership of these assets that is not open and transparent also creates significant accountability questions. Was there truly a policy "problem" to be addressed? What was the status of the town's finances? Were there any conflicts of interest for the consultants that produced the proprietary reports? What did the reports recommend? What alternative options were explored?

The issue of management capacity in the case of the town docks represents a slightly different issue. By contracting the management of the facility to a private company, the town was arguably solving a perplexing problem. However, the lack of bids suggests a lack of competition. Moreover, the town's decision to offer the contract to an existing tenant in the harbor also meant that the same management company controlled what are, in effect, competing businesses in the same location. The management company keeps all of the revenue it earns from the facility it owns, but must share revenue from the other with the town. It should be no surprise that the management company steers as much business as possible to the facility it owns, rather than the one it manages. In essence, a lack of true competition at the bid stage helped ensure a lack of competition for the operation of the asset.

Some of these issues might have been removed with a stronger contract. For example, the town could have insisted on a contract that based the management fee on the number of slips occupied per day, or provided incentive clauses for higher performance. Large corporations are generally not shy about retaining highly competent legal services, while many small towns tend to rely on a local attorney who serves as the town attorney on retainer. This is not meant to disparage the legal skills of small town lawyers, but rather to suggest that the skills (and experience) at the negotiating table are more likely to favor the private sector.

Conclusion

The experiences in Cape Charles, VA are, in many respects, replicated almost daily around the nation. The benefits of privatization can seem exceptionally enticing, especially to a small community. The promise of privatization is that a community can turn over a service to the private sector, relieve themselves of responsibility for the service, and allow citizens to reap the benefits of an increased quality of service at a lower cost. Structured correctly, there is no reason why a privatized arrangement can't achieve these goals.

The reality of privatization, especially for small, rural communities, is often very different. A lack of true competition among both buyers and sellers often results in limited, imperfect markets, which in turn limits the positive effects of competition. Asymmetric information about the true costs of a good or service often favors the private sector; coupled with an often distinct advantage in the quality of legal advice for the private sector, often puts the public sector at a significant disadvantage in negotiations.

However, the benefits of privatization can be made more likely if the following points are considered:

1. Have a clear goal for what the effort to privatize is meant to accomplish, and what the limitations of the existing arrangements are.
2. Have a clear strategy for how to proceed, and a clear decision tree to determine a path if things do not go to plan. For example, if an RFP is issued and only one firm responds, there is no competition. In this case, what is the next step?
3. Create a decision process that is open, transparent, accountable, and fair. Seek input from all stakeholders in the process.
4. If the process leads to contract negotiation, remember that the private sector has a strong incentive (and a clear advantage) to create a strong position for themselves. Contracts allocate risk; the public sector should not assume all the risk. It may cost more to retain experienced legal services, but the expense on the front end will be overwhelmed by the savings from a fair and equitable contract.
5. Remember that privatization is not the "golden bullet" that can fix all the problems of government. Indeed, as Morris (2007) points out, solving perceived problems of government with poorly executed privatization simply creates new (and often more expensive) problems.

References

13 News Now. (2022). Toll investigation reveals hundreds of millions in revenue, plus how many drivers pass through without paying. www.13newsnow.com/article/news/local/13news-now-investigates/downtown-midtown-tunnel-tolls-revenue-investigation/291-5899d4f8-2b6b-42f7-b86d-b0f60b012cf7 (accessed March 17, 2022)

dotrelief.com. (2022). Toll relief, Elizabeth River Crossings. www.vdottollrelief.com (accessed March 17, 2022)

Heilman, J. G., & Johnson, G. W. (1992). *The Politics and Economics of Privatization: The Case of Wastewater Treatment*. University of Alabama Press.

Johnson, G. W., & Watson, D. J. (1991). Privatization: Provision or production of services? *State & Local Government Review, 23*(2), 82–89.

Kettl, D. F. (1993). *Sharing Power: Public Governance and Private Markets*. Brookings.

Ley, A. (2017). Women plead for relief from expensive tunnel toll bills. APNews.com. https://apnews.com/article/8c0635b3c1b5420283df130c496f1d14 (accessed March 17, 2022).

Morris, J. C. (2007). Government and market pathologies of privatization: The case of prison privatization. *Politics & Policy, 35*(2), 318–341.

Salamon, L., Ed. (2002). *The Tools of Government: A Guide to the New Governance*. Oxford University Press.

Savas, E. (2000). *Privatization and Public-Private Partnerships*. Chatham House.
Saywitz, R. (2013). Is privatization the answer? https://icma.org/blog-posts/privat
  ization-answer
Tortmuseum.org. (2022). Grimshaw v. Ford Motor Company, 1981. Available at
  www.tortmuseum.org/ford-pinto/
Weimer, D. L., & Vining, A. R. (1999). *Policy Analysis: Concepts and Cases* (3rd
  ed.). Prentice Hall.

20

THE ROLE OF FEDERALISM IN THE ATTAINMENT OF COLLABORATIVE SUSTAINABILITY OUTCOMES IN SMALL COMMUNITIES

Jayce L. Farmer

Over the last decade, scholars have taken burgeoning interest in how and why local governments collaborate to achieve outcomes for sustainable development. Many of the conclusions within this research emphasize the incentives and disincentives of collective action among mid-sized to large jurisdictions (Carr & Hawkins, 2013; Hawkins, 2011; Percoco, 2016; Yi et al., 2018). Within this vein, work has recognized how federal and state influences affect collaborative sustainability efforts for urban and large metropolitan areas (Hawkins, 2011; Youm & Feiock, 2019). However, research that explores these same federalism effects within the context of rural and smaller-sized communities is curiously lacking.

The purpose of this chapter is to address this knowledge gap by exploring the connection between the intervening roles of the federal and state governments and interlocal collaboration for sustainable development among small cities. Thus, the substantive focus of this study is on the policy and fiscal influences of higher-level governments on sustainability partnerships for economic development among small local government jurisdictions. I approach this focus by gleaning understanding from the concept of contested federalism. Here, I outline how the competing incentives between centralized and lower-level governments impact the achievement of collaborative policy outcomes (Farmer, 2021; Rabe, 2011; Youm & Feiock, 2019). As larger urban local governments can overcome policy impediments with more localized resources (Benton, 2002; Wang & Pagano, 2017) smaller jurisdictions may be more dependent on federal and state assistance (Benton, 1992). Thus, the reliance of smaller governments

DOI: 10.4324/9781003287766-38

on the resource and policy interventions of higher-level governments might come with greater costs for these localities.

This chapter proceeds as follows. I first provide a discussion that outlines key differences between larger and smaller communities and how these differences impact their collaborative development efforts. I then lead into a discussion on contested federalism, highlighting what the interventions of higher-level governments mean for collaborative endeavors among small and large jurisdictions, and present testable hypotheses. Subsequent sections present the research design and results. While providing a contrast with larger cities, the analysis highlights the implications of multilevel governance influences on interlocal collaboration endeavors among smaller jurisdictions in their efforts to pursue development that emphasizes sustainability.

City Size and Implications for Interlocal Collaboration

Whether a local jurisdiction resides within a rural or metropolitan area will determine its predisposition to collaborate on policy issues. The choice to collaborate to achieve policy outcomes can be linked with a city's ability to produce labor, access capital, and maximize its economies of scale (Feiock, 2007). A community's access and use of these resources will be driven by attributes tied to its population size, economic resources, and service production capabilities. These attributes can have a significant influence on how jurisdictions approach the pursuit of policy outcomes (Oakerson, 1999; Ostrom, 1999). On one hand, larger jurisdictions can have the capabilities to make investments in policies that may be impractical for their smaller counterparts. On the other hand, smaller communities may be forced to overcome this issue through collaborative policy efforts that allow them to leverage their resources and maximize economies of scale.

Labor Market

A city's population size dictates its available market for human capital. Drawing on Paul Peterson's (1981) export hypothesis, we can assume that larger cities, having larger populations, will have more access to labor, and in some cases more highly skilled labor. This human workforce gives cities the capacity to enhance their economic position by exporting local products. When cities are able to export products, the local economy prospers through increased wages, property values, tax revenues, and improved local public service delivery. Larger cities generally seek to maintain a diverse workforce with highly and semi-skilled workers. According to Peterson, increases in the supply of unskilled workers increase the cost of social services. Therefore, cities will generally attempt to attract workers with higher skill levels to maintain a competitive economic base.

Having a skilled labor market gives cities a higher capacity for production. Having a higher capacity for production in turn leads to lower costs in producing public services. If the labor and materials to supply a service are in short supply, production costs increase, along with the levels of public expenditures (Peterson, 1981). Thus, cities with an adequate labor market will have the capacity to produce public services and therefore maintain lower service production costs. Meanwhile, smaller communities that lack highly skilled workers may be forced to seek alternative service production through means such as interlocal partnerships or some other external production mechanisms.

Financial Capital

Closely related to the labor market issue, is the issue of a city's economic and tax base. Simply put, a larger population with a diverse labor market can improve a city's fiscal position (Peterson, 1981; Shi et al., 2018). As mentioned above, a stronger labor market highlights a city's ability to maintain a stronger economic base, which results in higher wages and higher property values. Higher wages and higher property values generally equate to a city having a stronger tax base.

Because local governments are heavily reliant upon taxes to pay for services, a stronger tax base means that, theoretically, a municipality will have a greater fiscal capacity to fund a broader range of services without imposing an additional burden on its taxpayers. Thus, larger municipalities with a greater financial capital will be in better positions to fund services internally than smaller jurisdictions. Because internal spending capacity can crowd out the need for municipalities to seek partners, larger jurisdictions may be less reliant on partnerships to augment service spending (Kwon et al., 2014). Conversely, rural communities with less financial capital may be more incentivized to seek collaborative efforts to support service delivery.

Maximizing Economies of Scale

Because all cities seek to improve their economic standing, large and small cities alike will attempt to make investments in development. As larger cities, with more capital and production opportunities, will have more resources to invest in development, smaller cities will also find it in their interests to spend on programs that develop their economic base (Peterson, 1981). Cities with the requisite capital to create and export production can be in better positions to absorb the costs of development opportunities. Meanwhile, smaller cities may be more apt to seek development to leverage their resources through interlocal collaboration. While both larger and smaller jurisdictions can potentially receive collective benefits from interlocal cooperation, the latter may stand to obtain higher efficiency gains by enhancing their economies of scale.

Cooperating to enhance development can be the result of local officials seeking economies of scale in production, especially in the case of capital-intensive goods (Feiock, 2007). Jurisdictions in rural areas that lack resources may have greater difficulties matching the quantities and qualities of services with community service preferences. In communities with fewer taxpayers, the average output costs of producing capital intensive or specialized services may go up as output increases. Therefore, service production can become increasingly expensive for communities if there are not enough citizen consumers in a jurisdiction to produce services at a minimum cost (Feiock, 2007). Consequently, smaller jurisdictions may seek to overcome their size constraints through interlocal collaboration endeavors that enhance their production efficiency.

Contested Federalism and Interlocal Collaborations among Small Communities

Scholars have asserted that the interventions of higher-level governments could theoretically resolve the scale and resource constraint problems of local jurisdictions (Farmer, 2021; Homsy & Warner, 2015; Payson, 2020). However, scholars also believe that an increased dependence on centralized governments can increase the costs to local governments due to the loss of autonomy that can create certain agency and administrative inefficiencies (Rabe, 2011; Wood & Bohte, 2004; Youm & Feiock, 2019). For smaller jurisdictions, this issue might be magnified by their increased dependence on higher-level government transfers to offset their lack of capital, infrastructure, and financial resources.

Hierarchical intergovernmental relations can encompass a complicated set of interdependent relationships that can lead to contested federalism (Rabe, 2011; Youm & Feiock, 2019). From a contested federalism perspective, higher-level and lower-level governments can coordinate or collide on policy actions to increase their individual or mutual benefits (Farmer, 2021; Youm & Feiock, 2019). While coordination is often desirable, collisions can result in vertical dependence dilemmas as competition and asymmetries in policy goals can increase administrative and agency costs. Agency costs arise when the coercive authority of centralized governments imposes vertical influences that are misaligned with lower-level governments' policy actions. Administrative costs manifest when local governments lack the administrative flexibility to control and adapt to policy decisions. Larger cities are impacted by the positive and negative implications of these vertical influences, but smaller jurisdictions that may be more dependent on external support might be impacted to a higher degree.

The Administrative Costs of State Constraints over Local Autonomy

State governments can have substantial control over the functional and fiscal abilities of their local governments (Bunch, 2014). States that employ the Dillon's Rule principle generally only allow local governments to engage in activities as explicitly sanctioned by their state legislatures. Therefore, states that conform to this principle largely prohibit local governments from adopting home rule charters. Local governments that lack home rule can succumb to higher administrative costs, as they will lack the functional and fiscal autonomy to make decisions that allow them to adapt to policy problems.

Policy problems with poorly understood solutions decrease certainty about bureaucratic effectiveness, and the efficacy of policy prescriptions (Wood & Bohte, 2004). In state systems where local governments have greater autonomy, officials have more leeway to adapt policy and spending decisions when faced with uncertainty. Meanwhile, states with more constrained governing authority can require local officials to spend a considerable amount of time lobbying their state legislatures for bills that authorize local policy changes. Cities with greater functional and fiscal autonomy are more adaptable and will therefore produce lower administrative costs due to their ability to navigate agency performance around the uncertainties of fluctuating circumstances (Wood & Bohte, 2004).

State grants of governing authority and the application of Dillon's Rule are not the same for every city within every state. Population size can often dictate the degree of authority afforded by a state. States such as Illinois and Texas, for example, only allow cities that meet a population threshold to adopt home rule charters. Thus, the powers of smaller and more rural jurisdictions are generally heavily constrained by their states. Likewise, Indiana implements a similar mandate that precludes townships from establishing home rule. Here, smaller and unincorporated localities are limited in their abilities to function, spend, and generate revenue.

Although state restrictions on local governing can impact both smaller and larger jurisdictions, the impacts may not come equally (Bunch, 2014). Governing limitations placed on larger more prominent areas might be better absorbed by their inherent resources realized through their economic and labor related capital. Conversely, smaller communities, with their limited capacity to garner resources might be more constrained by state mandated restrictions. Even with state restrictions on functional and fiscal autonomy, metropolitan areas can still have thriving economies due to the transboundary flows of people and trade that transpire within urban areas (Feiock, 2002; Ramaswami et al., 2018).

For larger jurisdictions, demands resulting from increased urbanization can require localities to enhance their efforts for development (Benton, 2002). Thus, having the administrative capabilities to adjust policy decisions can be advantageous for these entities in addressing these demands. While smaller jurisdictions may be less likely to succumb to urban pressures for development, the pursuit of policies that enhance the economic base can still be important. For larger jurisdictions, functional and fiscal autonomy may give them the ability to seek alternative production while relying on internally generated mechanisms. The resource attributes of larger cities can allow them to maximize output, while having the capacity to absorb output costs. The limited attributes of smaller localities, however, may force them to rely more on external sources. Their lack of exporting abilities may prompt them to import service production through service contracting and interlocal partnerships. Where local government autonomy can give larger cities the freedom to enhance internal production, it gives smaller communities the authority to overcome service deficiencies through interlocal partnerships.

H1: Home rule granted by a state will have a positive relationship with interlocal contracting for sustainable development but will have a greater effect for smaller jurisdictions.
H2: Taxation and expenditure limitations will have a negative relationship with interlocal contracting for sustainable development but will have a greater effect for smaller jurisdictions.

The Agency Costs of Federal and State Involvement in Local-Level Policy Actions

Agency costs can manifest when the mandates of higher-level centralized governments conflict with the goals of local-level units (Gerber & Teske, 2000; Youm & Feiock, 2019). However, higher-level governments often seek to offset these costs by providing incentivized mechanisms of compliance to their lower-level units. That is, the state and federal governments can minimize their agency costs and encourage policy compliance among decentralized governments when they provide resources for them to do so (Farmer, 2021; Youm & Feiock, 2019). However, central government transfers can bring stipulations that limit the recipient's ability to prioritize local objectives, thus increasing the agency costs for local governments (Oates, 1993).

State governments have a heavier hand in the affairs of local governments than the federal government. Therefore, the regulatory mandates of the states can potentially have greater effects (Gerber & Teske, 2000). Hence, dollars tied to state mandates may serve more as a regulatory mechanism to guide local behavior (Gerber & Teske, 2000; Kim, 2019). Meanwhile federal dollars can have a lesser regulatory effect for localities as these dollars tend to be viewed as "outside money" tied to grant-in-aid systems (Benton, 1992; Farmer, 2011). Additionally, a significant portion of federal transfers are passed through the states and allocated down to the local governments. Therefore, any regulatory effects may be affiliated more with state regulation rather than federal.

When it comes to interlocal collaboration, the regulatory effect of centralized governments may be countering for local jurisdictions. Prior research suggests that centralized activities can at times crowd out the voluntary cooperation activities of local units (Kwon et al., 2014; Youm & Feiock, 2019). When state agencies provide sufficient resources, localities may have less need to seek horizontal partnerships with other local governments. That is, the provision of state resources reduces agency costs for the state, while enhancing legislative control over local-level policy directions and alleviating the need for interlocal exchanges. We can expect this effect to occur for both large and small local jurisdictions.

Meanwhile, federal activities might produce a stimulative effect for interlocal collaboration, but only in smaller jurisdictions. The grant-in-aid nature of federal dollars can serve to support rather than control local endeavors. Therefore, federally funded transfers might go further to enhance local-level collaboration efforts (Farmer, 2015). Due to their weaker abilities to garner resources for production, smaller jurisdictions may be more reliant on federal grant-in-aid to support development efforts that pertain to issues, for example, like land use, transportation, and business incubation.

Federal programs, such as the Rural Economic Development Loan and Grant Program, for example, provide special direct monetary assistance to small and rural communities for the purpose of bolstering local economic development. Rural communities have traditionally had a direct line to federal financial assistance dating back to the inception of the Farm Security Administration program that was implemented as part of President Franklin D. Roosevelt's New Deal. Therefore, the grant-in-aid nature of federal aid can be expected to provide a mechanism for rural communities to circumvent the agency costs often associated with the provision of central government transfers.

H3: State fiscal transfers will have a negative relationship with interlocal collaboration for both larger and smaller local jurisdictions.

H4: Federal fiscal transfers will have a positive relationship with interlocal collaboration for smaller jurisdictions.

Data, Measures, and Estimation

Data for this analysis were sourced from the International City/County Management Association (ICMA), the 2015 *Local Government Sustainability Practices*. The survey was originally sent to 8,562 US cities and counties with populations greater than 2,500, with a response rate of 27 percent. The sample used for this study is limited to municipalities that also reported financial data in the 2012 US Census *Historical Finances for Individual Governments*. This produced an overall sample of 1,124 cities across 48 states. As the analysis was conducted in two steps to compare the effects of smaller versus larger cities, the sample size was split across two models. The first model, which assessed larger cities, those with a population of 10,000 or greater, consisted of a sub-sample of 682 cities. Population sizes within this model ranged from 10,019 to 3.7 million. The second model, which consisted of cities with populations less than 10,000 examined the remaining 442 cities from the overall sample. Here, city populations ranged from 2,317 to 9,933.

Dependent Variable

ICMA surveyed city officials about whether they cooperated with other localities within their regions across an array of 12 sustainability policies and programs. Included within these programs were three items that fell within the category of economic development as defined by prior research on sustainability policies (Opp & Saunders, 2013). Using these items, I created an ordinal outcome variable to capture municipal involvement in *economic sustainability collaborations*. This variable ranged from 0, denoting that a city did not participate in economic development collaborative sustainability endeavors, to 3, which represented that a city cooperated with other local partners across all three development policy tools. A higher value suggests a broader scope of interlocal collaboration on economic development policies.

Estimation Approach

The dependent variable was assessed using a Bayesian multilevel ordered logit to predict levels of collaborative engagement across economic development activities. The multilevel model captured the conditioned effects within states, while accounting for assumed random interstate effects. This technique provided probabilistic estimations of the choices of local officials to engage in interlocal collaboration. Therefore, this analysis relied on Markov chain Monte Carlo (MCMC) sampling algorithms that generated simulated probabilities to estimate the outcomes of the actors' decisions. This allowed for estimates based on updates determined by pre-established or anticipated prior information. Because the literature is mixed about multilevel governance effects on local collaboration choices (Farmer, 2021; Hawkins, 2011; Krause, 2011; Youm & Feiock, 2019), there is no prior theoretical information that consistently informs the question of interest. Therefore, this analysis used uninformative priors that allowed the data to drive predictions. Finally, the interpretations of this analysis were done using post-estimation hypothesis tests to determine the probability that the reported model parameters fell with a given interval ($\beta > 0$ or $\beta < 0$).

Administrative Cost Measures

I used two measures to capture administrative cost effects. First, I employed *functional home rule* to capture the levels of functional autonomy afforded to a municipality by a state. Functional home rule provides governing powers that can range from broad to limited that allow localities to autonomously manage their governing and administrative affairs. Broad functional home rule provides governments with comprehensive powers and wide discretion that allow them to operate with limited state interference (ACIR, 1993). Limited home rule means that localities are strictly constrained by their states and have restricted autonomy in conducting local affairs. For analysis, this variable was scaled from 1 to 3, with 1 indicating no functional autonomy, 2 representing limited autonomy, and 3 denoting that a city had the broadest functional powers of self-governing. Data for this measure were sourced from the ACIR (1993) and the 2010 state-by-state report from the National Association of Counties on county authority.

The second measure uses an additive index of state-imposed taxation and expenditure limits on municipalities (*municipal TELS*) to capture levels of fiscal autonomy. TELs are state mandated limitations on local governments' abilities to raise taxes, increase expenditures, and incur debt. State mandates of this nature can be imposed at varying levels of restrictiveness that can be binding or non-binding based on the ease of a local government to circumvent the limitation. This variable starts at zero and gains two points for each potentially non-binding constraint, and three points for each binding constraint. The categories used for this measure include property tax limit, specific tax limit, property tax revenue limit, assessment limit, general revenue limit and expenditure limits, and full disclosure (Carr & Farmer, 2011). The variable ranges from 0 to 11, with 11 indicating the most binding. Data for this analysis were sourced from Mullins and Wallin's (Mullins & Wallin, 2004) inventory on TELs.

Agency Cost Measures

The first agency cost measure used *federal transfers* to local governments. This variable captures the total amount of revenue received by a municipality from the federal government. The second measure captured *state transfers* to local governments. As with the first measure, this variable captured the total amount of revenue received by a municipality from state intergovernmental revenue. Data for both variables were sourced from the Census of Governments historical finances data for 2012.

Controls

The models include measures to control for the effects of fragmentation, a city's institutional arrangement, its taxation capacity, and its socioeconomic attributes. Prior research has demonstrated that the policy decisions and collaboration efforts of municipalities can be affected by other local actors within a region (Goodman, 2019; Stokan & Deslatte, 2019). Controls for regional fragmentation include political fragmentation and vertical fragmentation. Political fragmentation controls for the magnitude of fragmented units within a region. This variable borrows from Hendrick and Shi's (2015) fragmentation index to measure the number of local governments in a region per capita. Vertical fragmentation controls for service production overlap and captures the percentage of special districts to general purpose governments in a region. These controls were sourced from the US Census historical data for 2012.

The policy choices of municipalities are influenced by their institutional arrangement and fiscal capacity for service provision (Clingermayer & Feiock, 2001; Kim, 2019; Kwon et al., 2014). Institutional arrangements were measured with a dichotomous variable indicating whether a city had the council-manager form of government. A city's fiscal capacity was captured with per capita taxes received from city property and sales taxes. This variable was sourced from the Census historical finances data. Socioeconomic factors were used to control for attributes that might impact a city's labor market and capital (Peterson, 1981). These variables include the logged population of a city, the percent of a city population that was White and non-Hispanic, and a city's median property values. Data for these variables were sourced from the 2010 US Census. Finally, I employed dummy variables to capture group effects between state boundaries and US geographic regions. Table 20.1 highlights the descriptive statistics for all included variables.

Results and Discussion

Table 20.2 reports the estimated effects for municipal interlocal collaboration for sustainability endeavors with economic development outcomes for both large and small jurisdictions. The outputs reveal the parameter estimates, standard errors, credible intervals, and hypothesis

TABLE 20.1 Descriptive Statistics

	Mean/Prop.	SD	Min	Max
Dependent variable				
Economic development collaboration	1.866	1.032	0	3
Agency Cost Variables				
Home rule	2.163	0.481	1	3
Municipal TEL	5.536	2.656	0	11
Administrative cost variables				
Federal transfers	3.98E+03	2.00E+04	0	4.54E+05
State transfers	1.01E+04	4.19E+04	0	6.82E+05
Controls				
Political fragmentation	0.172	0.331	0.002	3.45
Vertical fragmentation	0.798	0.195	0	0.997
Council-manager	0.674	0.468	0	1
Per capita tax municipal tax revenue	0.622	5.36	0	5.62
Logged population	9.722	1.256	7.75	15.15
% White non-Hispanic	0.798	0.171	0.057	1
Median property value	25641	4.94E+05	405	9.74E+06
Group variables				
State	----	----	0	1
US region (dummies)				
Midwest	.335	.472	0	1
South	.323	.468	0	1
West	.252	.434	0	1

TABLE 20.2 Bayesian Estimates of Sustainable Development Collaborations

Variables	Large Cities Model			Small Cities Model		
	Odds Ratio (MCSE)	Credible Interval	Hypothesis Test	Odds Ratio (MCSE)	Credible Interval	Hypothesis Test
Administrative Costs						
Home rule	0.271 (0.008)	-0.254, 0.802	0.818	0.503 (0.008)	0.050, 0.981	0.939
Municipal TEL	-0.055 (0.002)	-0.143, 0.032	0.951	-0.0298 (0.006)	-0.098, 0.039	0.907
Agency Costs						
Federal transfers	3.75E-06 (2.04E-06)	8.46E-05, 4.35E-04	0.252	2.30E-04 (3.10E-06)	1.07E-05, 4.4E-04	0.900
State transfers	-2.39E-06 (2.04E-06)	-3.31E-04, -1.41E-04	0.086	5.82E-05 (1.90E-06)	-9.94E-04, 2.21E-04	0.658
Controls						
Political fragmentation	0.402 (0.008)	-0.366, 1.19	0.821	-0.4569 (0.006)	-0.869, 0.052	0.961
Vertical fragmentation	-0.116 (0.013)	-1.007, 1.098	0.498	-0.007 0.009	-1.12, 0.856	0.583
Council-manager	0.017 (0.004)	-0.731, 0.099	0.515	0.053 0.007	-0.322, 0.327	0.483
Per capita tax municipal tax revenue	-0.397 (0.004)	-0.738, 0.099	0.963	0.040 (0.003)	-0.214, 0.297	0.597
Logged population	0.28 (0.004)	0.371, 0.632	0.975	0.421 (0.006)	0.126, 0.720	0.974
% White non-Hispanic	0.927 (0.011)	-1.002, 1.331	0.972	1.246 (0.019)	-0.310, 2.05	0.973
Median property value	8.71E-08 (3.70E-09)	-1.78E-07, 3.73E-07	0.711	3.31E-08 (8.80E-09)	-4.53E-07, 5.33E-07	0.521
Group variation effects						
State	0.179 (0.004)	0.012, 0.533		0.082 (0.006)	0.005, 0.573	
US region	0.172 (0.019)	0.006, 0.1.00		0.100 (0.002)	0.005, 0.302	
MCMC sample size	450,000			450,000		
Burn-ins	90,000			90,000		
Acceptance rate	0.325			0.376		
N	682			442		

Note: Bold values denote greater strength of evidence. Cut point values have been omitted.

tests for each model. The findings in bold produced the strongest evidence, as suggested by their respective hypothesis tests.

Administrative Cost Effects

The results support H1 and suggest that home rule granted within states positively affects interlocal collaboration for economic development within smaller communities. The model reveals that there is a 93.9 percent chance of a positive relationship between home rule and interlocal collaboration. Conversely, no strength of evidence was shown under the model for larger cities. As illustrated in prior studies, greater functional autonomy provides local governments the ability to seek alternative service arrangements (Benton, 2002; Choi et al., 2010). However, this is only the case for smaller communities. It appears that functional autonomy in smaller cities goes further in allowing them to expand service options. Communities with fewer resource capabilities seem to be more affected by the ability to manage their governing affairs. Therefore, home rule can go a long way in reducing administrative costs for small and rural cities.

The results support H2, by showing a negative relationship between municipal TELs and interlocal collaboration activities. The models showed countering effects for both large and smaller jurisdictions. Specifically, the large cities model revealed a 95.1 percent chance of a negative relationship between municipal TELs and sustainable development collaborations. Meanwhile, the small cities model revealed a 90.7 percent chance of an occurring effect. While the models go in the direction as predicted, the results counter the argument regarding greater effects existing for smaller communities. Instead, this finding speaks to the connection between fiscal decentralization within states and local government activities for economic development. As evidenced in prior research, states that constrain local government fiscal autonomy also stymie local economic activity (Stokan & Deslatte, 2019). Rather than effects being more pronounced within rural areas, metropolitan areas with reduced fiscal authority may experience greater challenges in improving allocative efficiency through development on a larger scale. Thus, reduced fiscal autonomy raises the administrative costs for larger jurisdictions.

Agency Cost Effects

For H3, the models revealed no evidence connecting state transfers with interlocal collaboration. These findings are not consistent with the arguments of contested federalism, where state-level fiscal intervention can serve as a mechanism for legislatures to reduce agency costs for the states, while increasing agency costs for localities. Meanwhile, the results support H4 and show a positive relationship between federal transfers and interlocal collaboration within smaller communities. The model reveals modest evidence for this finding, with a 90 percent chance of federal transfers having a stimulative effect on sustainable development collaborations for small cities. The grant-in-aid nature of federal dollars seems to take on a supportive, rather than a regulative role in the activities of small local jurisdictions. Where state funding was projected to serve more as a regulatory mechanism that directs local actions, federal funding appears to serve more as a supplement that supports local government actions. From a sustainable development perspective, this supplemental support may stabilize collaborative partnerships.

Not only can federal funding enhance local collaborative efforts for sustainability actions, but it can also serve to reduce agency costs for state governments. Because states can have substantial stake in sustainability outcomes, it is likely that local sustainability actions will at least partially align with state goals. Federal dollars can, therefore, aid local governments in following state goals, while potentially not interfering with local objectives. Although the policy intent behind federal assistance in small communities may not be regulative, states can benefit from this external support through local compliance with state directives.

Summary and Conclusion

This chapter investigated the link between state and federal interventions and interlocal collaboration within small cities. This study approached this objective by outlining and assessing the key differences between larger and smaller jurisdictions, and how they might be affected by higher-level governments. Using an argument grounded in contested federalism, this analysis outlined four hypotheses that proposed how small cities would be affected by state and federal influences, in contrast to larger local governments. Several key differences between smaller and larger cities dictate how they might be impacted by the fiscal and policy influences of the federal and state governments. Key attributes such as their labor markets, their ability to garner capital, and their capacity to maximize production can impact how much they might rely on higher-level governments.

The overall findings suggest that access to greater functional autonomy enables small localities to forge partnerships to achieve sustainability outcomes. However, having access to more fiscal autonomy appears to have greater influence in larger jurisdictions. While federal inaction has been the cause for states to take the mantle in sustainability endeavors, federal funding was shown to be important in supporting the endeavors of small local governments. As the current findings point out key differences between large and small local jurisdictions and their implications for collaborative sustainability action, further inquiry needs to investigate this issue across a broader array of policy areas to glean better understanding regarding collaborative sustainability actions within and among small and rural jurisdictions.

References

Advisory Commission on Intergovernmental Relations. (1993). *State Laws Governing Local Government Structure and Administration*. Advisory Commission on Intergovernmental Relations.

Benton, J. E. (1992). The effects of changes in federal aid on state and local government spending. *Publius: The Journal of Federalism*, 22(1), 71–82. https://doi.org/10.1093/oxfordjournals.pubjof.a037997

Benton, J. E. (2002). County service delivery: Does government structure matter? *Public Administration Review*, 62(4), 471–479. https://doi.org/10.1111/0033-3352.00200

Bunch, J. (2014). Does local autonomy enhance representation? The influence of home rule on county expenditures. *State and Local Government Review*, 46(2), 106–117. https://doi.org/10.1177/0160323x14536589

Carr, J. B., & Farmer, J. (2011). Contingent effects of municipal and county TELs on special district usage in the United States. *Publius: The Journal of Federalism*, 41(4), 709–733.

Carr, J. B., & Hawkins, C. v. (2013). The costs of cooperation. *State and Local Government Review*, 45(4), 224–239. https://doi.org/10.1177/0160323x13508793

Choi, S. O., Bae, S. S., Kwon, S. W., & Feiock, R. (2010). County limits: Policy types and expenditure priorities. *American Review of Public Administration*, 40(1), 29–45. https://doi.org/10.1177/0275074008328171

Clingermayer, J. C., & Feiock, R. C. (2001). *Institutional Constraints and Policy Choice: An Exploration of Local Governance*. SUNY Press.

Farmer, J. L. (2011). County government choices for redistributive services. *Urban Affairs Review*, 47(1), 60–83. https://doi.org/10.1177/1078087410384235

Farmer, J. L. (2015). County–nonprofit service arrangements: The roles of federal and state fiscal involvement. *Publius: The Journal of Federalism*, 45(1), 117–138. https://doi.org/10.1093/publius/pju024

Farmer, J. L. (2021). State-level influences on community-level municipal sustainable energy policies. *Urban Affairs Review*, Advance online publication, 1078087421995262.

Feiock, R. C. (2002). A quasi-market framework for development competition. *Journal of Urban Affairs*, 24(2), 123–142. https://doi.org/10.1111/1467-9906.00118

Feiock, R. C. (2007). Rational choice and regional governance. *Journal of Urban Affairs*, 29(1), 47–63. https://doi.org/10.111/j.1467-9906.2007.00322.x

Gerber, B. J., & Teske, P. (2000). Regulatory policymaking in the American states: A review of theories and evidence. *Political Research Quarterly*, 53(4). https://doi. org/10.1177/106591290005300408

Goodman, C. B. (2019). Local government fragmentation: What do we know? *State and Local Government Review*, 51(2), 134–144. https://doi.org/10.1177/ 0160323X19856933

Hawkins, C. v. (2011). Smart growth policy choice: A resource dependency and local governance explanation. *Policy Studies Journal*, 39(4), 679–704.

Hendrick, R., & Shi, Y. (2015). Macro-level determinants of local government interaction: How metropolitan regions in the United States compare. *Urban Affairs Review*, 51(3), 414–438. https://doi.org/10.1177/1078087414530546

Homsy, G. C., & Warner, M. E. (2015). Cities and sustainability: Polycentric action and multilevel governance. *Urban Affairs Review*, 51(1), 46–73. https:// doi.org/10.1177/1078087414530545

Kim, Y. (2019). Limits of property taxes and charges: City revenue structures after the great recession. *Urban Affairs Review*, 55(1), 185–209. https://doi.org/ 10.1177/1078087417697199

Krause, R. M. (2011). Policy innovation, intergovernmental relations, and the adoption of climate protection initiatives by U.S. cities. *Journal of Urban Affairs*, 33(1), 45–60. https://doi.org/10.1111/j.1467-9906.2010.00510.x

Kwon, S. W., Feiock, R. C., & Bae, J. (2014). The roles of regional organizations for interlocal resource exchange: Complement or substitute? *American Review of Public Administration*, 44(3), 339–357. https://doi.org/10.1177/027507401 2465488

Mullins, D. R., & Wallin, B. A. (2004). Tax and expenditure limitations: Introduction and overview. *Public Budgeting & Finance*, 24(4), 2–15. https://doi.org/10.111/ j.0275-1100.2004.00344.x

Oakerson, R. J. (1999). *Governing Local Public Economies: Creating the Civic Metropolis*. ICS Press.

Oates, W. E. (1993). Fiscal decentralization and economic development. *National Tax Journal*, 46(2), 237–243. https://doi.org/10.1086/NTJ41789013

Opp, S. M., & Saunders, K. L. (2013). Pillar talk: Local sustainability initiatives and policies in the United States-finding evidence of the "Three E's": Economic development, environmental protection, and social equity. *Urban Affairs Review*, 49(5), 678–717. https://doi.org/10.1177/1078087412469344

Ostrom, E. (1999). Institutional rational choice. In P. A. Sabatier (Ed.), *Theories of the Policy Process* (pp. 21–64). Westview Press.

Payson, J. A. (2020). Cities in the statehouse: How local governments use lobbyists to secure state funding. *Journal of Politics*, 82(2), 403–417. https://doi.org/ 10.1086/706767

Percoco, M. (2016). Strategic planning and institutional collective action in Italian cities. *Public Management Review*, 18(1), 139–158. https://doi.org/10.1080/ 14719037.2014.969758

Peterson, P. E. (1981). *City Limits*. University of Chicago Press.

Rabe, B. (2011). Contested federalism and American climate policy. *Publius: The Journal of Federalism*, 41(3), 494–521. https://doi.org/10.1093/publius/ pjr017

Ramaswami, A., Bettencourt, L., Clarens, A., Das, S., Fitzgerald, G., Irwin, E., Pataki, D., Pincetl, S., Seto, K., Waddell, P., Nichols, L. G., & Tabory, S. (2018). *Sustainable Urban Systems: Articulating a Long-Term Convergence Research Agenda.* www.nsf.gov/ere/ereweb/ac-ere/sustainable-urbansystems.pdf

Shi, Y., Aydemir, N. Y., & Wu, Y. (2018). What factors drive municipal fiscal policy adoption? An empirical investigation of major cities in the United States. *State and Local Government Review*, *50*(3), 177–188. https://doi.org/10.1177/01603 23x18813418

Stokan, E., & Deslatte, A. (2019). Beyond borders: Governmental fragmentation and the political market for growth in American cities. *State and Local Government Review*, *51*(3), 150–167. https://doi.org/10.1177/0160323X2 0915497

Wang, S., & Pagano, M. A. (2017). Cities and fiscal federalism in the Trump era. *State and Local Government Review*, *49*(3), 184–198. https://doi.org/10.1177/ 0160323x17741527

Wood, B. D., & Bohte, J. (2004). Political transaction costs and the politics of administrative design. *Journal of Politics*, *66*(1), 176–202.

Yi, H., Suo, L., Shen, R., Zhang, J., Ramaswami, A., & Feiock, R. C. (2018). Regional governance and institutional collective action for environmental sustainability. *Public Administration Review*, *78*(4), 556–566. https://doi.org/ 10.1111/puar.12799

Youm, J., & Feiock, R. C. (2019). Interlocal collaboration and local climate protection. *Local Government Studies*, *45*(6), 777–802. https://doi.org/ 10.1080/03003930.2019.1615464

CASE STUDY: ONE FOOD BASKET AT A TIME: ADDRESSING FOOD INSECURITY

Clara Gerhardt

Introduction

If bread is the staff of life, then sharing nutrition with others is exponentially powerful. As a Practicum supervisor I have experienced the other side of a local charitable community that focuses on food distribution to the needy. I see the powerful effect of being part of the cycle of service; how the hearts of those who share are impacted by the power of the gesture, and how it creates a life of its own by giving forward. Generosity touches on the foundational principle of sharing our bread, and thereby sharing our hearts. Our students are learning about the power of giving, serving, and making a difference. A priceless life lesson is best learned in a practical setting such as community distributing food.

According to Maslow's hierarchy of needs, the complexity of our existence rests upon foundational needs for nourishment, safety, and shelter. If any of these are under threat, the effects spill over into related areas of functioning. A variety of *growth needs* may be affected, even sacrificed, because the focus shifts to *deficiency needs* (Noltemeyer et al., 2021). Food insecurity is an example of the challenges faced by those in poverty or a variety of crises affecting families.

DOI: 10.4324/9781003287766-39

Outline of Initiatives

Attempts have been made to address food insecurity at various systemic levels, ranging from macro- through to microsystemic levels.

- *Governmental interventions*: focusing on those in need through food stamps, subsidies, welfare, and the like.
- *Local council and county initiatives*: repurposing space in underserved areas for nonprofit grocery stores.
- *Legislative interventions*: such as initiatives minimizing food waste in the hospitality and food industries through redistribution of safe and edible food.
- *Indemnity reduction*: legislative protection for redistribution of safe and edible food without major risks of litigation.
- *Nonprofit initiatives*: providing community support, e.g., food banks, food redistribution centers, and education on wise stewardship, resourcefulness, reallocation of resources, money management, nutrition, food preservation and gardening. May be supported with grants and tax benefits.

Policies Pertaining to Food Insecurity

Food insecurity is generally defined as a situation in which individuals do not have reliable access to safe, nutritious food in quantities that meet their caloric needs. In the state of Alabama, a 2021 estimate is that one out of five children face food insecurity and hunger, and that the prevalence of *household* food insecurity tends to be above the US average. According to the United States Department of Agriculture (USDA) in 2020, about 10.5 percent of US households faced ongoing and persistent threats of significant food insecurity, while another 4 percent of households had very low food security. Importantly, *each household affects multiple children*, translating to a quarter or 25 percent of growing children. Food insecurity can also affect the elderly; "Senior Hunger." The percentages are even larger when intermittent and occasional food insecurity are considered. These children depend on a balanced diet to meet developmental needs (USDA, 2023; Feeding America, n.d.).

Limited food accessibility, often termed a "food desert," can be addressed with the creation of nonprofit grocery stores, pop-up food distributions, or community refrigerators. The incentives are humanitarian, rather than financial, and these tasks are typically undertaken by charitable and community-oriented organizations to contribute to the betterment of all. Dealing with these challenges "needs systemic change ... everything from a higher minimum wage or better public transit that would make food more accessible" (Ahmed, 2022).

The State of California introduced various initiatives addressing food waste. In 2020 about 23 percent of the Californian population had insufficient food to eat and displayed food insecurity. One angle of attack is keeping compostable food out of landfills. Individuals and businesses need to manage household waste responsibly. The consumer of food should be included if we attempt a holistic approach. Educational initiatives that address the consumer are important: family food preparation, taking responsibility for nutritional food choices, and avoiding waste within family kitchens are some entry points in addressing the complexity of food insecurity. Just as the country must learn to address food waste, the consumer must consider how they are wasting food. If change starts with the proverbial "me" it is more sustainable.

A second allied approach deals with food recovery. Senate bill 1383 requires that by 2025 California will recover 20 percent of edible food to safely feed people in need. The food rescue or food recovery initiative also keeps the food out of landfills. A trickle-down effect of this legislation requires the establishment of food recovery programs and the strengthening of existing ones. Donors are responsible for recovering as much of the edible food as possible to prevent unnecessary waste. Food recovery organizations and services must document their participation in programs pertaining to SB 1383. Donors have commented how transportation costs can be an obstacle. Nevertheless, each meal, feeding a hungry mouth, contributes to the greater good on many levels. California Recycle estimated significant reduction in the carbon footprint, while creating employment opportunities. In a three-year period since 2018, these programs have been able to repurpose 86 million meals in California (California Recycle, n.d.).

These large-scale initiatives require that donor organizations be matched with distributing networks and food banks. Supporting materials can include guides to safe surplus-food handling, to setting up partnerships, and guidance concerning tax benefits and grants. The food rescue initiative must be addressed at several entry-points and has the potential of positively affecting the community on a number of levels.

Case Study

The following case study describes a local initiative, Grace Klein Community, in Alabama (Grace Klein Community, n.d.). A grassroots effort started by citizens Jason and Jenny Waltman, as a nonprofit enterprise in April 2010, recovered and distributed over 1 million pounds of food in 2021 responding to food insecurity in 40 of 67 Alabama counties. Several

Human Development and Family Science students at Samford University have completed practicum experiences in this setting. They learn about the systemic effects of food redistribution, the economic challenges for recipients as well as for the distributor as a nonprofit organization. There is complexity in maintaining such a large-scale initiative, especially as this food bank deals with perishable food items as well, and the timeframe for collecting and subsequent redistribution can affect food safety. The food is received and redistributed within 24 hours.

The intent of such an initiative is manifold. On the one hand, food rescue prevents large-scale waste affecting environmental concerns, by making it feasible to donate left-over and excessive food. In many areas the tendency is to dispose of good food through the waste system as opposed to taking a longer term responsibility and asking where does this food cycle continue and with what outcomes? The reasons for food disposal and waste are many; fear of being sued for providing food not considered the "best by date" or freshness, interpretation by consumers of food being unsafe due to lack of education, the cost of delivery and the labor entailed to redistribute. In short, the effort of implementing sustainable solutions may be more challenging than taking the short-term route reflecting short-range vision and creating more waste.

Grace Klein Community goes beyond addressing food waste and focuses on edible food distribution and composting. Their vision is to share resources, and in that manner build relationships "to ignite restoration of individuals, families, and communities" (Grace Klein Community, n.d.). Its mission is encapsulated in the phrase: "Love. Serve. Share. Repeat." The aim is to meet physical and spiritual needs both locally and globally.

Student Reflection

As practicum supervisor, I have asked my students: "What skills, insights are you gathering from this experience?" The following reflection was written by an intern:

I have loved working at Grace Klein Community. My supervisor has been such an amazing part of this practicum. Something she said recently that I thought was pivotal, was "*if we lived simply, others can simply live.*" The idea of living simply allows one to help others who need basics; to meet their needs, which may be greater than simply the need for food.

Families need community to thrive. Community is built through the sharing of resources pertaining to families. Our students learned to be part of these greater families. They were able to adopt the values epitomized by Grace Klein, namely:

- Embrace community by building valued relationships;
- Compassionate interactions by caring deeply;
- Respect and honoring diversity;
- Teamwork by focusing on a common vision;
- Stewardship of gifts, while inspiring resourcefulness.

The combined standards and goals of Grace Klein Community inspire opportunities to exemplify the values required to build character. They are also the building blocks for greater resilience—the process from which communities are strengthened: one food basket at a time.

Acknowledgment

The author gratefully acknowledges the support of Grace Klein Community in offering meaningful practicum opportunities to students in Human Development and Family Science.

References

Ahmed, Amal (2022). Our unequal earth. Market with a mission: Non-profit grocery stores help heal 'food deserts. *The Guardian*, 3 April. Retrieved from: www.theguardian.com/environment/2022/apr/03/non-profit-grocery-store-food-desert-texas

California Recycle. (n.d.). https://calrecycle.ca.gov/organics/slcp/foodrecovery

Feeding America. (n.d.). Hunger in America. www.feedingamerica.org/hunger-in-america

Grace Klein Community. (n.d.). Retrieved from https://gracekleincommunity.com/

Noltemeyer, A., James, A. G., Bush, K., Bergen, D., Barrios, V., & Patton, J. (2021). The relationship between deficiency needs and growth needs: The continuing investigation of Maslow's theory. *Child & Youth Services*, 42(1), 24–42.

United States Department of Agriculture. (2023). Food and nutrition assistance. www.ers.usda.gov/topics/food-nutrition-assistance/

21

INTERLOCAL ECONOMIC DEVELOPMENT COLLABORATION IN RURAL AMERICA

A Case of West Texas

Sung-Wook Kwon and Xiaoou Cheng

Economic development has been recognized as one of the important goals for local governments (Peterson, 1981). Cities of all sizes participate in economic development activities for various reasons, including to expand the local tax base, create more job positions, and cope with decreasing funds from the federal government (England et al., 2017). Current studies on economic development have paid much more attention to metropolitan areas than to rural areas. Much like cities in urbanized areas, rural cities and small towns recognize the importance of a healthy economy to support the overall wellbeing of the city.

Abundant literature reveals that an essential aspect of economic development activities is competition because cities compete with each other for jobs, economic growth, and economic development resources such as personnel and funding opportunities (Hawkins, 2010; Kwon & Gonzalez-Gorman, 2014; Lee, 2011). Despite the competitive nature of local economic development, a growing number of studies show that interlocal cooperation has become the primary mechanism for economic development (Ha et al., 2016; Kwon & Feiock, 2010; Kwon & Gonzalez-Gorman, 2014; Lee, 2016; Lee & Lee, 2020). Even in this stream of interlocal economic development research, rural areas continue to be understudied.

In an effort to improve our understanding of interlocal economic development collaboration in rural areas, we examine local governments in three regions of West Texas (South Plains, Panhandle, and Permian Basin). In West Texas, cities are expected to collaborate with others for economic development while dealing with challenges such as their own

DOI: 10.4324/9781003287766-40

limited agriculture-based economies and geographically scattered local governments.

In this chapter, we will first discuss factors that influence economic development activities focusing on West Texas, including economic development and political institutional factors and network characteristics. In the second section, we elaborate on the data collection process, measurements, and empirical analysis and results. We conclude this chapter with discussions of the findings.

Factors of Interlocal Economic Development Collaboration in Rural Regions

Collaborative action on economic development activities is affected by a variety of political, economic, and social factors. In this section, we discuss economic development factors (competition between cities, opportunities and challenges, and budgetary capacity), a political institution factor (form of city government), and network characteristics (density and centrality).

Interlocal Competition

Although interlocal competition is commonly observed in large metropolitan areas, competition also exists in rural areas. Compared to large metropolitan regions, rural regions have a smaller number of local governments competing with each other. However, the limited resources for economic development in rural areas make the competitive environment not so different from that in large metropolitan areas. As the economy is heavily dependent on agriculture in most rural cities, the development of technologies and outmigration of young people have become challenges for rural regions (Monchuk et al., 2007). Cities in rural regions are constrained by both fiscal and personnel resources, so these cities are likely to compete with others to secure their economic base when facing such constraints (Lee, 2016). Moreover, the declining funds from higher levels of government push rural cities with limited budgets to a higher level of competition for those funding opportunities allocated to rural regions (Lackey et al., 2002; Porter et al., 2004).

Scholars have observed that competition influences a city's economic development collaboration. Competition can limit the capacity to solve common problems and can also lead to collaboration risks (Feiock et al., 2012) such as reluctance to share information (Lee et al., 2012), inequities, and inefficiencies (Gordon, 2007). Interestingly, however, those problems caused by competition increase the demand for cities to collaborate with other cities. Previous literature suggests that, while excessive competition results in negative economic externalities, it helps cities recognize potential benefits they can gain through collective actions (Lee, 2016). Therefore, we assume that rural cities tend to collaborate with other cities when confronting a higher level of competition in their regions.

Opportunities and Challenges

Opportunities are precious and intangible resources for economic development in cities. The diversity of local business types can create development opportunities through collaboration with other local governments. While generally relying on agriculture, cities in rural areas differ in how much their economic bases are diversified. When cities conduct economic development activities in a variety of business areas, these activities will produce more opportunities to collaborate with other cities to expand their economic base by taking advantage of experiences and resources that cities share with each other. In contrast, when cities rely heavily on just one or a few businesses, they will have difficulty seeking economic development goals through collaboration because of a limited number of opportunities to work together. We argue that, when rural cities seek economic development in more diverse areas, they will be more motivated to collaborate.

While seeking more opportunities for economic activities, cities also confront challenges that hinder economic development. The existing literature suggests that rural communities face a variety of challenges such as lower education levels, limited skilled labor, ageing population, and lack of capital to finance economic development activities (Agranoff & McGuire, 2003; Monchuk et al., 2007). Notably, the unique characteristic of geographic distances between cities should be considered when discussing the constraints on rural economic development collaboration. City officials tend to make frequent interactions to collaborate when they share similar challenges (Post, 2014), and the long distances between cities in rural areas increases the need for more interactions to collectively address economic development challenges. We argue that, when cities in rural areas are constrained by more local economic challenges, they are more likely to collaborate with other activities to overcome those challenges.

Budgetary Capacity

Budgetary capacity determines the scope and size of economic activities. It is imperative for rural cities to collaborate on economic development if they do not have sufficient budgets to implement economic development activities by themselves. Organizations that have limited resources are involved in interactions with their environment to obtain external resources (Pfeffer & Salancik, 1978) and are more likely to collaborate with other organizations (Cepiku et al., 2020). We assume that the relationship between weak budget capacity and collaborative efforts is salient in rural communities. Although some cities can pursue economic development based on a strong budget, most rural cities have difficulty generating sufficient budgets for economic development. Thus, we argue that rural cities with smaller economic development budgets are more likely to seek collaboration with other cities to cope with their budget limitations.

Form of Government

Local government leaders in different forms of government represent distinctive leadership styles and affect policy outcomes in different ways (Song et al., 2018). Therefore, it is important to discuss the influence of institutional forms on the formation and patterns of interlocal collaboration regarding economic development activities. Since mayor-council and council-manager are two forms found in West Texas, we examine the impact of these two institutional forms on economic development collaboration among cities in the regions. Elected city mayors focus on being reelected, while appointed city managers seek to advance their professional administrative capacity and potentially find a future job in a larger city (Feiock & Park, 2006; Hawkins, 2010). Under the mayor-council form, mayors are hindered from focusing on one specific policy arena such as economic development because they are more risk averse due to their desire for reelection and their concern for the diverse preferences of their constituents (Lee, 2016). In contrast, city managers seek higher efficiency in local government operation and can devote more to economic development activities (England et al., 2017; Kwon & Gonzalez-Gorman, 2014). In sum, we expect that cities in rural areas with a council-manager form of government are more likely to participate in interlocal economic development collaboration than cities with a mayor-council form.

Network Characteristics

Interlocal economic development collaboration is also influenced by networks that local governments create and maintain. Networks facilitate information sharing among actors within the network, which increases efficiency in cooperation and enhances trust among actors (Lee, 2011; Feiock et al., 2012). The combined effects of jurisdictional fragmentation and competition embedded in economic development activities make collaboration more risky and uncertain (Lee et al., 2012). Networks serve as a crucial approach to addressing the negativity caused by jurisdictional and institutional fragmentation (Lee et al., 2012; Reid and Smith, 2012). In addition, partaking in informal policy networks helps decrease the level of collaborative uncertainty and maintain relationships with existing participants (Hawkins et al., 2016).

The smaller number of cities in geographically large areas explain why rural cities have fewer potential network collaborators. Because networks can provide social capital to participating members (Compion et al., 2015), rural cities may actively seek benefits of networking with other cities in spite of the challenges. Economic development networks are not unique to large metropolitan areas; cities in rural regions are equally motivated to participate in regional networks to achieve the goal of developing their local economies.

The specific characteristics of a network will then influence each member city's economic development collaboration efforts (Hawkins et al., 2016). We utilize network density and centrality which are two levels of measurement of network characteristics that are viewed as the best captures of a network structure (Carr et al., 2017; Compion et al., 2015; Lee et al., 2012; Hawkins, 2010; Monge & Contractor, 2003). First, we assume that rural cities in a denser network tend to initiate ties with other cities for economic development. Second, cities with higher outdegree centrality are more likely to form connections with other cities for economic development. Last, the higher the betweenness centrality, the more likely cities are to collaborate with other cities for economic development.

Research Design

The West Texas Local Economic Development Survey we conducted from 2018 to 2019 covers three regions of West Texas encompassing 134 cities: 45 in South Plains, 60 in Panhandle, and 29 in Permian Basin. This survey covers each city's economic development and political institution data. We also collected socioeconomic data from the Bureau of Census' 2017 American Community Survey.

Dependent Variable

The dependent variable in this study is the level of interlocal collaboration on economic development activities which was measured by the total number of cities that a city is collaborating in the region where the city is located. The data are drawn from the West Texas Local Economic

Development Survey, in which we asked each city to check all the cities that it has cooperated with in its respective region.

Economic Development Factors

We included four variables that capture the economic development condition of each city: competition, opportunities, challenges, and budget. All these variables are obtained from the West Texas Local Economic Development Survey. We asked the cities to check other cities with which they are competing within their region for economic development and summed up the number of competitors they checked to measure the level of economic development competition. Economic development opportunities were measured by the number of business areas on which a city focuses. The survey provided eight business areas and asked each city to check the extent to which it focuses on each of them using a five-point Likert scale. If a city chose very little extent, little extent, and some extent, the answer was coded as 0, and 1 was given to cities that answered great extent and very great extent. Economic development challenges were measured in the same way as the opportunity variable. The survey listed 19 areas of challenges. Each city's economic development budget size is the per capita budget amount allocated for local economic development.

Political Institution

The local political institution was measured by each city's form of government. The data were collected through the West Texas Local Economic Development Survey by asking which form of government a city is currently using. It is coded 1 for cities that adopt the council-manager form, and 0 for cities with the mayor-council form.

Network Characteristics

We tested three variables that capture the network characteristics using the West Texas Local Economic Development Survey data. Network density evaluates the network density of the overall network. It is calculated by the existing ties over the potential ties in a network which provides an overall picture of the structure of a whole network (Wasserman & Faust, 1994). A higher density of a network indicates more existing economic development ties within this network. Outdegree centrality measures the expansiveness of a network (Wasserman & Faust, 1994) which is calculated by the total number of cities that are nominated by an ego-centered city.

Outdegree centrality will be higher when cities act proactively to initiate collaboration with other cities on economic development in their region. Betweenness centrality means an interaction between two actors not sitting next to each other in a network that may depend on the other participants, so it is measured by the number of times that an actor sits between other two actors in a network (Wasserman & Faust, 1994). In other words, cities with high betweenness centrality play a more bridging role by linking two cities that are not directly connected. Network characteristics data were calculated through the *statnet* package of the R program.

Control Variables

We controlled for the general socioeconomic factors of the surveyed cities. First, we included racial homogeneity measured by the percentage of the majority racial residents over the overall population. Second, education level was measured by the percentage of citizens holding a bachelor's degree or higher. Third, city size was measured by the population of each city in thousand residents. Last, median household income in thousand dollars was included. The data on all of the control variables were collected from the 2017 American Community Survey data of the Bureau of Census. The descriptive statistics and measures for the variables are reported in Table 21.1.

Methods

We employ a negative binomial regression model in this study since this model best fits our dependent variable that is a count measure with an over-dispersed nature (Long, 1997). The number of cities with which a city cooperates for its economic development is a count variable that is over-dispersed from 0 to 17. Most of the counts per city remain at relatively low values, and there are 25, 13, and 10 cities that reported the number of collaborators as 0, 1, 2, respectively. In running the model, we identified outliers by employing Cook's Distance, which detects highly influential data points by calculating the changes in the estimated coefficients when potential outliers are excluded from the estimation. While we obtained complete data for 72 cities, we dropped two cities that were more than three standard deviations away from the mean Cook's value. Consequently, we conducted our analysis for 70 observations in the dataset.

Results

The results of the negative binomial regression are reported in Table 21.2. Before obtaining robust standard errors by clustering cities by regions,

TABLE 21.1 Descriptive Statistics and Measurements

Variables	Measurement	Mean	SD	Min	Max
Dependent variable					
Level of interlocal cooperation	Number of cities that a city has cooperated with for economic development	2.11	3.19	0	16
Economic development factors					
Level of interlocal competition	Number of cities that a city has competed with for economic development	0.89	1.58	0	11
Focused business areas	Number of business areas on which a city is focusing	3.87	2.09	0	8
Challenges	Number of challenges a city confronts in developing the local economy	10.91	3.34	3	18
Budget	Per capita budget allocated for economic development	30.36	38.46	0	183.93
Political institution					
Form of government	1 = Council-Manager, 0 = Mayor-Council	0.51	0.50	0	1
Network characteristics					
Network density	Percentage of extant ties over the potential ties in each region	0.06	0.01	0.05	0.08
Outdegree centrality	Number of outgoing ties that a city initiates	1.30	1.91	0	7
Betweenness centrality	Number of times that a city sits between other two cities	2.00	4.63	0	21.08
Control variables					
Racial homogeneity	Percentage of the majority racial residents over the overall population	63.11	13.63	43	92
Education level	Percentage of residents with bachelor's degree or higher	15.67	8.71	4.60	52.20
Population size	City population size (in thousands)	13.75	41.81	0.08	247.32
Median household income	Median household income of the residents (in thousands)	49.43	12.72	29.61	97.37

Note: N = 70 (cities that are analyzed in our analysis).

TABLE 21.2 Negative Binomial Regression Results

Variable	Coefficient	Robust Std. Err.
Economic development factors		
Level of interlocal competition	-0.0812	0.4110
Focused business areas	0.1305 ***	0.0080
Challenges	-0.0731 **	0.0330
Budget	-0.0068	0.1530
Political institution		
Form of government	-0.3484	0.2850
Network characteristics		
Network density	-29.3418 ***	0.0000
Outdegree centrality	0.5333 ***	0.0000
Betweenness centrality	0.0166 ***	0.0020
Control variables		
Ethnic homogeneity	-0.0051	0.2930
Education level	0.0131	0.4910
Population size	0.0039 *	0.0660
Median household income	-0.0203 **	0.0470
Constant	2.9869 ***	0.0000
N = 70		
Pseudo R² = 0.2830		

Note: *p<0.1, **p<0.05, ***p<0.01; standard errors are clustered by three regions.

we conducted the likelihood ratio test to check whether the dependent variable is over-dispersed. The test was significant at the 0.01 level which supports our use of the negative binomial model.

Two economic development factor variables, opportunities and challenges, are statistically significant and explain interlocal collaboration in our model. The number of focused business areas is statistically significant at the 0.01 level, and the positive coefficient shows that when a city has more opportunities, it is likely to collaborate with more neighboring cities. The number of challenges that a city faces is estimated at the 0.05 significance level. The negative coefficient of economic development challenges indicates that the city is less likely to collaborate with other cities when confronting more challenges. Two other economic development related variables and the form of government variable do not have a statistically significant influence on interlocal collaboration for economic development.

All three network characteristics variables are statistically significant at the 0.01 level. The negative coefficient of network density suggests that cities are less motivated to collaborate in a denser network. The outdegree centrality has a positive coefficient, meaning that the more ties a city sends out, the more likely the city is to collaborate on economic development with other cities. The betweenness centrality has a positive coefficient, indicating that as the importance of a city increases in the network, the city will be less inclined to collaborate.

The results for control variables demonstrate a significant influence of socioeconomic conditions in each community on interlocal economic development collaboration. Population size is estimated at the 0.1 significance level, and the coefficient is positive, indicating that larger cities tend more to collaborate with other cities. Median household income has a negative and significant impact at the 0.05 level, which shows that a city with better economic conditions at the community level is more likely to cooperate. Racial homogeneity and education level do not have a significant effect on the interlocal economic collaboration actions.

Discussion and Conclusion

Interestingly, cities in rural areas exhibit similar collaborative patterns of economic development to those in large urbanized metropolitan areas while still retaining distinctive characteristics. The analysis presents evidence that more focal business areas increase collaboration among rural cities. When cities operate economic activities in more business areas, they are motivated to collaborate with other cities because they enjoy advantages from their experiences or knowledge in those respective economic activities. However, economic challenges frustrate the development of local economies, and cities find it more difficult to collaborate with other cities dealing with these challenges. Rural areas confront more challenges compared with large urbanized metropolitan areas in the economic development context. Because of the lack of resources in labor and capital, rural cities have difficulties developing and expanding their economy. Furthermore, globalization and shifts to service and technology industries make rural cities more vulnerable to economic development (Porter et al., 2004).

The level of economic competition does not influence collaborative efforts in West Texas regions. As most cities in West Texas regions are small and lack economic bases, competition has minimal influence on these cities. No impact of the budget size can be understood in the same context. Although some cities, particularly larger ones, have a significant budget allocated for their economic development activities, many small cities in rural West Texas regions have no, or very small, budget for this goal, resulting in no impact of economic development budget.

Furthermore, form of government does not influence city efforts for collaboration for economic development in the case of West Texas rural regions. While the mayor-council and council-manager forms are more popular in very small and larger cities in West Texas, respectively, our analysis does not show any consistent pattern regarding city form of government and economic development collaboration, suggesting that non-institutional factors are more critical in explaining their collaboration.

It is noteworthy that the network characteristics present a unique picture of interlocal economic development collaboration in rural West Texas regions. We find network density negatively affects collaborative actions, which is opposite to previous findings in large metropolitan area studies (Hawkins, 2010; Lee, 2016). Our result shows that increasing incident lines decrease the collaboration among cities, which may result from an untested latent variable of perception of the risk of collaboration. For instance, scholars find that the increase of network density increases the likelihood that cities perceive interlocal collaboration as a highly risky task (Carr et al., 2017) which will then decrease cities' motivation to collaborate with other cities. This requires further study to unpuzzle this negative relationship between network density and interlocal collaboration. The results of centrality measures are consistent with previous findings in metropolitan areas.

When cities have higher outdegree centrality, they are likely to have a greater number of cooperative cities. This shows that, although cities in rural areas are relatively small and have limited economic development resources, they are actively contacting other cities in the region to achieve economic growth. The positive impact of betweenness centrality shows that when cities play a bridging role more often, they are more likely to have a greater number of collaborators. Although the geographical distances between rural cities in West Texas make it difficult to form strong ties among cities, some cities, particularly big ones, act as bridges and help to establish economic development connections between smaller cities. The result shows that Granovetter's (1973) "strength of weak ties" works in the case of economic development collaboration in West Texas regions.

Our analysis also shows that general socioeconomic variables are important in explaining economic development collaboration among rural cities. Cities with larger population sizes will seek more collaboration for economic development to satisfy diverse service and development demands from citizens. Cities that have higher median household incomes are less likely to collaborate on economic development activities as they are less motivated to seek collaborative development activities, since they are less constrained by a poor economy and have more latitude to choose their own development strategies.

We summarize our study with three implications. First, we emphasize the importance of studying collaboration in rural regions which have received relatively less attention in the literature. The unique characteristics of rural cities distinguish them from those in large urbanized metropolitan areas in a variety of ways. As this study is focused on one specific part of the country, we need more studies in other regions to better explain the dynamics of interlocal economic development collaboration in rural regions. Second, we examined the factors that were expected to be influential in both urban and rural areas and found that most of these factors explained interlocal collaboration in rural areas. Last, this study sheds light on the critical roles that rural cities play in local and regional governance. While constrained by the resource and geographical barriers, many rural cities are proactively seeking collaboration to expand their local economy rather than staying as passive actors.

Acknowledgment

This research was supported by Texas Tech University's Scholarship Catalyst Program and Center for Public Service.

References

Agranoff, R., & McGuire, M. M. (2003). *Collaborative Public Management: New Strategies for Local Governments*. Georgetown University.

Carr, J. B., Hawkins, C. V., & Westberg, D. E. (2017). An exploration of collaboration risk in joint ventures: Perceptions of risk by local economic development officials. *Economic Development Quarterly, 31*(3), 210–227.

Cepiku, D., So, H. J., & Jesuit, D. K. (2020). *Collaborative Governance for Local Economic Development: Lessons from Countries around the World*. Routledge.

Compion, S., Ofem, B., Ferrier, W., Borgatti, S., Cook-Craig, P., Jensen, J., & Nah, S. (2015). The collaboration networks of economic development organizations in Eastern Kentucky. *Journal of Appalachian Studies, 21*(1), 105–127.

England, R. E., Pelissero, J. P., & Morgan, D. R. (2017). *Managing Urban America* (8th ed.). CQ.

Feiock, R. C., Lee, I. W., & Park, H. J. (2012). Administrators' and elected officials' collaboration networks: Selecting partners to reduce risk in economic development. *Public Administration Review, 72*(1), 58–68.

Feiock, R. C., & Park, H. J. (2006). Institutional collective action, social capital and regional development partnership. *International Review of Public Administration, 11*(2), 57–69.

Gordon, V. (2007). Partners or competitors? Perceptions of regional economic development cooperation in Illinois. *Economic Development Quarterly, 21*(1), 60–78.

Granovetter, M. S. (1973). The strength of weak ties. *American Journal of Sociology, 78*(6), 1360–1380.

Ha, H., Lee, I. W., & Feiock, R. C. (2016). Organizational network activities for local economic development. *Economic Development Quarterly, 30*(1), 15–31.

Hawkins, C. V. (2010). Competition and cooperation: Local government joint ventures for economic development. *Journal of Urban Affairs, 32*(2), 253–275.

Hawkins, C. V., Hu, Q., & Feiock, R. C. (2016). Self-organizing governance of local economic development: Informal policy networks and regional institutions. *Journal of Urban Affairs, 38*(5), 643–660.

Kwon, S.-W., & Feiock, R. C. (2010). Overcoming the barriers to cooperation: Intergovernmental service agreements. *Public Administration Review, 70*(6), 876–884.

Kwon, S.-W, & Gonzalez-Gorman S. (2014). Links between performance measures and local economic development: Examination of a two-stage model of internal and external factors. *Public Performance & Management Review, 37*(4), 658–678.

Lackey, S. B., Freshwater, D., & Rupasingha, A. (2002). Cooperation in rural areas: Evidence from the Tennessee valley. *Economic Development Quarterly, 16*(2), 138–154.

Lee, I. W., Feiock, R. C., & Lee, Y. (2012). Competitors and cooperators: A micro-level analysis of regional economic development collaboration networks. *Public Administration Review, 72*(2), 253–262.

Lee, Y. (2011). Economic development networks among local governments. *International Review of Public Administration, 16*(1), 113–134.

Lee, Y., Lee, I. W., & Feiock, R. C. (2012). Interorganizational collaboration networks in economic development policy: An exponential random graph model analysis. *Policy Studies Journal, 40*(3), 547–573.

Lee, Y. (2016). From competition to collaboration: Intergovernmental economic development policy networks. *Local Government Studies, 42*(2), 171–188.

Lee, Y., & Lee, I. W. (2020). A longitudinal network analysis of intergovernmental collaboration for local economic development. *Urban Affairs Review, 58*(1), 229–257.

Long, J. S. (1997). *Regression models for categorical and limited dependent variables*. Sage.

Monchuk, D. C., Miranowski, J. A., Hayes, D. J., & Babcock, B. A. (2007). An analysis of regional economic growth in the U.S. Midwest. *Review of Agricultural Economics, 29*(1), 17–39.

Monge, P. R., & Contractor, N. S. (2003). *Theories of Communication Networks*. Oxford University Press.

Peterson, P. E. (1981). *City Limits*. University of Chicago.

Pfeffer, J., & G. R. Salancik, G. R. (1978). *The External Control of Organizations: A Resource Dependence Perspective*. Harper & Row.

Porter, M. E., Ketels, C. H. M., Miller, K., & Bryden, R. T. (2004). Competitiveness in rural US regions: Learning and research agenda. *Policy*, 1–70.

Post, S. (2014). Metropolitan area governance and institutional collective action. In R. C. Feiock (ed.), *Metropolitan Governance: Conflict, Competition, and Cooperation* (pp. 67–92). Georgetown University.

Reid, N., & Smith, B. W. (2012). Collaboration in local economic development: The case of Toledo. *Urbani Izziv, 23*(1), 85–93.

Song, M., Park, H. J., & Jung, K. (2018). Do political similarities facilitate interlocal collaboration? *Public Administration Review, 78*(2), 261–269.

Wasserman, S., & Faust K. (1994). *Social Network Analysis: Methods and Applications.* Cambridge University Press.

CONCLUSION

James C. Clinger, Donna M. Handley, and
Wendy L. Eaton

This volume has examined the experiences and the institutional context of local government in small American communities. Some of what our contributors report is fairly obvious. Small town governments lack the resources in budget, staff, and professional expertise that their counterparts in larger communities have. They often do have connections to their people and places that are more tenuous in bigger jurisdictions. Those connections may in some ways be a blessing but also a curse. What we see is that close-knit personal ties may facilitate communication, trust, and cooperation among people in dense networks, but they can also limit collaboration with those outside their communities or their own circles. Feuding may occur between cliques within communities and isolation from state, federal, and other local governments may result when no effort is made to reach beyond one's own locality.

This book has shown that the resource deficits that small communities face can sometimes be overcome when communities are willing to collaborate with one another or with the entities inside and outside of government and inside and outside of their own jurisdiction. Our book contains narratives of nonprofit organizations that leverage resources from their local small town government and its local businesses while at the same time finding grants from state and federal governments and philanthropic foundations. Some of our chapters report collaboration and communication within local networks but also across statewide networks of local officials. Some of our chapters show how grantsmanship can bring in resources from across the nation to rural areas that could never finance projects on their own.

DOI: 10.4324/9781003287766-41

In many ways, collaboration is the overarching theme of this book. Collaboration makes many policy efforts possible that might never be conceivable through one government's own self-reliance. Collaboration does not merely occur between jurisdictions. Local governments work with businesses, churches, nonprofits, and private citizens within their own jurisdictions. However, there are sometimes serious obstacles to collaboration. Local governments in small communities often are led by elected officials with little of what Thomas Schlesinger called progressive ambition. They have very little interest in rising to higher and higher political office. They may have somewhat more of what Schlesinger called static ambition, meaning that they wish to retain the offices that they currently have for an extended period of time. Probably most have discrete ambition, which means that they are willing and able to serve in a particular capacity for a term or two, perhaps three, but they want no long-term political career. They wish to provide some civic service, but they do not wish to leave private life, at least not for long.

By the same token, most government employees and administrators may have somewhat limited career ambitions, or if they do have some sort of desire to advance to a more prestigious and usually higher paying position they do not stay in small town government for long. Many have a deep-rooted commitment to their communities and are happy to stay there. Those that wish to rise in their professions may strive to be successful at their present positions, but they do not intend to make a career out of their current jobs. They wish to rise to greater heights, which normally means leaving for a larger community, often in the state or national capital.

These characteristics of both political and administrative leadership of small towns can be both attractive and frustrating to local residents. The lack of progressive ambition may cause local politicians to focus on the concerns of their immediate constituents. They have no desire to appeal to much larger, often more diverse potential constituencies that would be relevant to them if they wanted higher office. If they desire to remain in office, as they would if they have static ambition, they would have an incentive to cater to their local voters' preference. If they have discrete ambition, they may have a Burkean conception of duty to guide their actions. They may act on principle rather than on a vote-seeking basis. There is certainly something to be said for static and discrete ambition. But without progressive ambition, politicians may not have an incentive to reach out far beyond their communities' borders to curry favor with state and federal office-holders, and all the resources that they may control. Local government administrators and public officers may also be valued for their commitment to their communities if they have no plans to move to other positions away from their present locations. But they may also have no career incentive to innovate or develop their skills to advance in their professions. This does not mean that they are unable or unwilling to improve their abilities to perform their jobs, but it does mean they have less extrinsic motivation to do so. What drives them must be an inner commitment to public service in their hometowns rather than a personal interest in career advantage.

Some aspects of the institutional context for small town governance can help or hinder collaboration. Many states require their local officers to participate in training to hold their jobs. Sometimes this training is delivered locally or regionally or at the state capital. Other times it is delivered over the internet. Some states have offices of local government or supra-local regional divisions that provide technical assistance for small communities, including help with preparing grant proposals, education about changing state requirements, and contacts with various government officers who can provide local assistance. Some state universities may also provide policy evaluation services, need assessments, and meetings and symposiums where professionals can gather. The quality and quantity of these state efforts differ dramatically. Some of the supposedly expert professionals are not as knowledgeable as they purport to be. Some state administrators take a condescending view of local personnel, particularly those from rural areas. In many cases, meetings and training sessions in which local public officers are invited to attend are held at inconvenient times or places. Most elected officials in small communities hold part-time public positions. They largely work during the day at their personal occupations. The best available times for them to attend meetings is at night, which is also when most city council meetings are scheduled. The administrators and civil servants in small towns and rural areas are largely on the clock during the day and could sometimes attend meetings, but it is important to realize that their duties in the field are often pressing. A small town fire chief may not simply work in an office. He or she will often be called to suit up for any fire runs if an alarm is sounded. Local public works directors may be called on short notice if a water or sewer main breaks. They may have to diagnose the problem and take remedial action almost immediately before the problem turns into a catastrophe.

What small town officials often find most helpful are opportunities to interact, talk, and share experiences with others in comparable circumstances. These interactions may be with other local government officers, or perhaps with state or federal government personnel or even retired professionals or academics with an interest in their roles in local government. These experiences help span the boundaries of local jurisdictions while at the same time they do not threaten the commitments and loyalties to the people and the places that they serve. These interactions are also of their own choosing. They are not mandated but are voluntary. Professional associations meetings of state chiefs of police or public works directors or HR managers or even city managers can create opportunities for collaboration that may produce significant results.

INDEX

healthcare access: broadband internet, poor rural access to 136, 138; Certificates of Need 134; clinical workforce rural shortages 129; community health centers 134; Community Needs Assessments 133; COVID-19, health inequities highlighted by 130; Healthy People program 131; hospital closures, rural 129, 132, 139; insurance coverage, rural lack of 129; literacy, lack of, as barrier 129; local leadership, importance of 140; Medicaid expansion 132, 134, 137; poorer health of rural populations 129; severe national health inequities 130; social determinants of health (SDOH) 131, 135, 140; *see also* maternal health

Health Resources & Services Administration 136

Healthy Start Program: Community Action Networks 146; health education 147; overview 146; success of 145–146; under-evaluated in rural areas 147

Help America Vote Act (HAVA, 2002) 70, 72, 75n14

Horace, KS 36, 37, 38–39

Hull House 205

Huntington, WV 47

Idaho 33, 246, 247

ideological chasm between metropolitan and rural areas 3

Illinois 322

independent school districts 8

Indiana 31, 32–33, 322

Infrastructure Investment and Jobs Act (2021) 53, 248, 314

in-migration 224

institutions, interests, and ideas 13–14

intergovernmental relations (IGR): block grants 285, 286–287; categorical grants 286; definition 283; digital rural infrastructure, importance of 298; Dillon's Rule 108, 112, 284, 322; early state dominance 284; federal redistribution to rural areas 291–294; fiscal federalism 285, 288; General Revenue Sharing 285;

home rule status for LGs 284, 287, 322, 323, 326, 330; Partnership for Sustainable Communities 291–292; party polarization, as disruptive 287, 297; post-9/11 assertions of federal power 285; post-Civil War growing federal power 285; preemption 289–290; Reaganite reduction of federal state 285; regional councils 286; redistributive and regulatory functions of 287–288, 291; reduced boundary governance 283; regional government support for rural areas 294–296; shared services agreements 295; siloed budgets and capacity, cooperation needed to overcome 293–294; state refusals of conditional federal funds 289; state redistribution to rural areas 293–294; subsidiarity principle 288; value differences, challenge of 297; *see also* collaborative sustainability; contested federalism, effects on interlocal collaboration; mayoral networking

interlocal economic development cooperation: budgetary capacity limitations, as motivating factor 342–343; challenges to economic development 342, 348, 349; council-manager vs. mayor-council government 343, 350; economic diversity as source of opportunity 342, 348, 349; general socioeconomic variables 350; interlocal competition 341–342, 349; networks, as enabling factor 343–344, 348–349, 350; research gap on rural areas 340, 351

International City/County Management Association (ICMA): annual survey 4, 325; continuing education, source of 22; financial condition, definition of 94; geographic informations systems, advocacy of 234, 237; 325

Iowa 22–26, 33

Johnson, Howard 232

Kane County, UT 195

Kansas: broadband access 246; county creation 33; Greeley County 36,

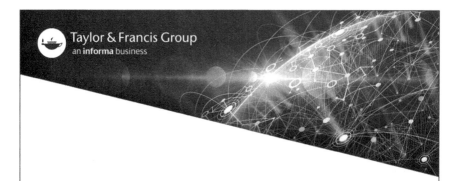